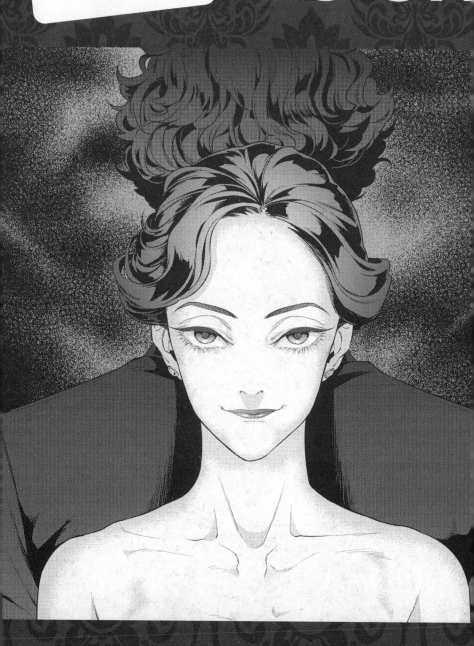

RLOCK

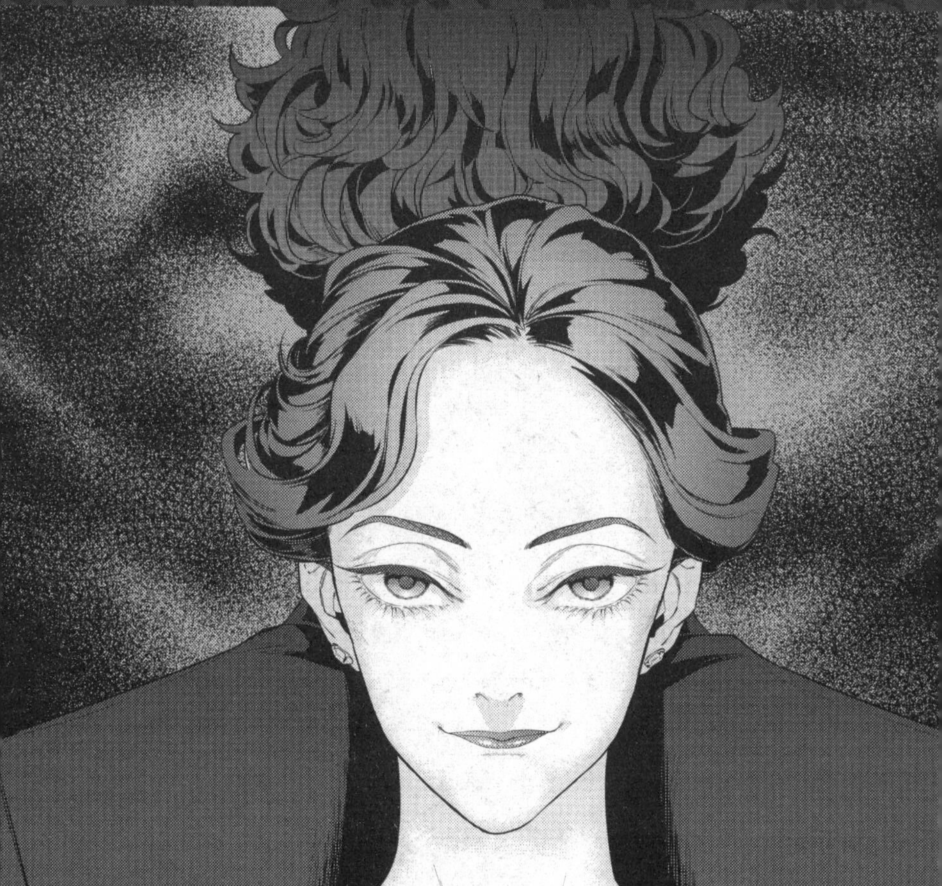

A SCANDAL IN BELGRAVIA

SHERLOCK
A SCANDAL IN BELGRAVIA
PART ONE

SCRIPT
STEVEN MOFFAT

ADAPTATION/ART
JAY.

LETTERING
AMOONA SAOHIN

Originally published in Japanese by Kadokawa.
This manga is presented in its original right-to-left
reading format.

Based on the TV series **SHERLOCK**
co-created by **STEVEN MOFFAT** & **MARK GATISS**
and adapting Episode Four: A Scandal in Belgravia.

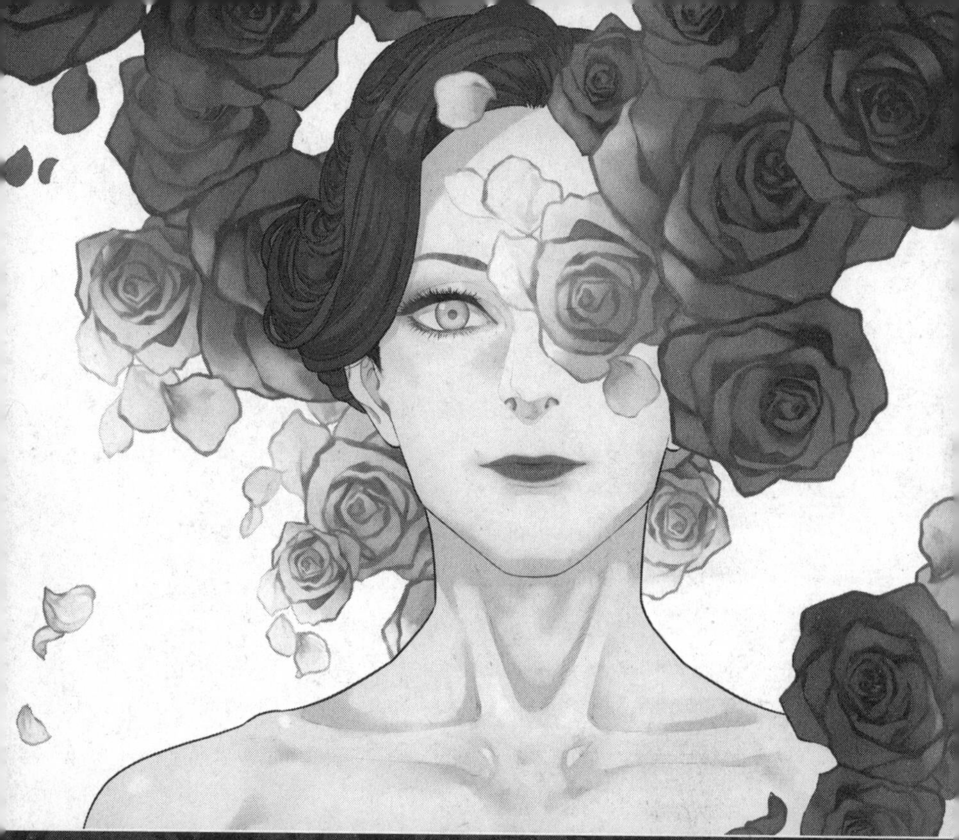

TITAN COMICS

EDITOR
JAKE DEVINE

MANAGING EDITOR
MARTIN EDEN

SENIOR DESIGNER
Andrew Leung

PRODUCTION CONTROLLER
Caterina Falqui

SENIOR PRODUCTION CONTROLLER
Jackie Flook

ART DIRECTOR
Oz Browne

SALES & CIRCULATION MANAGER
Steve Tothill

PRESS & PUBLICITY ASSISTANT
George Wickenden

PUBLICIST
Imogen Harris

MARKETING MANAGER
Ricky Claydon

EDITORIAL DIRECTOR
Duncan Baizley

OPERATIONS DIRECTOR
Leigh Baulch

EXECUTIVE DIRECTOR
Vivian Cheung

PUBLISHER
Nick Landau

SPECIAL THANKS TO: Steven Moffat, Mark Gatiss, Sue Vertue, Rachel Stone, and all at Hartswood, and Yuki Miyoshi, Mayumi Nagumo and all at Kadokawa.

Sherlock: A Scandal in Belgravia – Part One
ISBN: 9781787733169

10 9 8 7 6 5 4 3 2 1
Printed in India by Thomson Press
A CIP catalogue record for this title is available from the British Library.
www.titan-comics.com

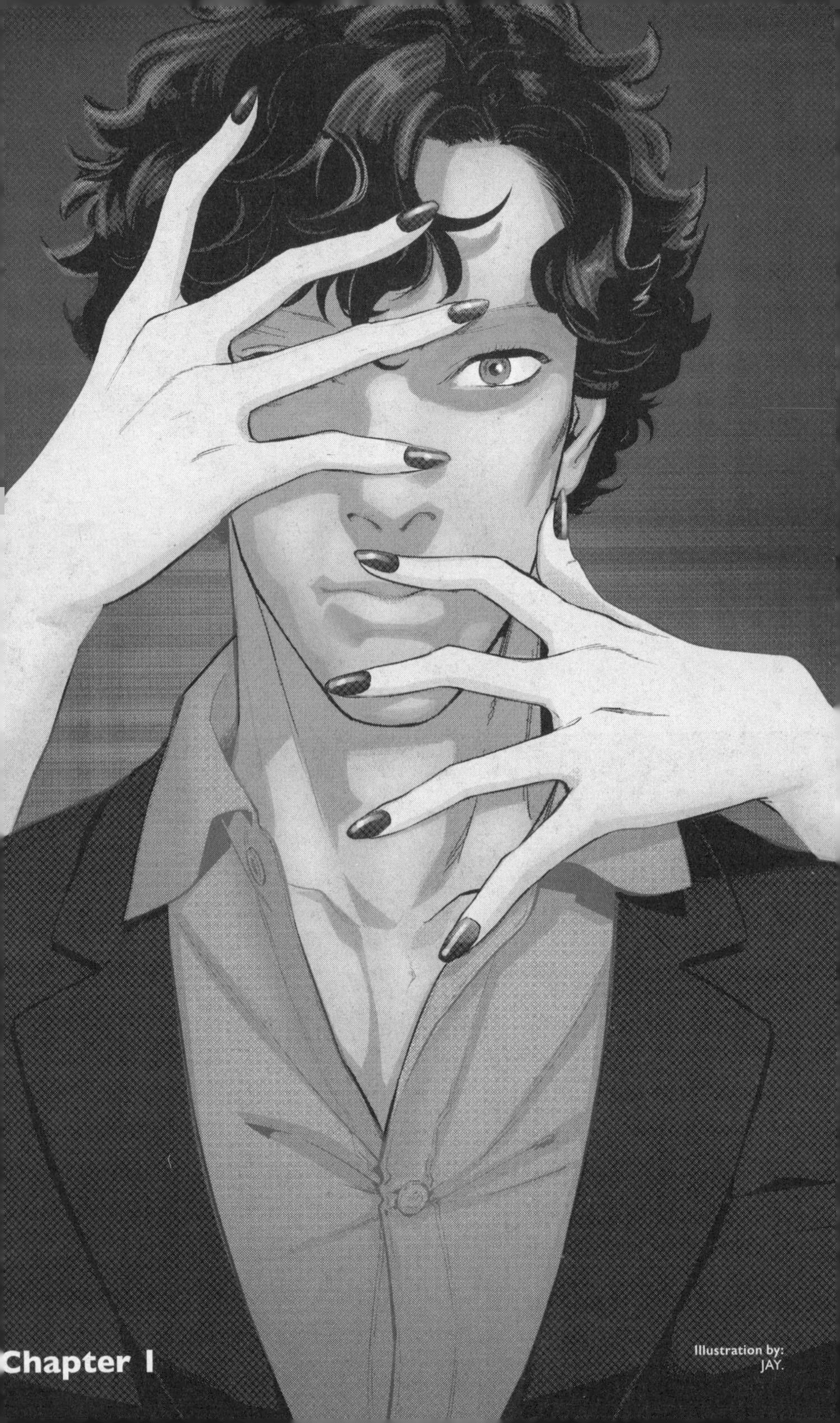

Chapter 1

Illustration by:
JAY.

PREVIOUSLY:

MASTER DETECTIVE SHERLOCK HOLMES WAS FORCED TO SOLVE NUMEROUS PUZZLES IN ORDER TO FREE HOSTAGES WHO HAD BOMBS STRAPPED TO THEM.

WHEN HIS FRIEND, JOHN WATSON, APPEARED AS AS A HOSTAGE, SHERLOCK CAME FACE TO FACE WITH THE CULPRIT -- MORIARTY. WITH A GUN TO HIS HEAD, SHERLOCK AIMED TO SHOOT THE BOMB, ENSURING BOTH OF THEIR DEMISE...

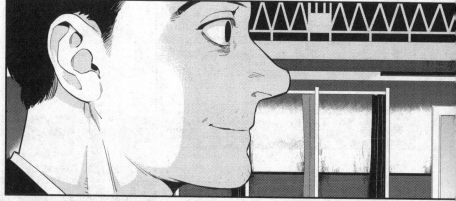

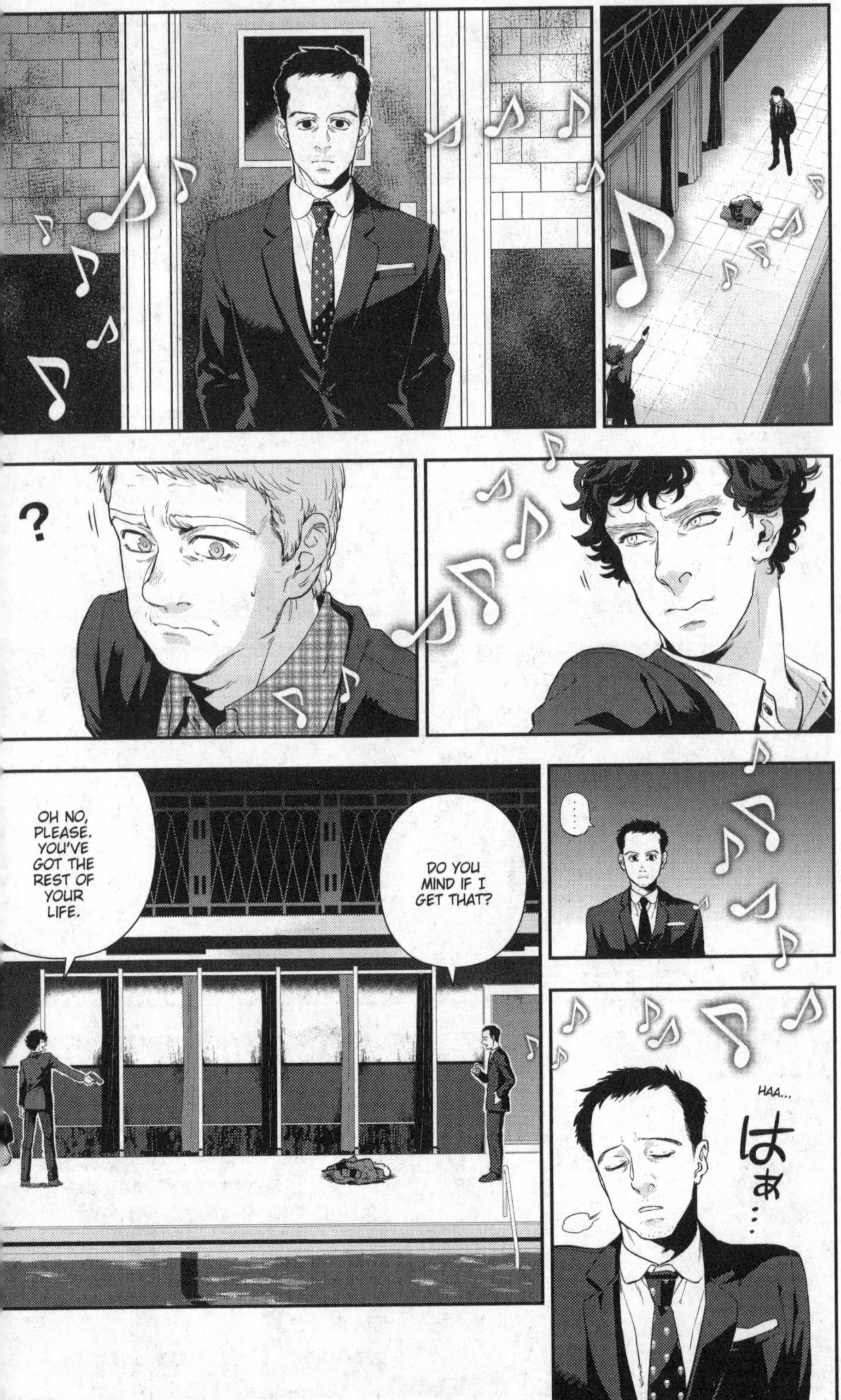
?
......
HAA...
はぁ...
DO YOU MIND IF I GET THAT?
OH NO, PLEASE. YOU'VE GOT THE REST OF YOUR LIFE.

HELLO?
SORRY.
IT'S FINE.
YES
OF COURSE IT IS.
WHAT DO YOU WANT?
...
SAY THAT AGAIN!

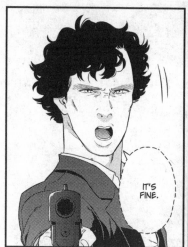

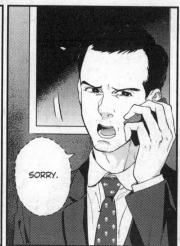

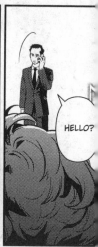

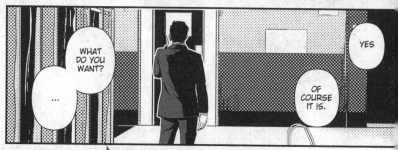

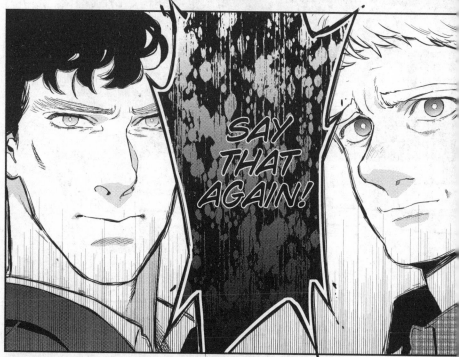

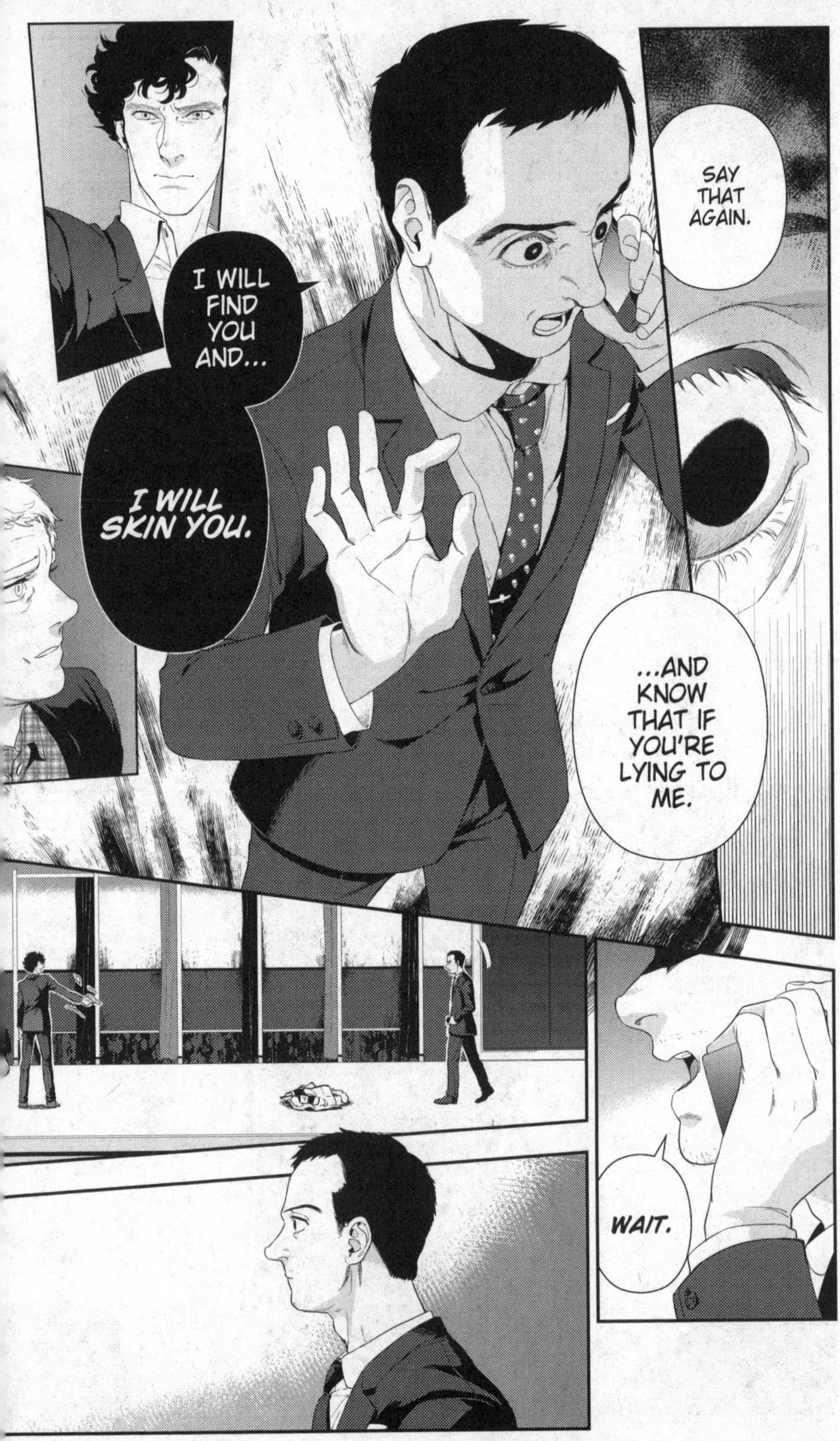
SAY THAT AGAIN.
...AND KNOW THAT IF YOU'RE LYING TO ME.
I WILL FIND YOU AND...
I WILL SKIN YOU.
WAIT.

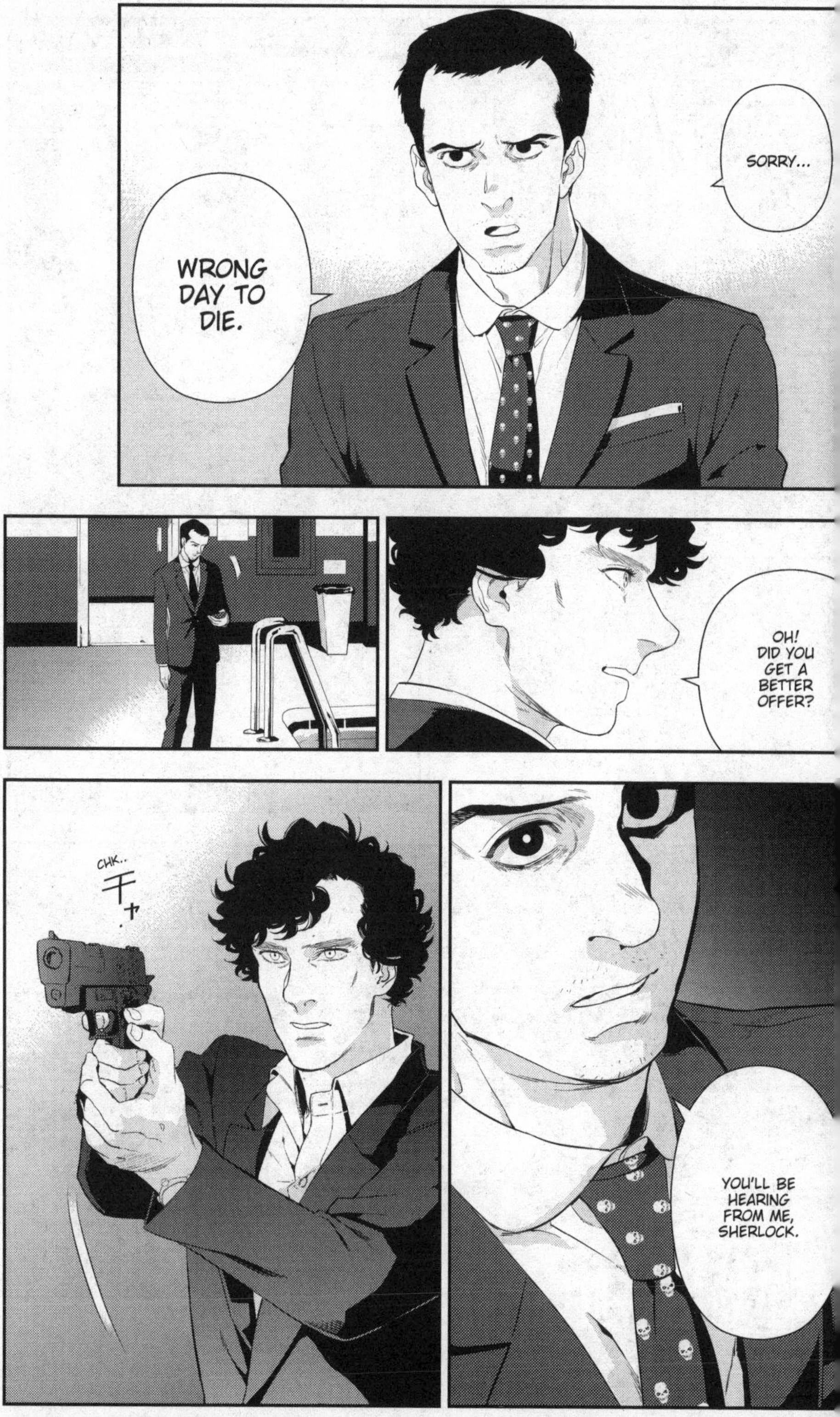
SORRY...
WRONG DAY TO DIE.
OH! DID YOU GET A BETTER OFFER?
YOU'LL BE HEARING FROM ME, SHERLOCK.
CHK..
チャ

SNAP パ

チ ン

SO IF YOU HAVE WHAT YOU SAY YOU HAVE...

I WILL MAKE YOU RICH.

IF YOU DON'T, I WILL MAKE YOU INTO SHOES.

FWIP

FWIP パ ッ

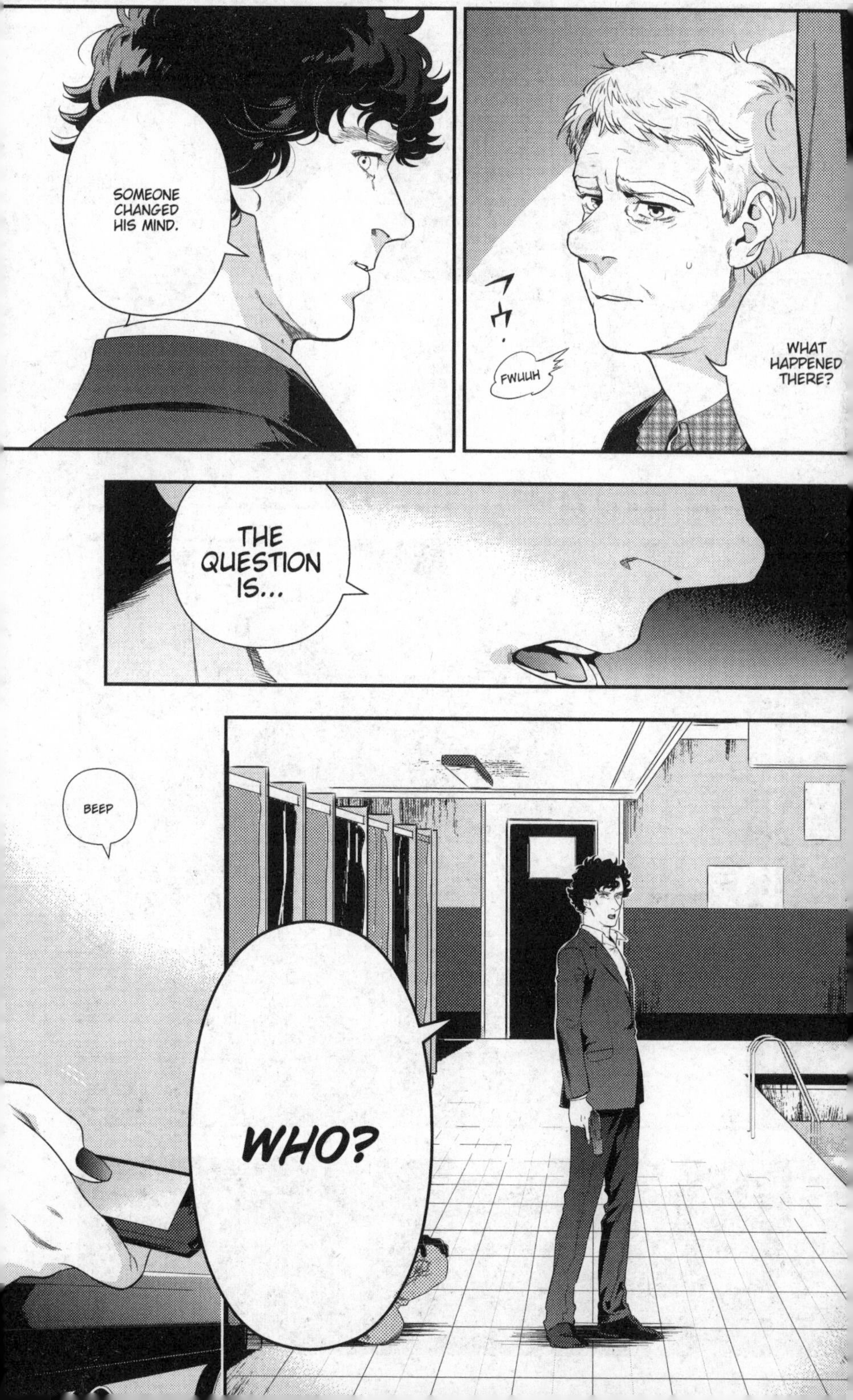
WHAT HAPPENED THERE?
フゥ
FWUUH
SOMEONE CHANGED HIS MIND.
THE QUESTION IS...
BEEP
WHO?

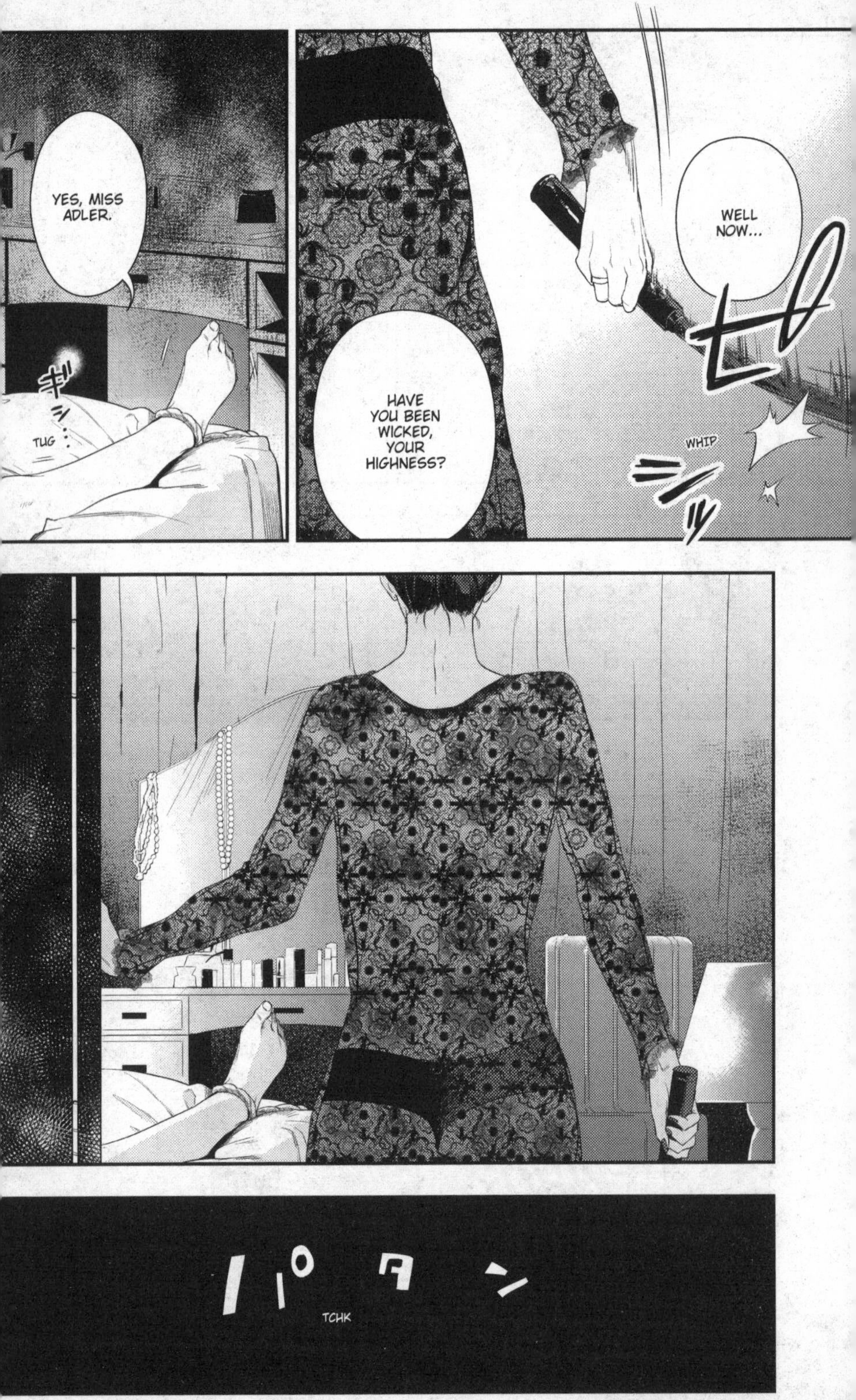
WELL NOW...
HAVE YOU BEEN WICKED, YOUR HIGHNESS?
WHIP
YES, MISS ADLER.
TUG
パタン
TCHK

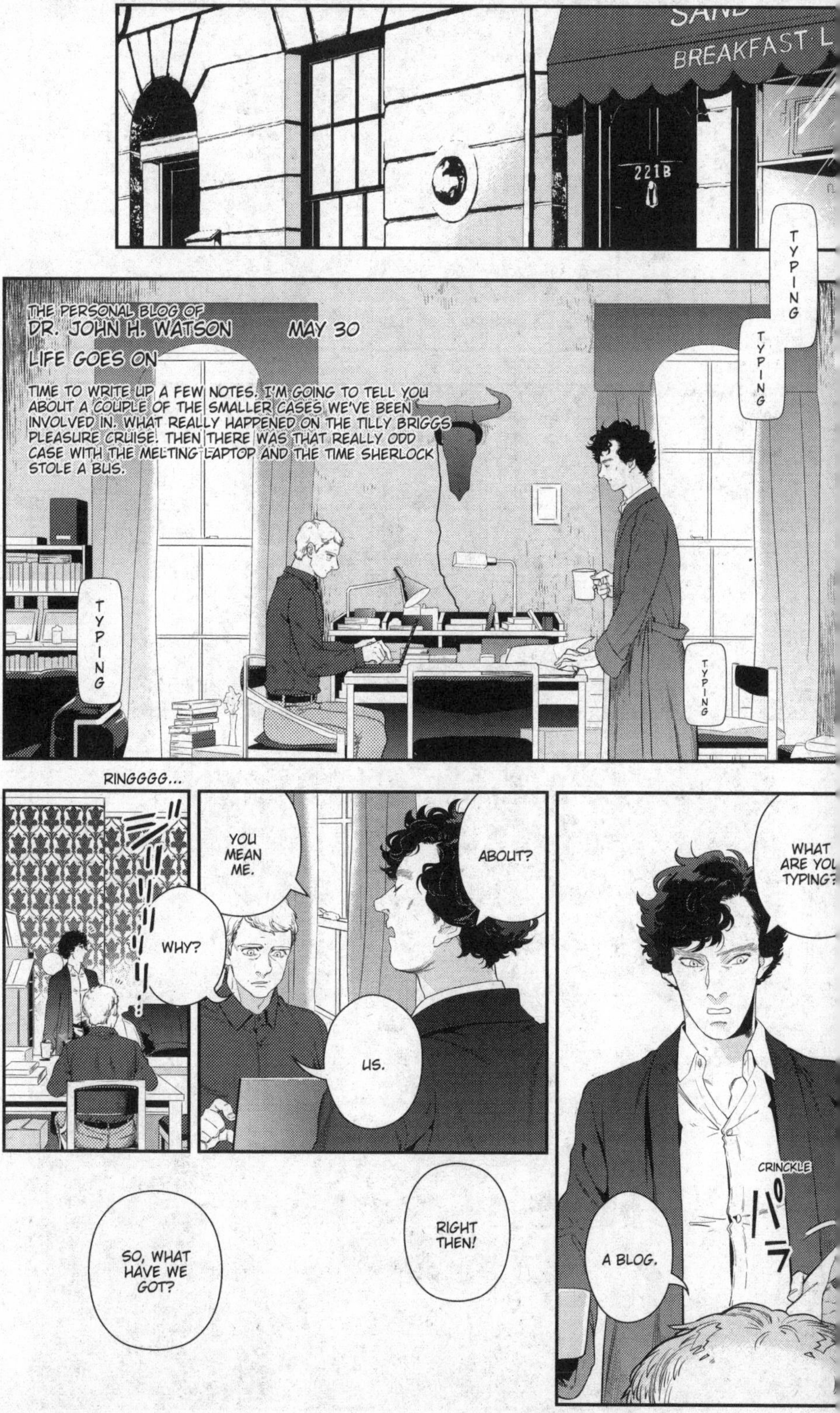

BREAKFAST
221B
TYPING
THE PERSONAL BLOG OF
DR. JOHN H. WATSON
MAY 30
LIFE GOES ON
TIME TO WRITE UP A FEW NOTES. I'M GOING TO TELL YOU ABOUT A COUPLE OF THE SMALLER CASES WE'VE BEEN INVOLVED IN. WHAT REALLY HAPPENED ON THE TILLY BRIGGS PLEASURE CRUISE. THEN THERE WAS THAT REALLY ODD CASE WITH THE MELTING LAPTOP AND THE TIME SHERLOCK STOLE A BUS.
TYPING
TYPING
TYPING
WHAT ARE YOU TYPING?
CRINCKLE
A BLOG.
ABOUT?
YOU MEAN ME.
WHY?
US.
RINGGGG...
RIGHT THEN!
SO, WHAT HAVE WE GOT?

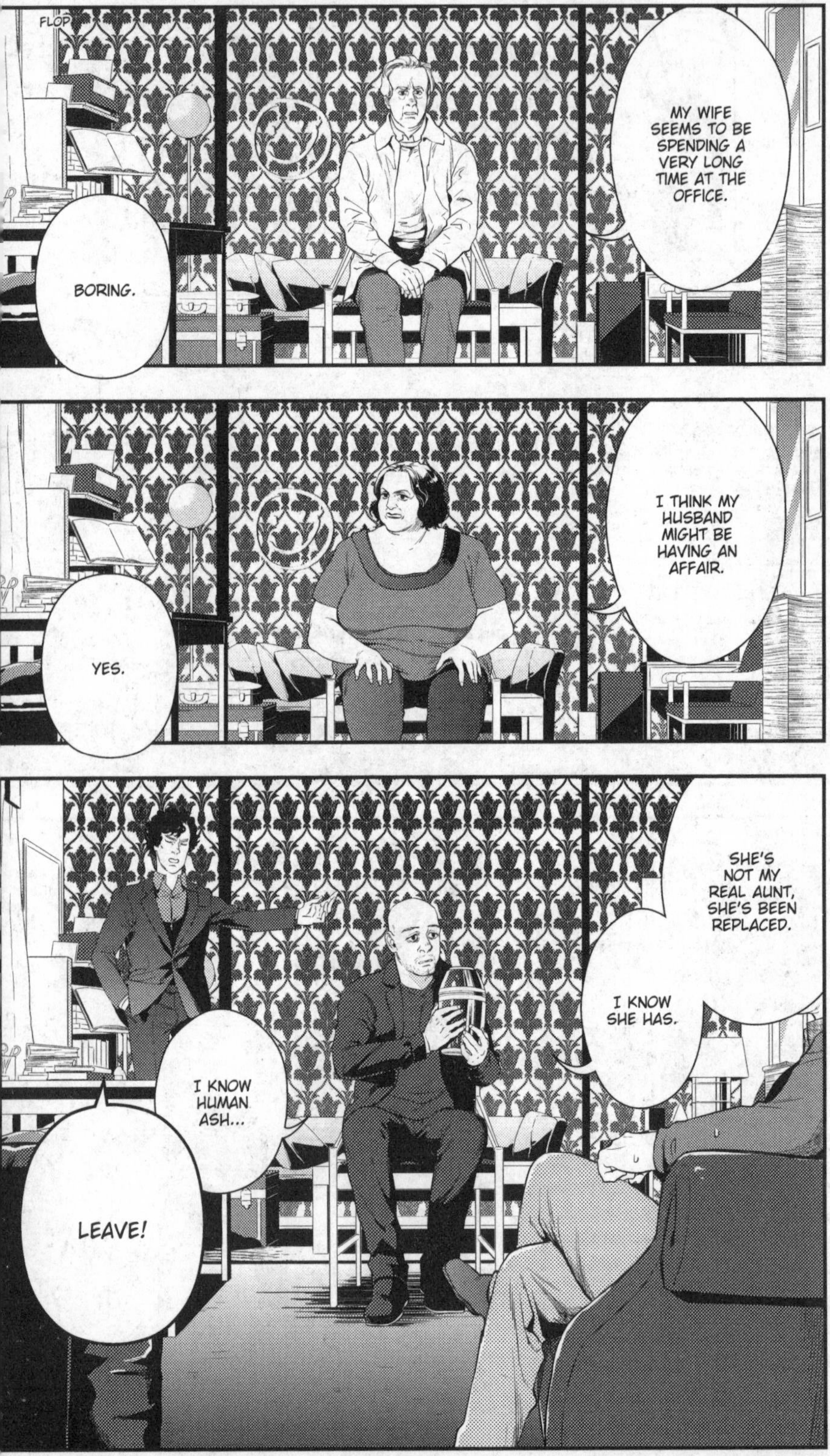
MY WIFE SEEMS TO BE SPENDING A VERY LONG TIME AT THE OFFICE.
FLOP
BORING.
I THINK MY HUSBAND MIGHT BE HAVING AN AFFAIR.
YES.
SHE'S NOT MY REAL AUNT, SHE'S BEEN REPLACED.
I KNOW SHE HAS.
I KNOW HUMAN ASH...
LEAVE!

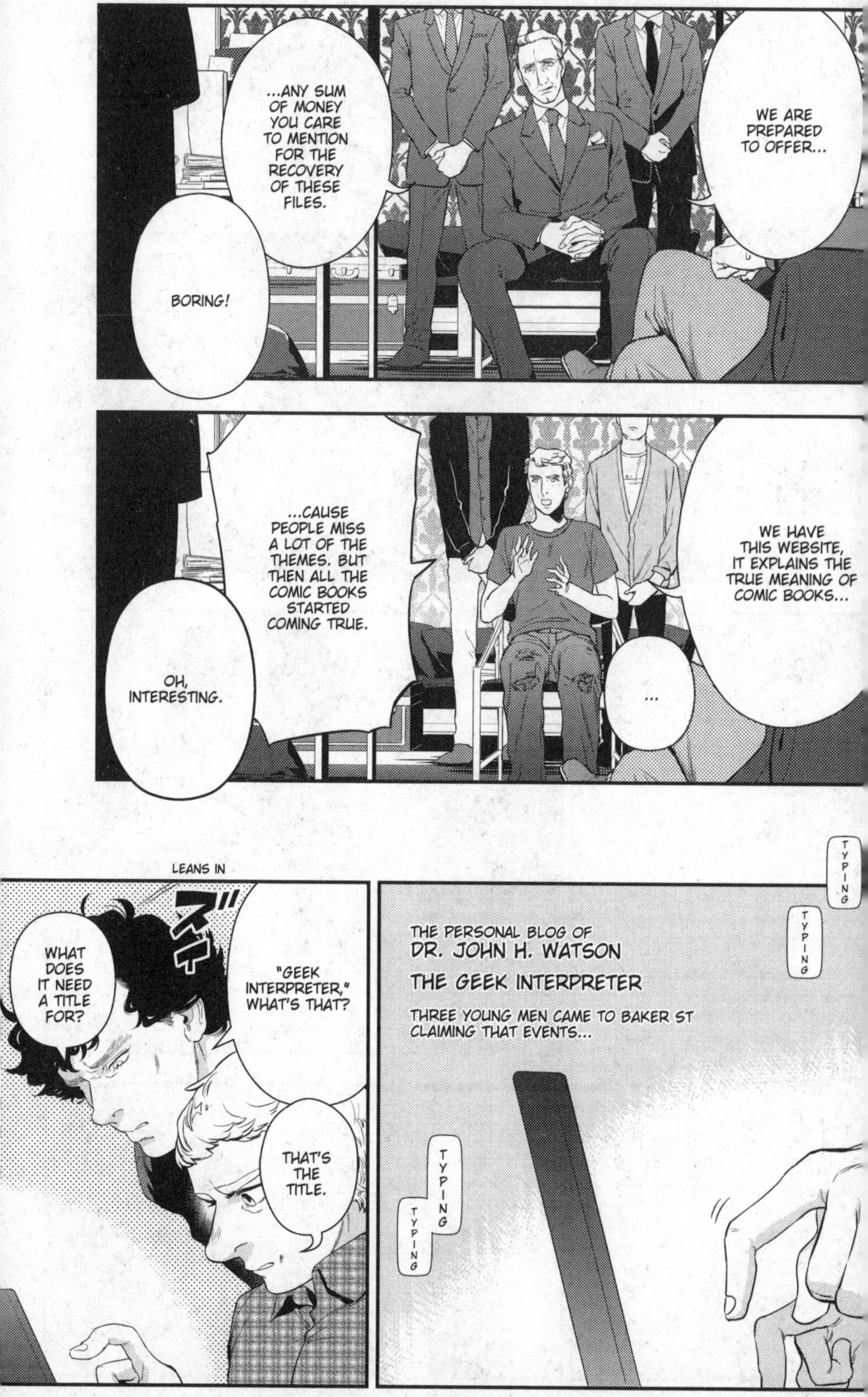

WE ARE PREPARED TO OFFER...
...ANY SUM OF MONEY YOU CARE TO MENTION FOR THE RECOVERY OF THESE FILES.
BORING!
WE HAVE THIS WEBSITE, IT EXPLAINS THE TRUE MEANING OF COMIC BOOKS...
...CAUSE PEOPLE MISS A LOT OF THE THEMES. BUT THEN ALL THE COMIC BOOKS STARTED COMING TRUE.
...
OH, INTERESTING.
TYPING
TYPING
THE PERSONAL BLOG OF
DR. JOHN H. WATSON
THE GEEK INTERPRETER
THREE YOUNG MEN CAME TO BAKER ST CLAIMING THAT EVENTS...
TYPING
TYPING
LEANS IN
"GEEK INTERPRETER," WHAT'S THAT?
WHAT DOES IT NEED A TITLE FOR?
THAT'S THE TITLE.

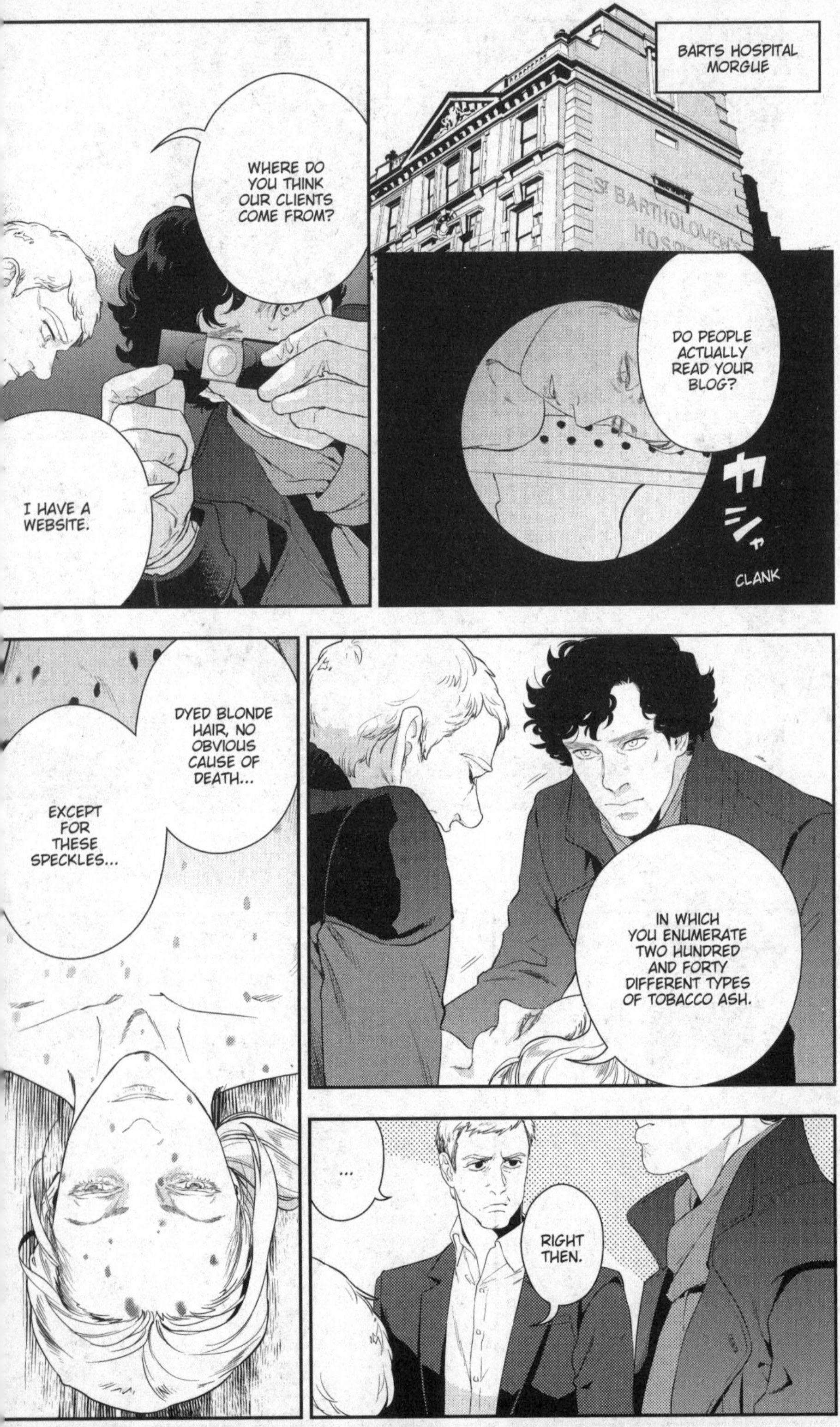
BARTS HOSPITAL MORGUE
DO PEOPLE ACTUALLY READ YOUR BLOG?
カシャ
CLANK
WHERE DO YOU THINK OUR CLIENTS COME FROM?
I HAVE A WEBSITE.
IN WHICH YOU ENUMERATE TWO HUNDRED AND FORTY DIFFERENT TYPES OF TOBACCO ASH.
...
RIGHT THEN.
DYED BLONDE HAIR, NO OBVIOUS CAUSE OF DEATH...
EXCEPT FOR THESE SPECKLES...

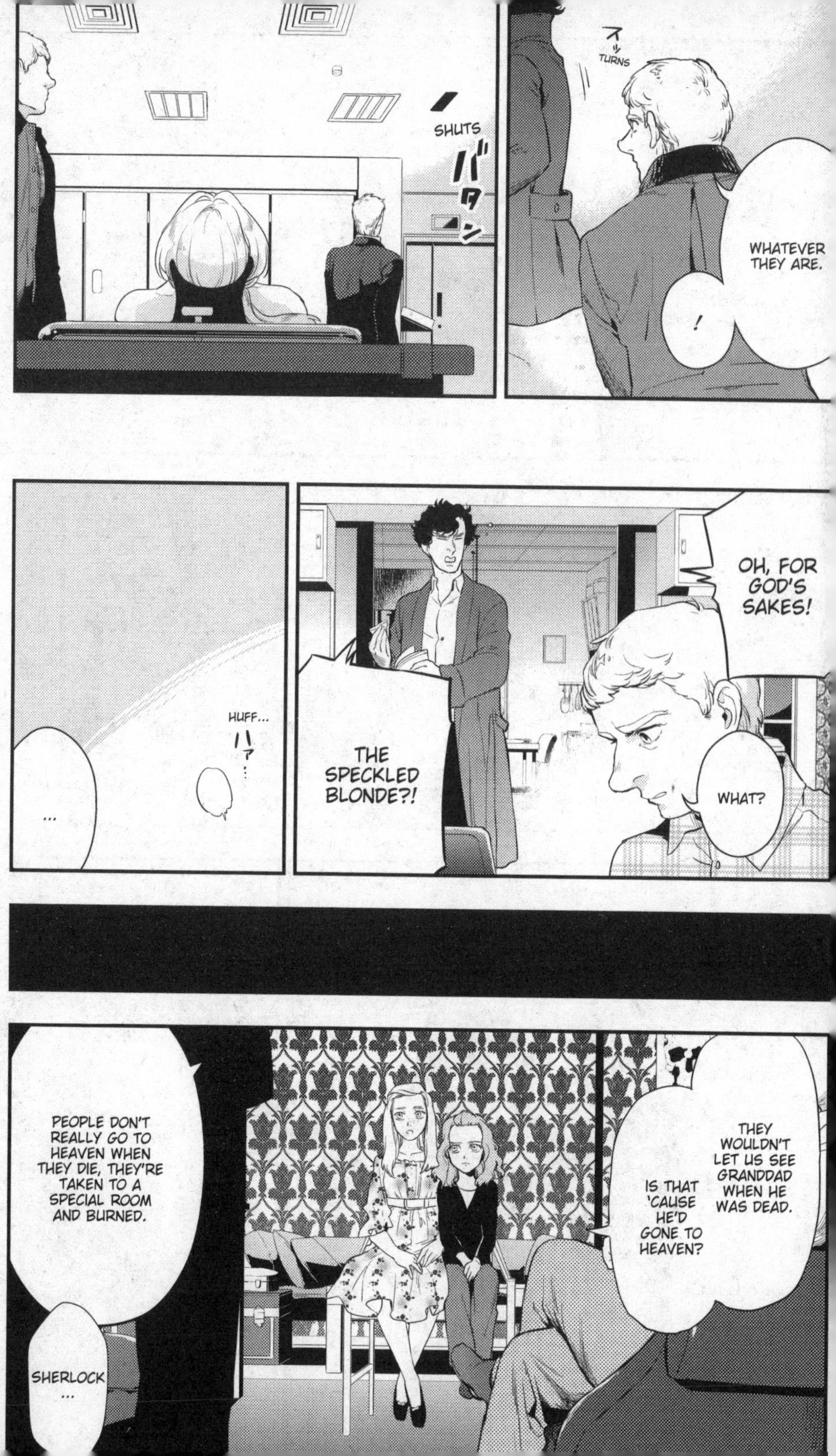
スッ
TURNS
WHATEVER THEY ARE.
!
SHUTS
バタン
OH, FOR GOD'S SAKES!
THE SPECKLED BLONDE?!
WHAT?
HUFF...
ハァ...
...
THEY WOULDN'T LET US SEE GRANDDAD WHEN HE WAS DEAD.
IS THAT 'CAUSE HE'D GONE TO HEAVEN?
PEOPLE DON'T REALLY GO TO HEAVEN WHEN THEY DIE, THEY'RE TAKEN TO A SPECIAL ROOM AND BURNED.
SHERLOCK...

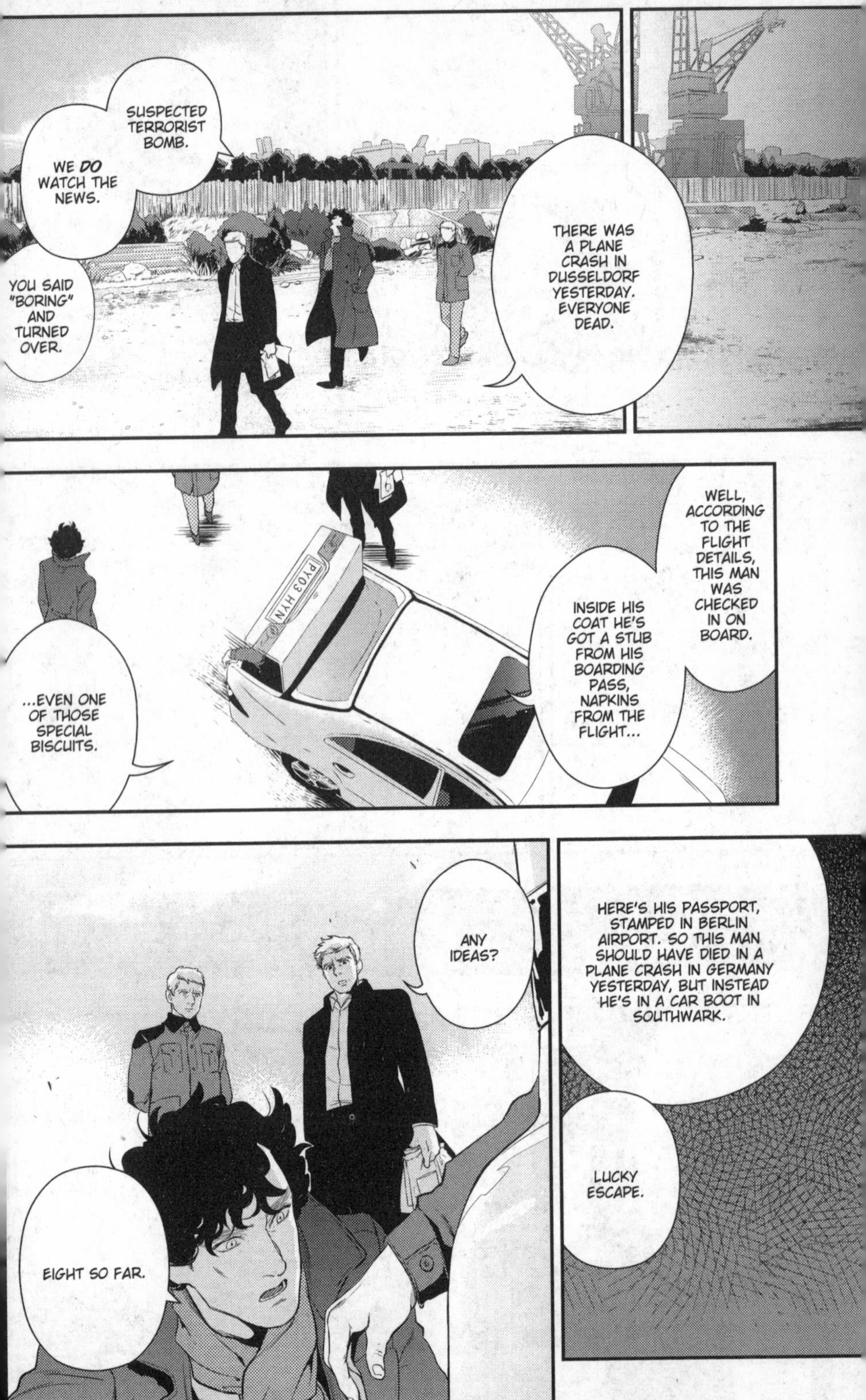

THERE WAS A PLANE CRASH IN DUSSELDORF YESTERDAY. EVERYONE DEAD.
SUSPECTED TERRORIST BOMB.
WE *DO* WATCH THE NEWS.
YOU SAID "BORING" AND TURNED OVER.
WELL, ACCORDING TO THE FLIGHT DETAILS, THIS MAN WAS CHECKED IN ON BOARD.
INSIDE HIS COAT HE'S GOT A STUB FROM HIS BOARDING PASS, NAPKINS FROM THE FLIGHT...
PY03 HYN
...EVEN ONE OF THOSE SPECIAL BISCUITS.
HERE'S HIS PASSPORT, STAMPED IN BERLIN AIRPORT. SO THIS MAN SHOULD HAVE DIED IN A PLANE CRASH IN GERMANY YESTERDAY, BUT INSTEAD HE'S IN A CAR BOOT IN SOUTHWARK.
LUCKY ESCAPE.
ANY IDEAS?
EIGHT SO FAR.

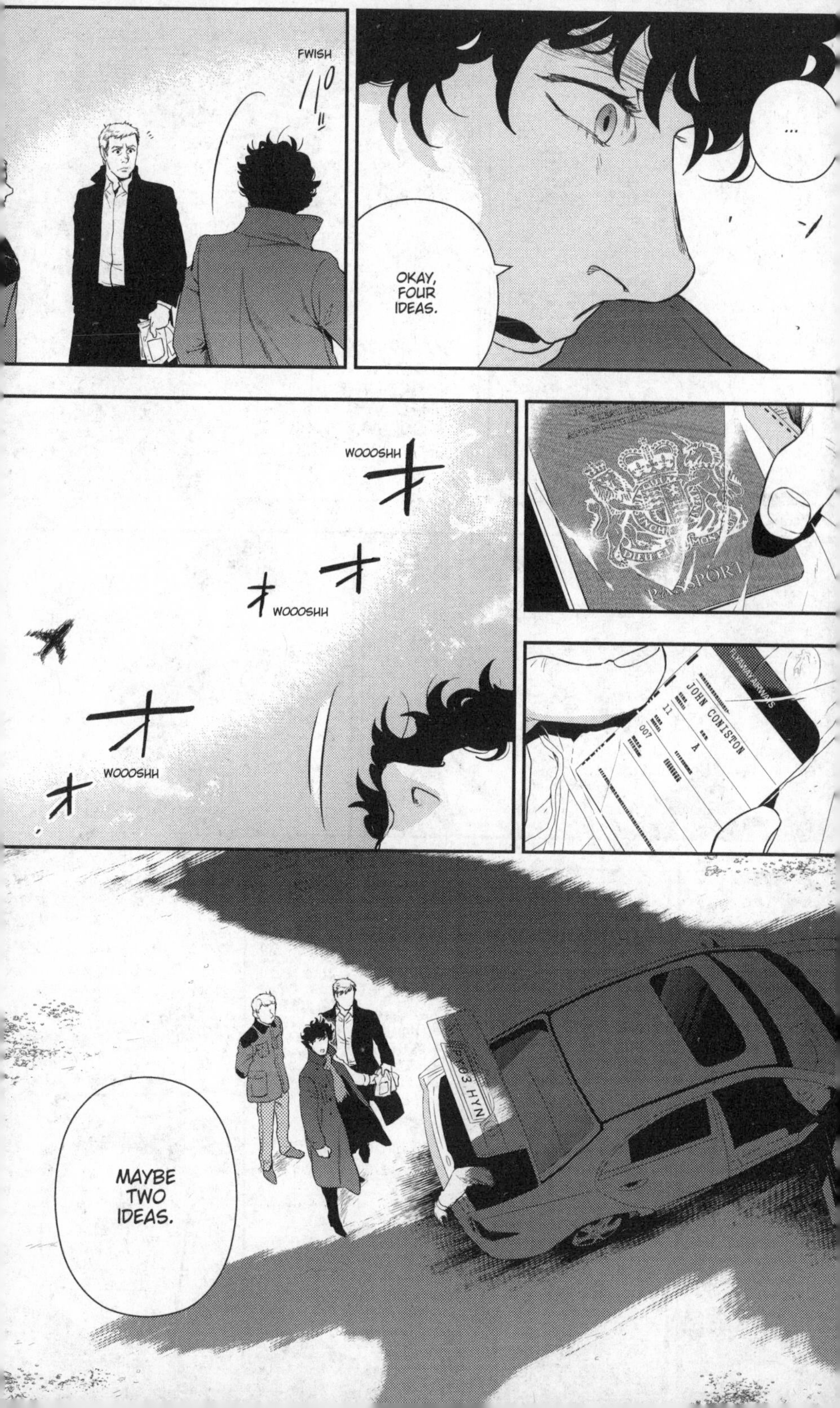
...
OKAY, FOUR IDEAS.
FWISH
PASSPORT
JOHN CONISTON
11
A
007
WOOOSHH
WOOOSHH
WOOOSHH
MAYBE TWO IDEAS.

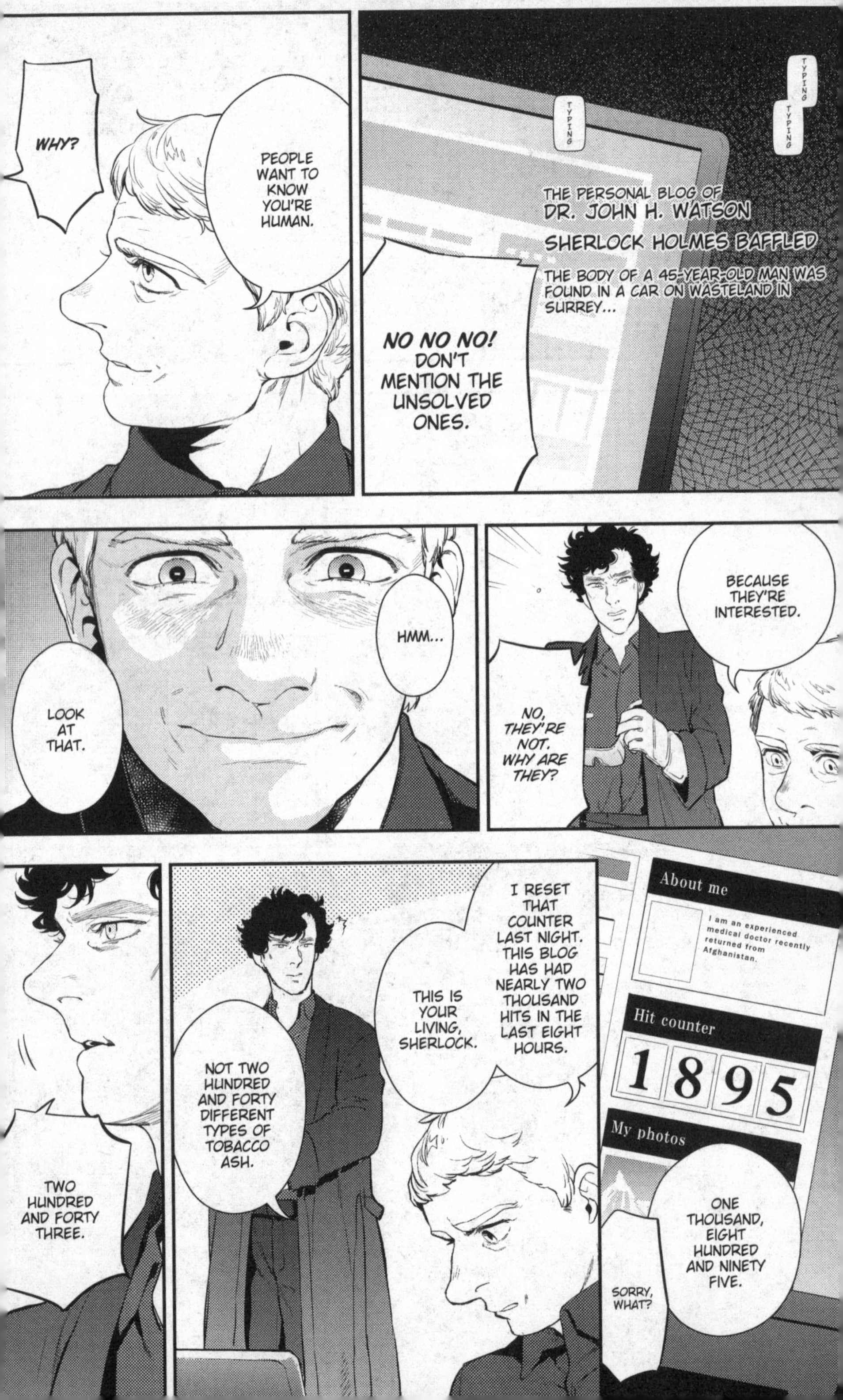

TYPING
TYPING
TYPING
THE PERSONAL BLOG OF
DR. JOHN H. WATSON
SHERLOCK HOLMES BAFFLED
THE BODY OF A 45-YEAR-OLD MAN WAS FOUND IN A CAR ON WASTELAND IN SURREY...
NO NO NO! DON'T MENTION THE UNSOLVED ONES.
WHY?
PEOPLE WANT TO KNOW YOU'RE HUMAN.
BECAUSE THEY'RE INTERESTED.
NO, THEY'RE NOT. WHY ARE THEY?
HMM...
LOOK AT THAT.
About me
I am an experienced medical doctor recently returned from Afghanistan.
Hit counter
1895
My photos
ONE THOUSAND, EIGHT HUNDRED AND NINETY FIVE.
SORRY, WHAT?
I RESET THAT COUNTER LAST NIGHT. THIS BLOG HAS HAD NEARLY TWO THOUSAND HITS IN THE LAST EIGHT HOURS.
THIS IS YOUR LIVING, SHERLOCK.
NOT TWO HUNDRED AND FORTY DIFFERENT TYPES OF TOBACCO ASH.
TWO HUNDRED AND FORTY THREE.

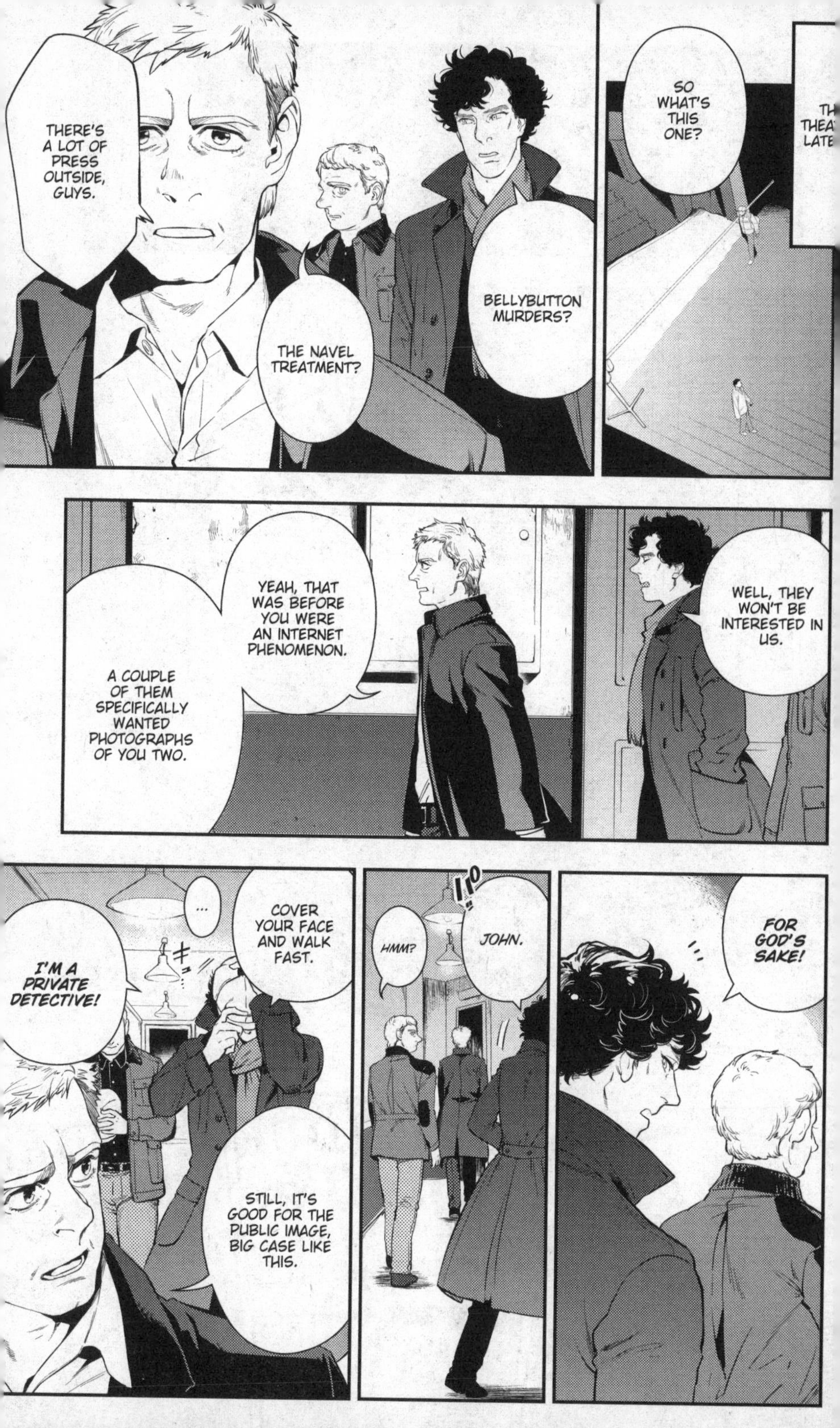
SO WHAT'S THIS ONE?
BELLYBUTTON MURDERS?
THE NAVEL TREATMENT?
THERE'S A LOT OF PRESS OUTSIDE, GUYS.
WELL, THEY WON'T BE INTERESTED IN US.
YEAH, THAT WAS BEFORE YOU WERE AN INTERNET PHENOMENON.
A COUPLE OF THEM SPECIFICALLY WANTED PHOTOGRAPHS OF YOU TWO.
FOR GOD'S SAKE!
JOHN.
HMM?
COVER YOUR FACE AND WALK FAST.
...
I'M A PRIVATE DETECTIVE!
STILL, IT'S GOOD FOR THE PUBLIC IMAGE, BIG CASE LIKE THIS.

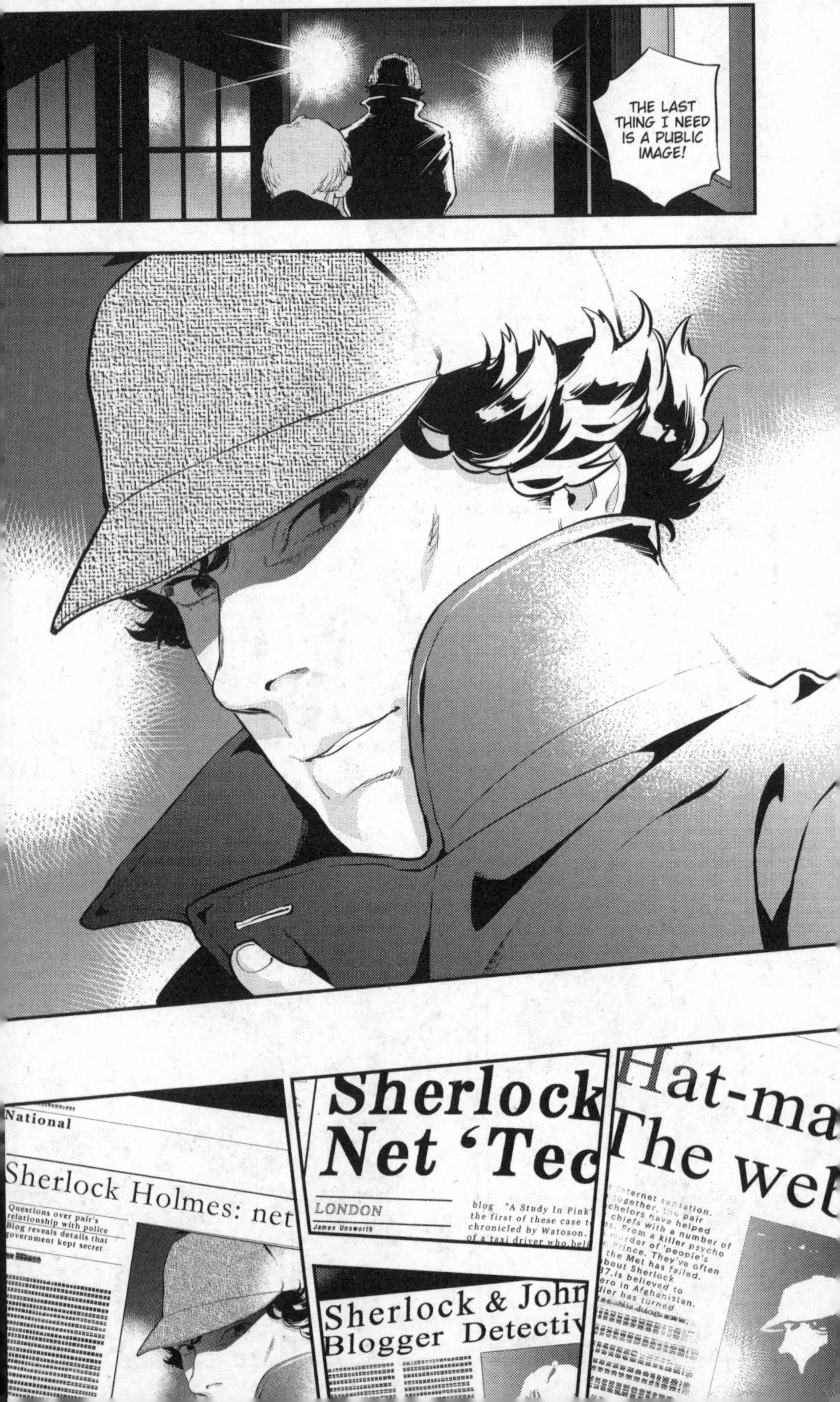
THE LAST THING I NEED IS A PUBLIC IMAGE!
Hat-ma
The wet
internet sensation.
together, the pair
chelors have helped
chiefs with a number of
es. From a killer psycho
murder of 'people's
Prince. They've often
the Met has failed.
bout Sherlock
37,is believed to
ero in Afghanistan.
dier has turned
Sherlock
Net 'Tec
LONDON
James Unsworth
blog "A Study In Pink"
the first of these case t
chronicled by Watoson.
of a taxi driver who beli
Sherlock & John
Blogger Detectiv
National
Sherlock Holmes: net
Questions over pair's relationship with police
Blog reveals details that government kept secret

National
Sherlock Holmes:
Questions over pair's
elationship with police
og reveals details that
ernment kept secret
TOUCH
BEEP
HELLO.
I THINK IT'S TIME, DON'T YOU?

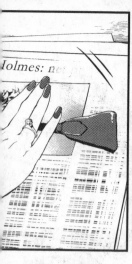

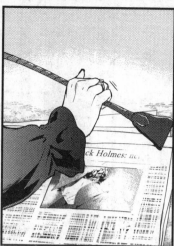

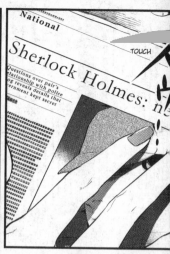

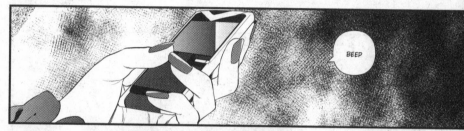

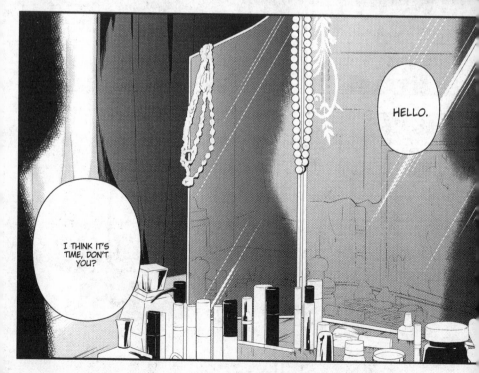

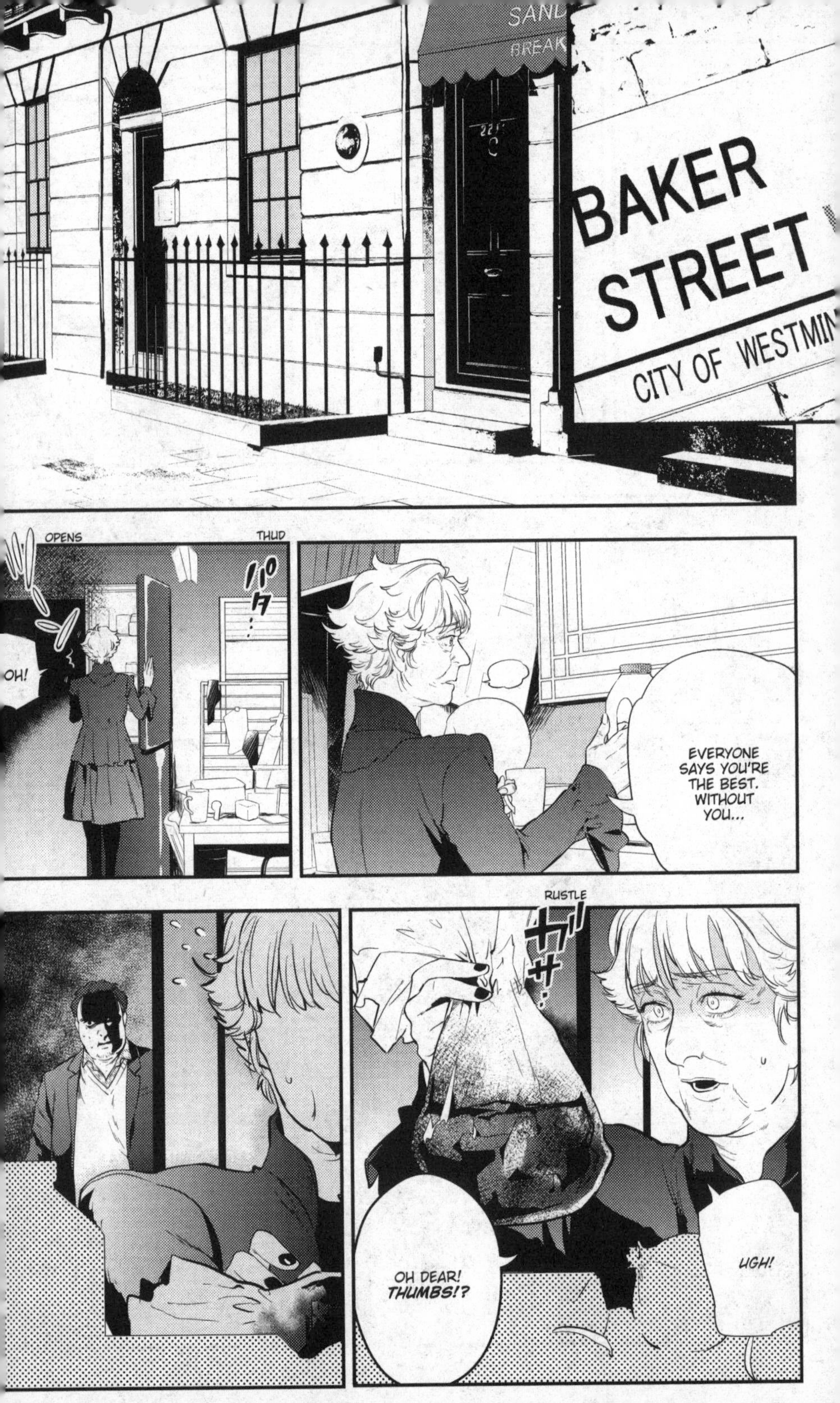
BAKER STREET
CITY OF WESTMIN
EVERYONE SAYS YOU'RE THE BEST. WITHOUT YOU...
THUD
パタ…
OPENS
OH!
RUSTLE
ガサッ
UGH!
OH DEAR! THUMBS!?

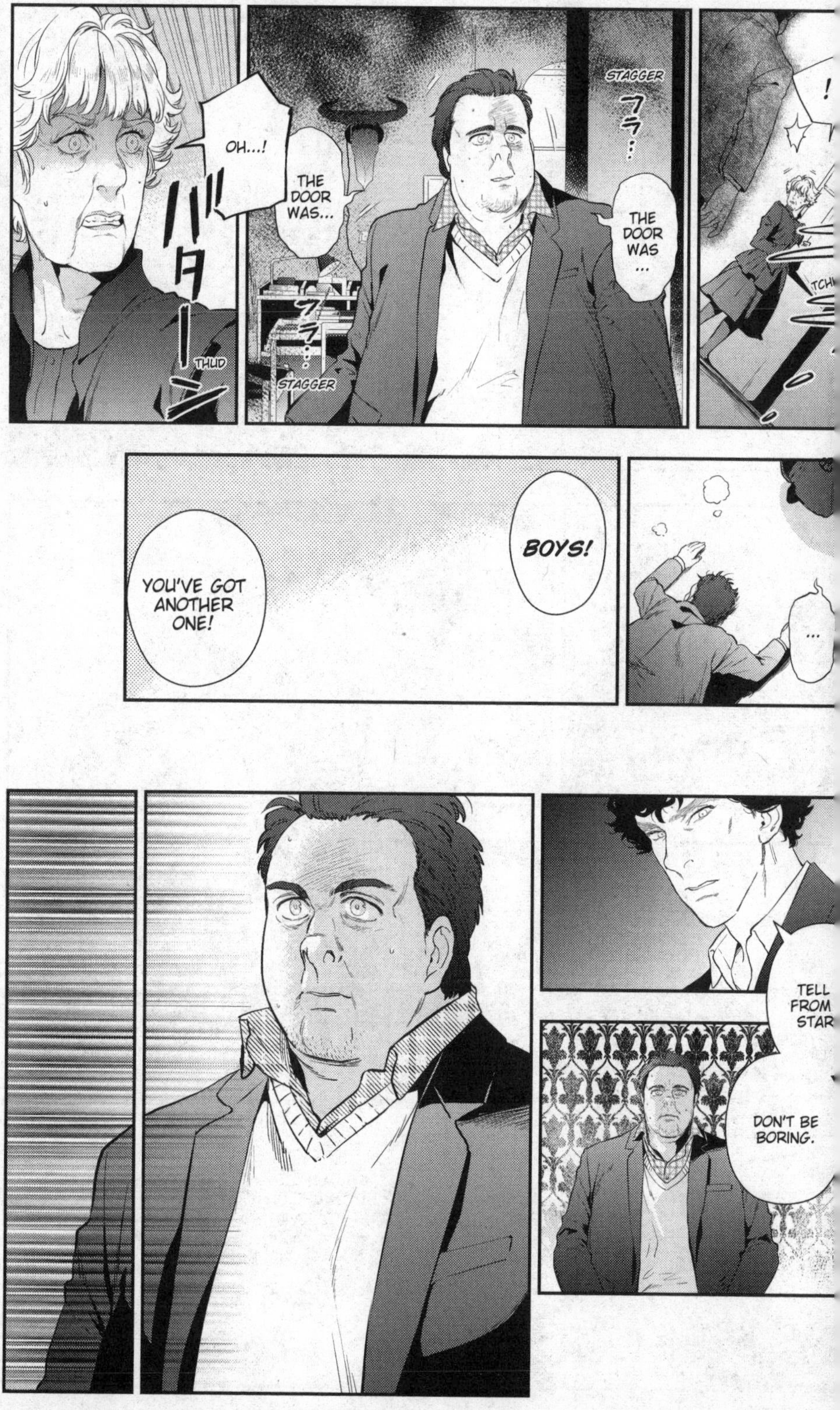
!
TCH
STAGGER
フラ…
THE DOOR WAS ...
THE DOOR WAS...
フラ…
STAGGER
OH...!
バタ―ン
THUD
...
BOYS!
YOU'VE GOT ANOTHER ONE!
TELL FROM STAR
DON'T BE BORING.

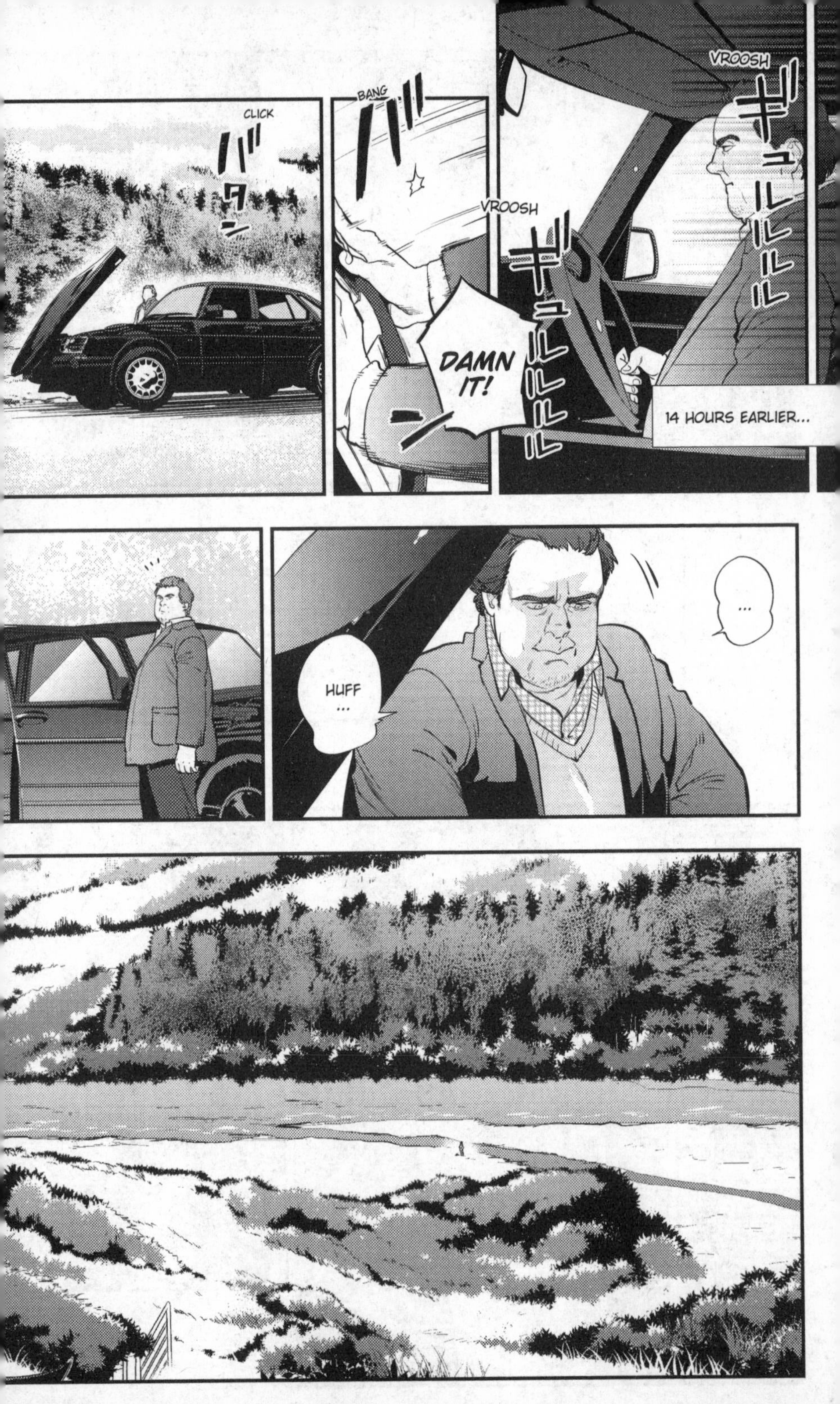
VROOSH
14 HOURS EARLIER...
VROOSH
BANG
DAMN IT!
CLICK
...
HUFF ...

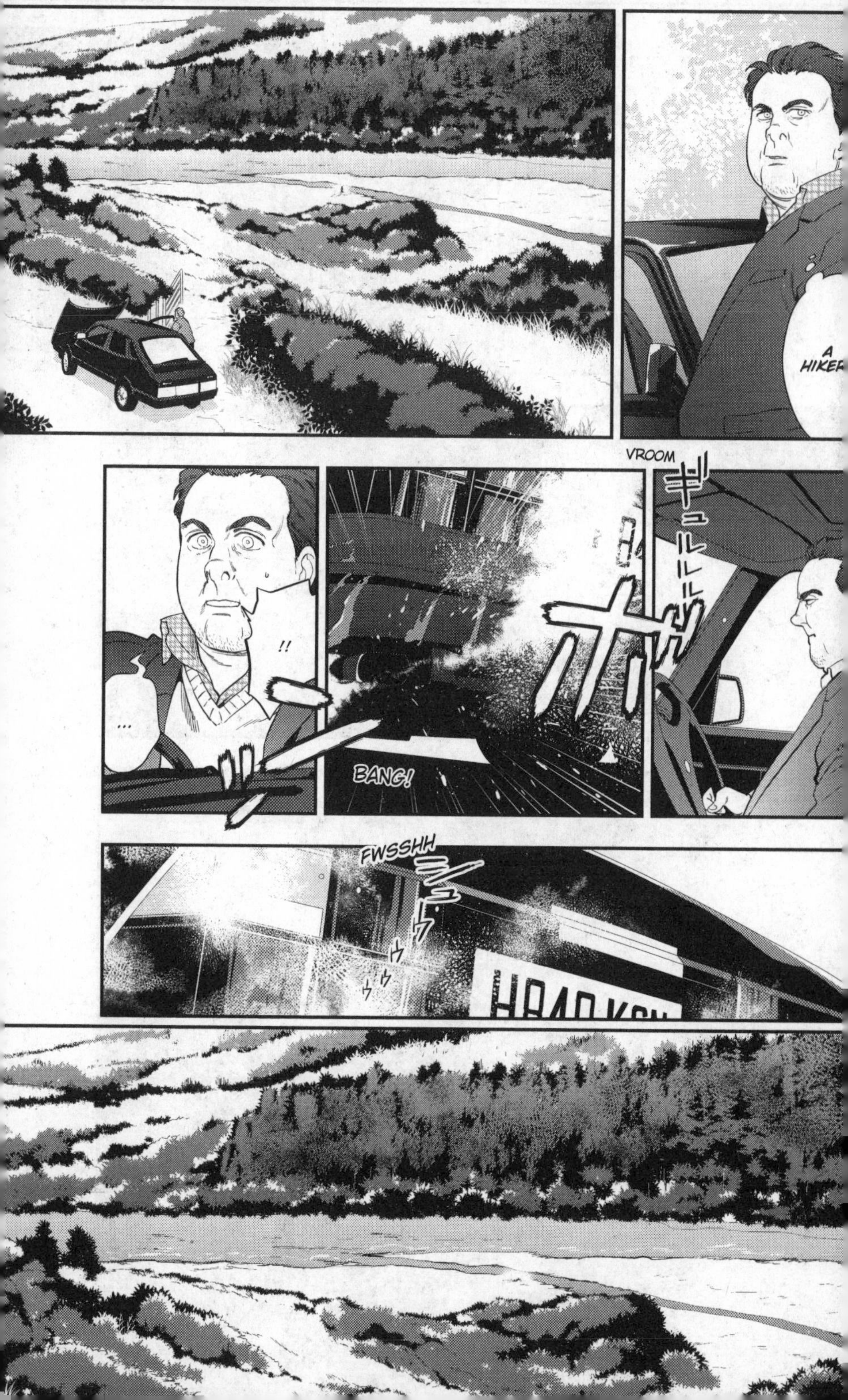
A HIKER
VROOM
BANG!
!!
...
FWSSHH

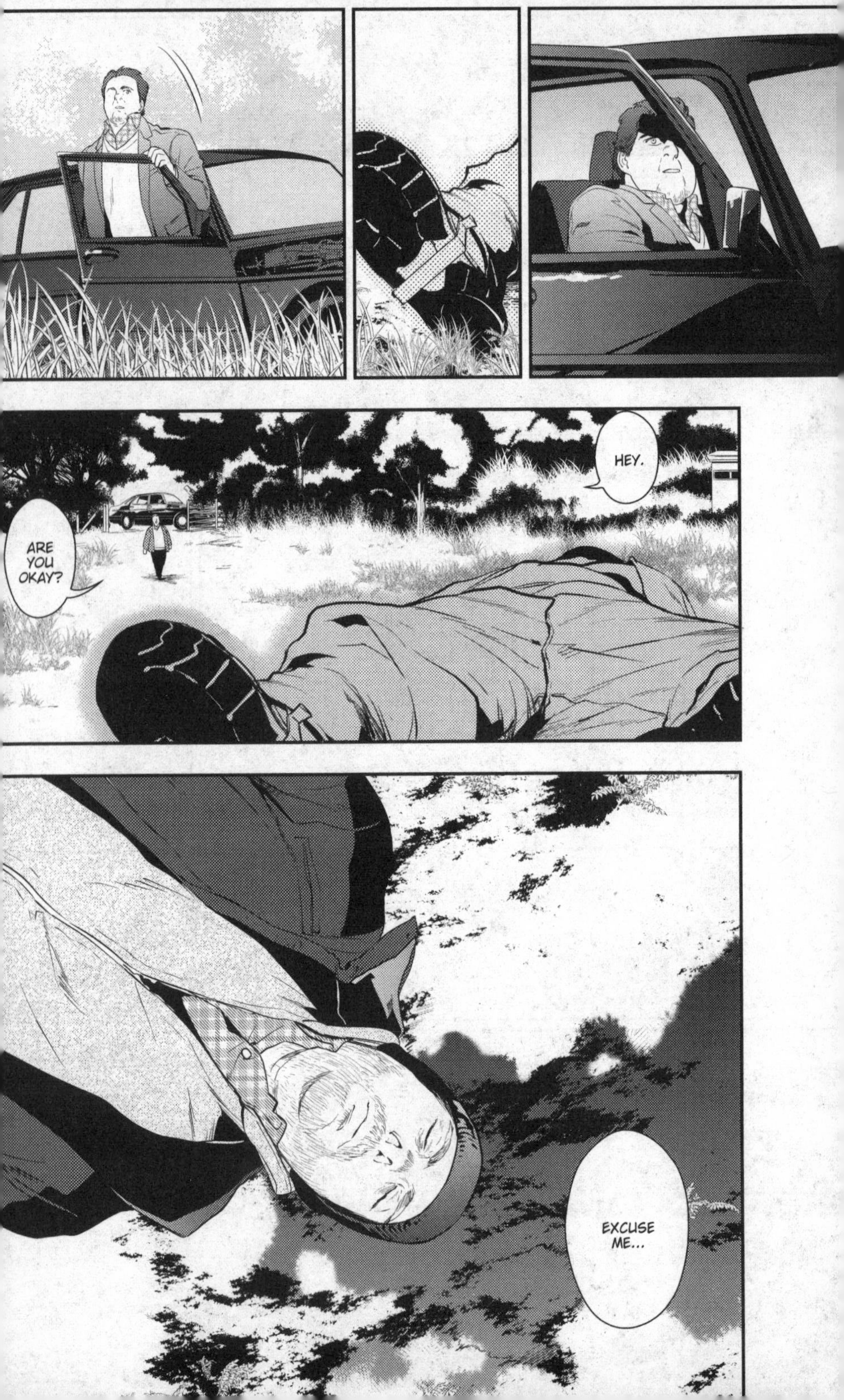
HEY.
ARE YOU OKAY?
EXCUSE ME...

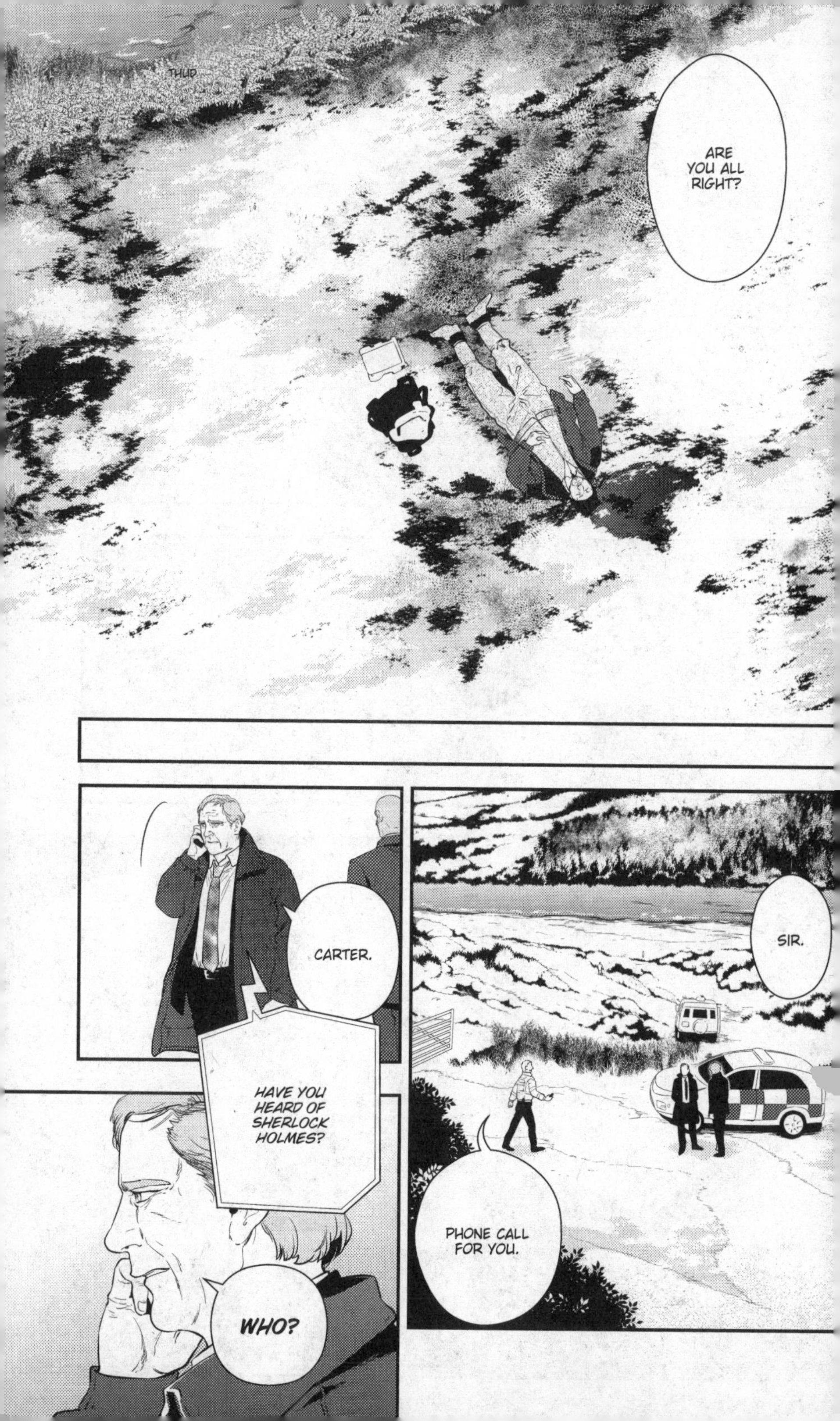
THUD
ARE YOU ALL RIGHT?
SIR.
PHONE CALL FOR YOU.
CARTER.
HAVE YOU HEARD OF SHERLOCK HOLMES?
WHO?

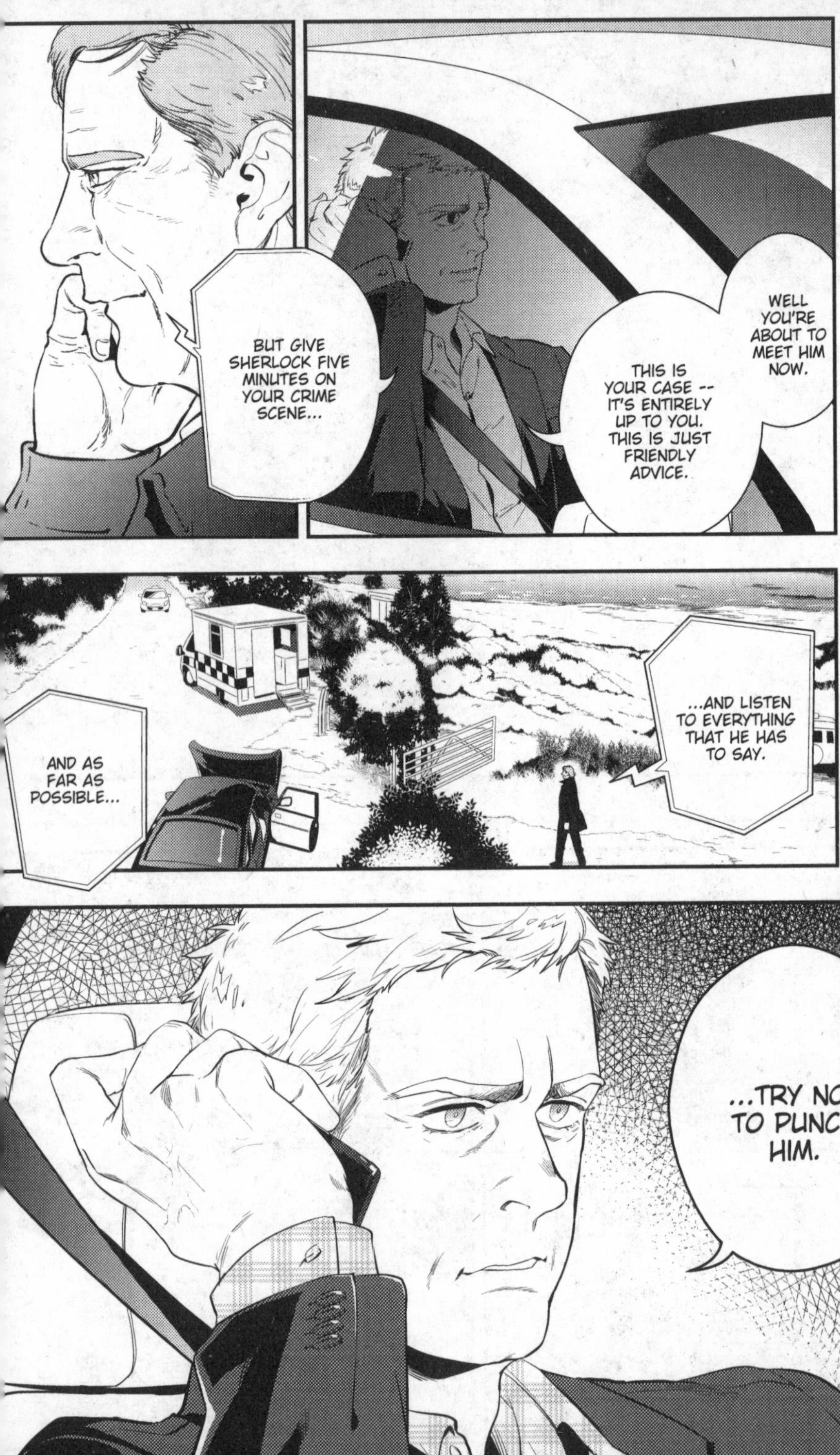
WELL YOU'RE ABOUT TO MEET HIM NOW.
THIS IS YOUR CASE -- IT'S ENTIRELY UP TO YOU. THIS IS JUST FRIENDLY ADVICE.
BUT GIVE SHERLOCK FIVE MINUTES ON YOUR CRIME SCENE...
...AND LISTEN TO EVERYTHING THAT HE HAS TO SAY.
AND AS FAR AS POSSIBLE...
...TRY NOT TO PUNCH HIM.

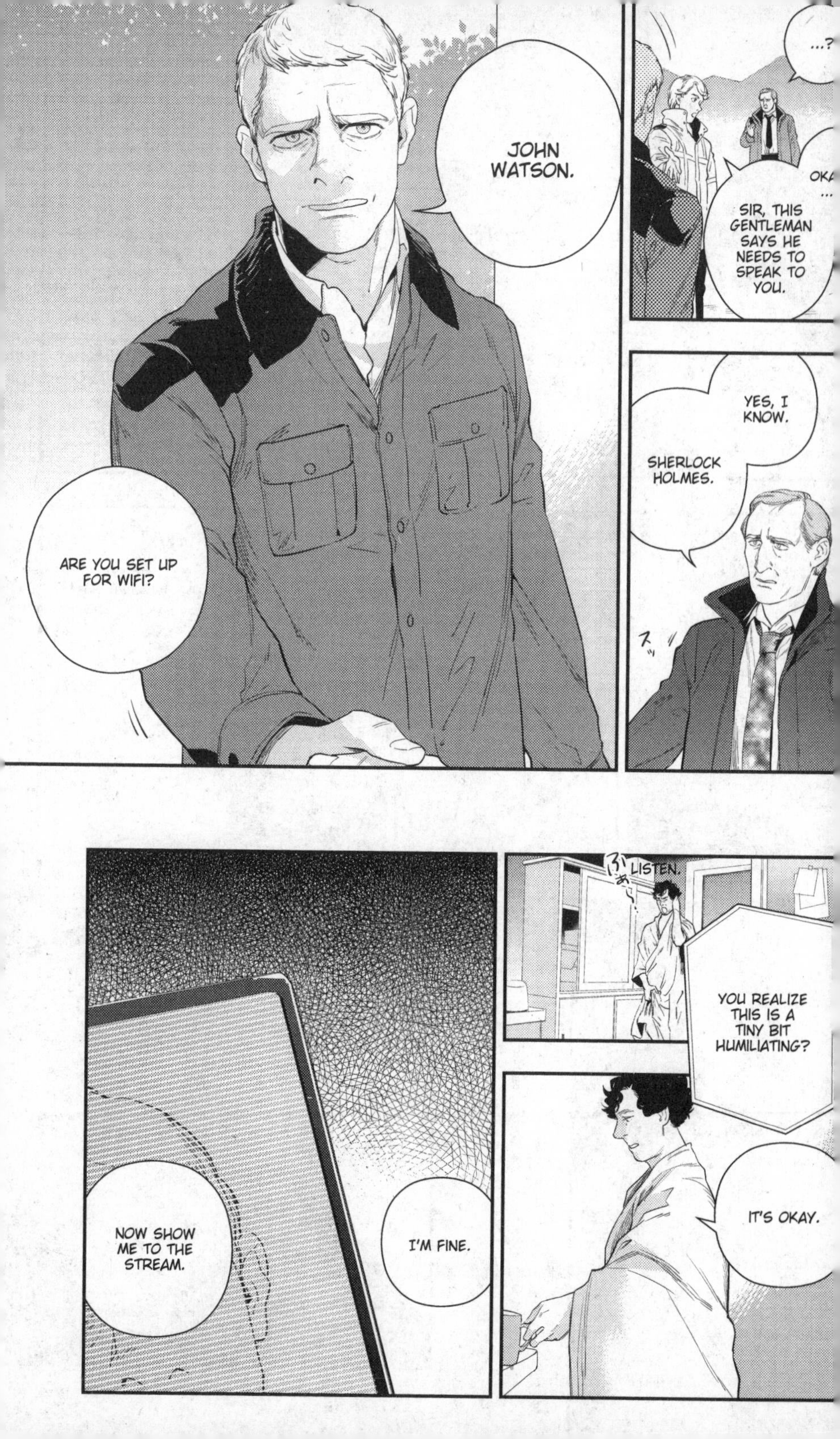
...?
OKA
...
SIR, THIS GENTLEMAN SAYS HE NEEDS TO SPEAK TO YOU.
YES, I KNOW.
SHERLOCK HOLMES.
JOHN WATSON.
ARE YOU SET UP FOR WIFI?
LISTEN.
YOU REALIZE THIS IS A TINY BIT HUMILIATING?
IT'S OKAY.
I'M FINE.
NOW SHOW ME TO THE STREAM.

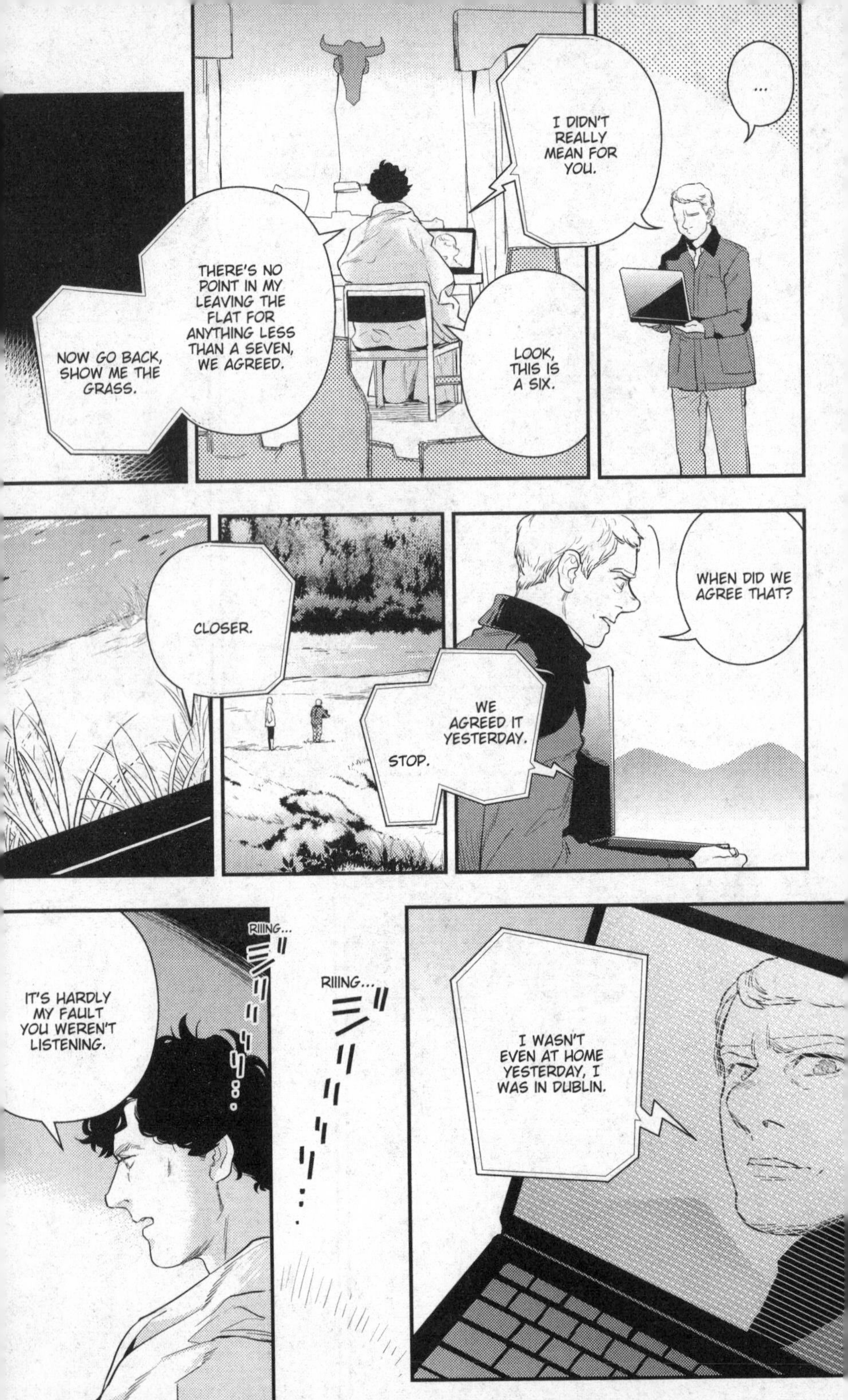
...
I DIDN'T REALLY MEAN FOR YOU.
THERE'S NO POINT IN MY LEAVING THE FLAT FOR ANYTHING LESS THAN A SEVEN, WE AGREED.
LOOK, THIS IS A SIX.
NOW GO BACK, SHOW ME THE GRASS.
WHEN DID WE AGREE THAT?
WE AGREED IT YESTERDAY.
STOP.
CLOSER.
I WASN'T EVEN AT HOME YESTERDAY, I WAS IN DUBLIN.
RIIING...
RIIING...
IT'S HARDLY MY FAULT YOU WEREN'T LISTENING.

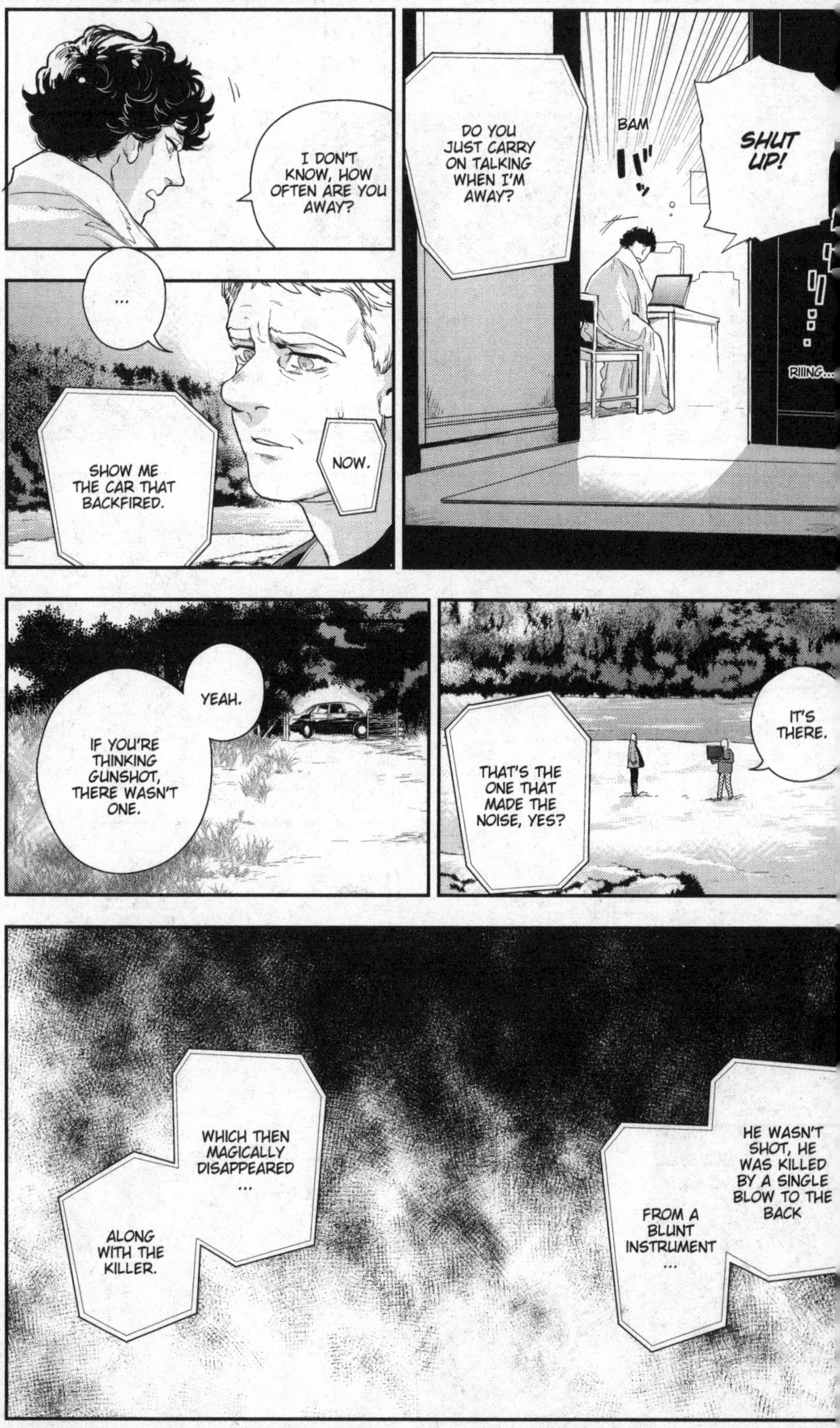
SHUT UP!
BAM
DO YOU JUST CARRY ON TALKING WHEN I'M AWAY?
RIIING...
I DON'T KNOW, HOW OFTEN ARE YOU AWAY?
...
SHOW ME THE CAR THAT BACKFIRED.
NOW.
IT'S THERE.
THAT'S THE ONE THAT MADE THE NOISE, YES?
YEAH.
IF YOU'RE THINKING GUNSHOT, THERE WASN'T ONE.
HE WASN'T SHOT, HE WAS KILLED BY A SINGLE BLOW TO THE BACK
FROM A BLUNT INSTRUMENT ...
WHICH THEN MAGICALLY DISAPPEARED ...
ALONG WITH THE KILLER.

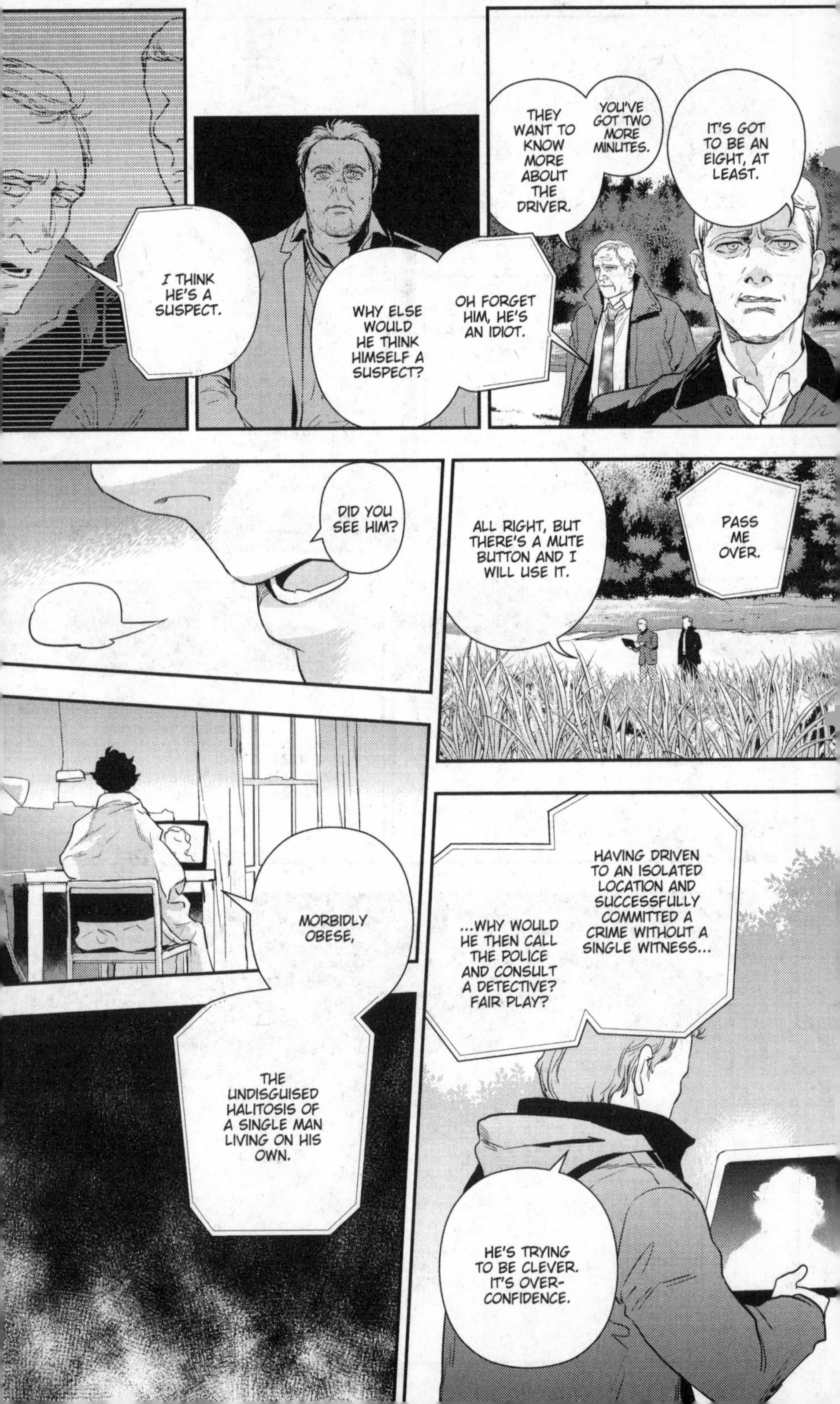
IT'S GOT TO BE AN EIGHT, AT LEAST.
YOU'VE GOT TWO MORE MINUTES.
THEY WANT TO KNOW MORE ABOUT THE DRIVER.
OH FORGET HIM, HE'S AN IDIOT.
WHY ELSE WOULD HE THINK HIMSELF A SUSPECT?
I THINK HE'S A SUSPECT.
PASS ME OVER.
ALL RIGHT, BUT THERE'S A MUTE BUTTON AND I WILL USE IT.
DID YOU SEE HIM?
HAVING DRIVEN TO AN ISOLATED LOCATION AND SUCCESSFULLY COMMITTED A CRIME WITHOUT A SINGLE WITNESS...
...WHY WOULD HE THEN CALL THE POLICE AND CONSULT A DETECTIVE? FAIR PLAY?
HE'S TRYING TO BE CLEVER. IT'S OVER-CONFIDENCE.
MORBIDLY OBESE,
THE UNDISGUISED HALITOSIS OF A SINGLE MAN LIVING ON HIS OWN.

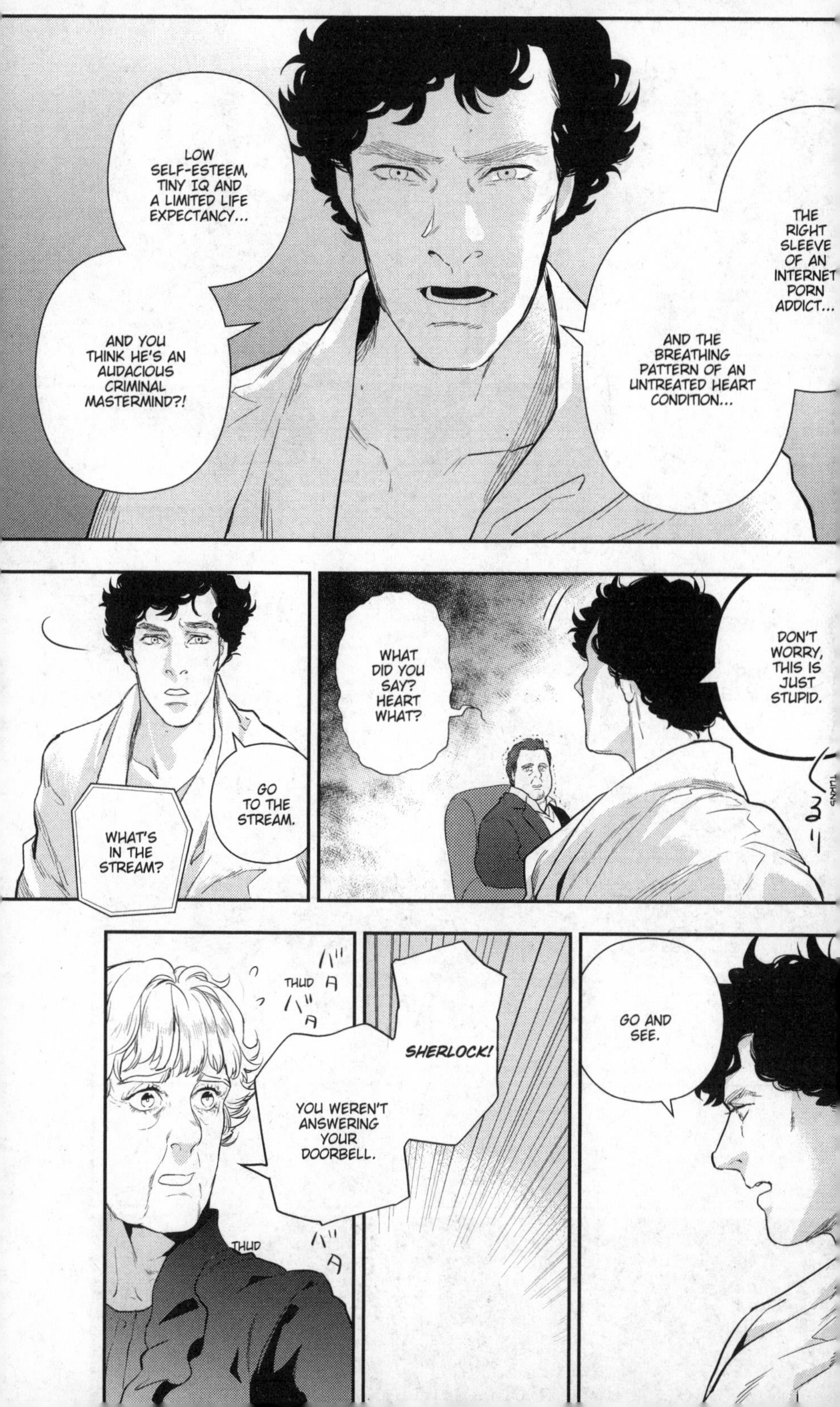
THE RIGHT SLEEVE OF AN INTERNET PORN ADDICT...
AND THE BREATHING PATTERN OF AN UNTREATED HEART CONDITION...
LOW SELF-ESTEEM, TINY IQ AND A LIMITED LIFE EXPECTANCY...
AND YOU THINK HE'S AN AUDACIOUS CRIMINAL MASTERMIND?!
DON'T WORRY, THIS IS JUST STUPID.
TURNS
WHAT DID YOU SAY? HEART WHAT?
GO TO THE STREAM.
WHAT'S IN THE STREAM?
GO AND SEE.
SHERLOCK!
YOU WEREN'T ANSWERING YOUR DOORBELL.
THUD
THUD

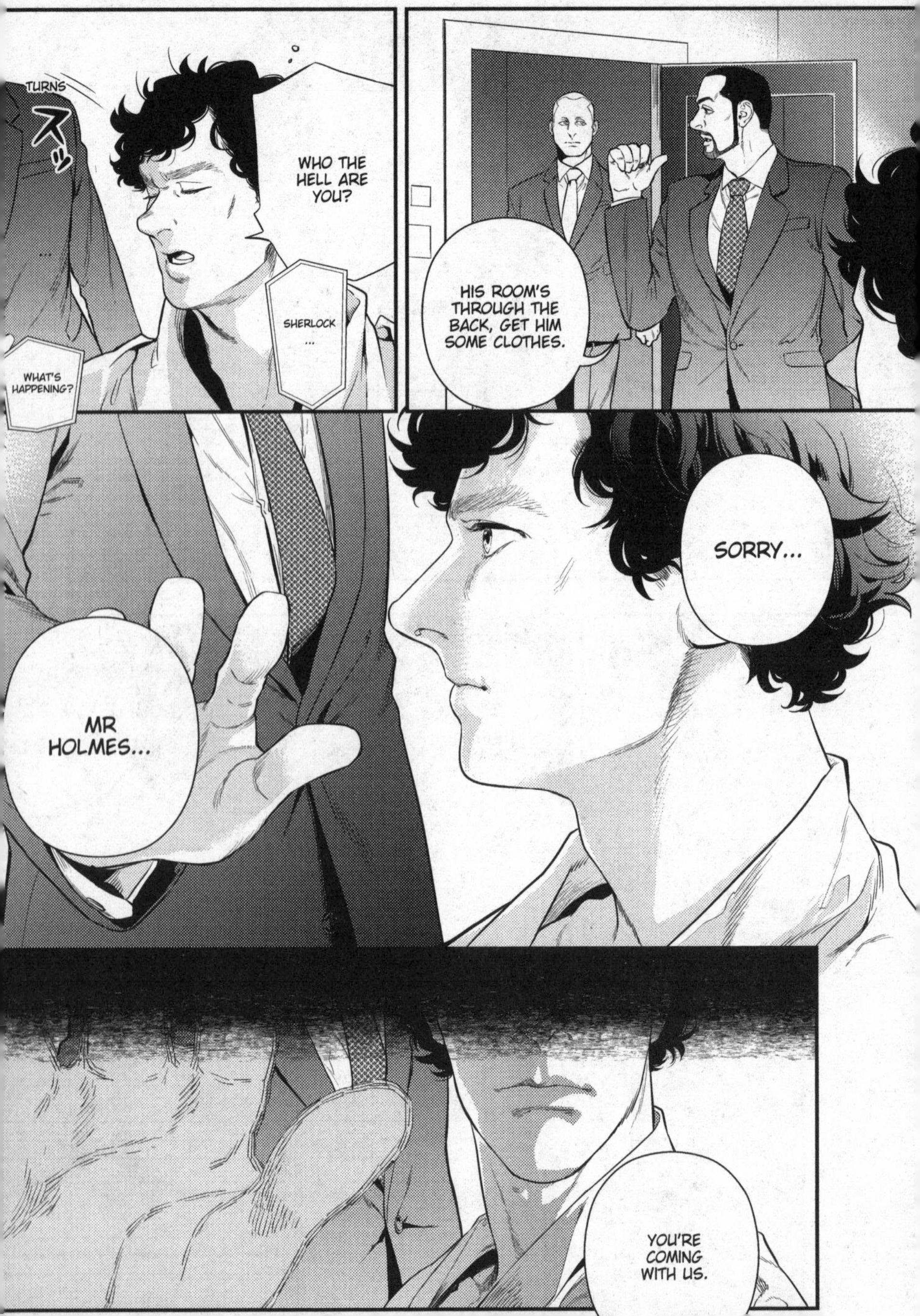
HIS ROOM'S THROUGH THE BACK, GET HIM SOME CLOTHES.
WHO THE HELL ARE YOU?
TURNS
スッ
SHERLOCK ...
WHAT'S HAPPENING?
SORRY...
MR HOLMES...
YOU'RE COMING WITH US.

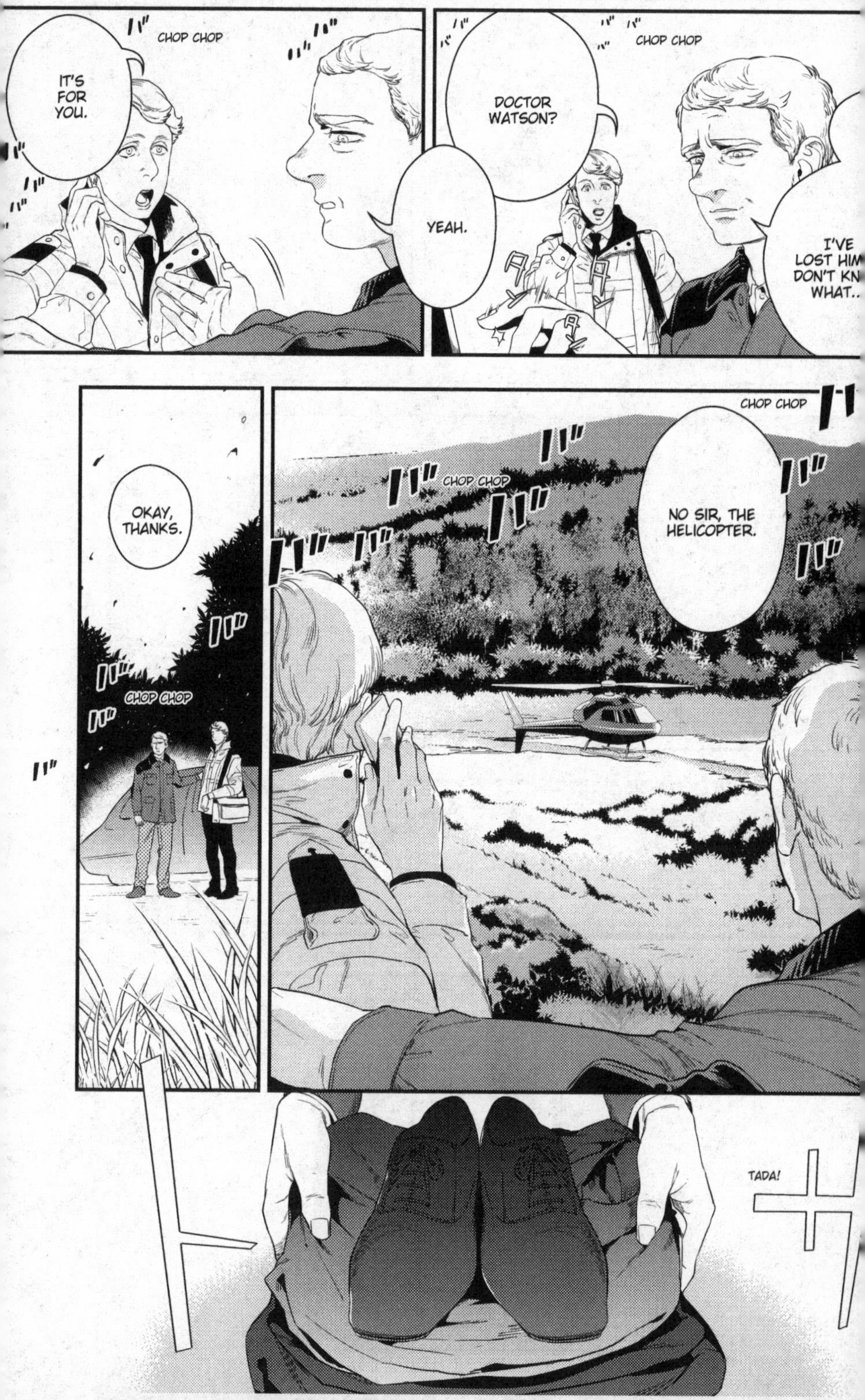
CHOP CHOP
DOCTOR WATSON?
YEAH.
I'VE LOST HIM DON'T KN WHAT..
CHOP CHOP
IT'S FOR YOU.
CHOP CHOP
CHOP CHOP
NO SIR, THE HELICOPTER.
OKAY, THANKS.
CHOP CHOP
TADA!

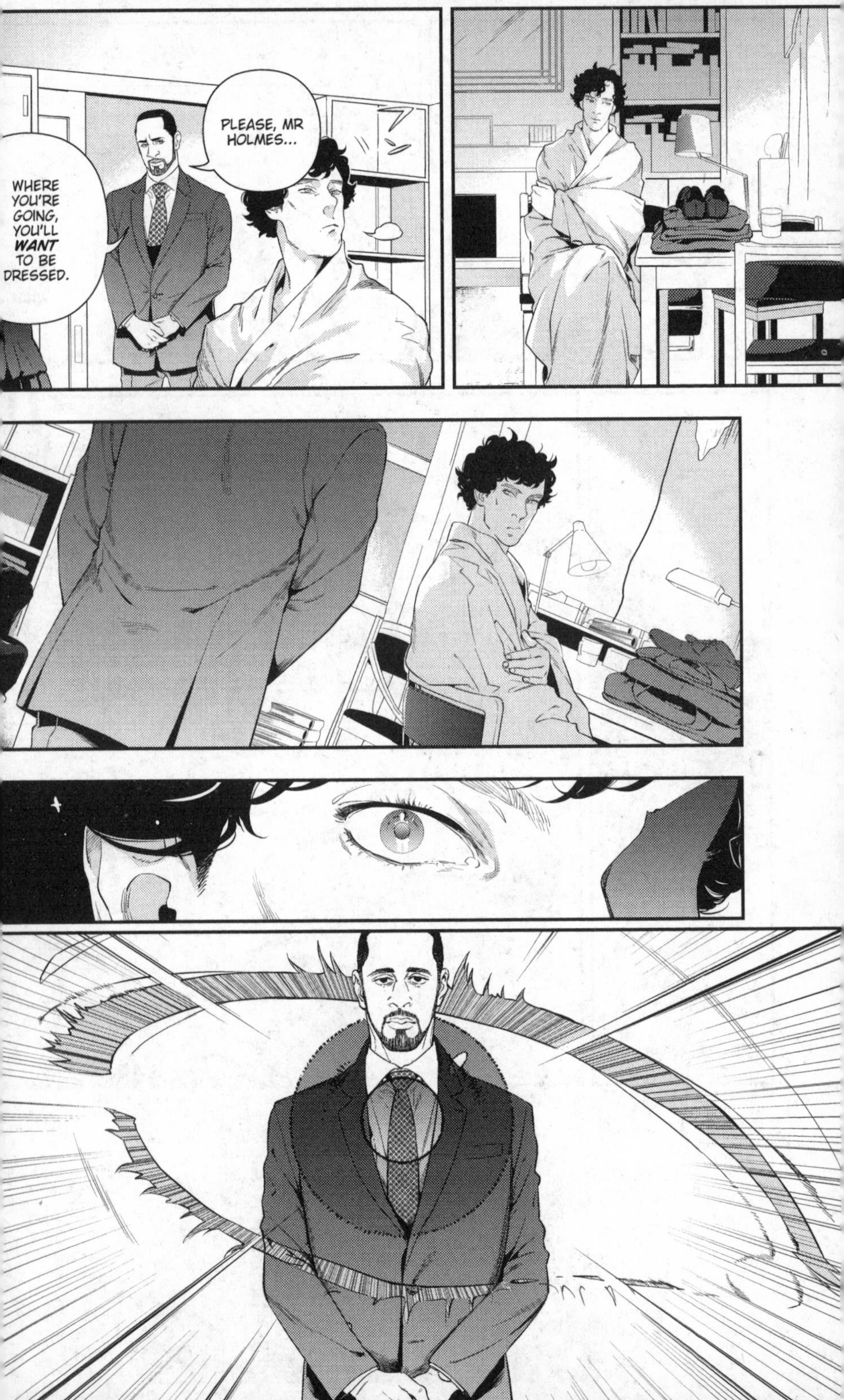
PLEASE, MR HOLMES...
WHERE YOU'RE GOING, YOU'LL *WANT* TO BE DRESSED.

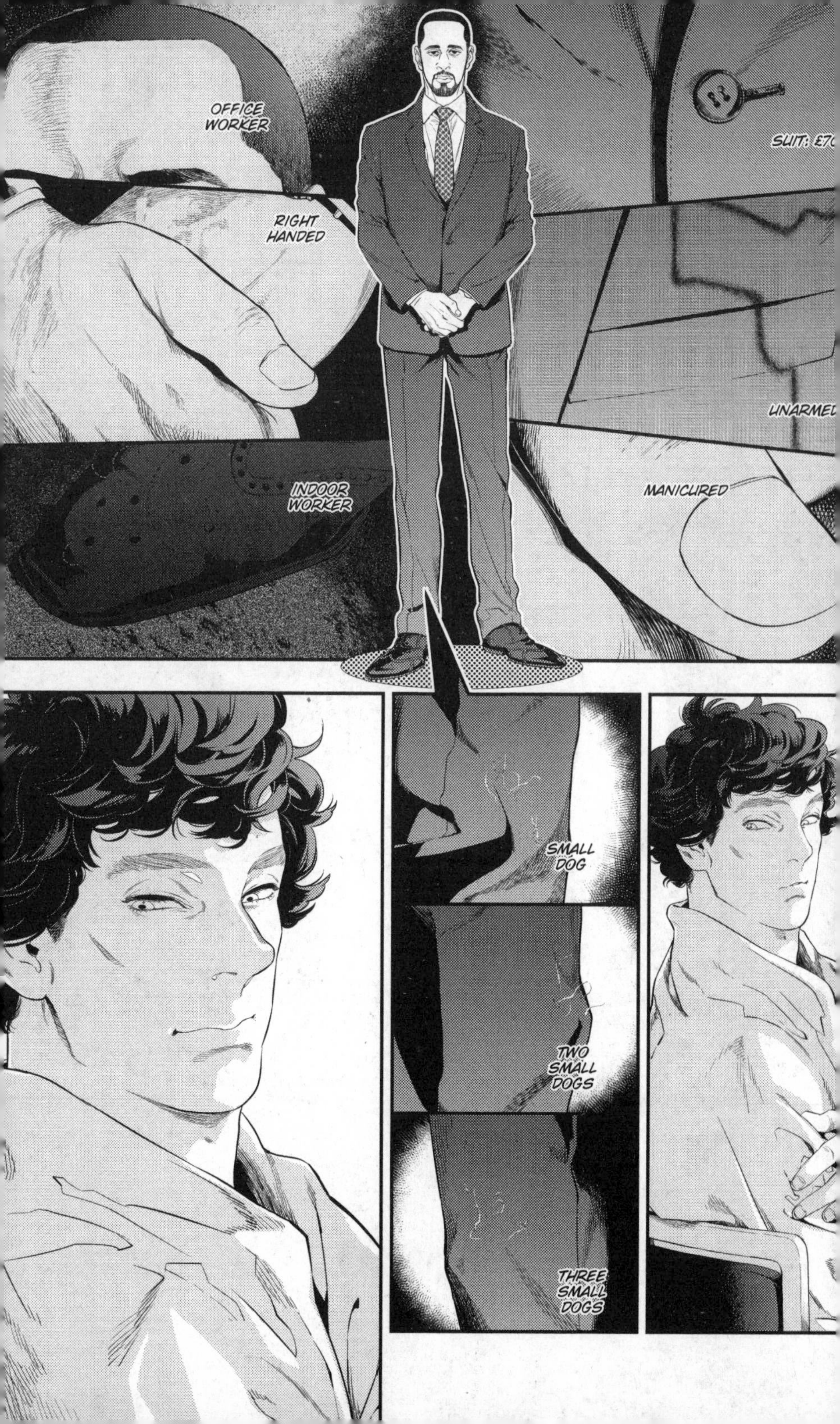
SUIT: £7
UNARME
MANICURED
OFFICE WORKER
RIGHT HANDED
INDOOR WORKER
SMALL DOG
TWO SMALL DOGS
THREE SMALL DOGS

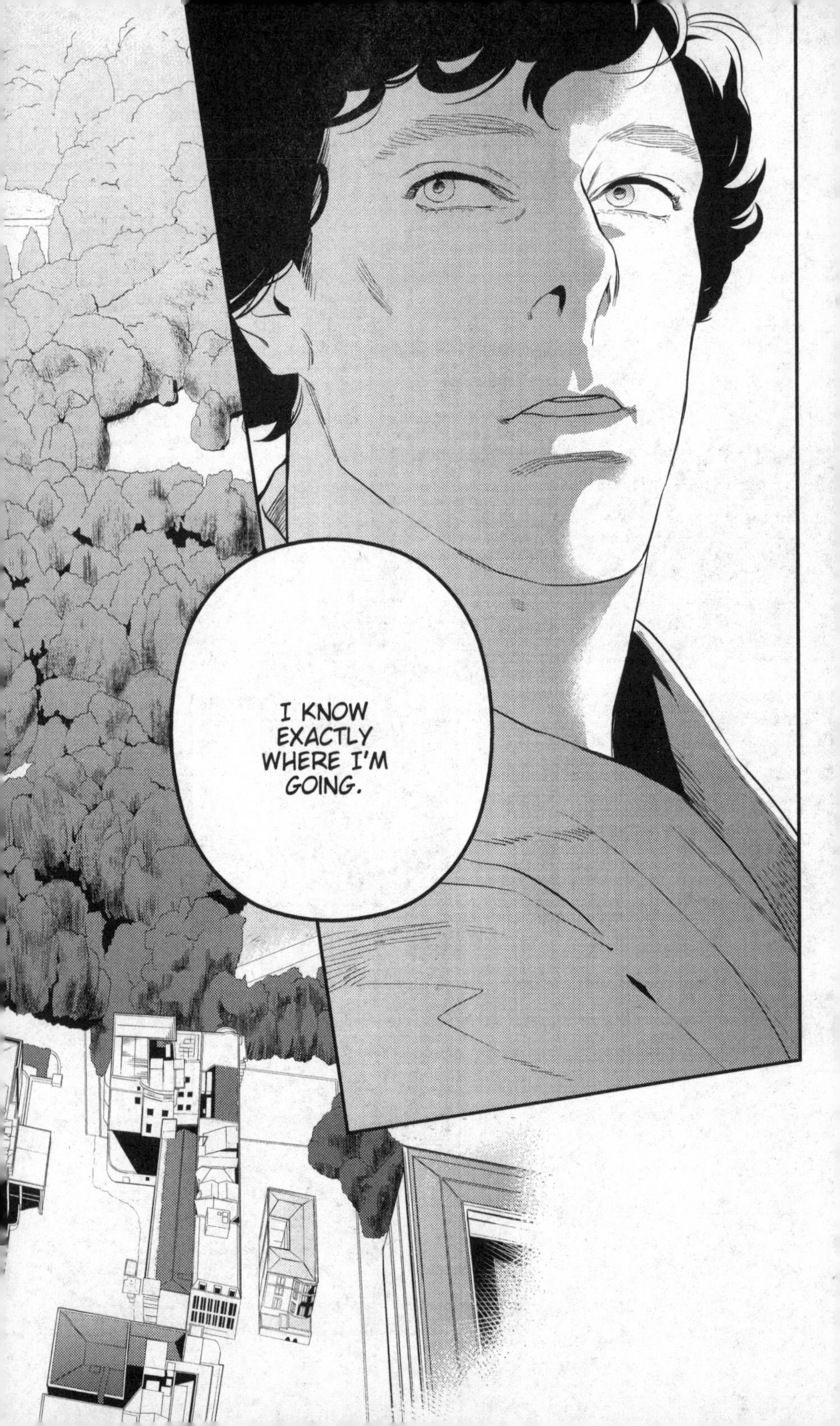
I KNOW EXACTLY WHERE I'M GOING.

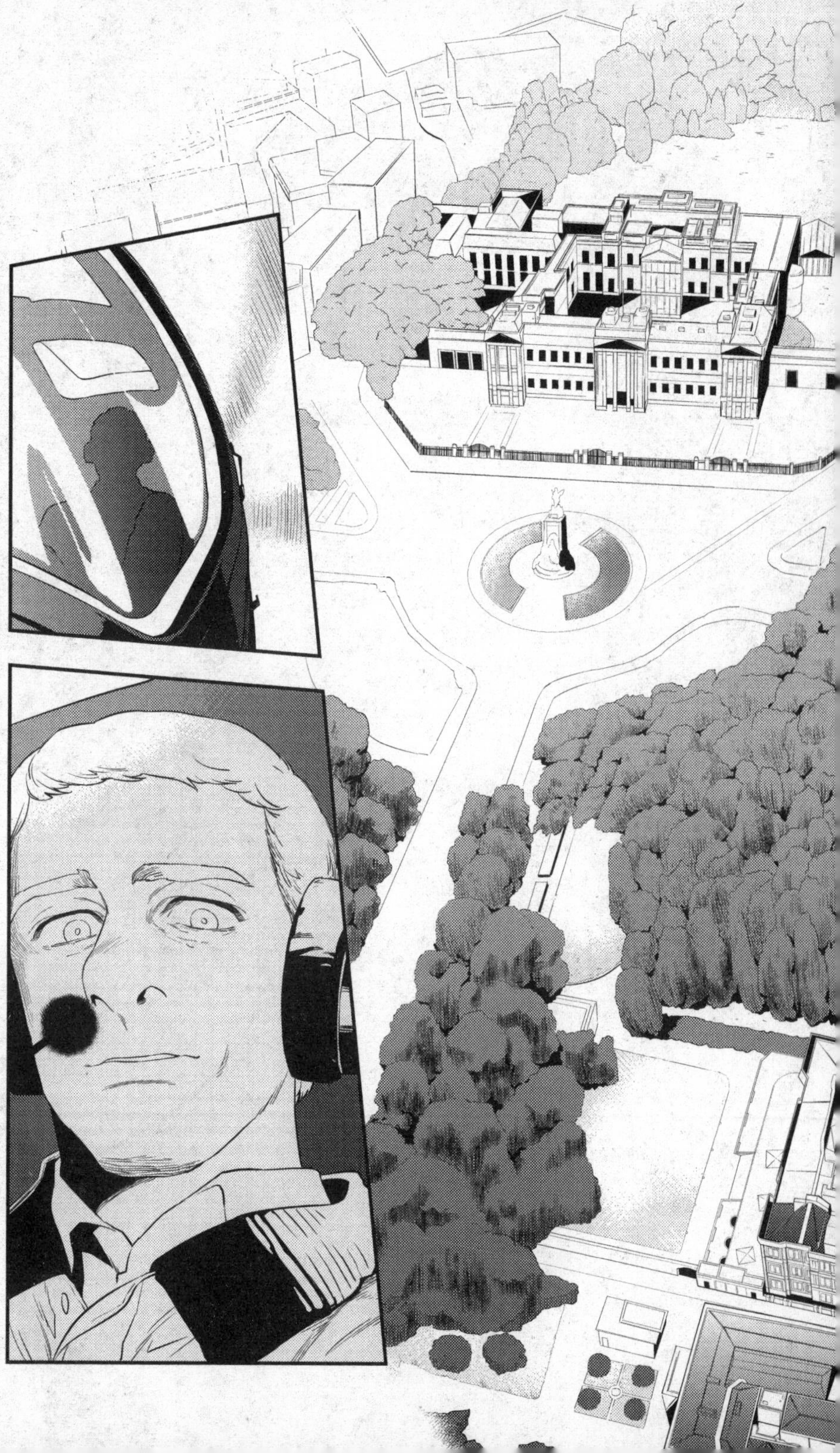

Chapter 2

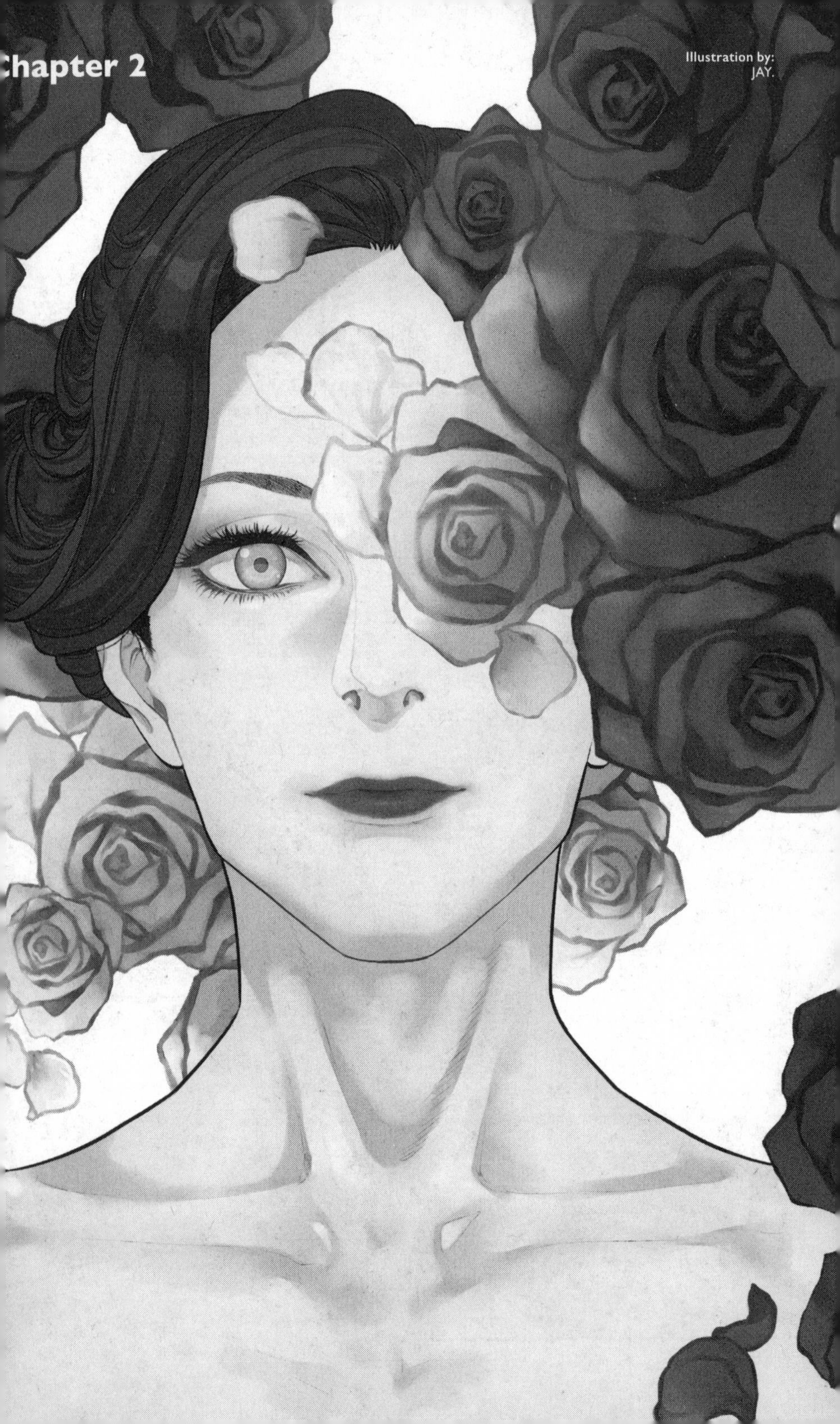

Illustration by:
JAY.

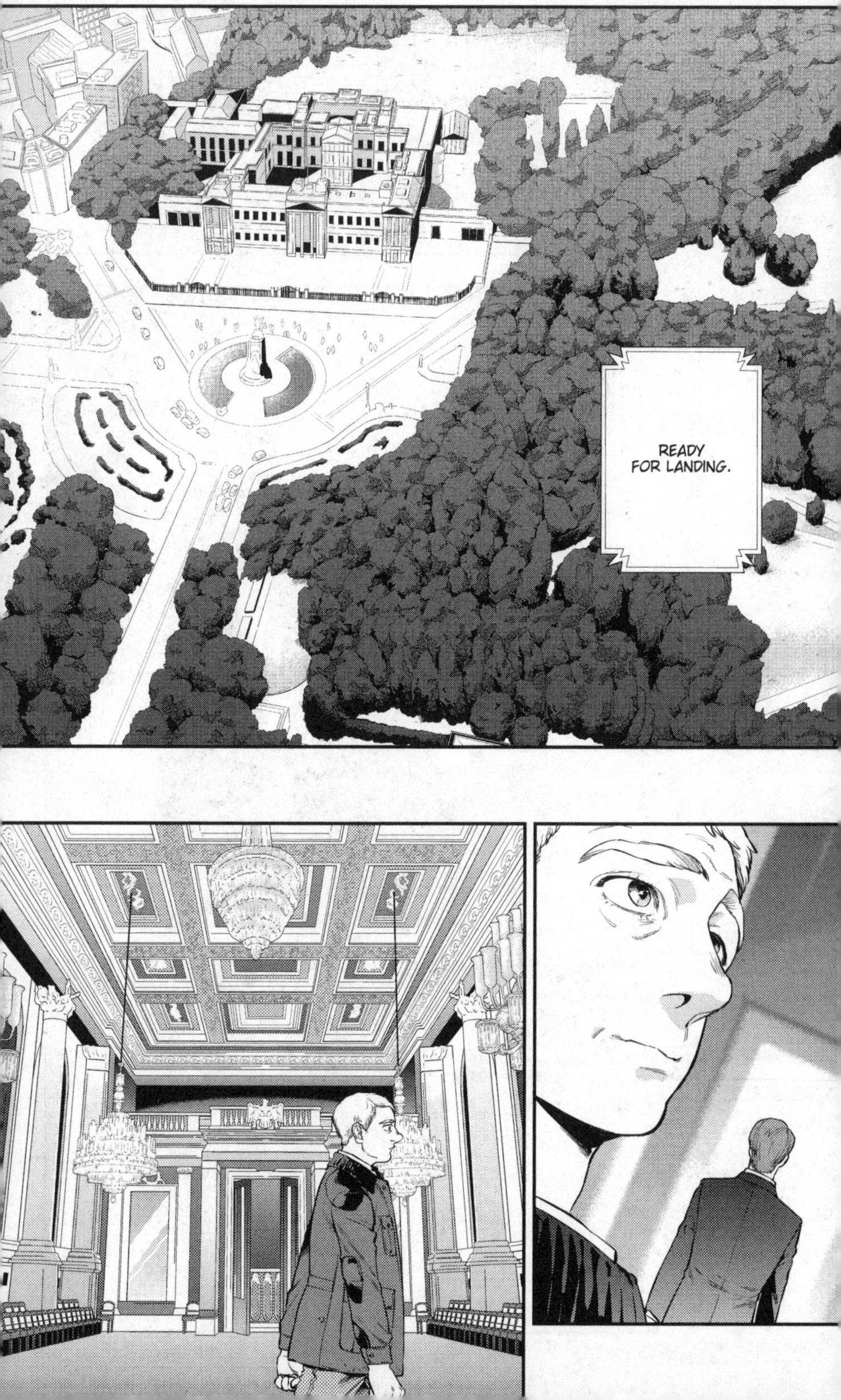
READY
FOR LANDING.

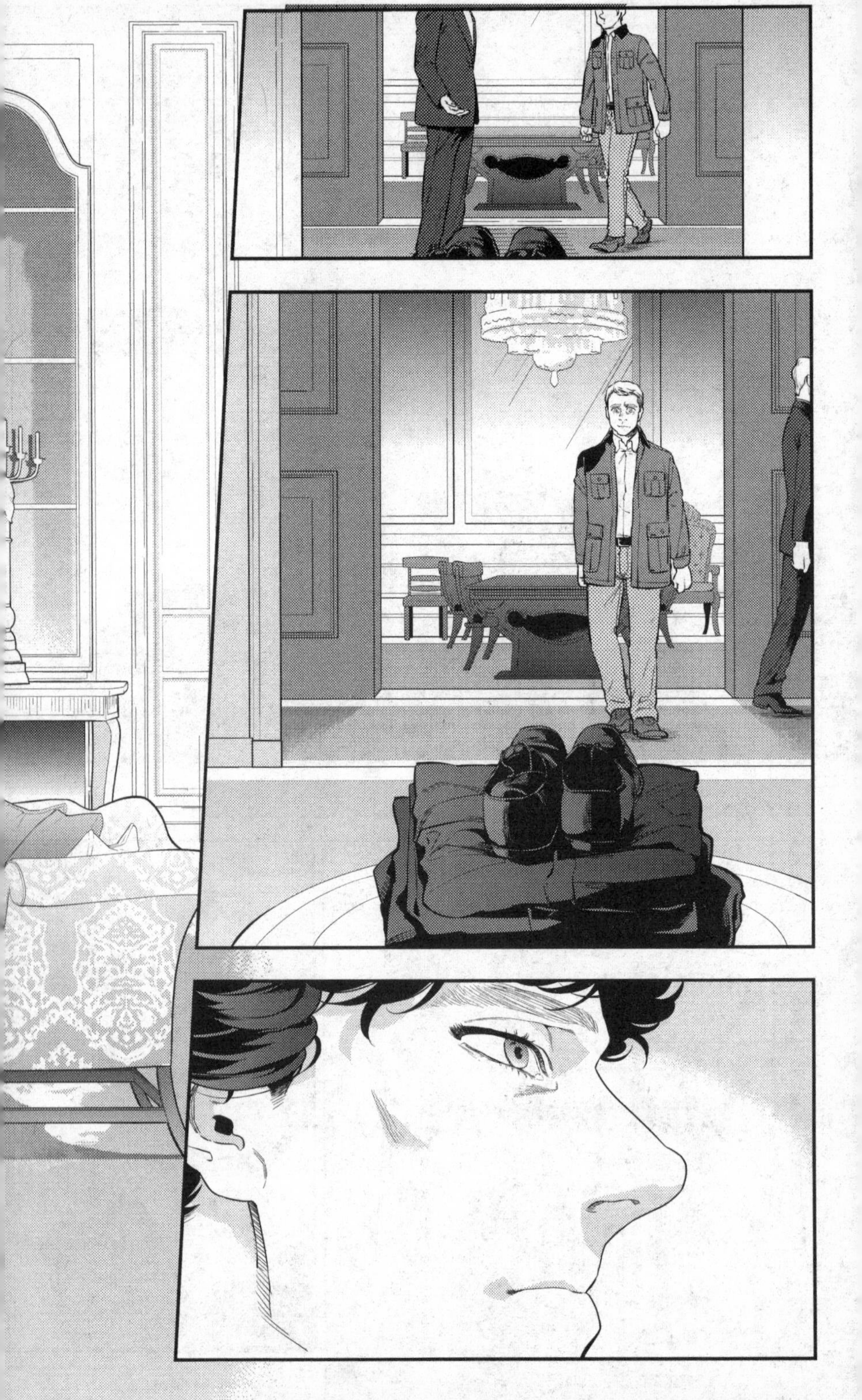

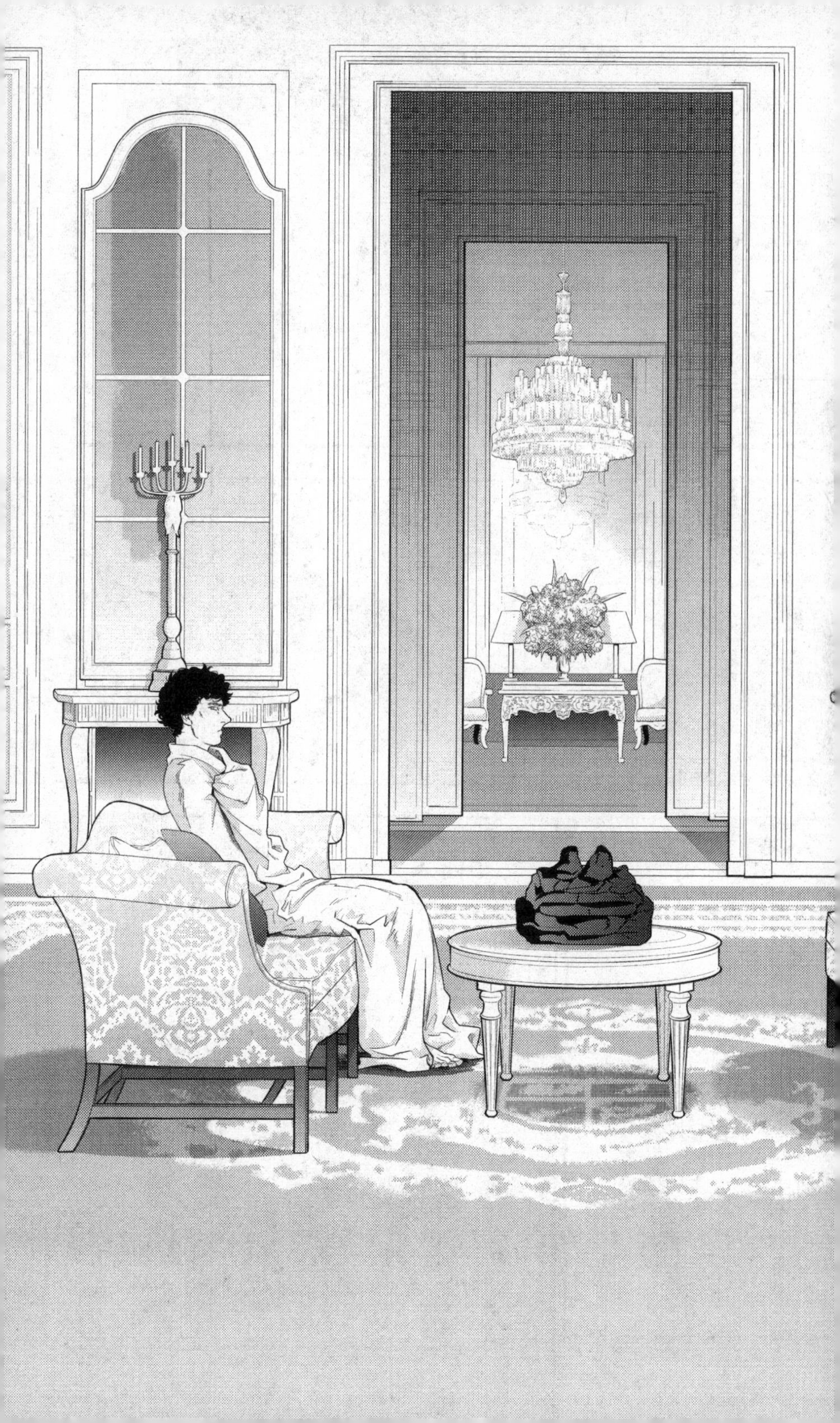

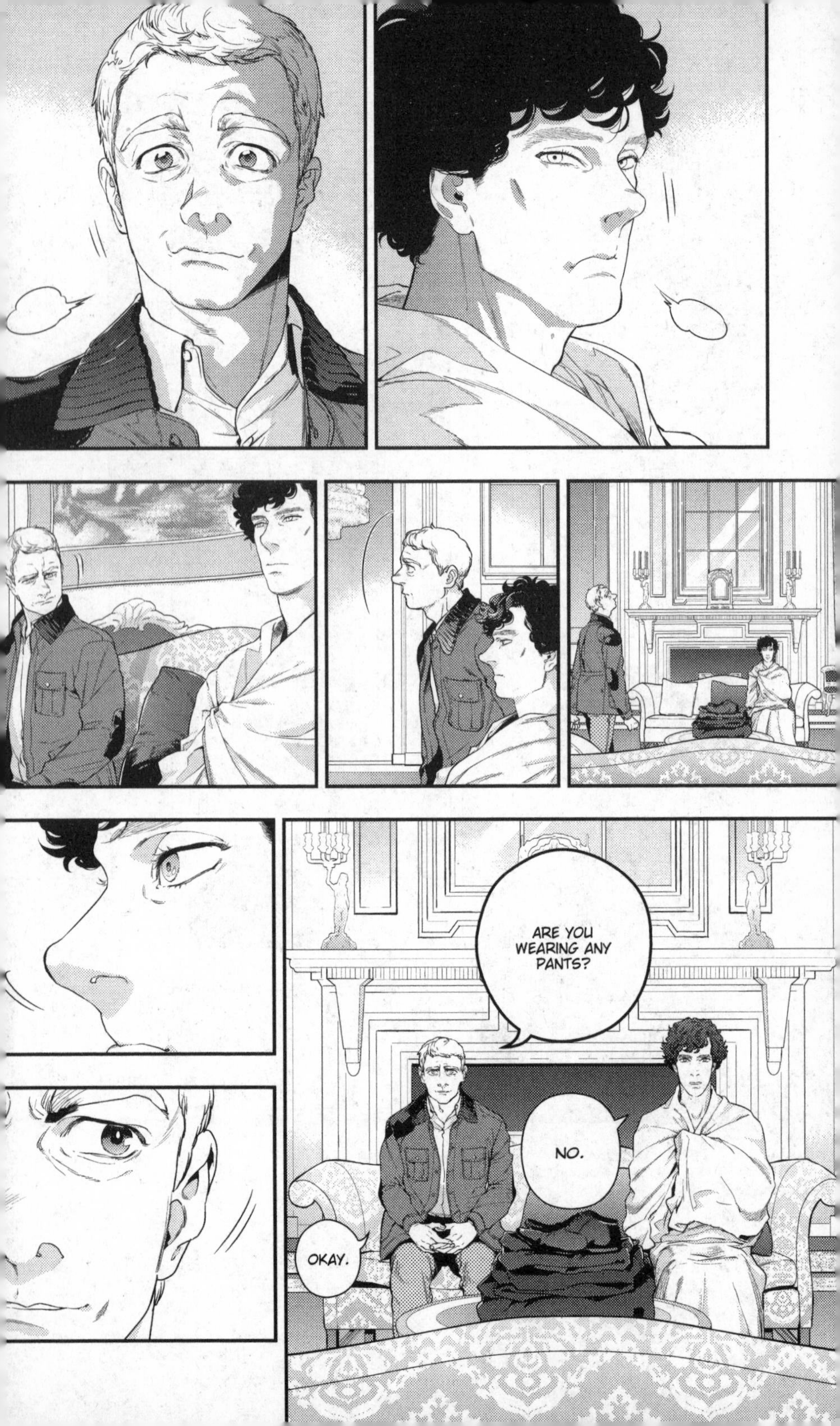
ARE YOU WEARING ANY PANTS?
NO.
OKAY.

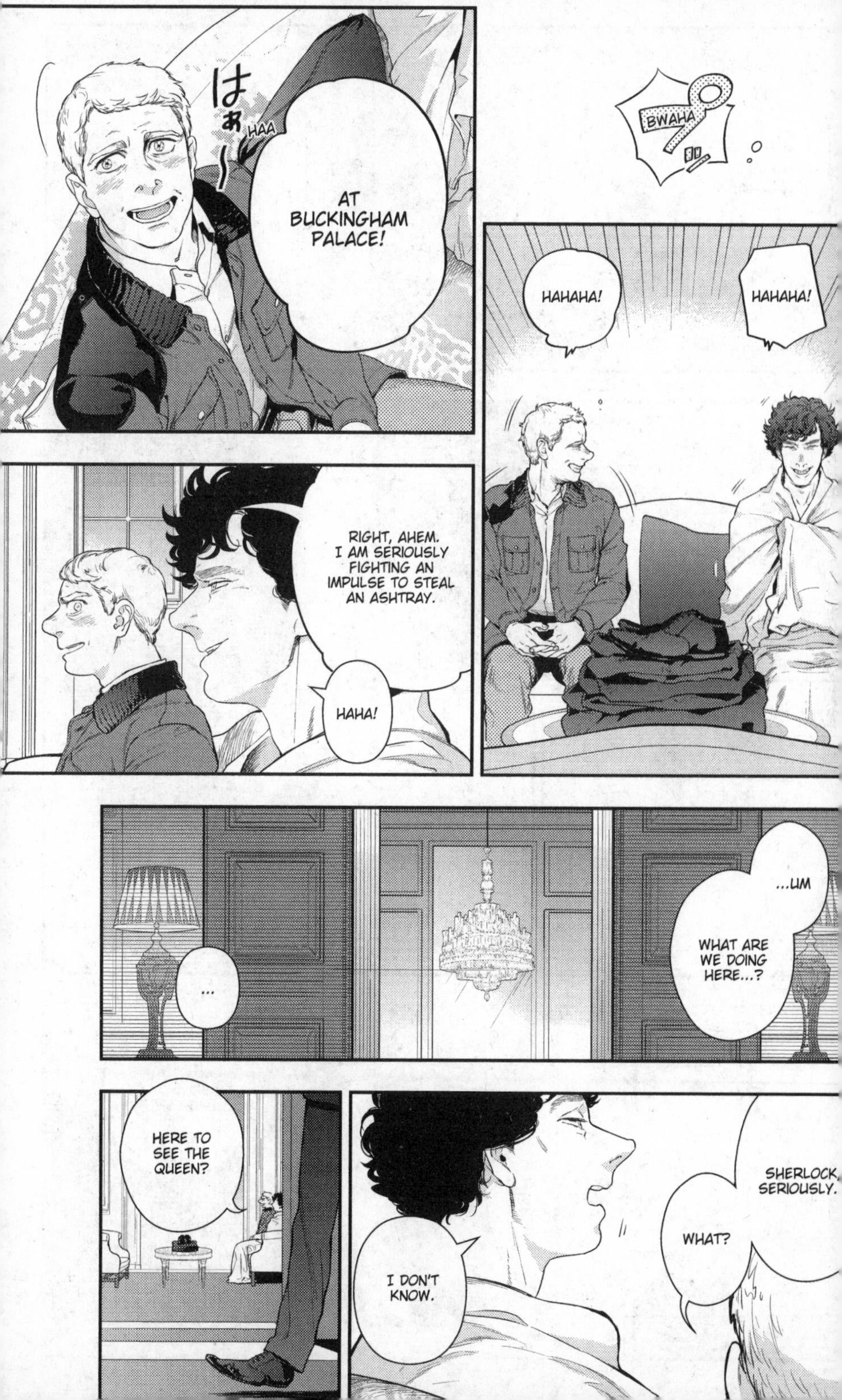
BWAHA
HAHAHA!
HAHAHA!
はぁ~
HAA
AT BUCKINGHAM PALACE!
RIGHT, AHEM. I AM SERIOUSLY FIGHTING AN IMPULSE TO STEAL AN ASHTRAY.
HAHA!
...UM
WHAT ARE WE DOING HERE...?
...
SHERLOCK. SERIOUSLY.
WHAT?
I DON'T KNOW.
HERE TO SEE THE QUEEN?

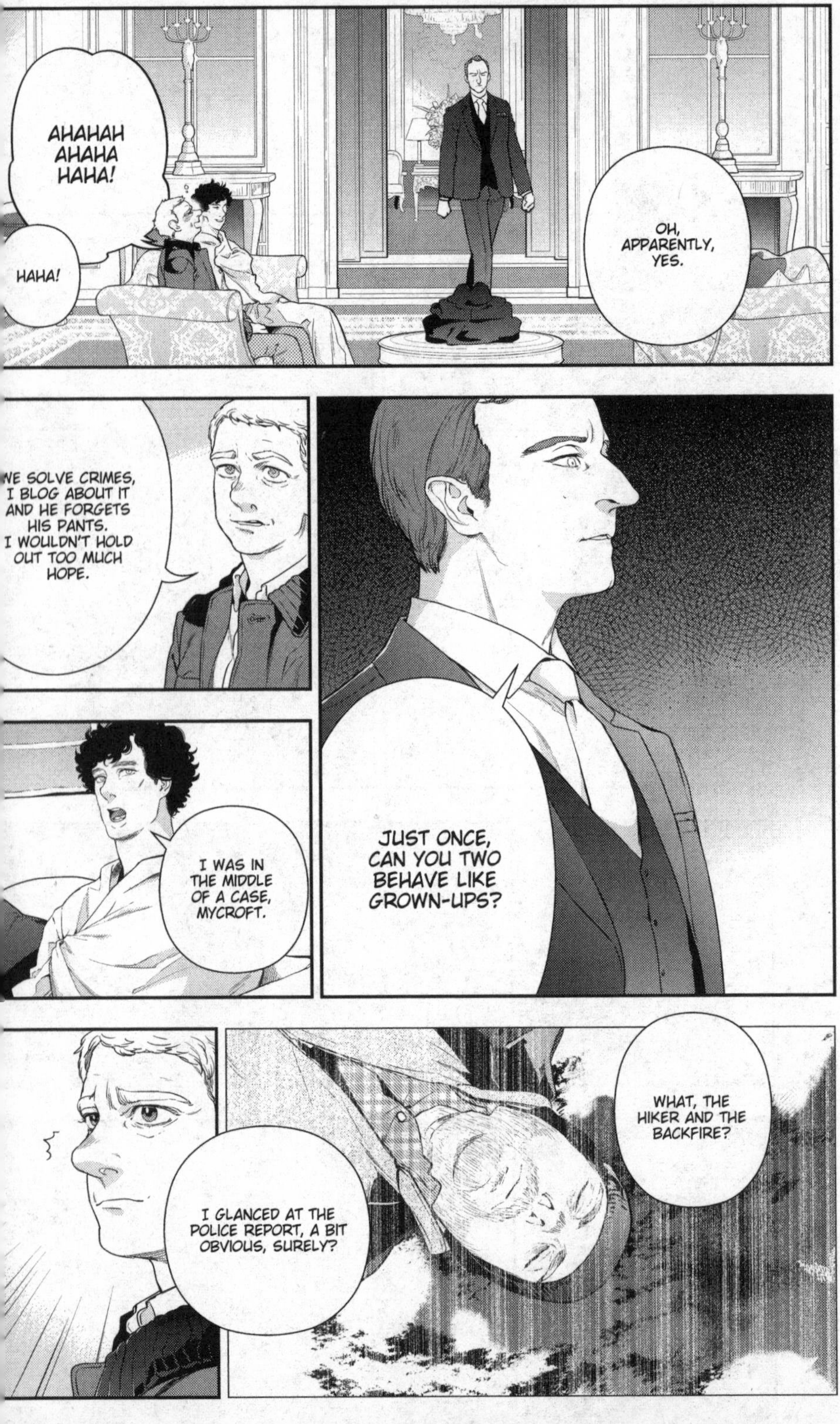
OH, APPARENTLY, YES.
AHAHAH AHAHA HAHA!
HAHA!
JUST ONCE, CAN YOU TWO BEHAVE LIKE GROWN-UPS?
WE SOLVE CRIMES, I BLOG ABOUT IT AND HE FORGETS HIS PANTS. I WOULDN'T HOLD OUT TOO MUCH HOPE.
I WAS IN THE MIDDLE OF A CASE, MYCROFT.
WHAT, THE HIKER AND THE BACKFIRE?
I GLANCED AT THE POLICE REPORT, A BIT OBVIOUS, SURELY?

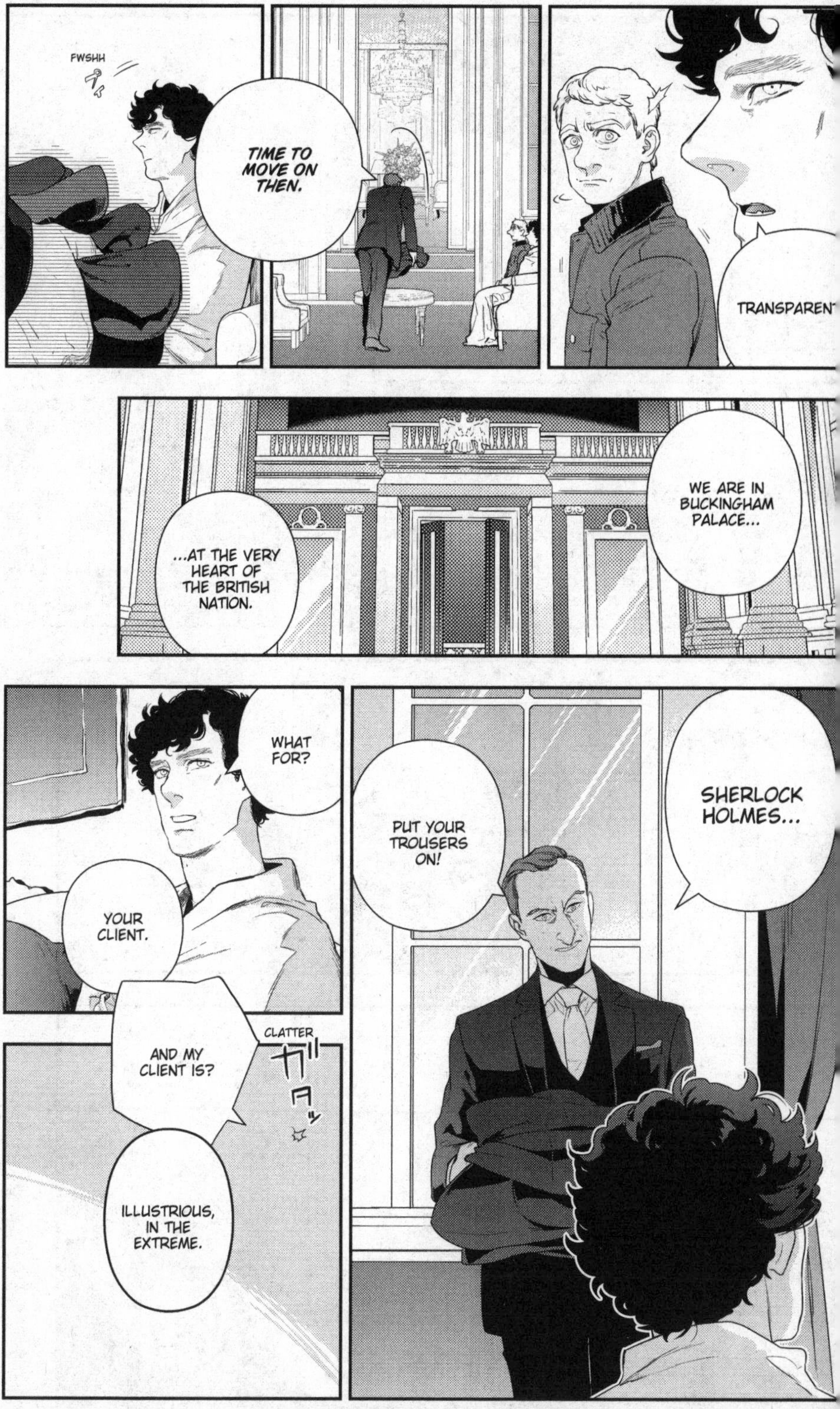

TRANSPARENT
TIME TO MOVE ON THEN.
FWSHH
WE ARE IN BUCKINGHAM PALACE...
...AT THE VERY HEART OF THE BRITISH NATION.
SHERLOCK HOLMES...
PUT YOUR TROUSERS ON!
WHAT FOR?
YOUR CLIENT.
AND MY CLIENT IS?
CLATTER
ILLUSTRIOUS, IN THE EXTREME.

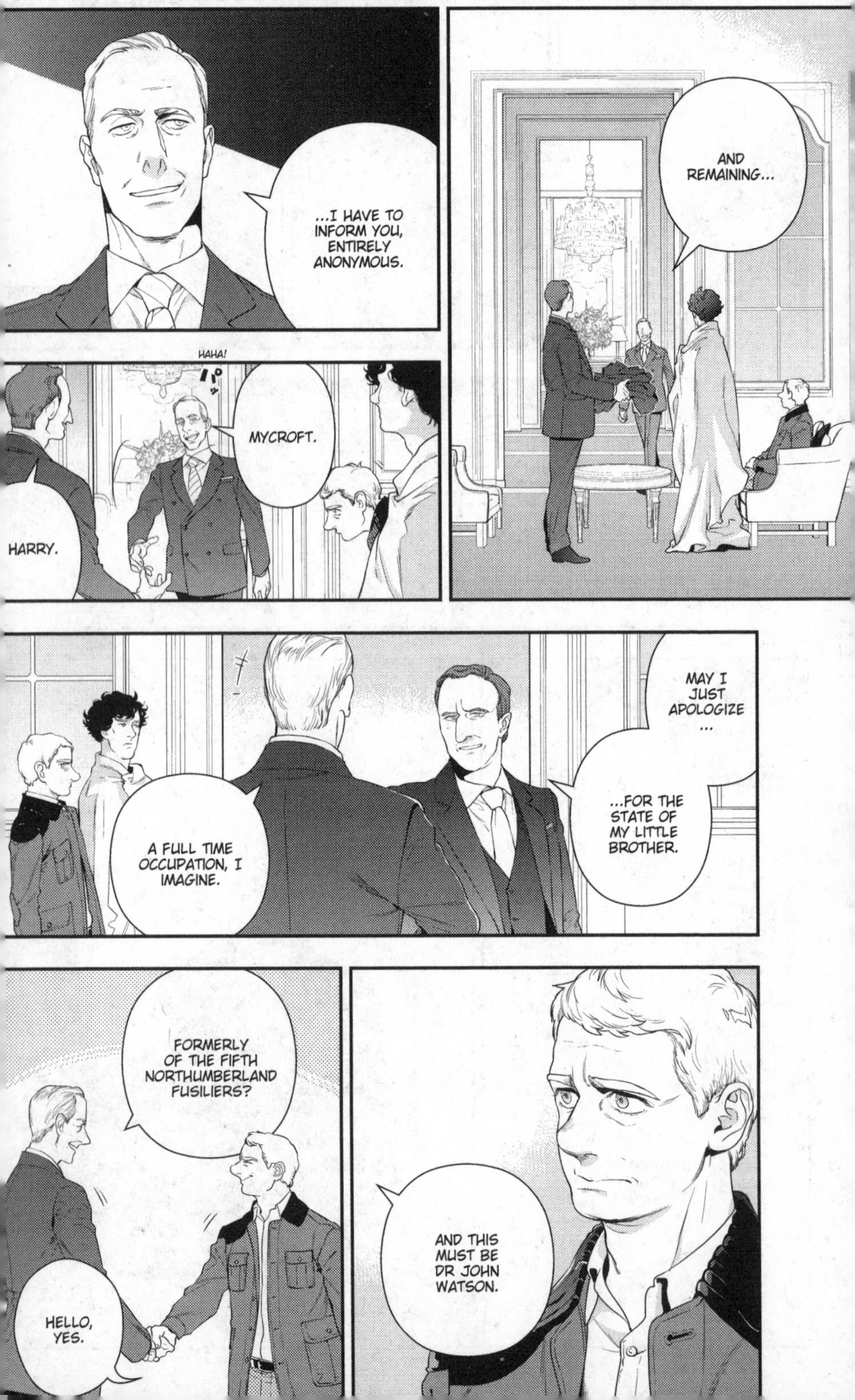

AND REMAINING...
...I HAVE TO INFORM YOU, ENTIRELY ANONYMOUS.
HAHA!
パッ
MYCROFT.
HARRY.
MAY I JUST APOLOGIZE ...
...FOR THE STATE OF MY LITTLE BROTHER.
A FULL TIME OCCUPATION, I IMAGINE.
AND THIS MUST BE DR JOHN WATSON.
FORMERLY OF THE FIFTH NORTHUMBERLAND FUSILIERS?
HELLO, YES.

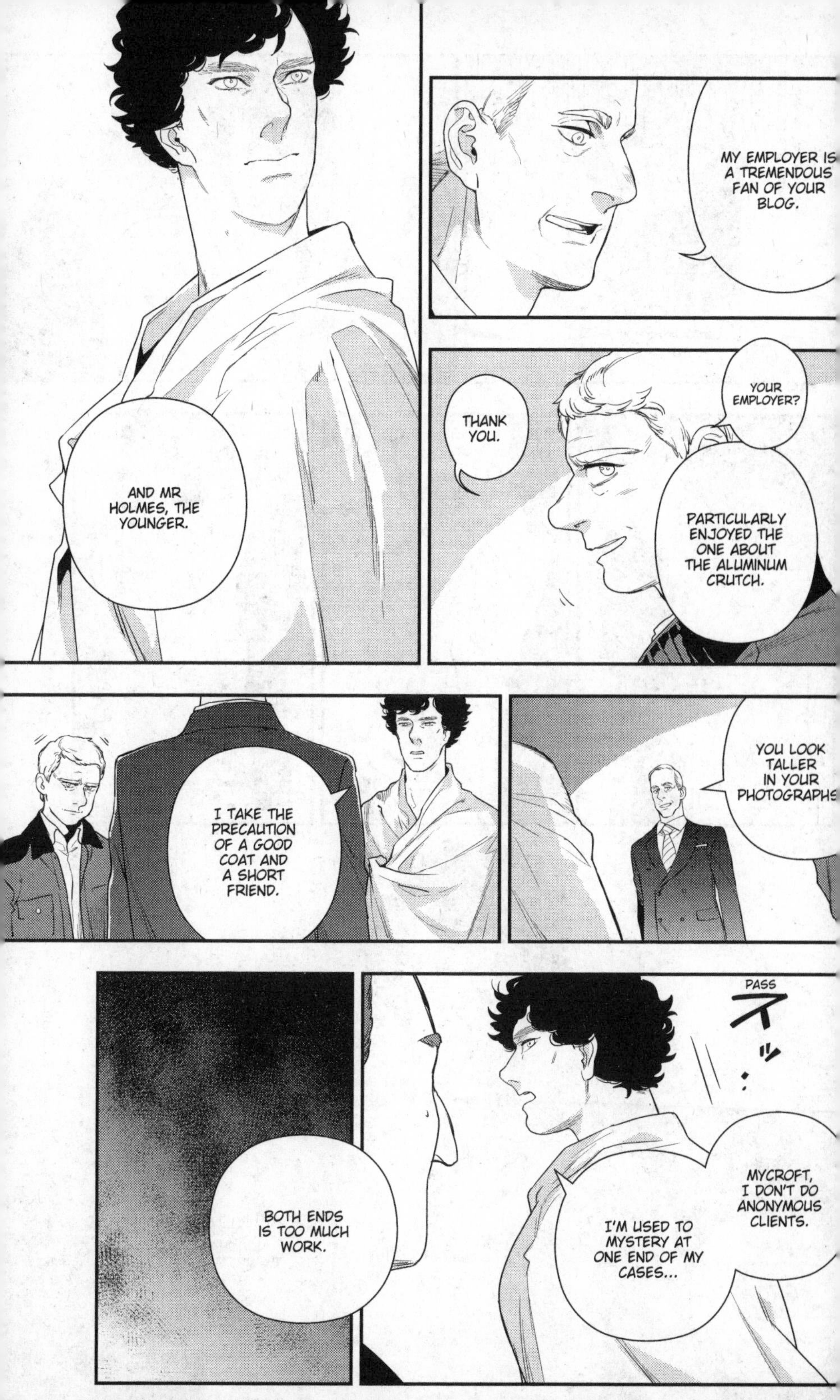
MY EMPLOYER IS A TREMENDOUS FAN OF YOUR BLOG.
YOUR EMPLOYER?
THANK YOU.
PARTICULARLY ENJOYED THE ONE ABOUT THE ALUMINUM CRUTCH.
AND MR HOLMES, THE YOUNGER.
YOU LOOK TALLER IN YOUR PHOTOGRAPHS
I TAKE THE PRECAUTION OF A GOOD COAT AND A SHORT FRIEND.
PASS
MYCROFT, I DON'T DO ANONYMOUS CLIENTS.
I'M USED TO MYSTERY AT ONE END OF MY CASES...
BOTH ENDS IS TOO MUCH WORK.

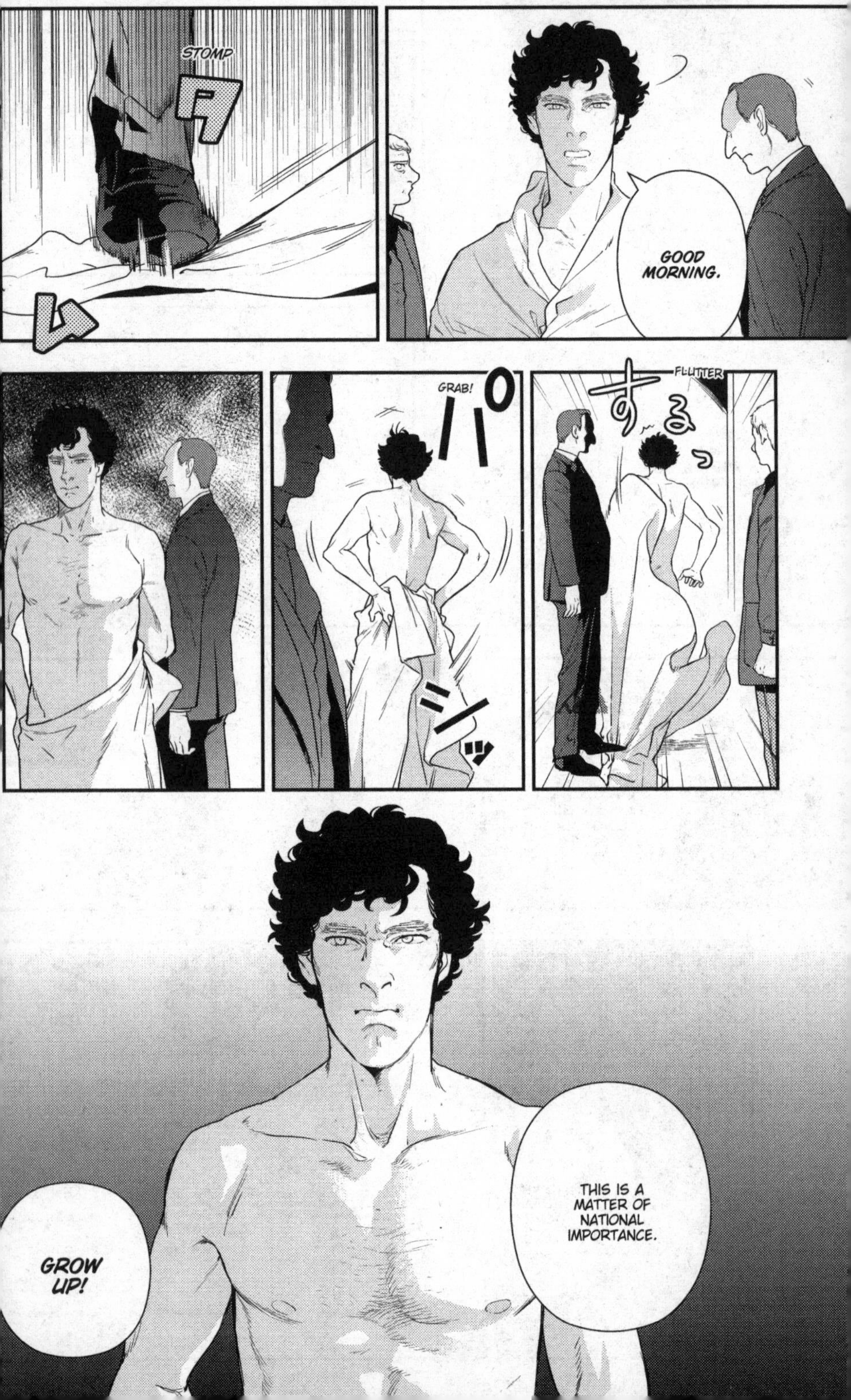
GOOD MORNING.
STOMP
FLUTTER
するっ
GRAB!
THIS IS A MATTER OF NATIONAL IMPORTANCE.
GROW UP!

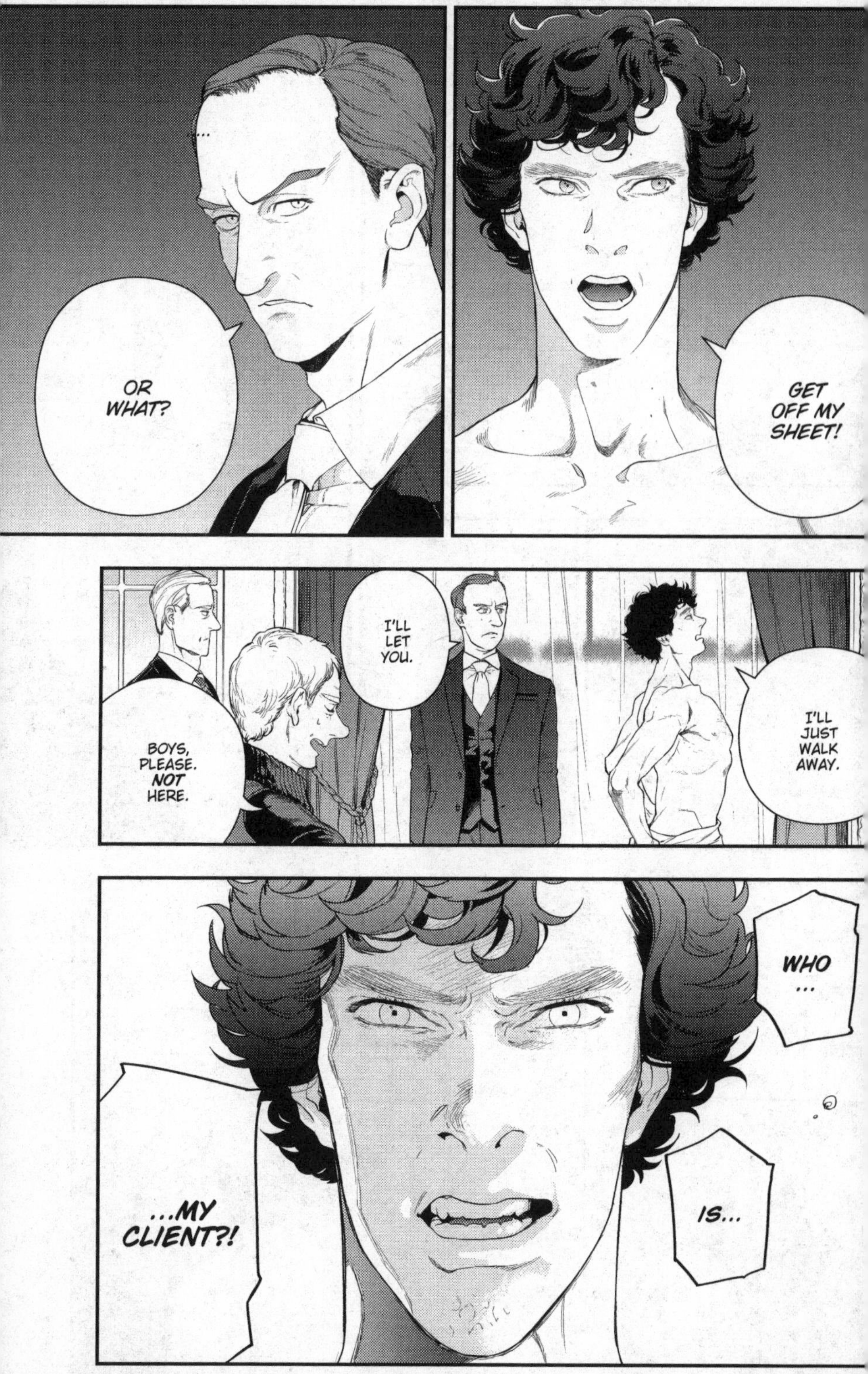

GET OFF MY SHEET!
...
OR WHAT?
I'LL JUST WALK AWAY.
I'LL LET YOU.
BOYS, PLEASE. NOT HERE.
WHO ...
IS...
...MY CLIENT?!

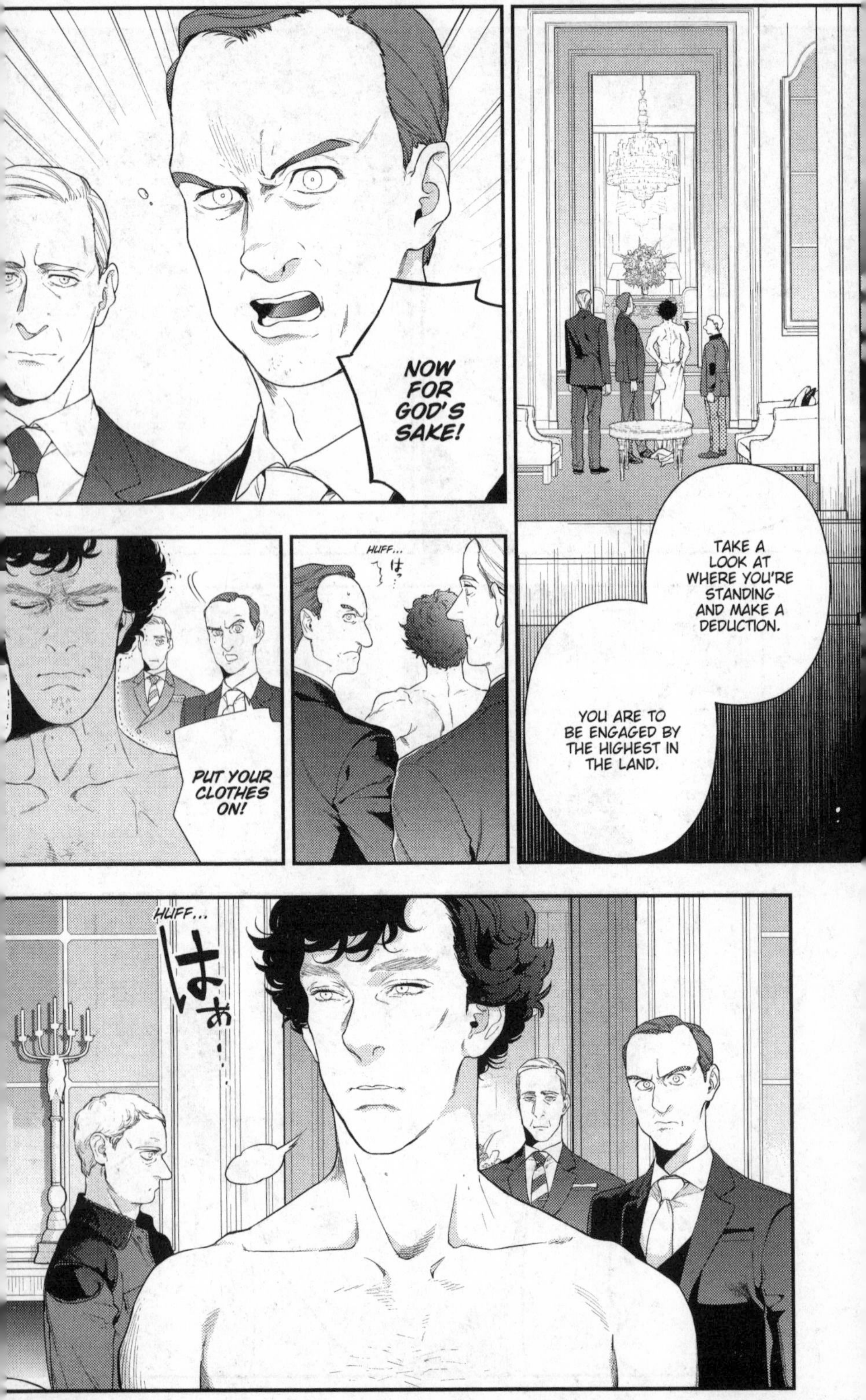
TAKE A LOOK AT WHERE YOU'RE STANDING AND MAKE A DEDUCTION.
YOU ARE TO BE ENGAGED BY THE HIGHEST IN THE LAND.
NOW FOR GOD'S SAKE!
HUFF...
は…
PUT YOUR CLOTHES ON!
HUFF...
はぁ…

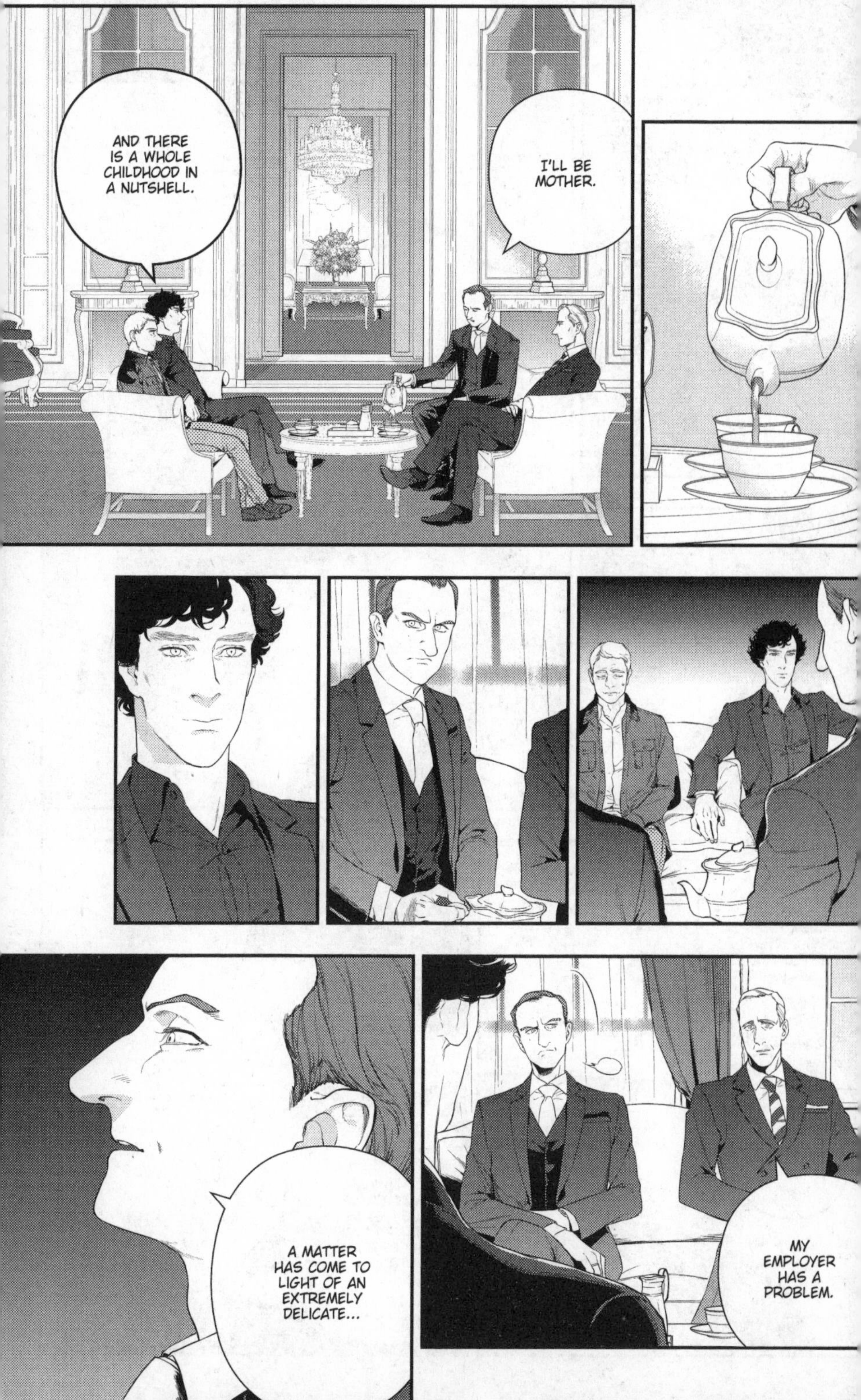
I'LL BE MOTHER.
AND THERE IS A WHOLE CHILDHOOD IN A NUTSHELL.
MY EMPLOYER HAS A PROBLEM.
A MATTER HAS COME TO LIGHT OF AN EXTREMELY DELICATE...

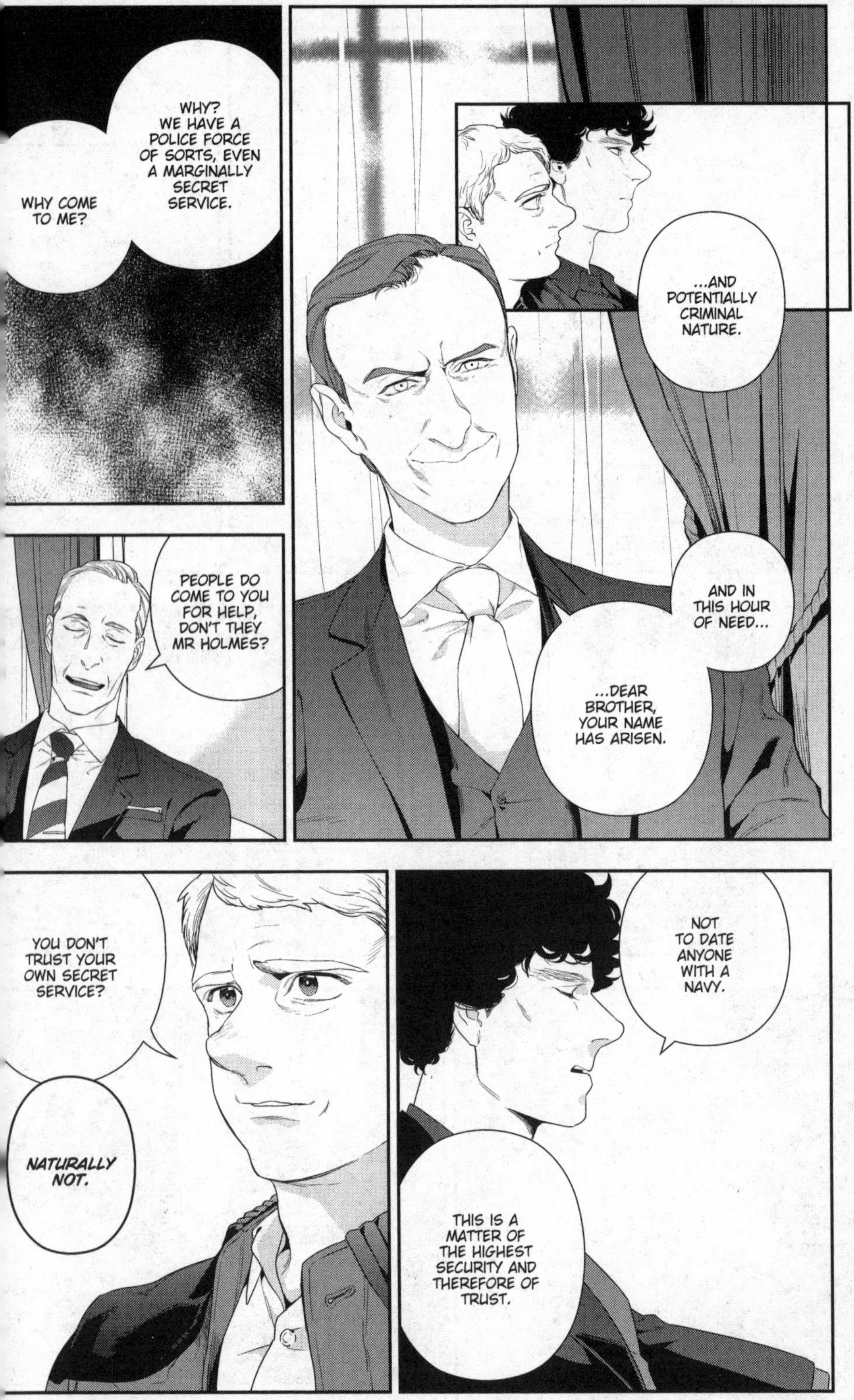
...AND POTENTIALLY CRIMINAL NATURE.
AND IN THIS HOUR OF NEED...
...DEAR BROTHER, YOUR NAME HAS ARISEN.
WHY? WE HAVE A POLICE FORCE OF SORTS, EVEN A MARGINALLY SECRET SERVICE.
WHY COME TO ME?
PEOPLE DO COME TO YOU FOR HELP, DON'T THEY MR HOLMES?
NOT TO DATE ANYONE WITH A NAVY.
THIS IS A MATTER OF THE HIGHEST SECURITY AND THEREFORE OF TRUST.
YOU DON'T TRUST YOUR OWN SECRET SERVICE?
NATURALLY NOT.

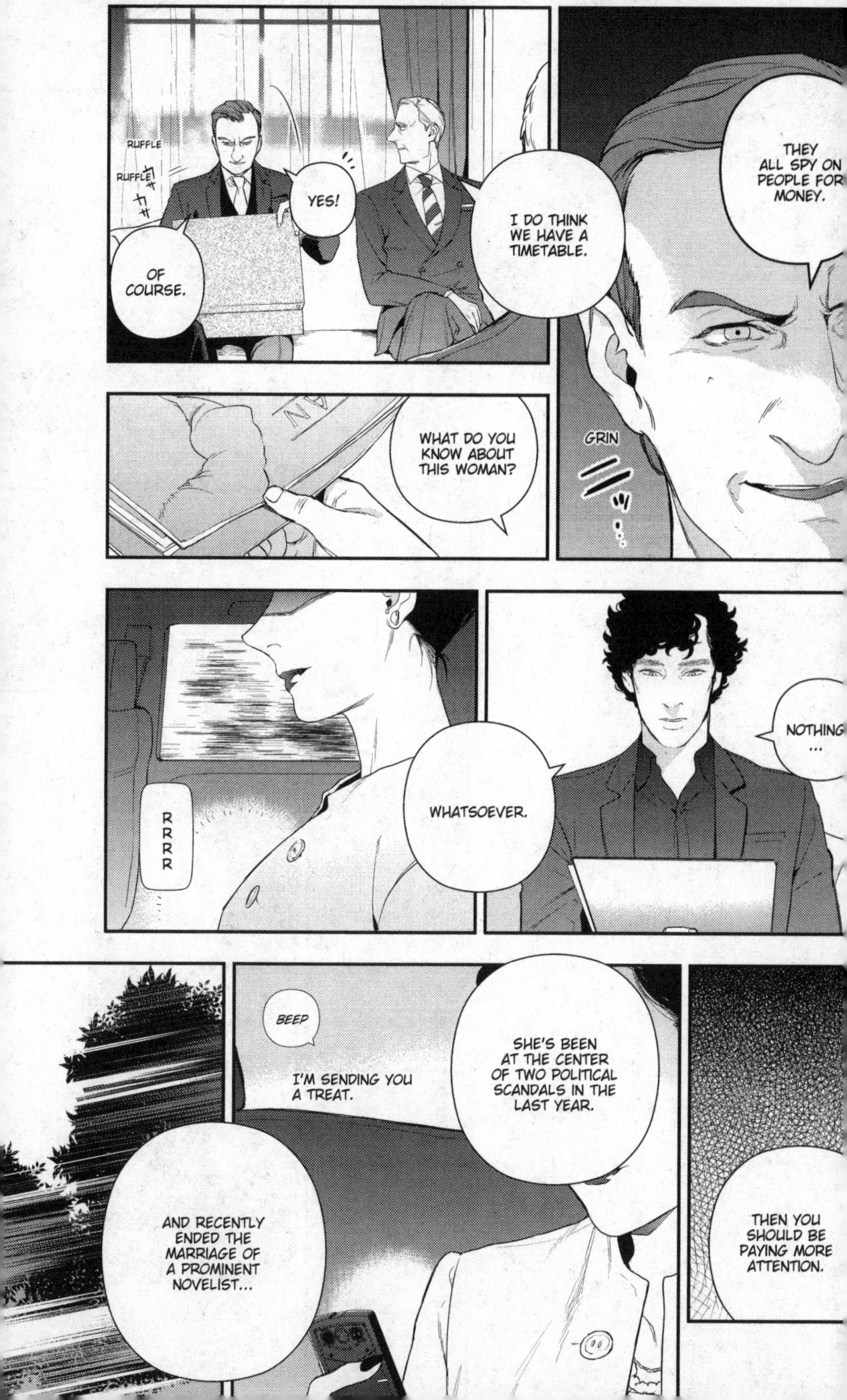
THEY ALL SPY ON PEOPLE FOR MONEY.
GRIN
I DO THINK WE HAVE A TIMETABLE.
YES!
RUFFLE
RUFFLE
OF COURSE.
WHAT DO YOU KNOW ABOUT THIS WOMAN?
NOTHING...
WHATSOEVER.
RRRR...
THEN YOU SHOULD BE PAYING MORE ATTENTION.
SHE'S BEEN AT THE CENTER OF TWO POLITICAL SCANDALS IN THE LAST YEAR.
BEEP
I'M SENDING YOU A TREAT.
AND RECENTLY ENDED THE MARRIAGE OF A PROMINENT NOVELIST...

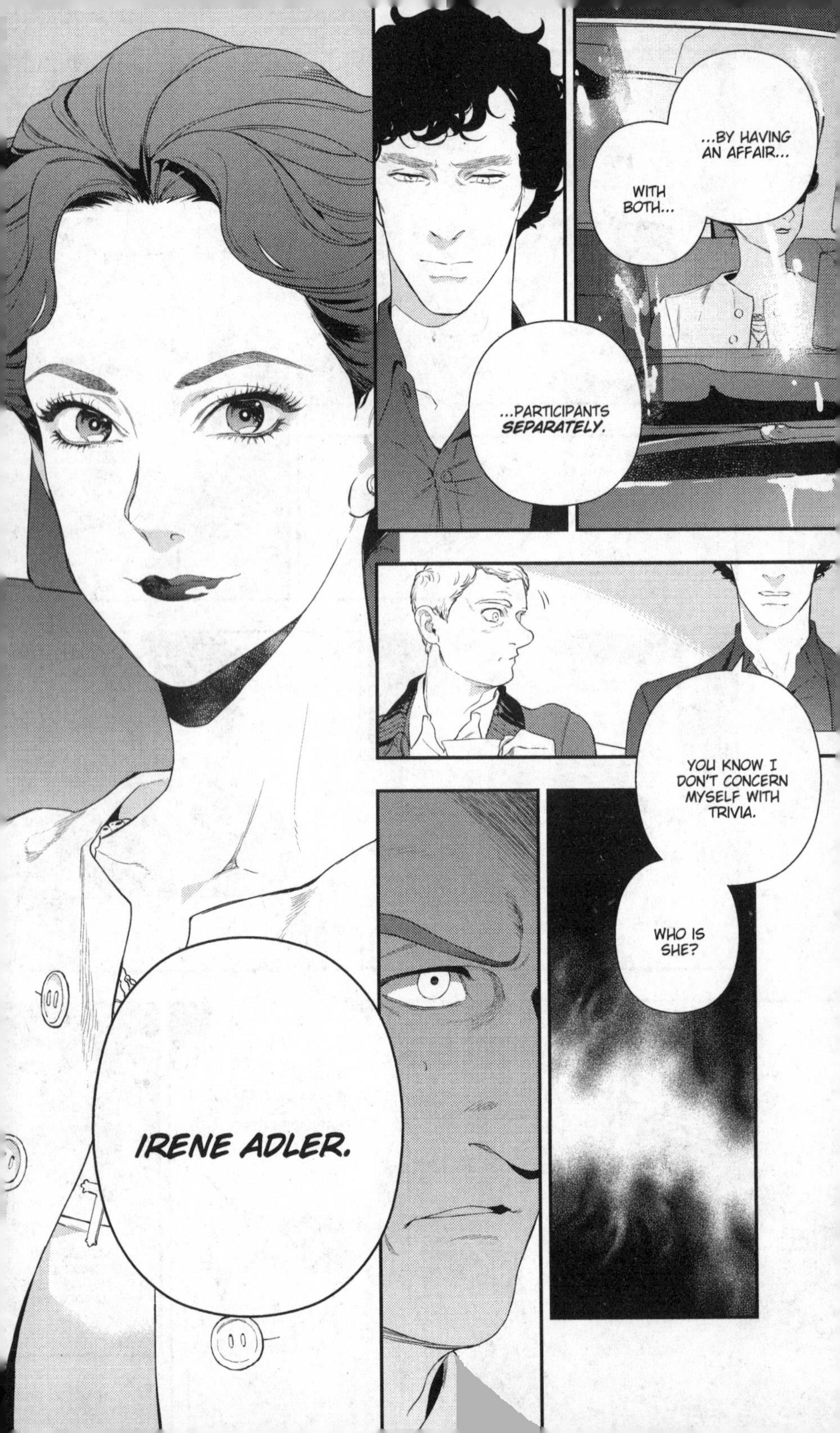
...BY HAVING AN AFFAIR...
WITH BOTH...
...PARTICIPANTS SEPARATELY.
YOU KNOW I DON'T CONCERN MYSELF WITH TRIVIA.
WHO IS SHE?
IRENE ADLER.

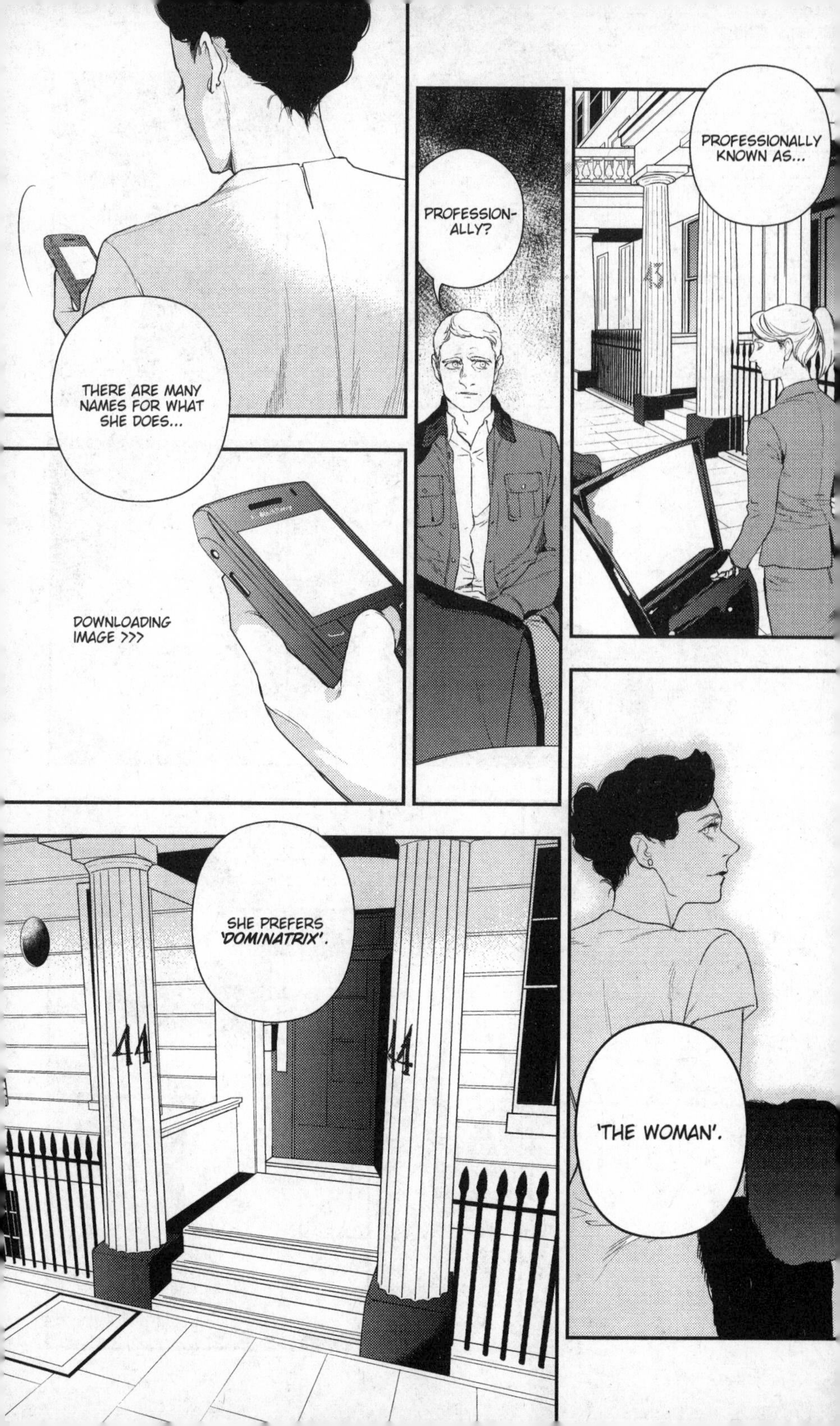
THERE ARE MANY NAMES FOR WHAT SHE DOES...
DOWNLOADING IMAGE >>>
PROFESSION-ALLY?
PROFESSIONALLY KNOWN AS...
SHE PREFERS 'DOMINATRIX'.
'THE WOMAN'.

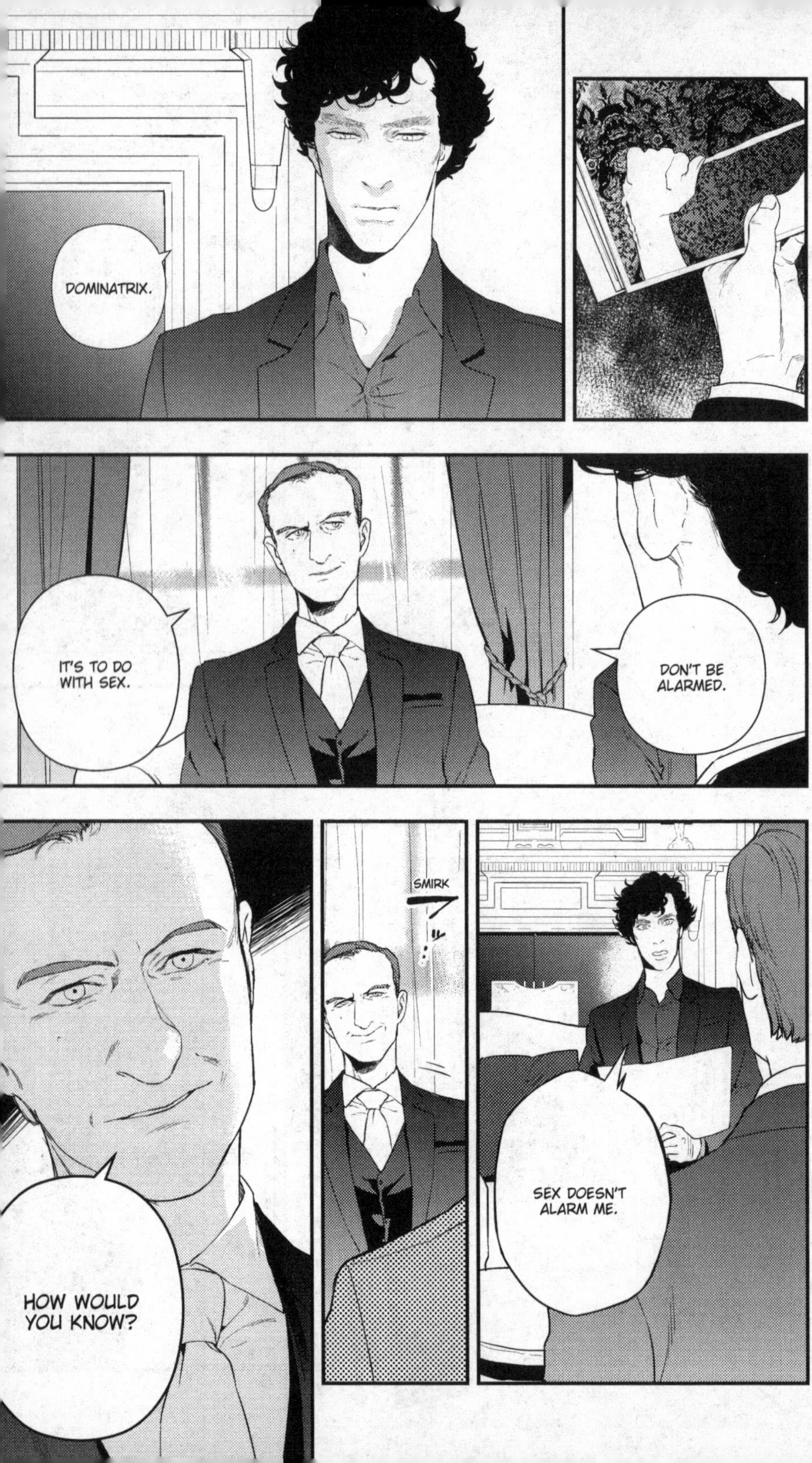
DOMINATRIX.
DON'T BE ALARMED.
IT'S TO DO WITH SEX.
SEX DOESN'T ALARM ME.
SMIRK
HOW WOULD YOU KNOW?

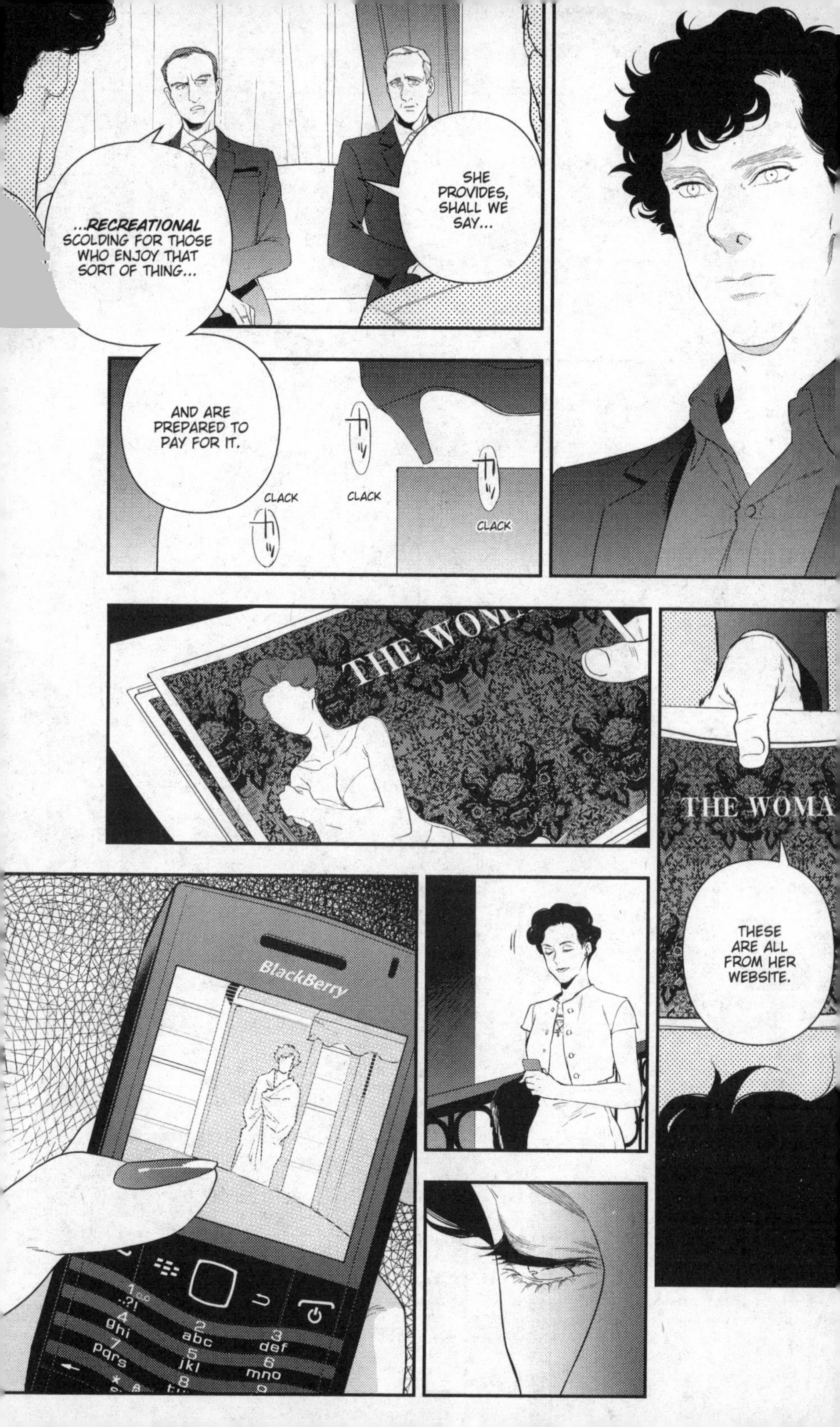
SHE PROVIDES, SHALL WE SAY...
...*RECREATIONAL* SCOLDING FOR THOSE WHO ENJOY THAT SORT OF THING...
AND ARE PREPARED TO PAY FOR IT.
CLACK
CLACK
CLACK
THE WOMA
THESE ARE ALL FROM HER WEBSITE.
THE WOM
BlackBerry

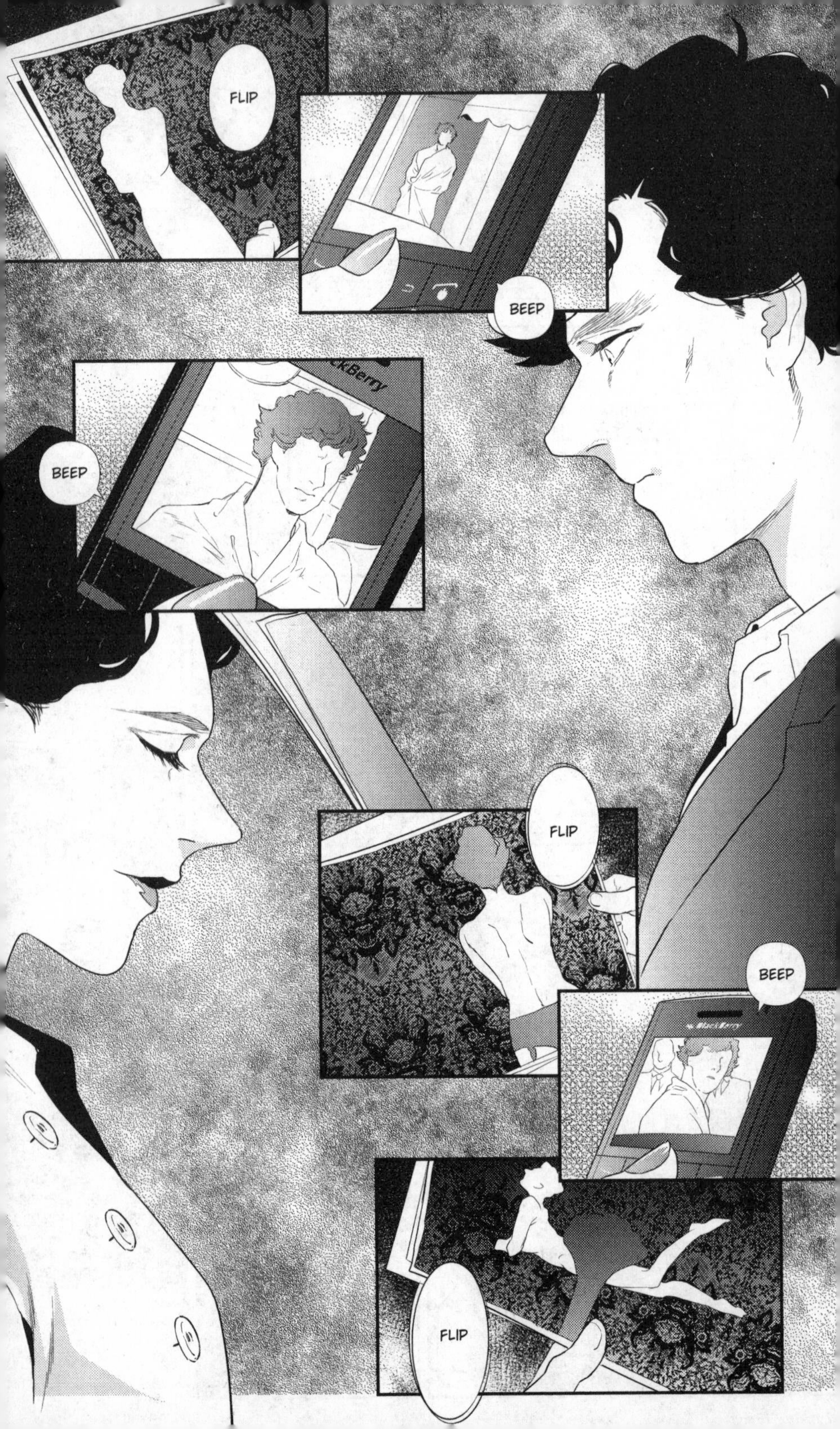
BEEP
FLIP
BEEP
FLIP
BEEP
FLIP

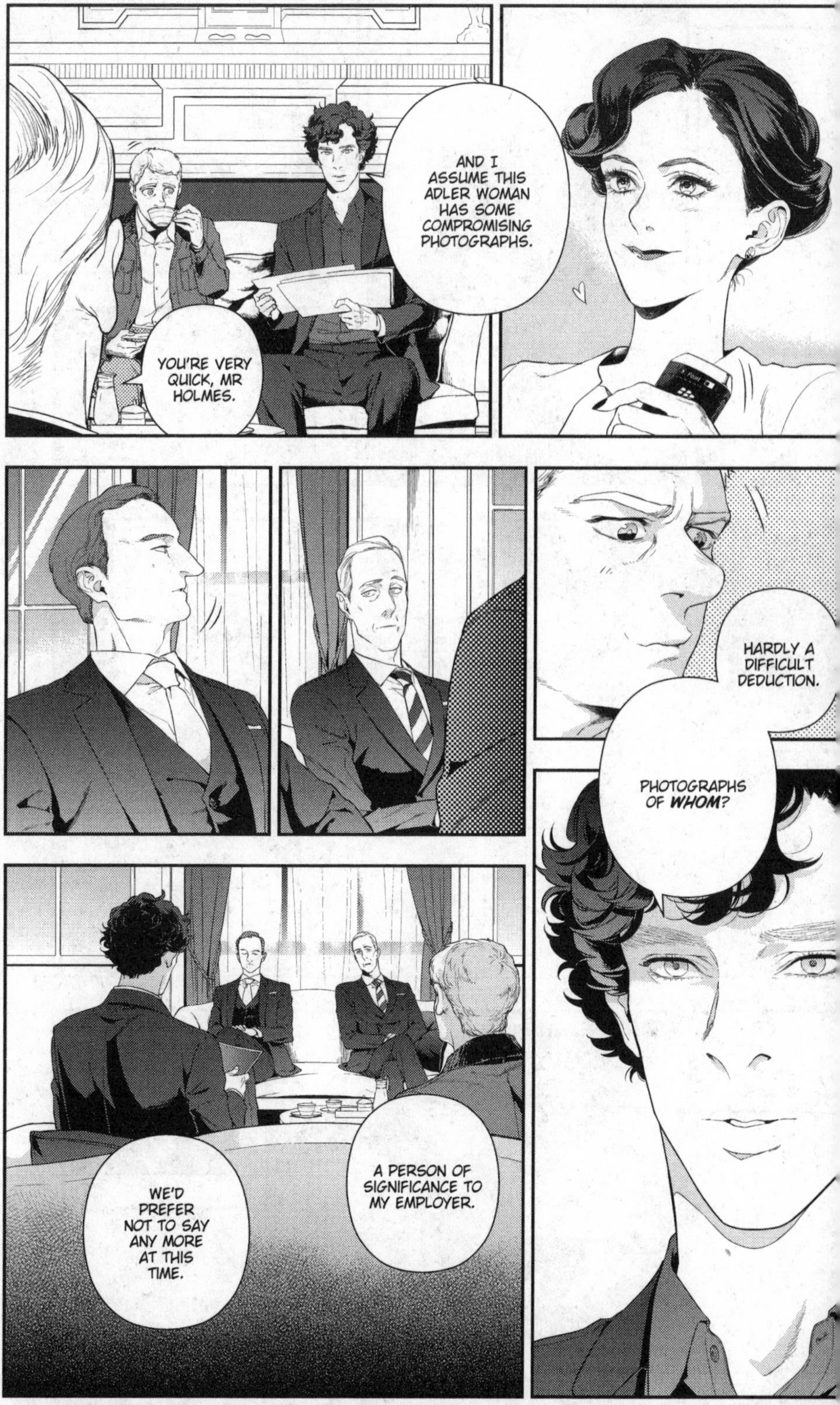
AND I ASSUME THIS ADLER WOMAN HAS SOME COMPROMISING PHOTOGRAPHS.
YOU'RE VERY QUICK, MR HOLMES.
HARDLY A DIFFICULT DEDUCTION.
PHOTOGRAPHS OF *WHOM*?
A PERSON OF SIGNIFICANCE TO MY EMPLOYER.
WE'D PREFER NOT TO SAY ANY MORE AT THIS TIME.

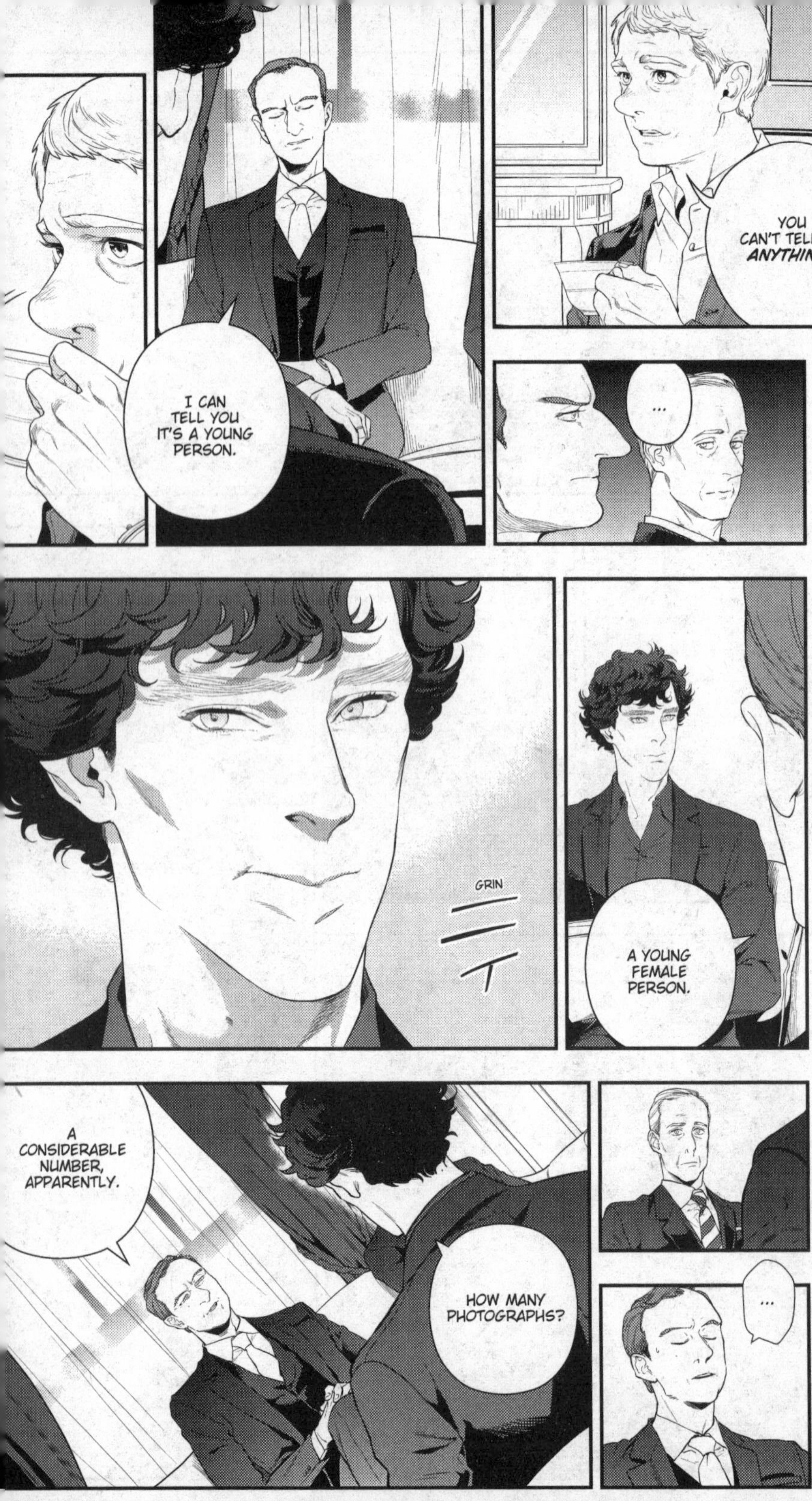
YOU CAN'T TELL US *ANYTHING?*
...
I CAN TELL YOU IT'S A YOUNG PERSON.
A YOUNG FEMALE PERSON.
GRIN
...
HOW MANY PHOTOGRAPHS?
A CONSIDERABLE NUMBER, APPARENTLY.

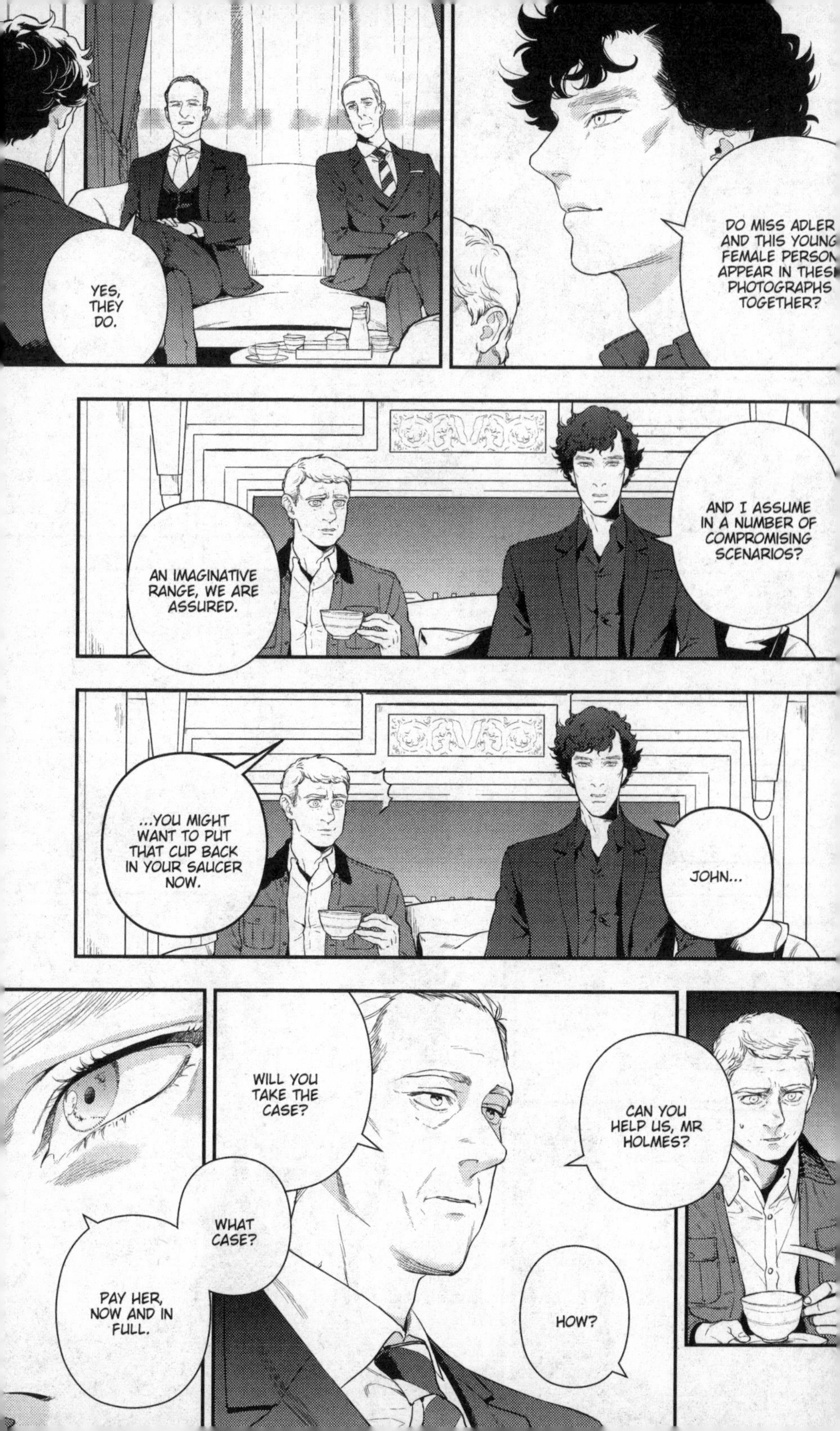
DO MISS ADLER AND THIS YOUNG FEMALE PERSON APPEAR IN THES PHOTOGRAPHS TOGETHER?
YES, THEY DO.
AND I ASSUME IN A NUMBER OF COMPROMISING SCENARIOS?
AN IMAGINATIVE RANGE, WE ARE ASSURED.
JOHN...
...YOU MIGHT WANT TO PUT THAT CUP BACK IN YOUR SAUCER NOW.
CAN YOU HELP US, MR HOLMES?
WILL YOU TAKE THE CASE?
WHAT CASE?
HOW?
PAY HER, NOW AND IN FULL.

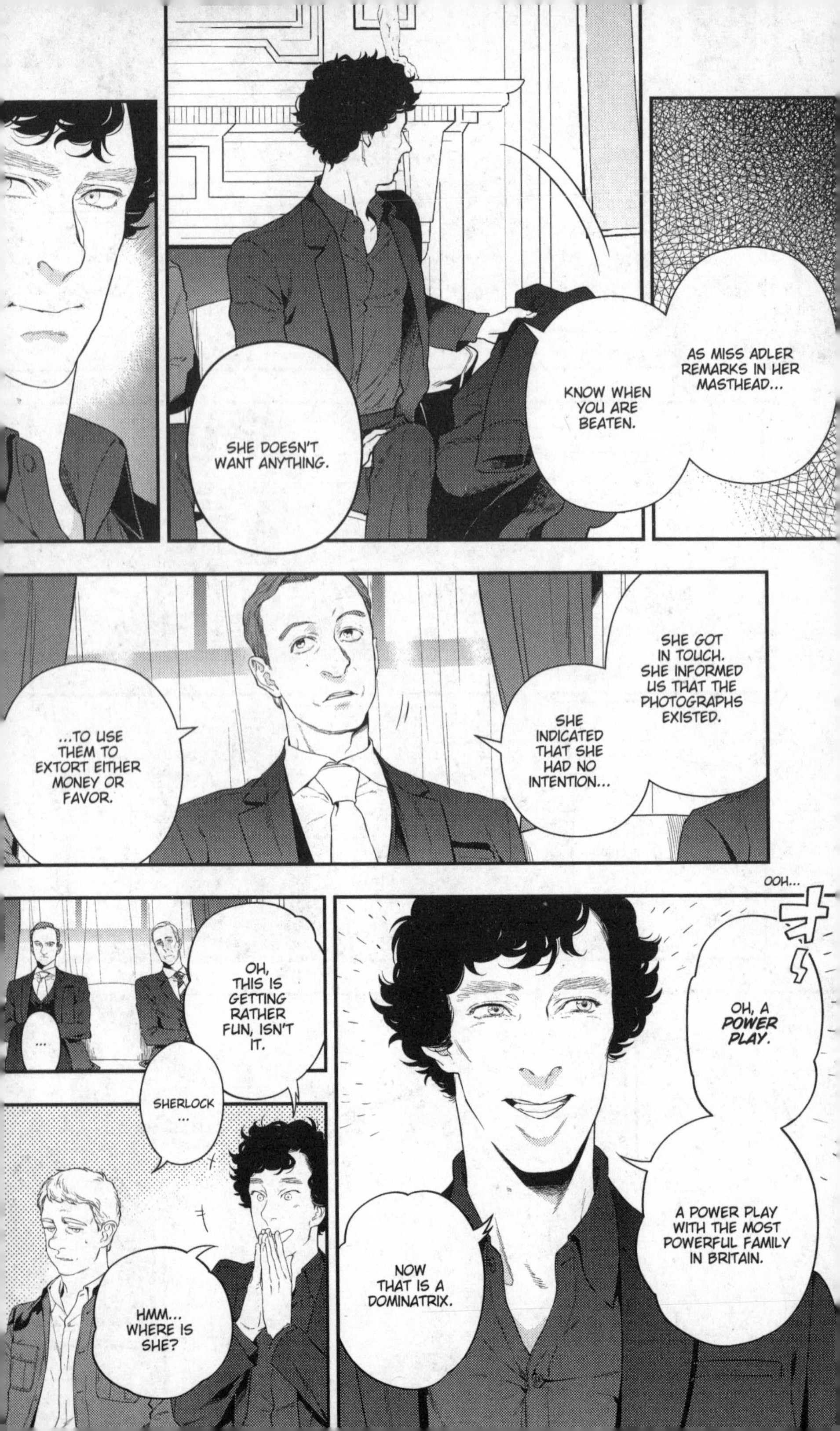
AS MISS ADLER REMARKS IN HER MASTHEAD...
KNOW WHEN YOU ARE BEATEN.
SHE DOESN'T WANT ANYTHING.
SHE GOT IN TOUCH. SHE INFORMED US THAT THE PHOTOGRAPHS EXISTED.
SHE INDICATED THAT SHE HAD NO INTENTION...
...TO USE THEM TO EXTORT EITHER MONEY OR FAVOR.
OOH...
OH, A *POWER PLAY*.
A POWER PLAY WITH THE MOST POWERFUL FAMILY IN BRITAIN.
NOW THAT IS A DOMINATRIX.
OH, THIS IS GETTING RATHER FUN, ISN'T IT.
...
SHERLOCK...
HMM... WHERE IS SHE?

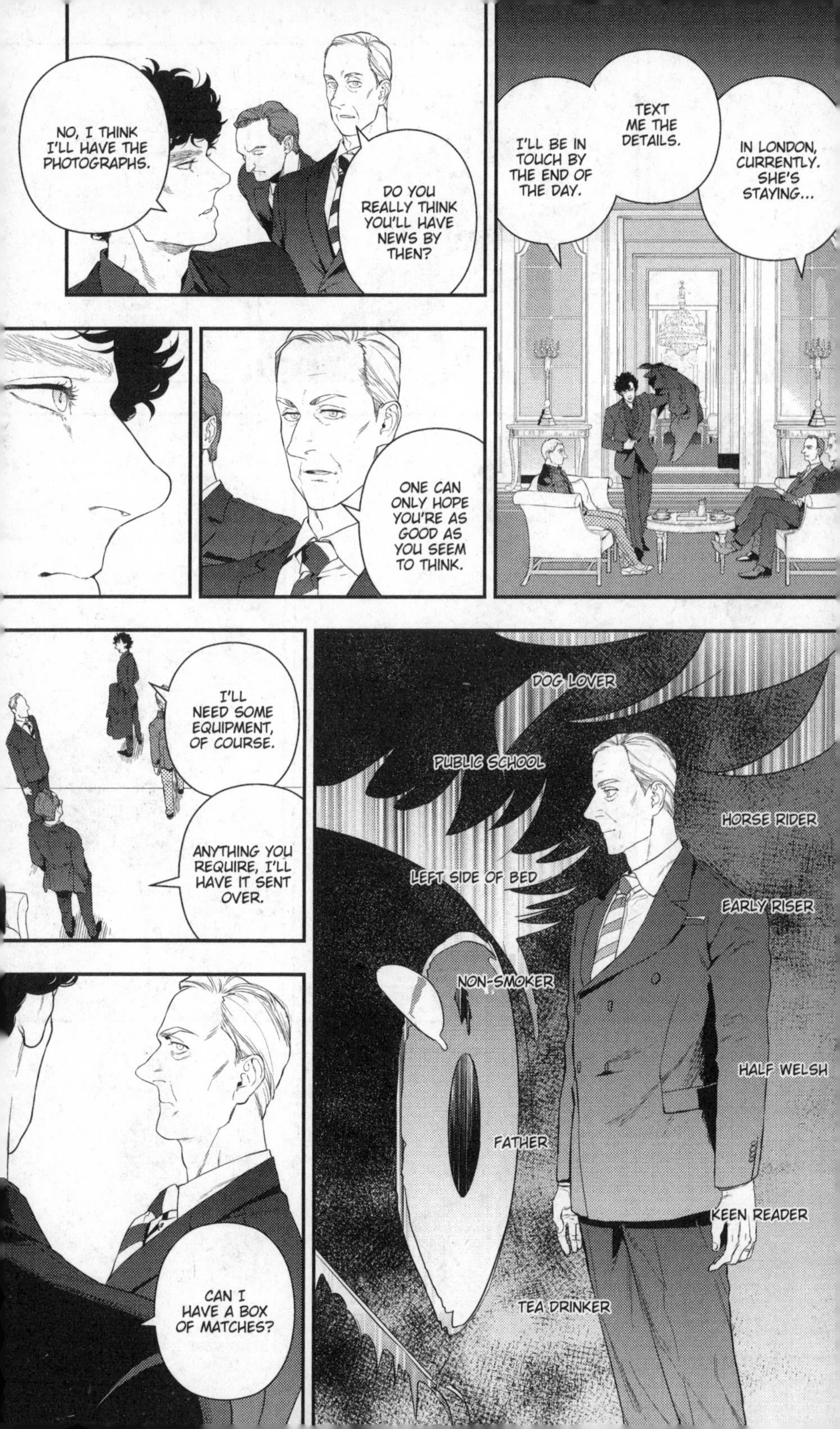
IN LONDON, CURRENTLY. SHE'S STAYING...
TEXT ME THE DETAILS.
I'LL BE IN TOUCH BY THE END OF THE DAY.
DO YOU REALLY THINK YOU'LL HAVE NEWS BY THEN?
NO, I THINK I'LL HAVE THE PHOTOGRAPHS.
ONE CAN ONLY HOPE YOU'RE AS GOOD AS YOU SEEM TO THINK.
DOG LOVER
PUBLIC SCHOOL
HORSE RIDER
LEFT SIDE OF BED
EARLY RISER
NON-SMOKER
HALF WELSH
FATHER
KEEN READER
TEA DRINKER
I'LL NEED SOME EQUIPMENT, OF COURSE.
ANYTHING YOU REQUIRE, I'LL HAVE IT SENT OVER.
CAN I HAVE A BOX OF MATCHES?

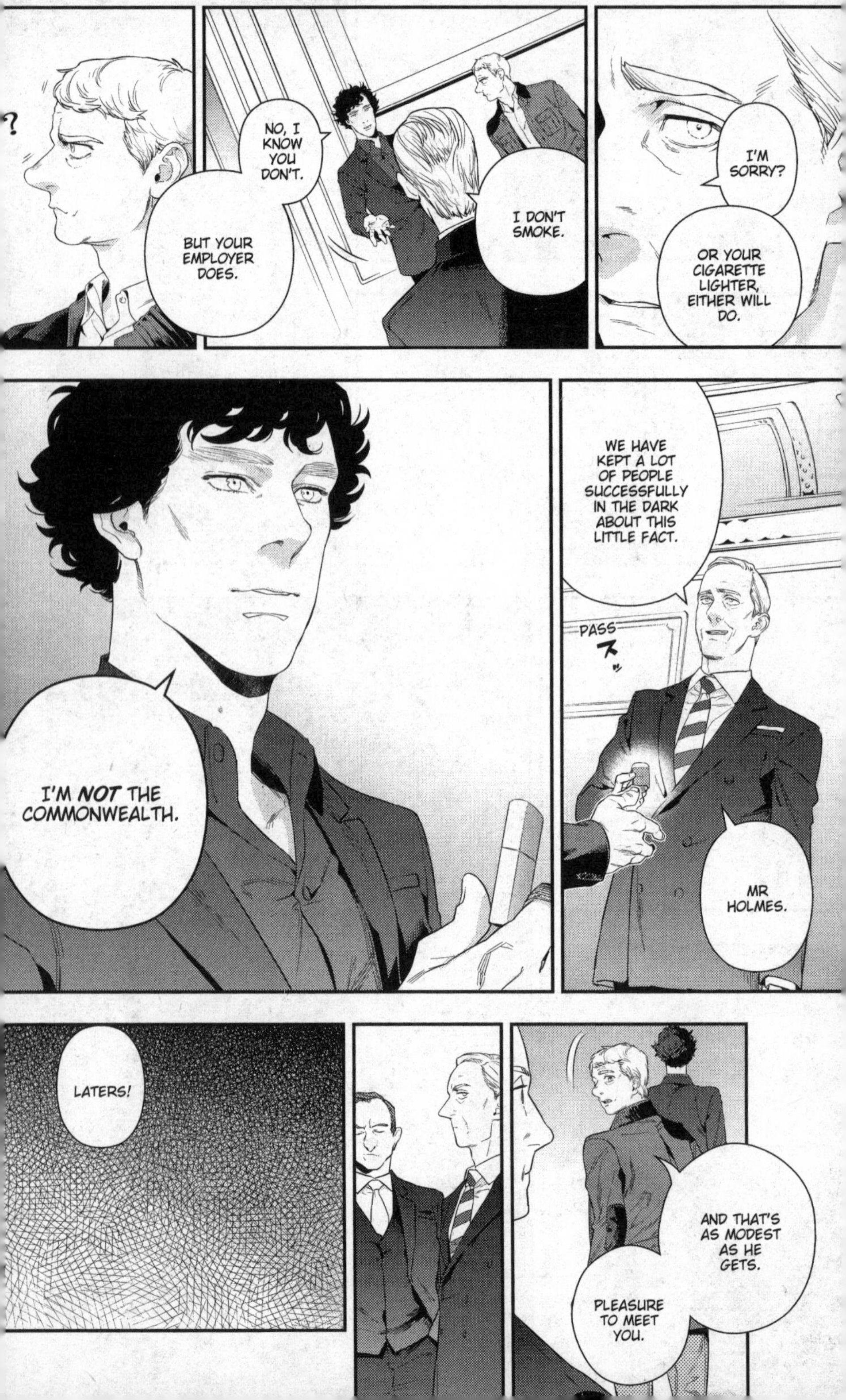
I'M SORRY?
OR YOUR CIGARETTE LIGHTER, EITHER WILL DO.
I DON'T SMOKE.
NO, I KNOW YOU DON'T.
BUT YOUR EMPLOYER DOES.
?
WE HAVE KEPT A LOT OF PEOPLE SUCCESSFULLY IN THE DARK ABOUT THIS LITTLE FACT.
PASS
MR HOLMES.
I'M **NOT** THE COMMONWEALTH.
AND THAT'S AS MODEST AS HE GETS.
PLEASURE TO MEET YOU.
LATERS!

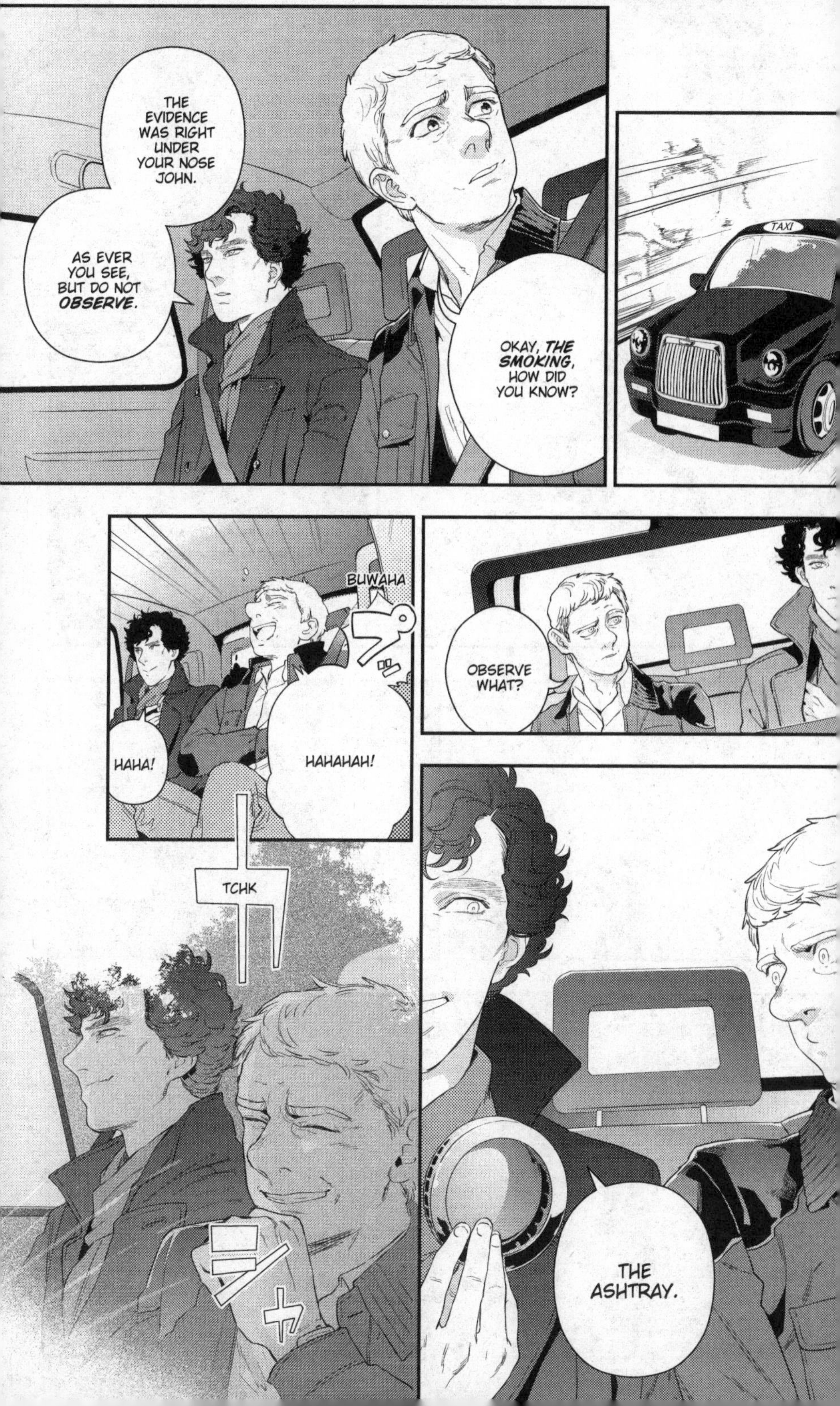
TAXI
OKAY, **THE SMOKING**, HOW DID YOU KNOW?
THE EVIDENCE WAS RIGHT UNDER YOUR NOSE JOHN.
AS EVER YOU SEE, BUT DO NOT **OBSERVE**.
OBSERVE WHAT?
BUWAHA
HAHAHAH!
HAHA!
THE ASHTRAY.
TCHK

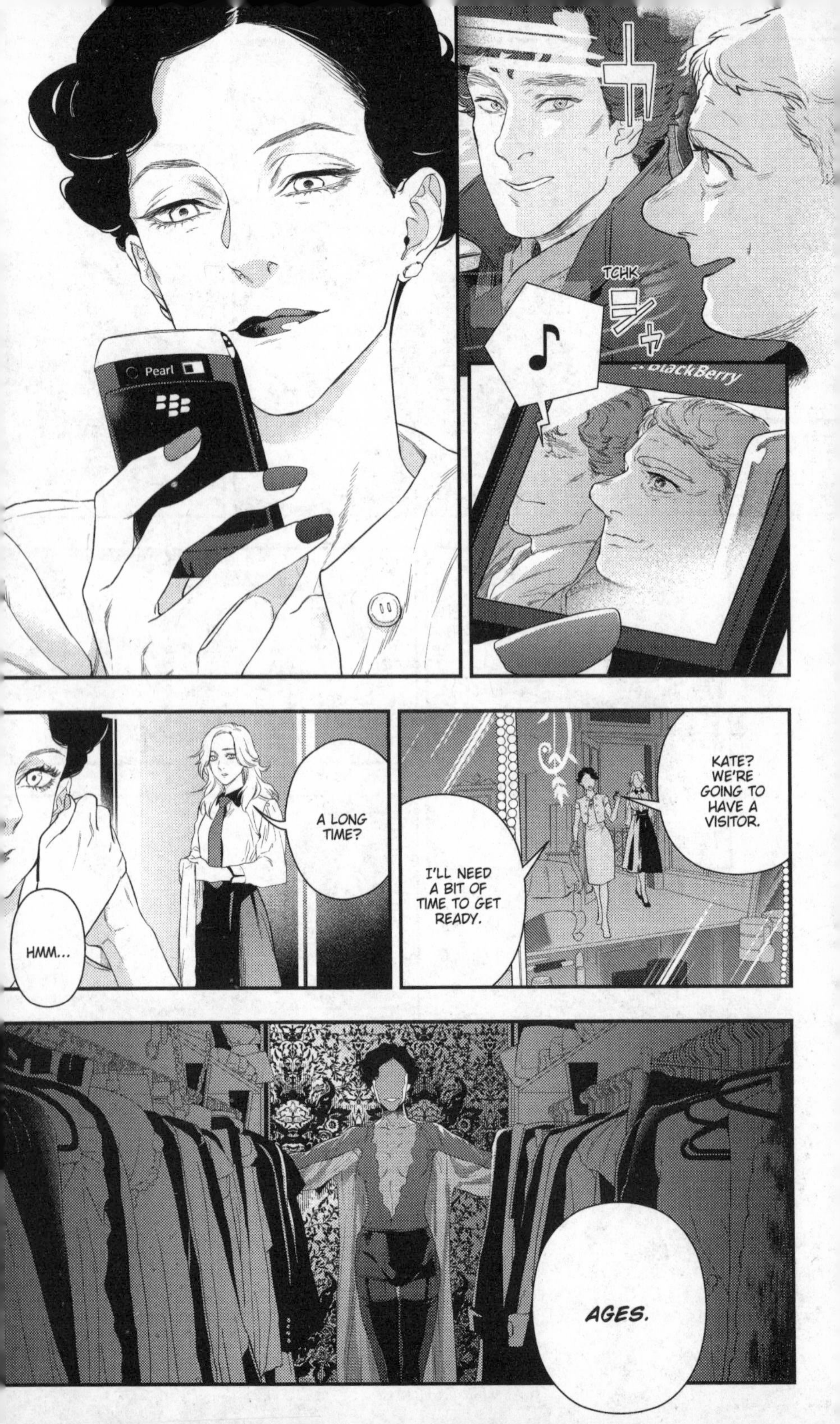
TCHK
シャ
♪
Pearl
KATE? WE'RE GOING TO HAVE A VISITOR.
I'LL NEED A BIT OF TIME TO GET READY.
A LONG TIME?
HMM...
AGES.

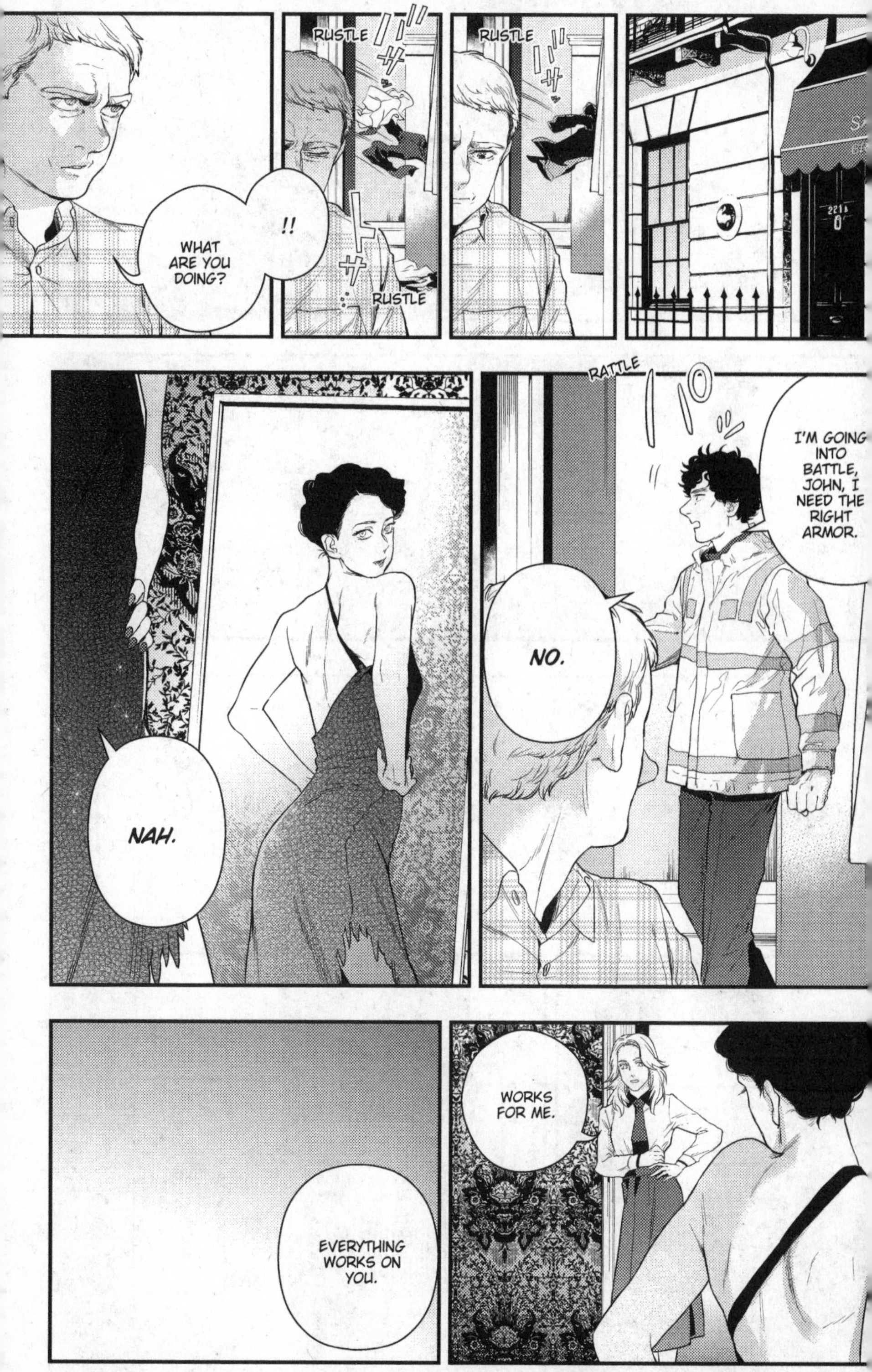
RUSTLE
RUSTLE
!!
RUSTLE
WHAT ARE YOU DOING?
RATTLE
I'M GOING INTO BATTLE, JOHN, I NEED THE RIGHT ARMOR.
NO.
NAH.
WORKS FOR ME.
EVERYTHING WORKS ON YOU.

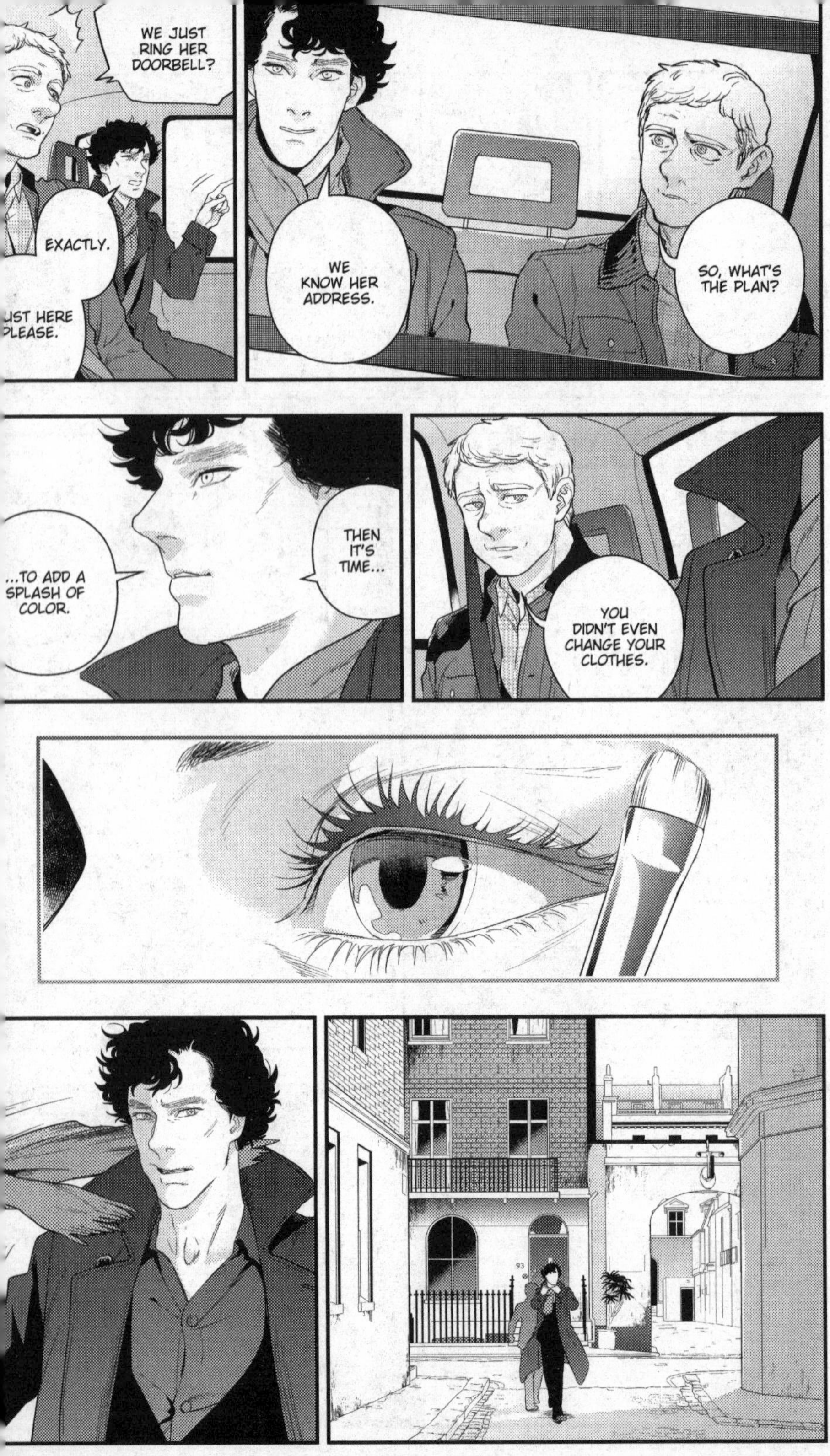
SO, WHAT'S THE PLAN?
WE KNOW HER ADDRESS.
WE JUST RING HER DOORBELL?
EXACTLY.
UST HERE PLEASE.
YOU DIDN'T EVEN CHANGE YOUR CLOTHES.
THEN IT'S TIME...
...TO ADD A SPLASH OF COLOR.

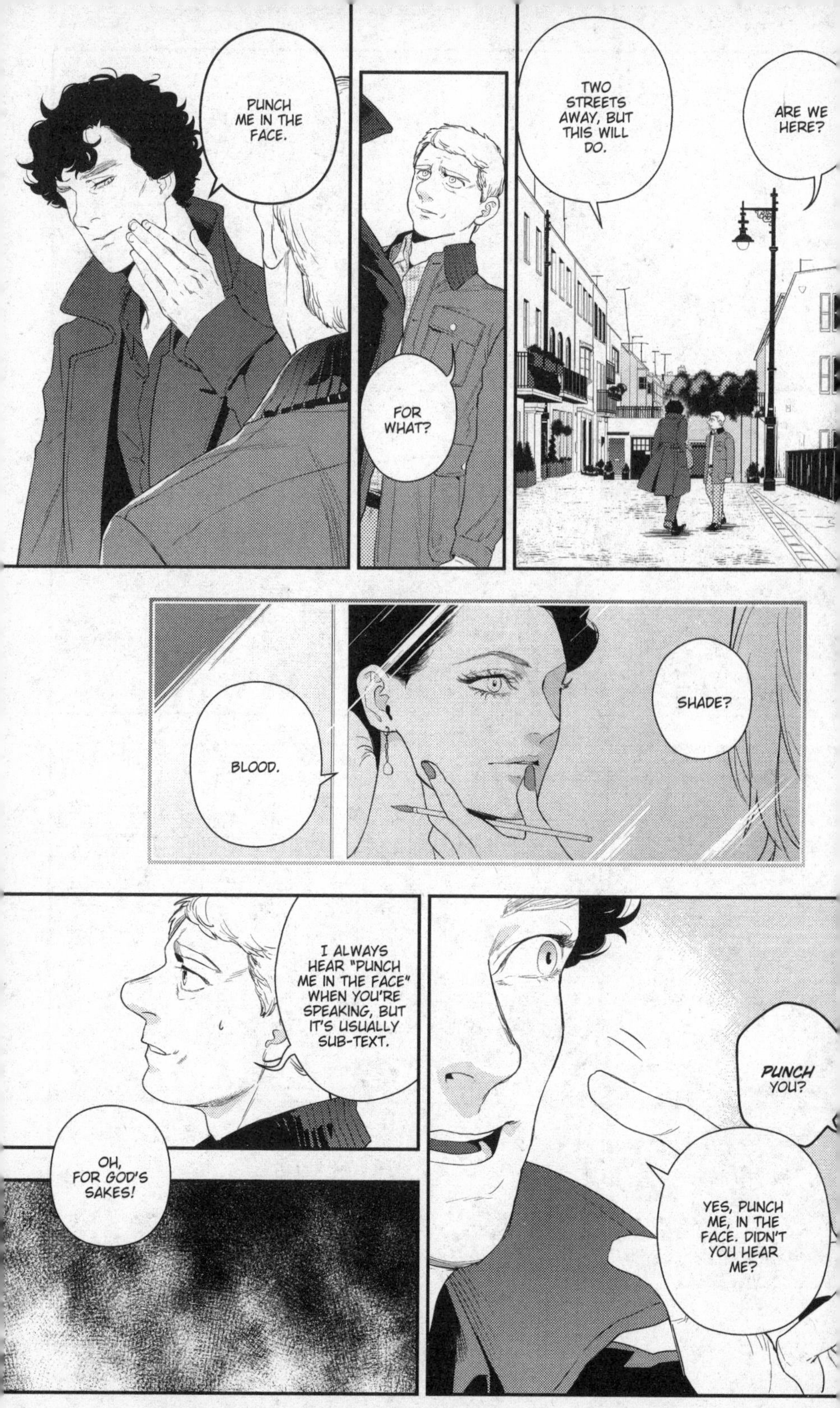
ARE WE HERE?
TWO STREETS AWAY, BUT THIS WILL DO.
FOR WHAT?
PUNCH ME IN THE FACE.
SHADE?
BLOOD.
PUNCH YOU?
YES, PUNCH ME, IN THE FACE. DIDN'T YOU HEAR ME?
I ALWAYS HEAR "PUNCH ME IN THE FACE" WHEN YOU'RE SPEAKING, BUT IT'S USUALLY SUB-TEXT.
OH, FOR GOD'S SAKES!

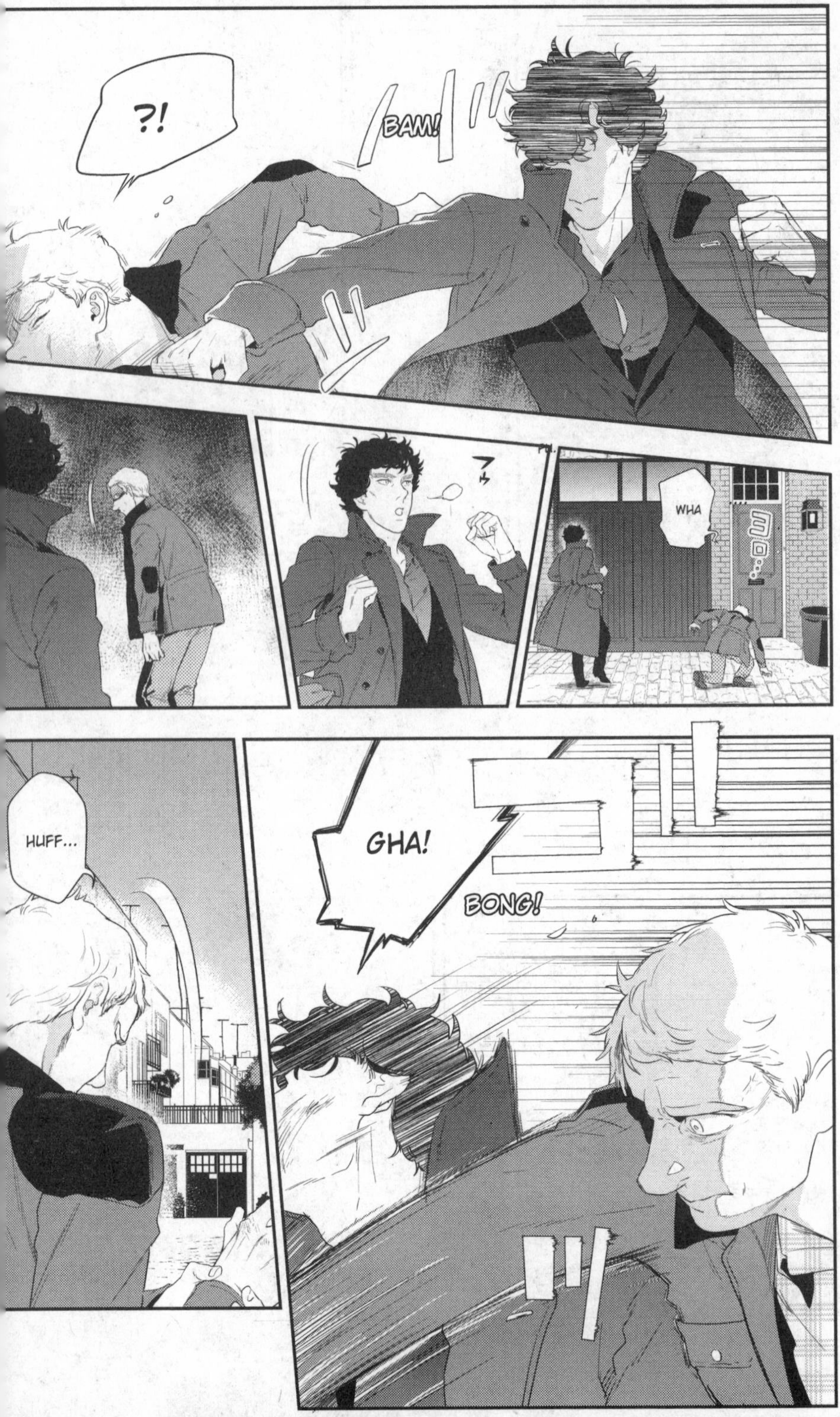
BAM!
?!
WHA
GHA!
BONG!
HUFF...

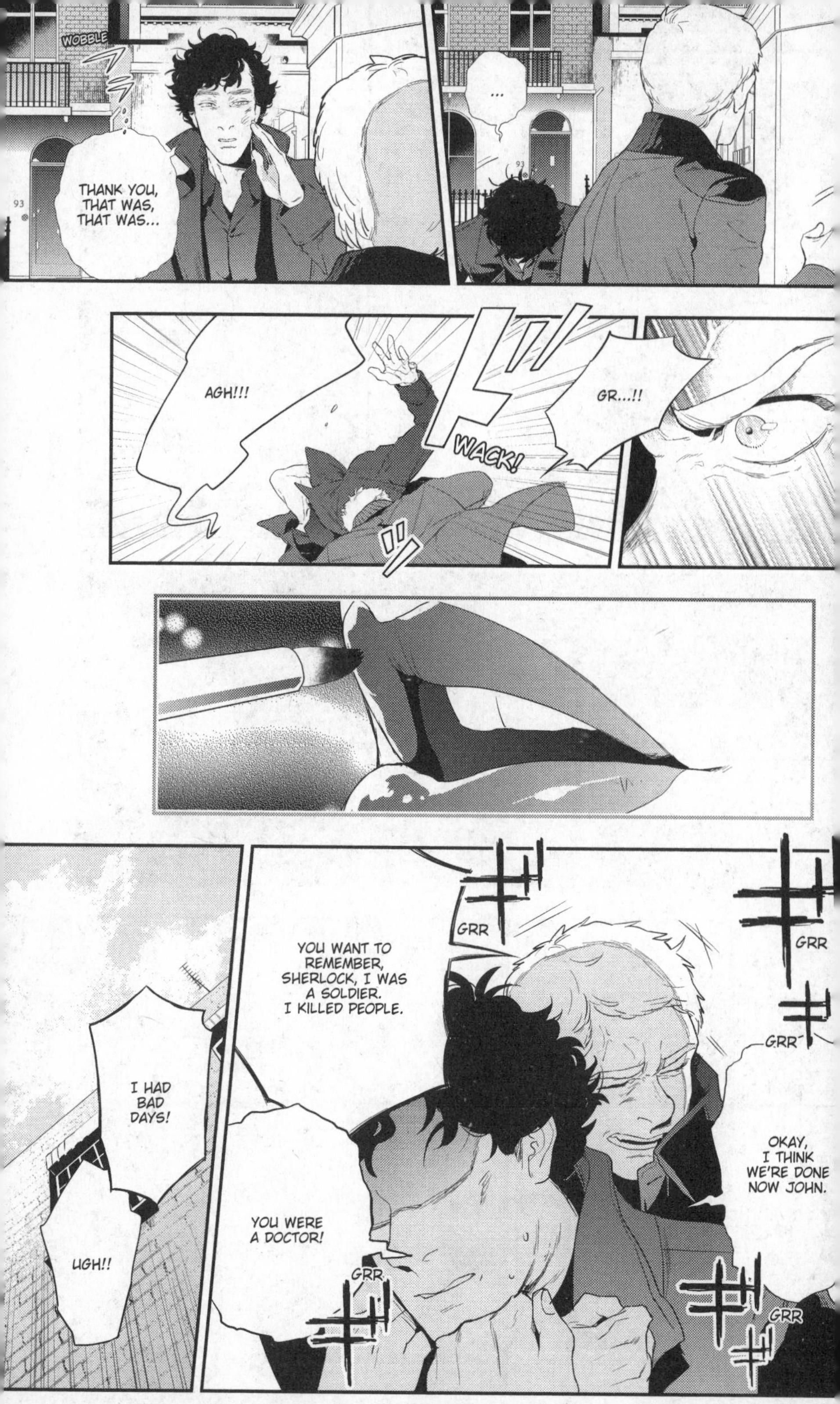
...
WOBBLE
THANK YOU, THAT WAS, THAT WAS...
GR...!!
AGH!!!
WACK!
GRR
GRR
GRR
YOU WANT TO REMEMBER, SHERLOCK, I WAS A SOLDIER. I KILLED PEOPLE.
OKAY, I THINK WE'RE DONE NOW JOHN.
YOU WERE A DOCTOR!
GRR
GRR
I HAD BAD DAYS!
UGH!!

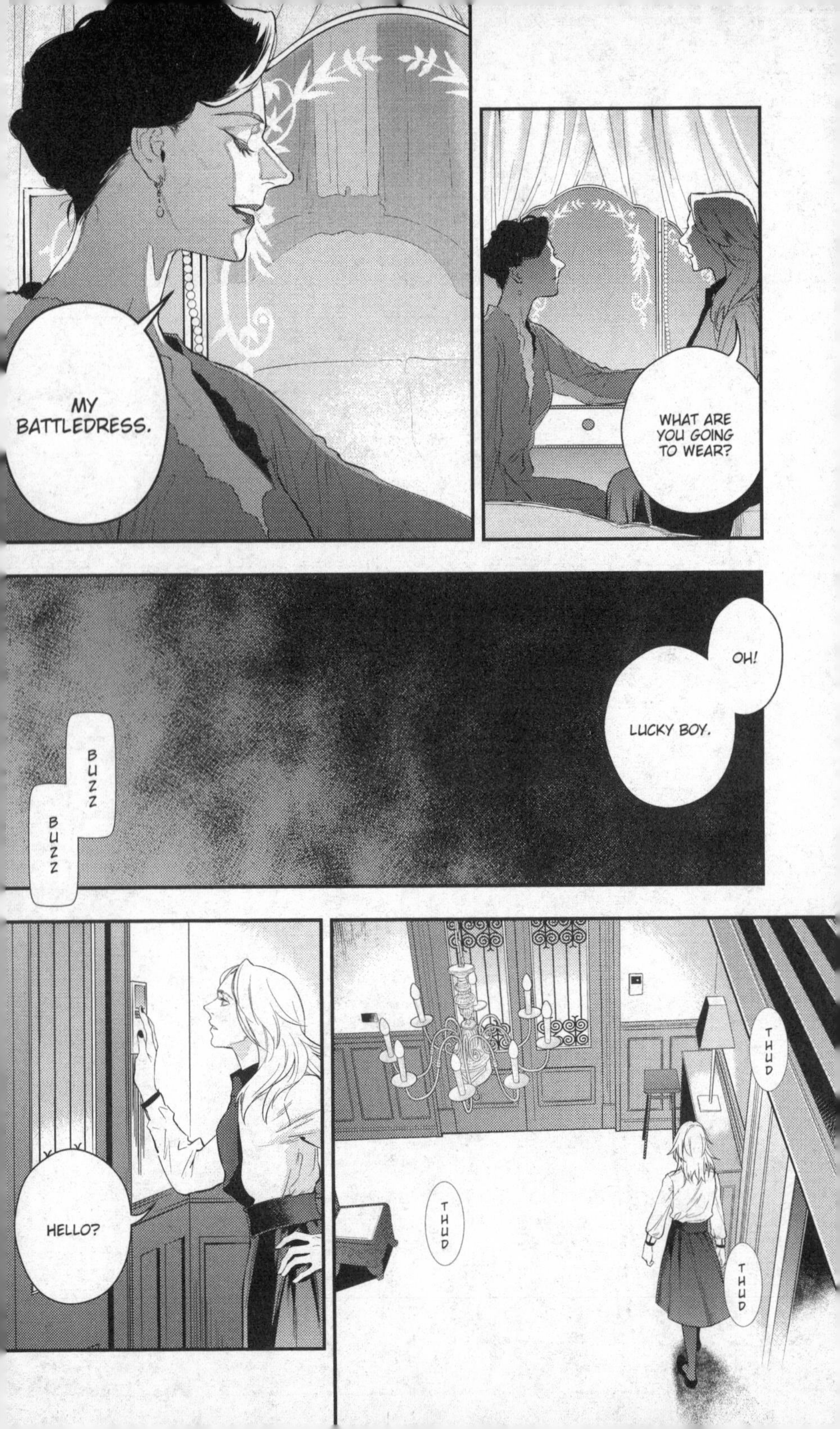
WHAT ARE YOU GOING TO WEAR?
MY BATTLEDRESS.
OH!
LUCKY BOY.
BUZZ
BUZZ
THUD
THUD
THUD
HELLO?

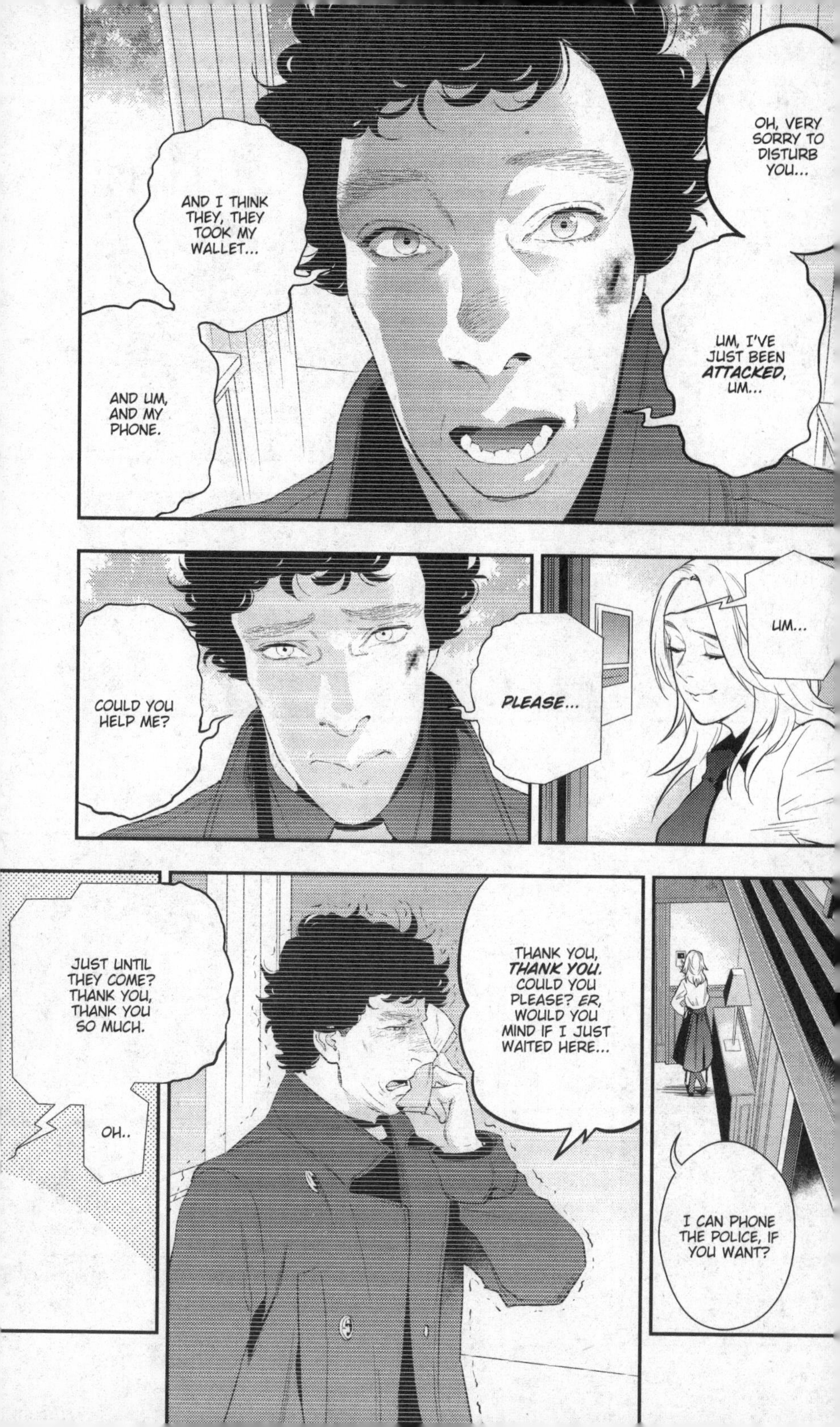
OH, VERY SORRY TO DISTURB YOU...
UM, I'VE JUST BEEN ***ATTACKED***, UM...
AND I THINK THEY, THEY TOOK MY WALLET...
AND UM, AND MY PHONE.
UM...
PLEASE...
COULD YOU HELP ME?
I CAN PHONE THE POLICE, IF YOU WANT?
THANK YOU, ***THANK YOU.*** COULD YOU PLEASE? *ER*, WOULD YOU MIND IF I JUST WAITED HERE...
JUST UNTIL THEY COME? THANK YOU, THANK YOU SO MUCH.
OH..

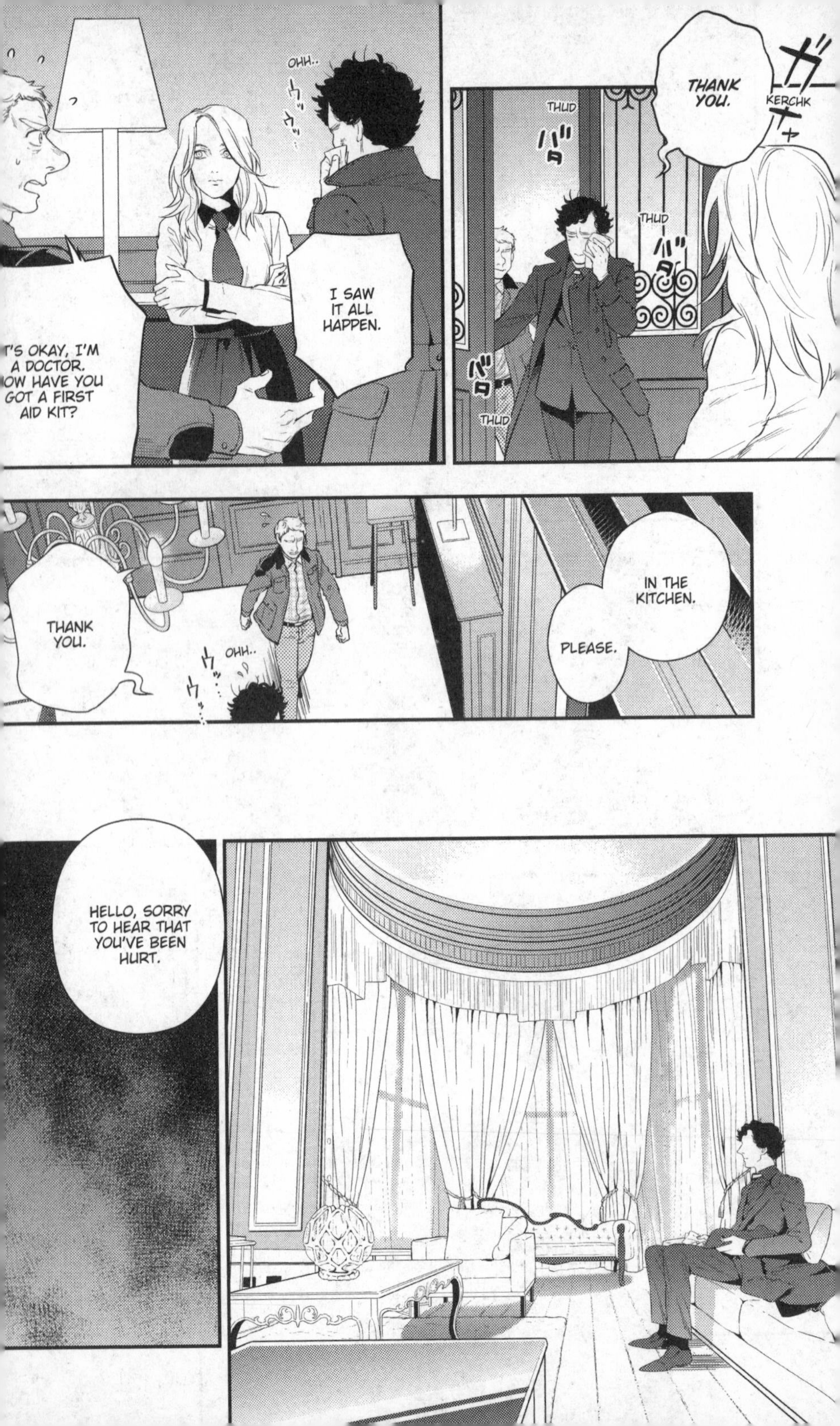
THANK YOU.
KERCHK
THUD
THUD
THUD
OHH..
I SAW IT ALL HAPPEN.
T'S OKAY, I'M A DOCTOR. OW HAVE YOU GOT A FIRST AID KIT?
IN THE KITCHEN.
PLEASE.
OHH..
THANK YOU.
HELLO, SORRY TO HEAR THAT YOU'VE BEEN HURT.

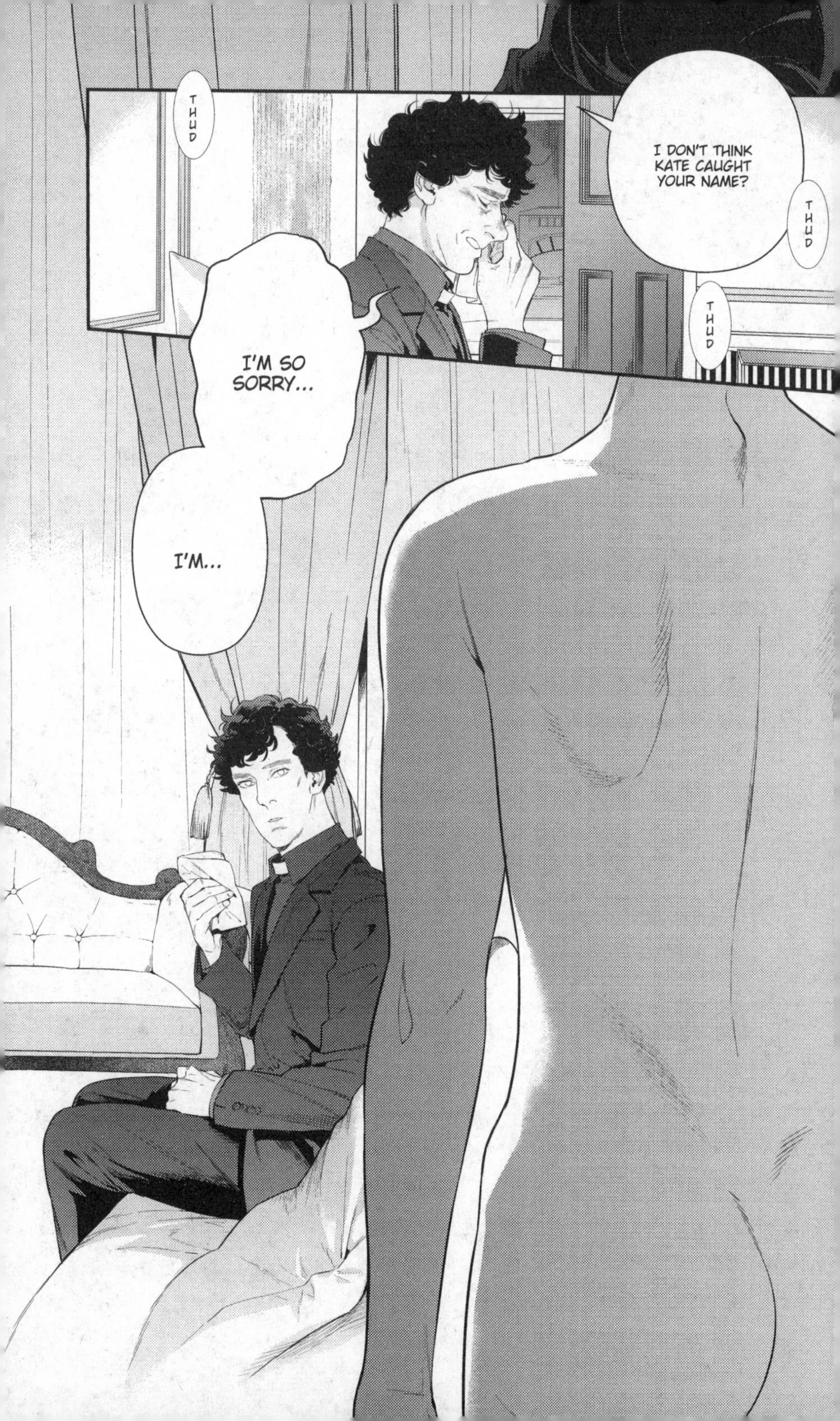
I DON'T THINK KATE CAUGHT YOUR NAME?
THUD
THUD
THUD
I'M SO SORRY...
I'M...

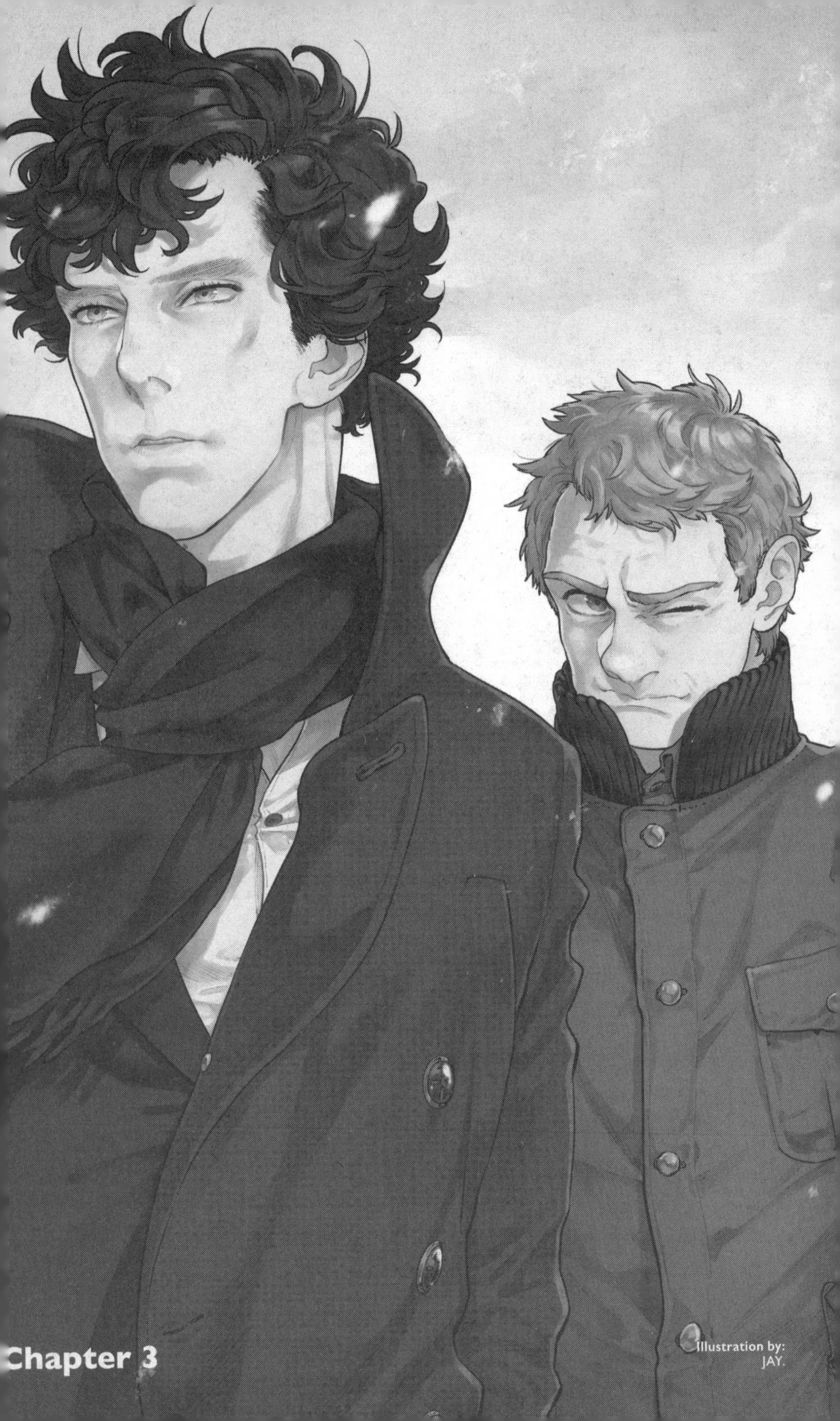

Chapter 3

Illustration by:
JAY.

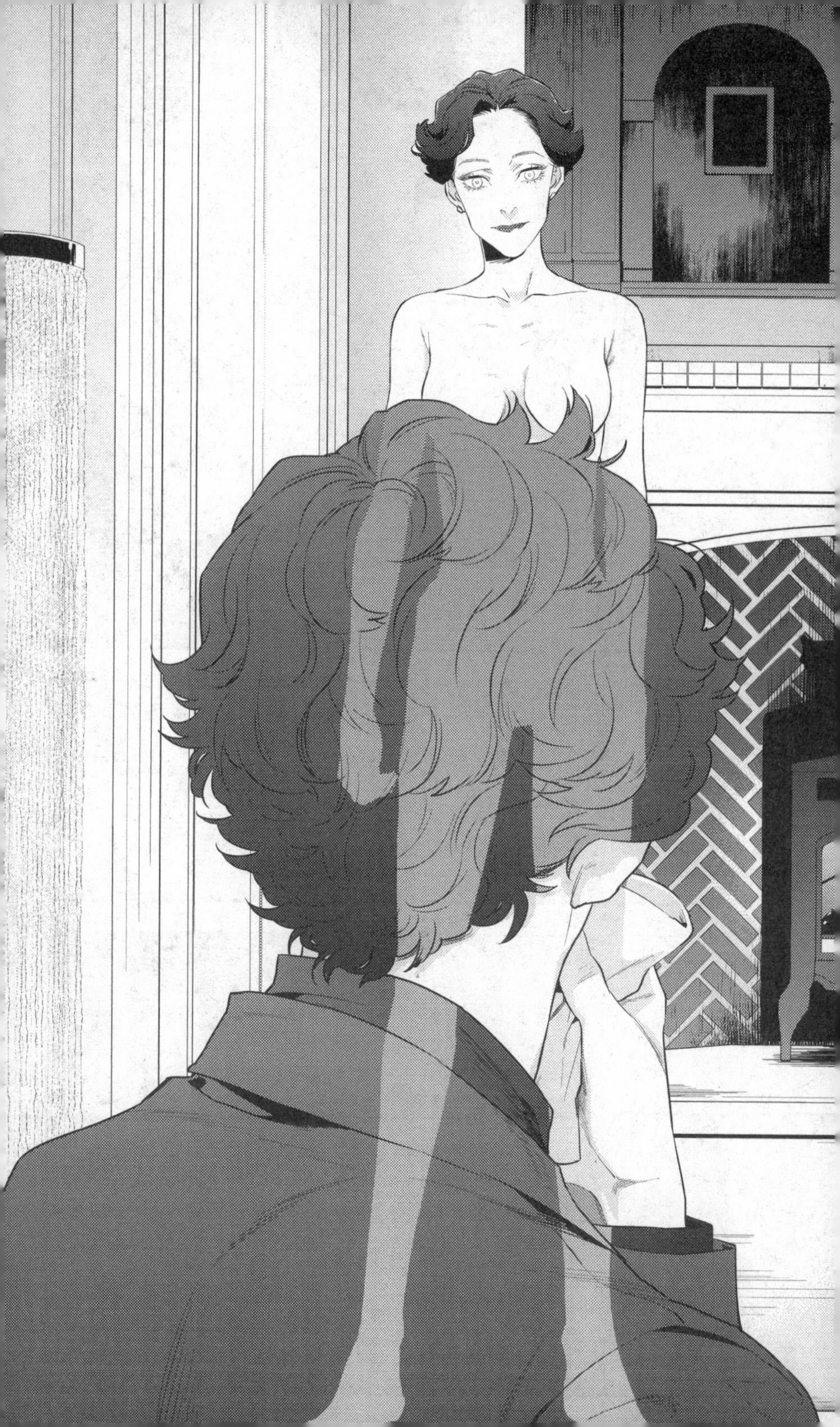

OH, IT'S ALWAYS HARD TO REMEMBER AN ALIAS WHEN YOU'VE HAD A FRIGHT.

ISN'T IT?

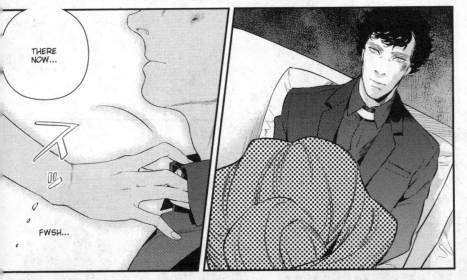

THERE NOW...

FWSH...

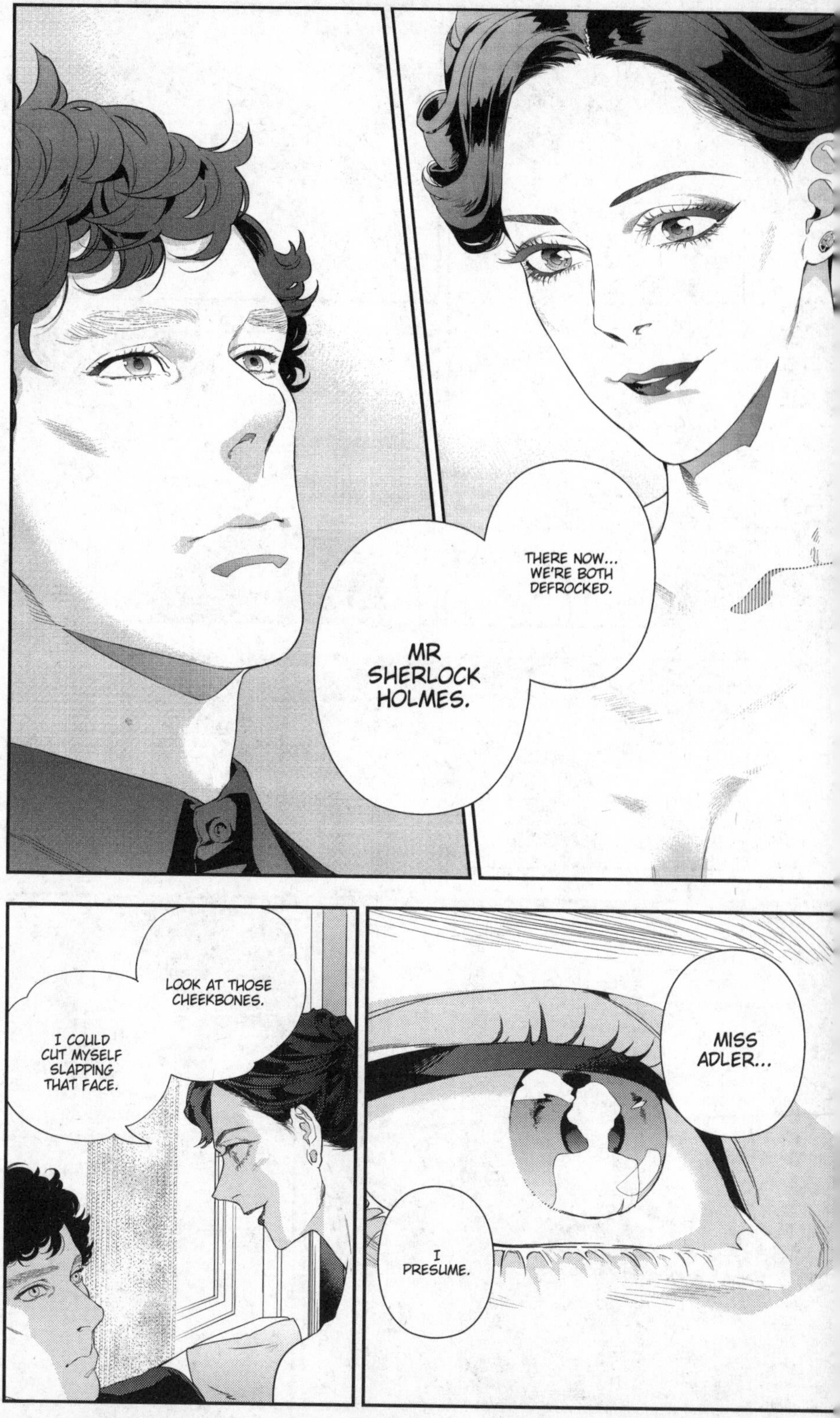
THERE NOW... WE'RE BOTH DEFROCKED.
MR SHERLOCK HOLMES.
MISS ADLER...
I PRESUME.
LOOK AT THOSE CHEEKBONES.
I COULD CUT MYSELF SLAPPING THAT FACE.

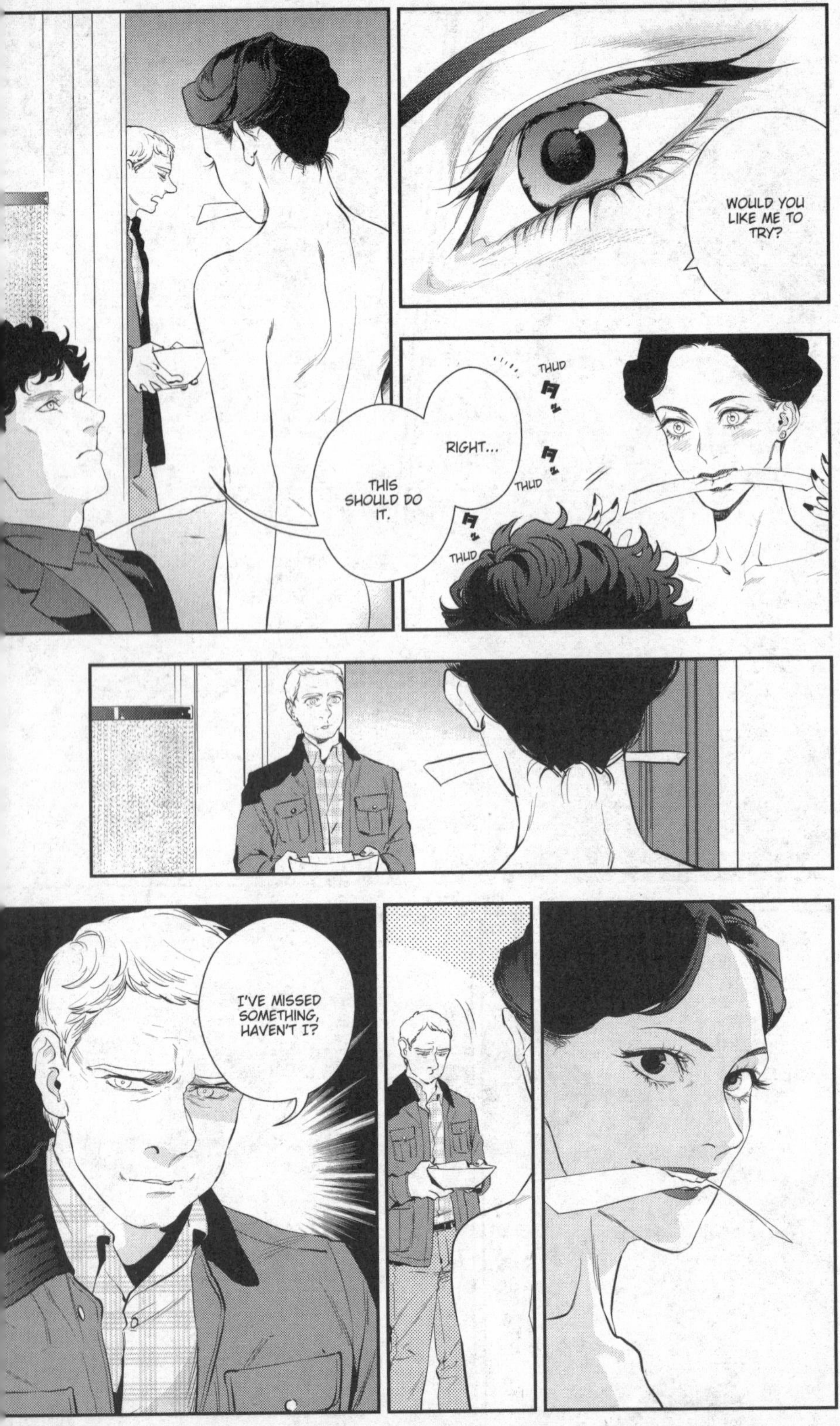

WOULD YOU LIKE ME TO TRY?
THUD
タッ
RIGHT...
THIS SHOULD DO IT.
タッ
THUD
タッ
THUD
I'VE MISSED SOMETHING, HAVEN'T I?

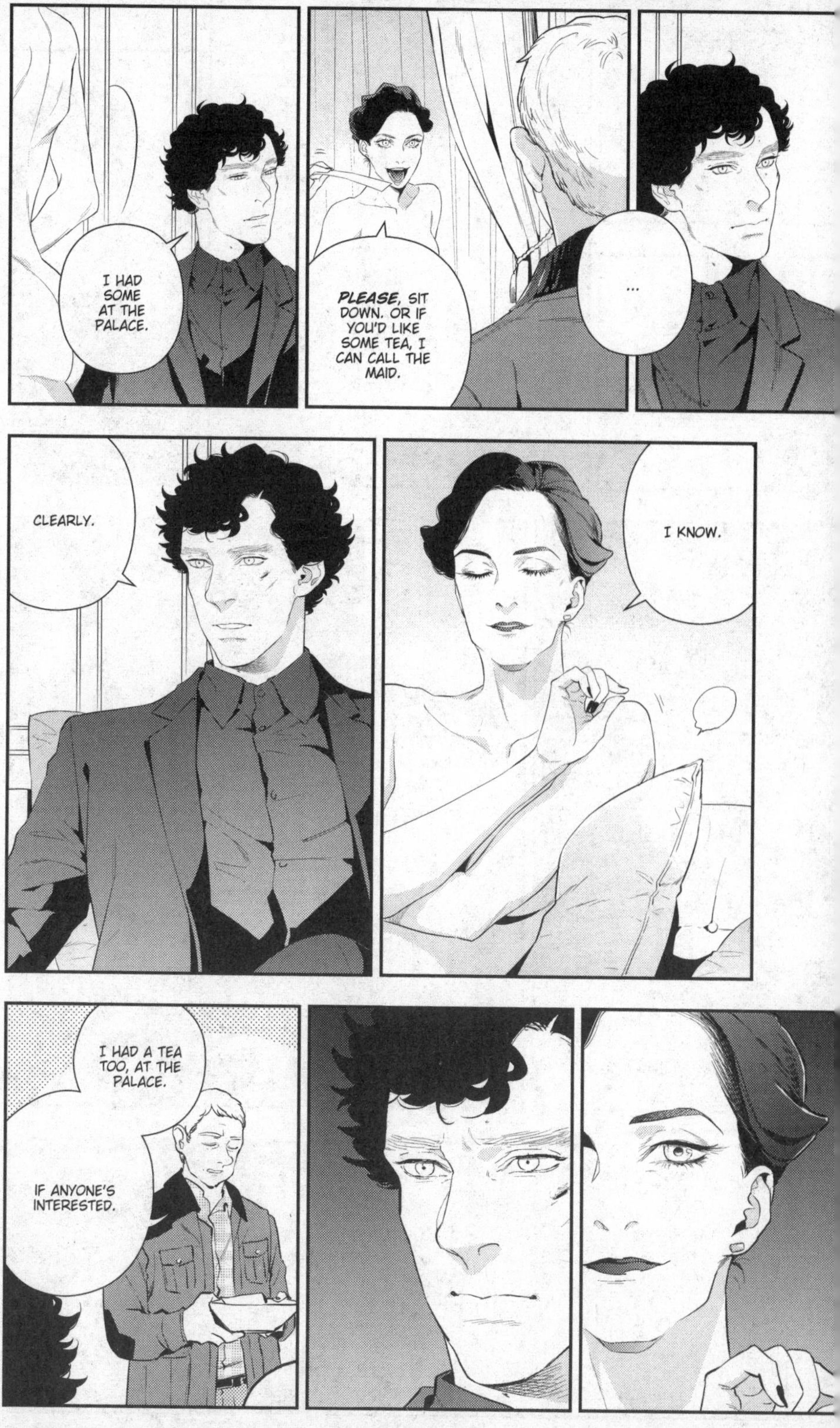
...
PLEASE, SIT DOWN. OR IF YOU'D LIKE SOME TEA, I CAN CALL THE MAID.
I HAD SOME AT THE PALACE.
I KNOW.
CLEARLY.
I HAD A TEA TOO, AT THE PALACE.
IF ANYONE'S INTERESTED.

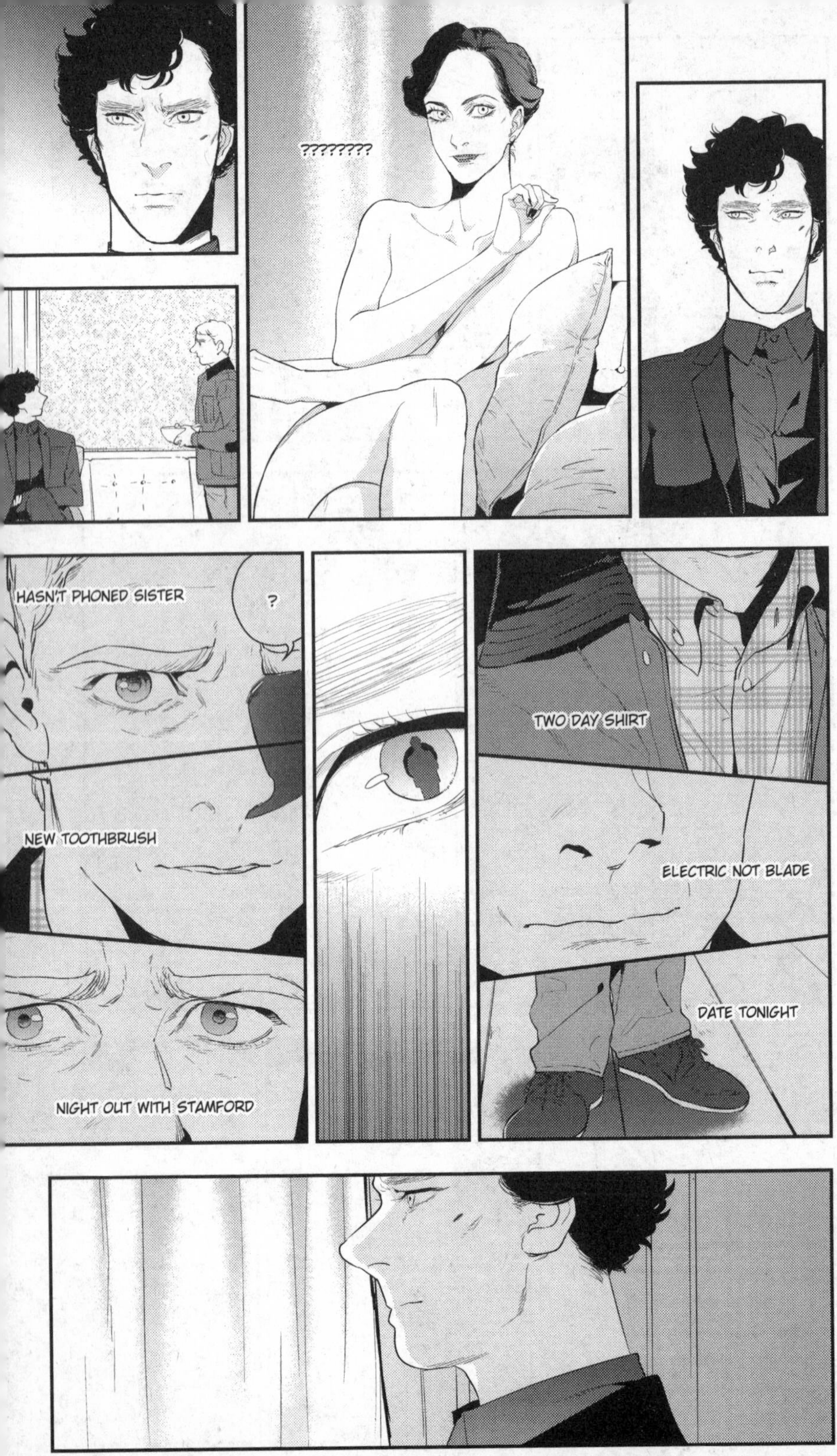
????????
TWO DAY SHIRT
ELECTRIC NOT BLADE
DATE TONIGHT
HASN'T PHONED SISTER
?
NEW TOOTHBRUSH
NIGHT OUT WITH STAMFORD

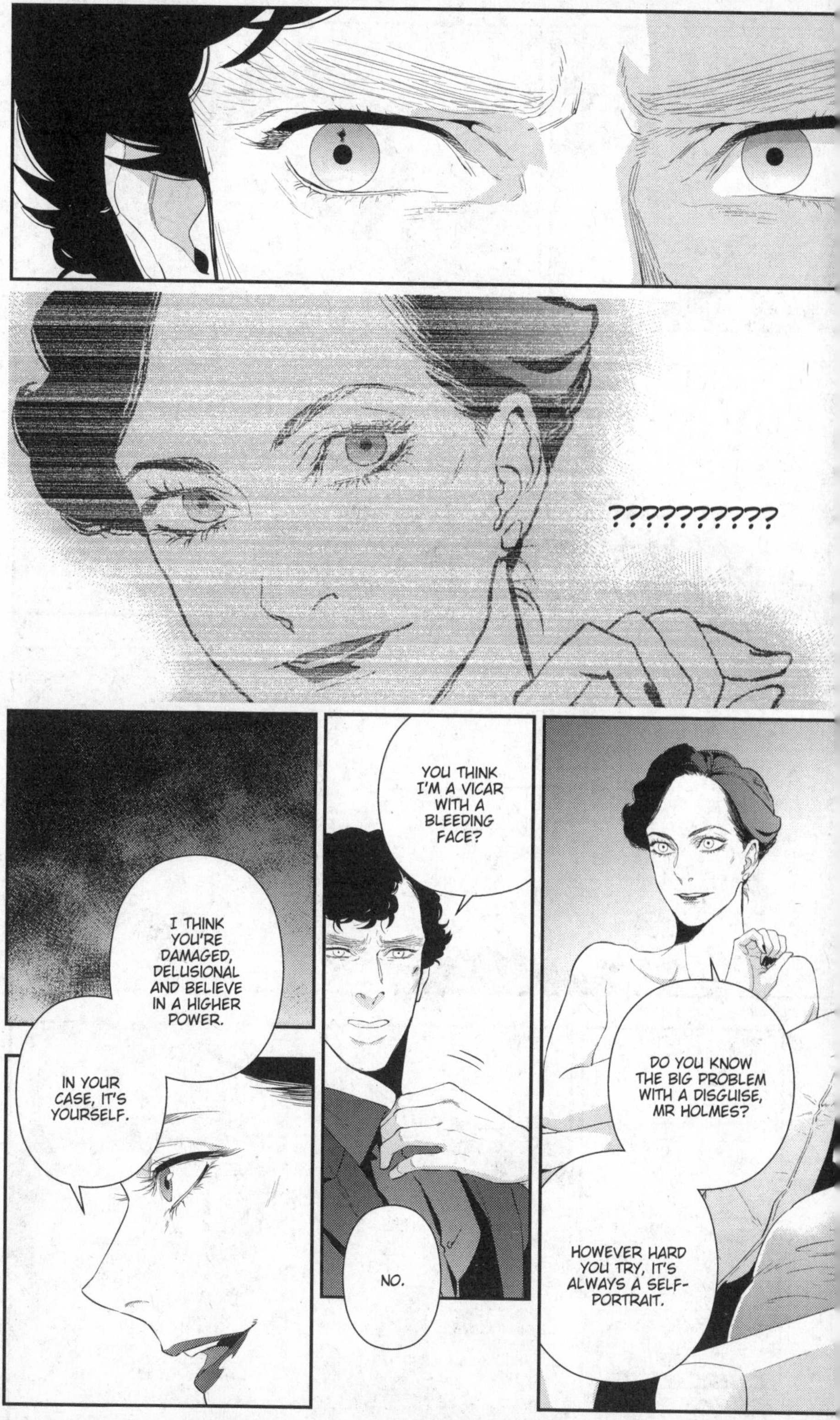
??????????
DO YOU KNOW THE BIG PROBLEM WITH A DISGUISE, MR HOLMES?
HOWEVER HARD YOU TRY, IT'S ALWAYS A SELF-PORTRAIT.
YOU THINK I'M A VICAR WITH A BLEEDING FACE?
NO.
I THINK YOU'RE DAMAGED, DELUSIONAL AND BELIEVE IN A HIGHER POWER.
IN YOUR CASE, IT'S YOURSELF.

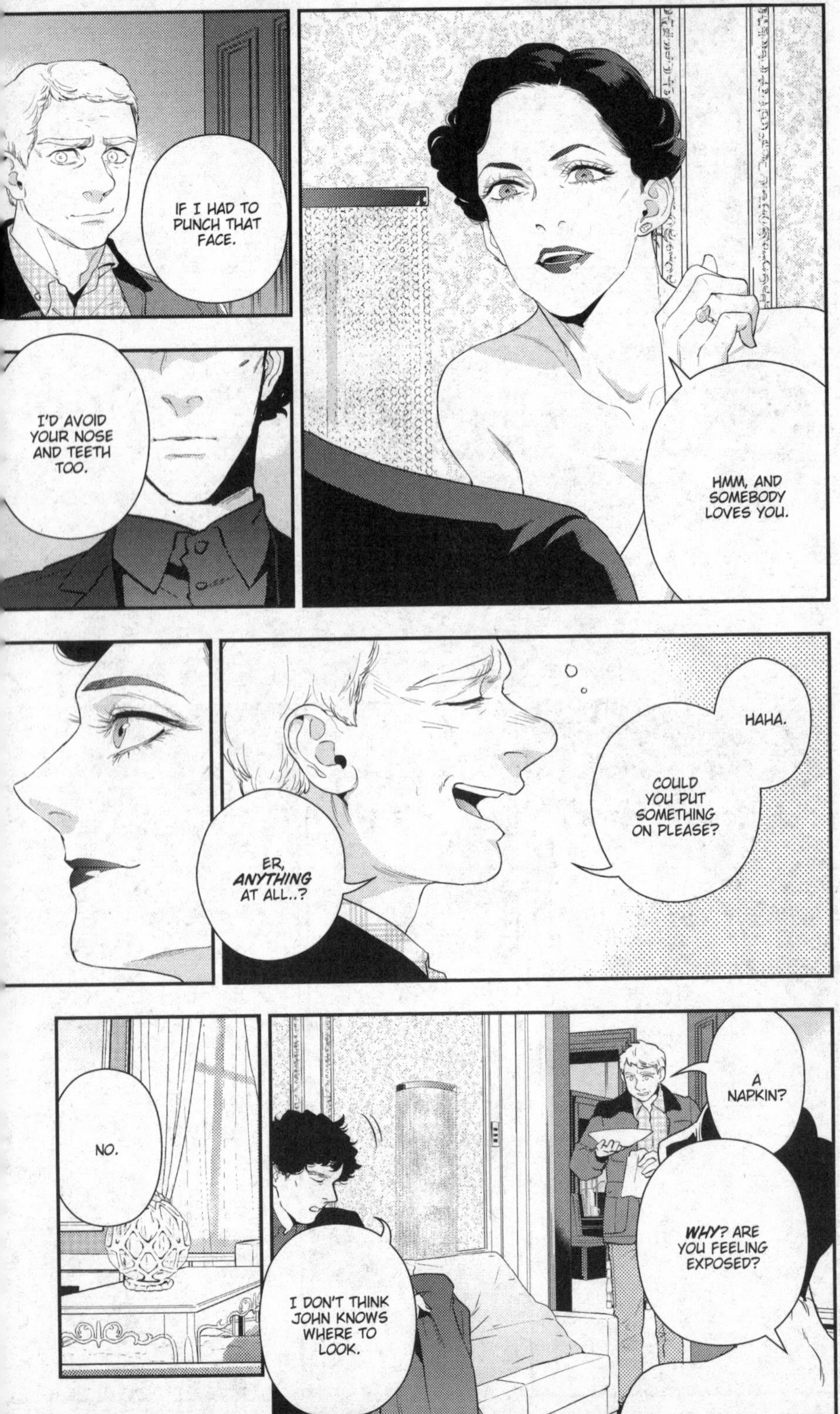
HMM, AND SOMEBODY LOVES YOU.
IF I HAD TO PUNCH THAT FACE.
I'D AVOID YOUR NOSE AND TEETH TOO.
HAHA.
COULD YOU PUT SOMETHING ON PLEASE?
ER, *ANYTHING* AT ALL..?
A NAPKIN?
WHY? ARE YOU FEELING EXPOSED?
I DON'T THINK JOHN KNOWS WHERE TO LOOK.
NO.

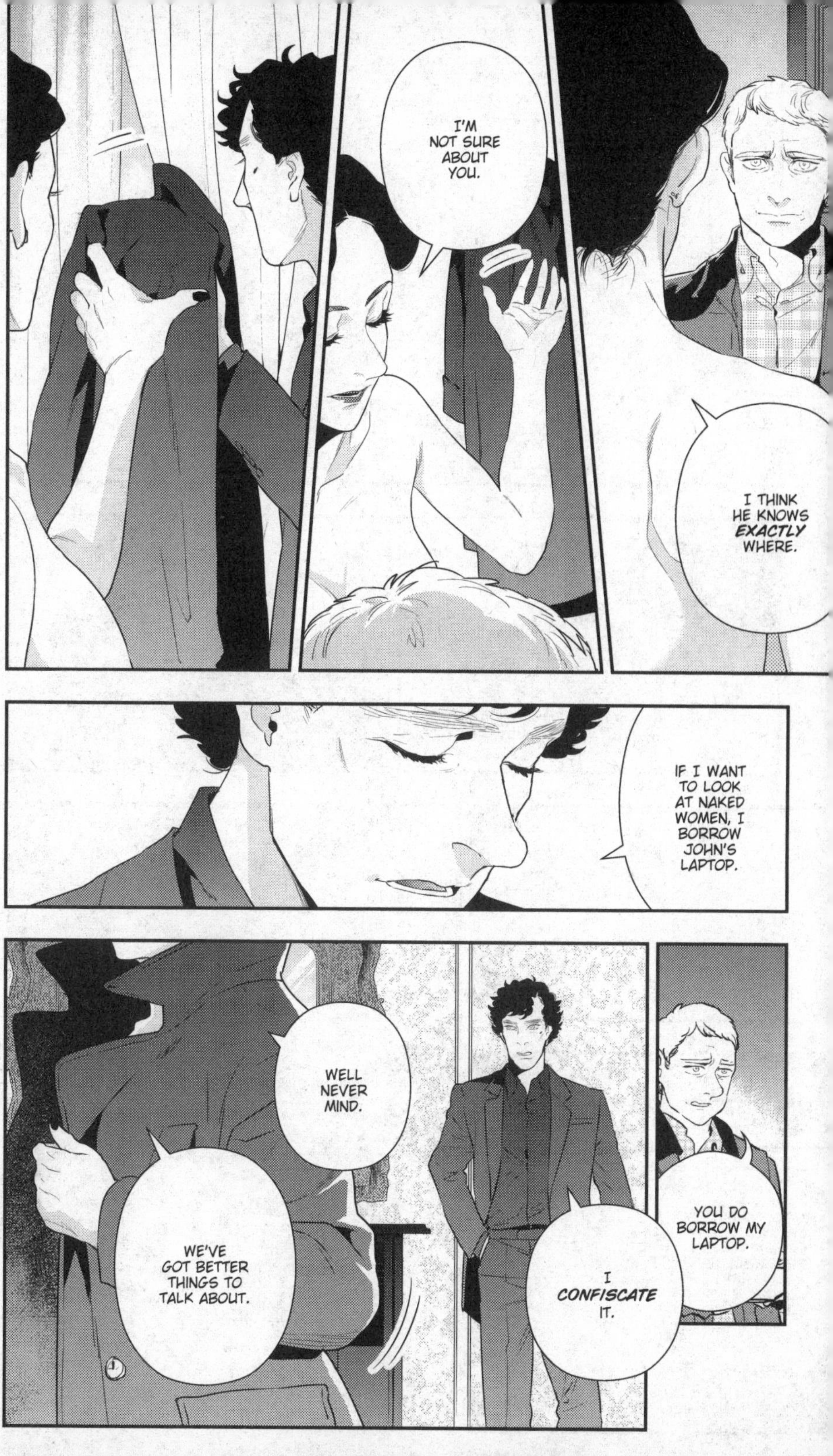
I THINK HE KNOWS ***EXACTLY*** WHERE.
I'M NOT SURE ABOUT YOU.
IF I WANT TO LOOK AT NAKED WOMEN, I BORROW JOHN'S LAPTOP.
YOU DO BORROW MY LAPTOP.
I ***CONFISCATE*** IT.
WELL NEVER MIND.
WE'VE GOT BETTER THINGS TO TALK ABOUT.

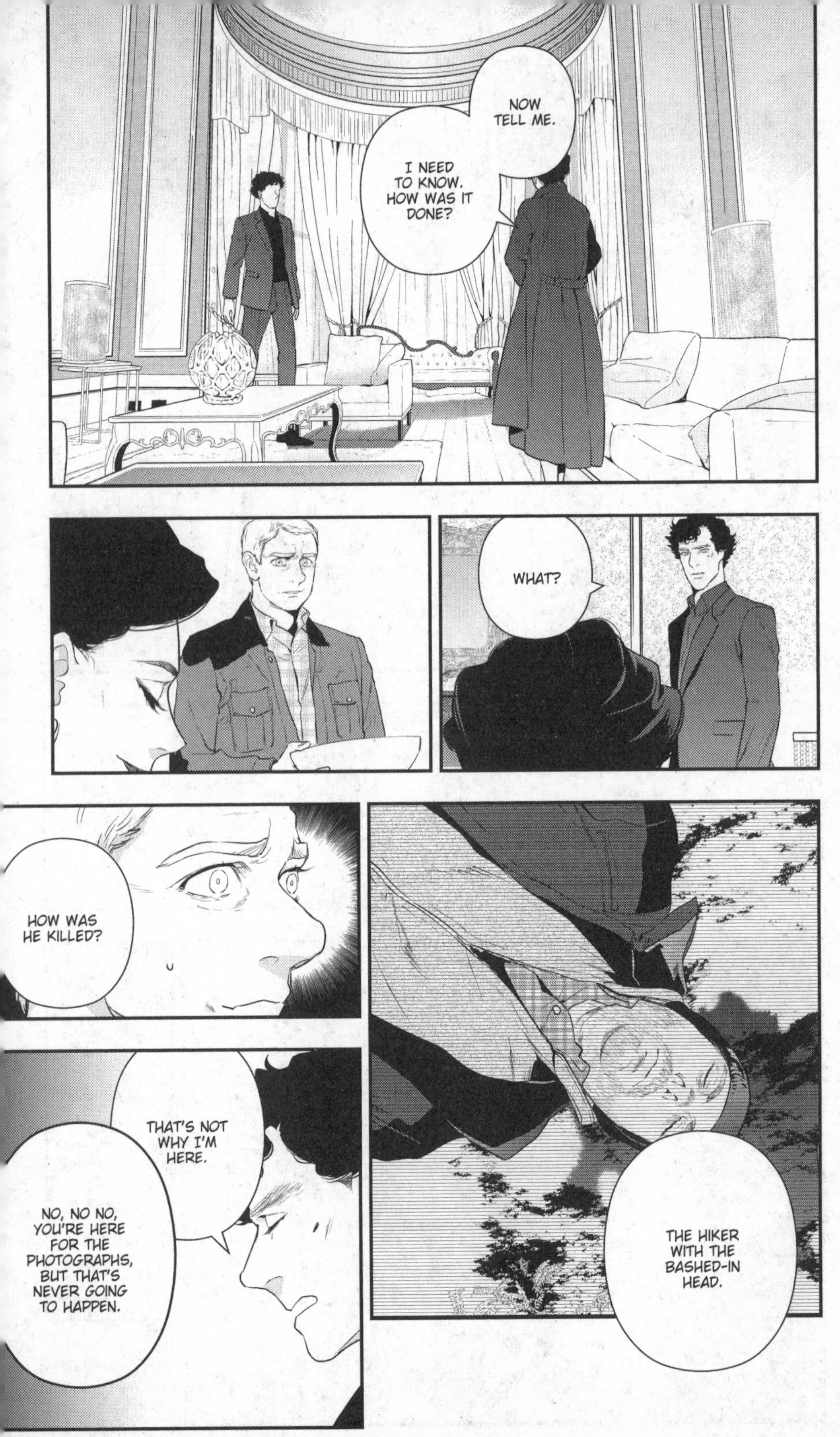
NOW TELL ME.
I NEED TO KNOW. HOW WAS IT DONE?
WHAT?
THE HIKER WITH THE BASHED-IN HEAD.
HOW WAS HE KILLED?
THAT'S NOT WHY I'M HERE.
NO, NO NO, YOU'RE HERE FOR THE PHOTOGRAPHS, BUT THAT'S NEVER GOING TO HAPPEN.

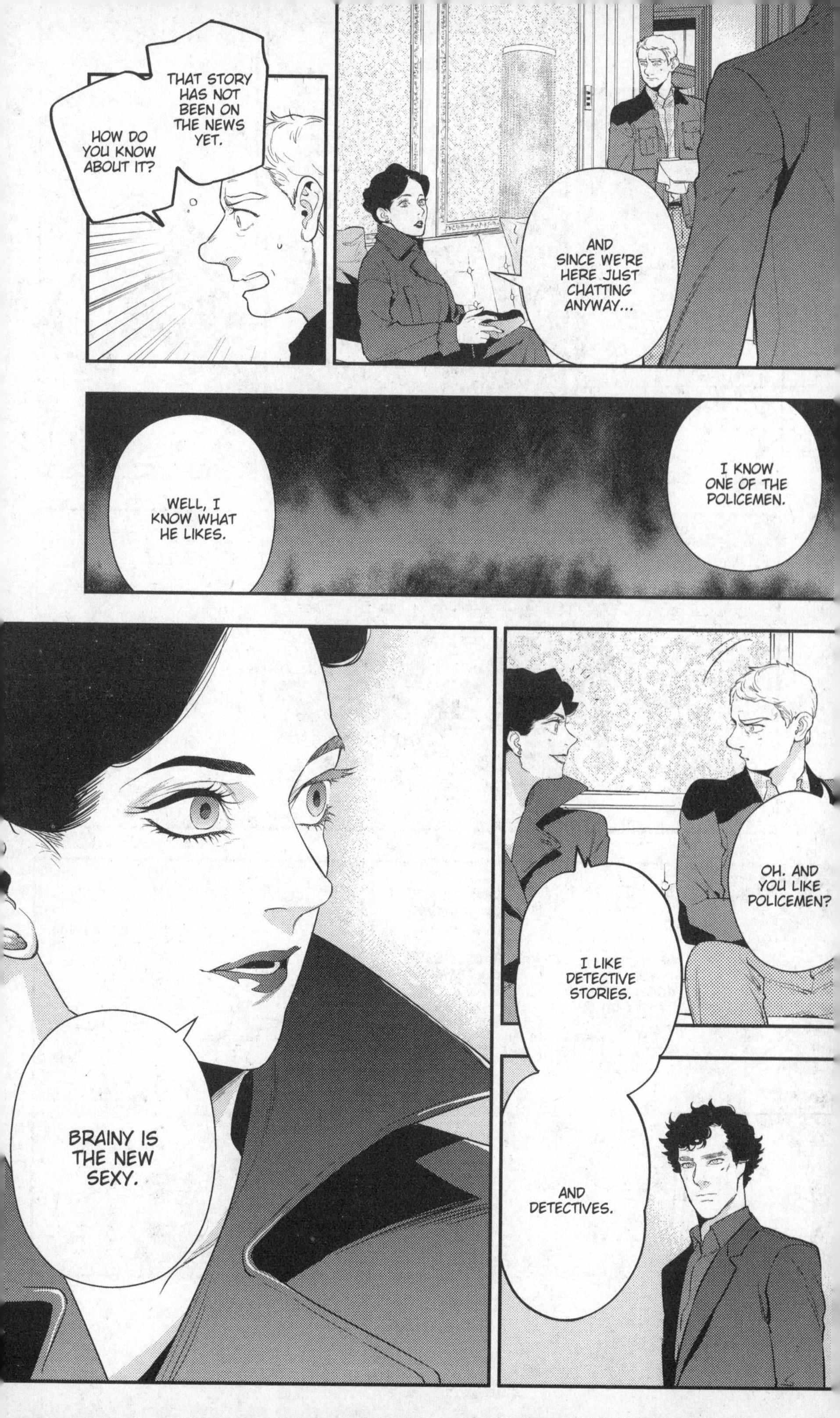
AND SINCE WE'RE HERE JUST CHATTING ANYWAY...
THAT STORY HAS NOT BEEN ON THE NEWS YET.
HOW DO YOU KNOW ABOUT IT?
I KNOW ONE OF THE POLICEMEN.
WELL, I KNOW WHAT HE LIKES.
OH. AND YOU LIKE POLICEMEN?
I LIKE DETECTIVE STORIES.
AND DETECTIVES.
BRAINY IS THE NEW SEXY.

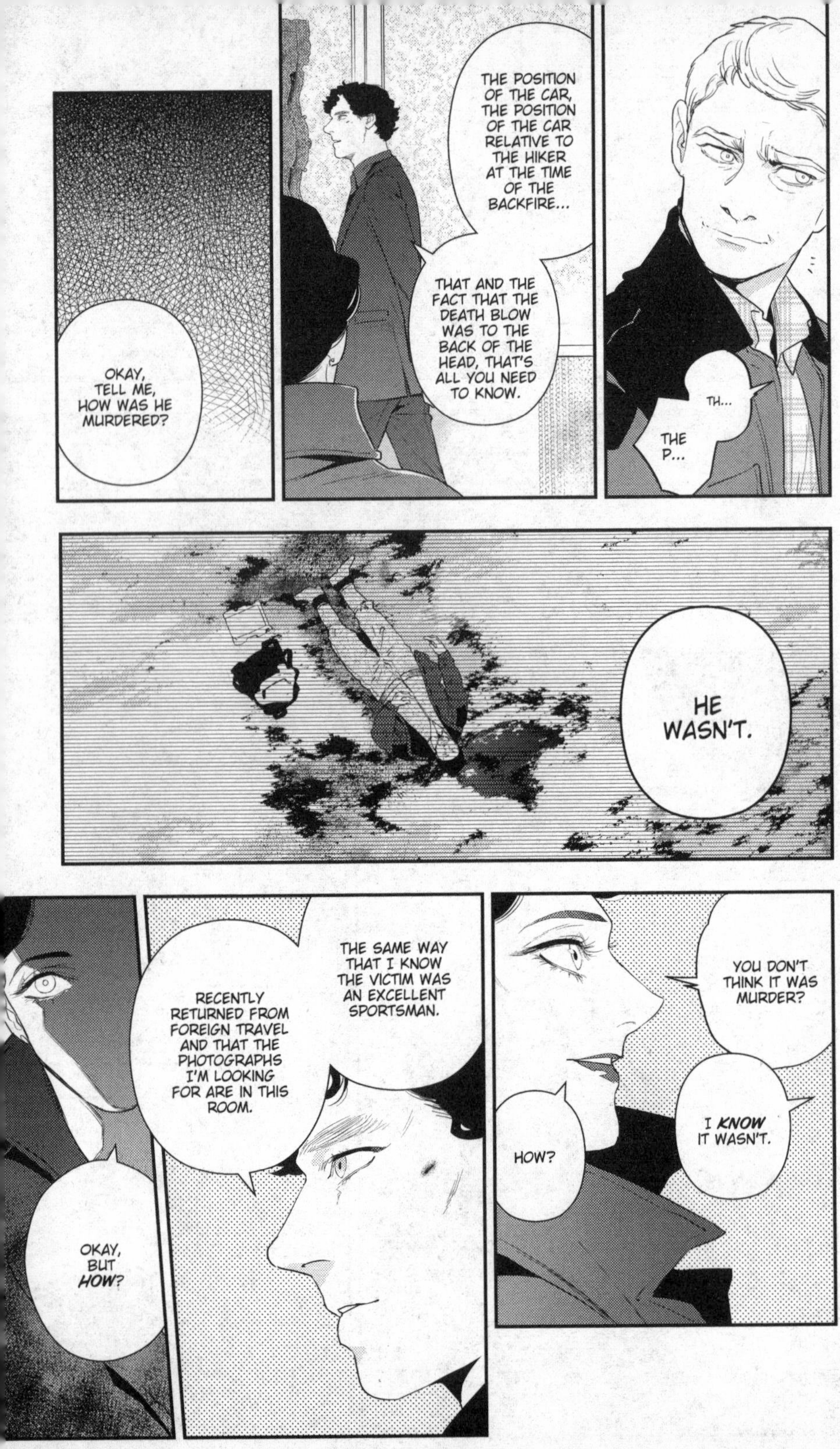
TH...
THE P...
THE POSITION OF THE CAR, THE POSITION OF THE CAR RELATIVE TO THE HIKER AT THE TIME OF THE BACKFIRE...
THAT AND THE FACT THAT THE DEATH BLOW WAS TO THE BACK OF THE HEAD, THAT'S ALL YOU NEED TO KNOW.
OKAY, TELL ME, HOW WAS HE MURDERED?
HE WASN'T.
YOU DON'T THINK IT WAS MURDER?
I ***KNOW*** IT WASN'T.
HOW?
THE SAME WAY THAT I KNOW THE VICTIM WAS AN EXCELLENT SPORTSMAN.
RECENTLY RETURNED FROM FOREIGN TRAVEL AND THAT THE PHOTOGRAPHS I'M LOOKING FOR ARE IN THIS ROOM.
OKAY, BUT ***HOW***?

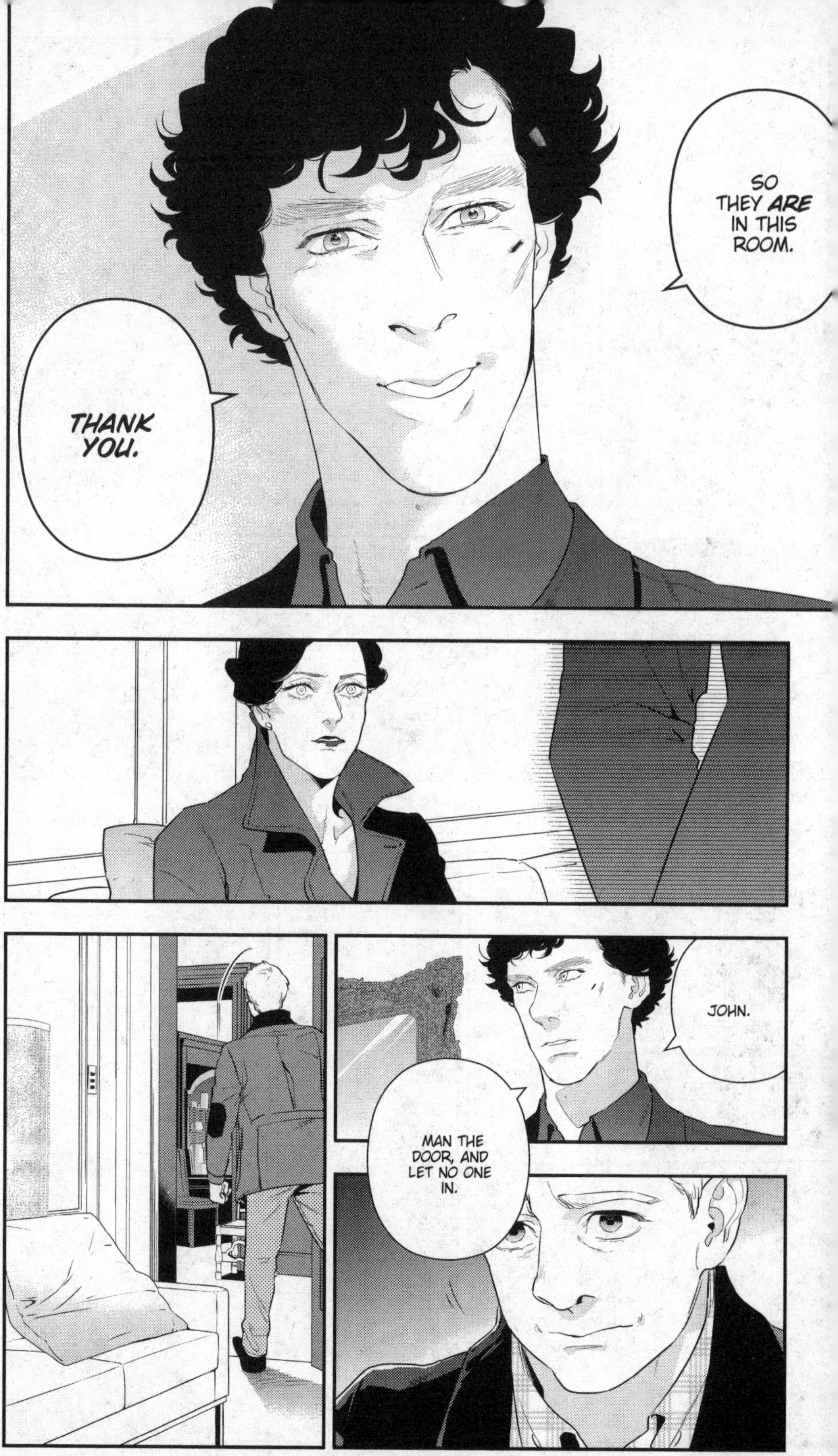
SO THEY ARE IN THIS ROOM.
THANK YOU.
JOHN.
MAN THE DOOR, AND LET NO ONE IN.

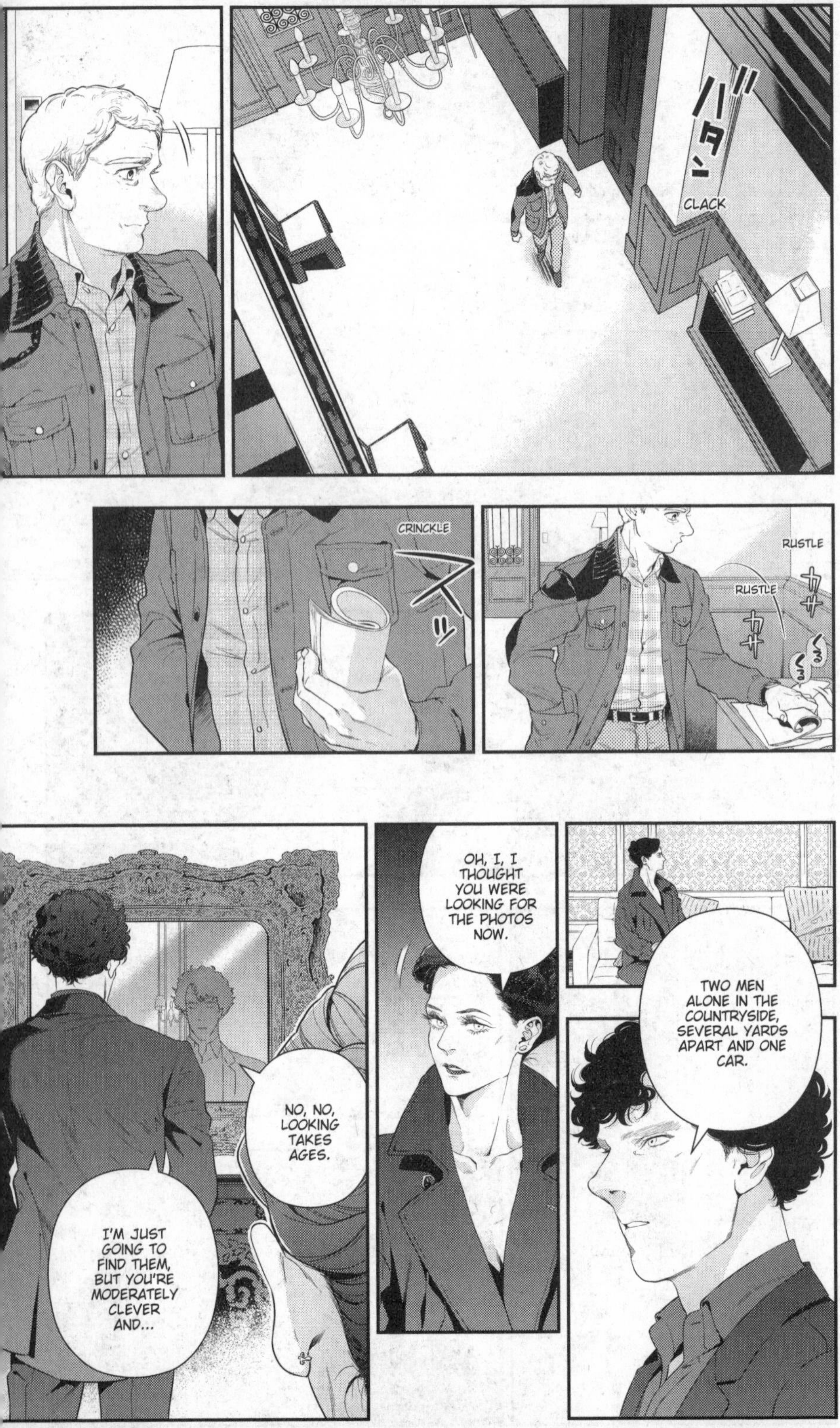

バタン
CLACK
RUSTLE
カサ
RUSTLE
カサ
CRINCKLE
スッ
TWO MEN ALONE IN THE COUNTRYSIDE, SEVERAL YARDS APART AND ONE CAR.
OH, I, I THOUGHT YOU WERE LOOKING FOR THE PHOTOS NOW.
NO, NO, LOOKING TAKES AGES.
I'M JUST GOING TO FIND THEM, BUT YOU'RE MODERATELY CLEVER AND...

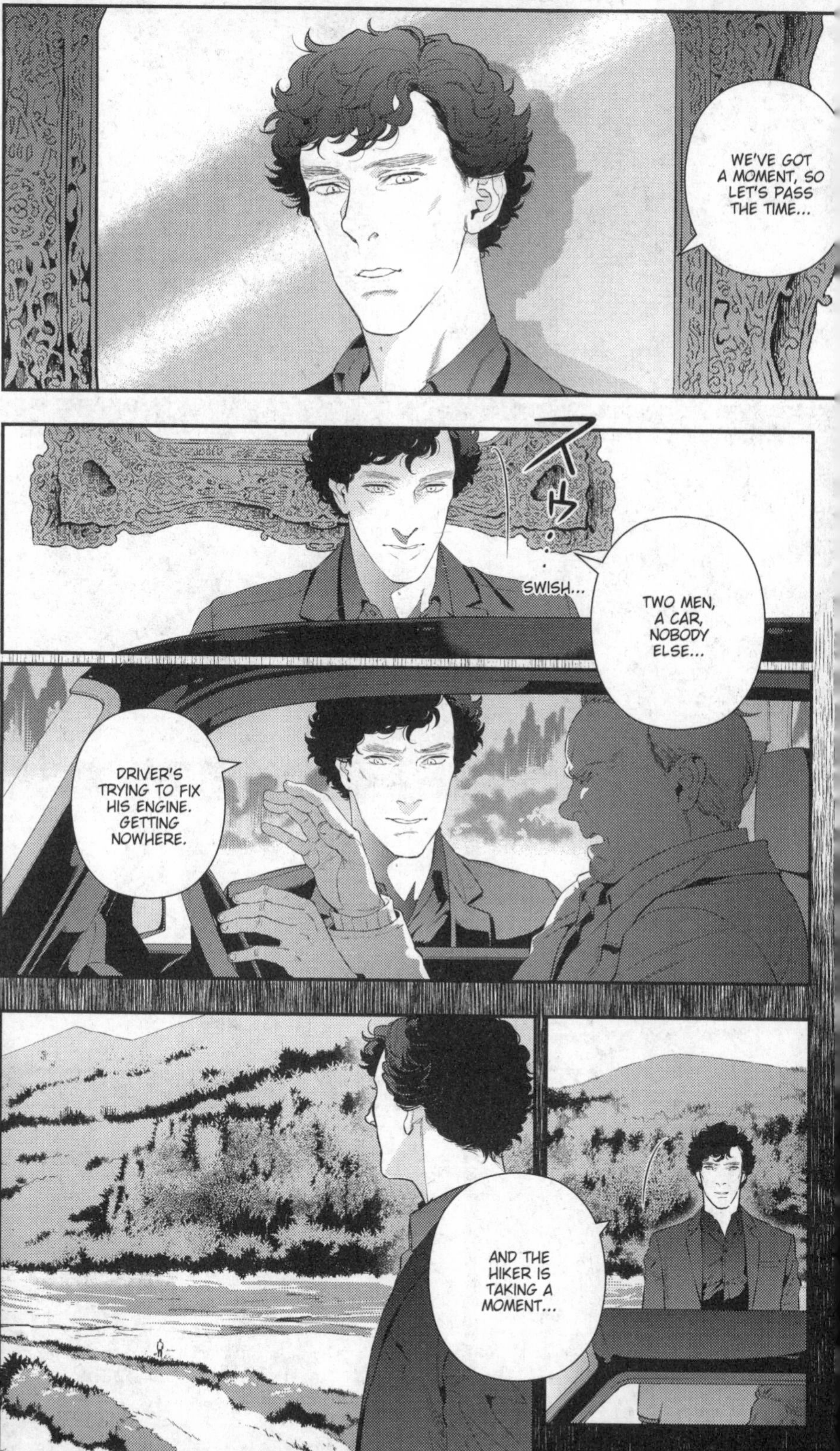
WE'VE GOT A MOMENT, SO LET'S PASS THE TIME...
スッ
SWISH...
TWO MEN, A CAR, NOBODY ELSE...
DRIVER'S TRYING TO FIX HIS ENGINE. GETTING NOWHERE.
AND THE HIKER IS TAKING A MOMENT...

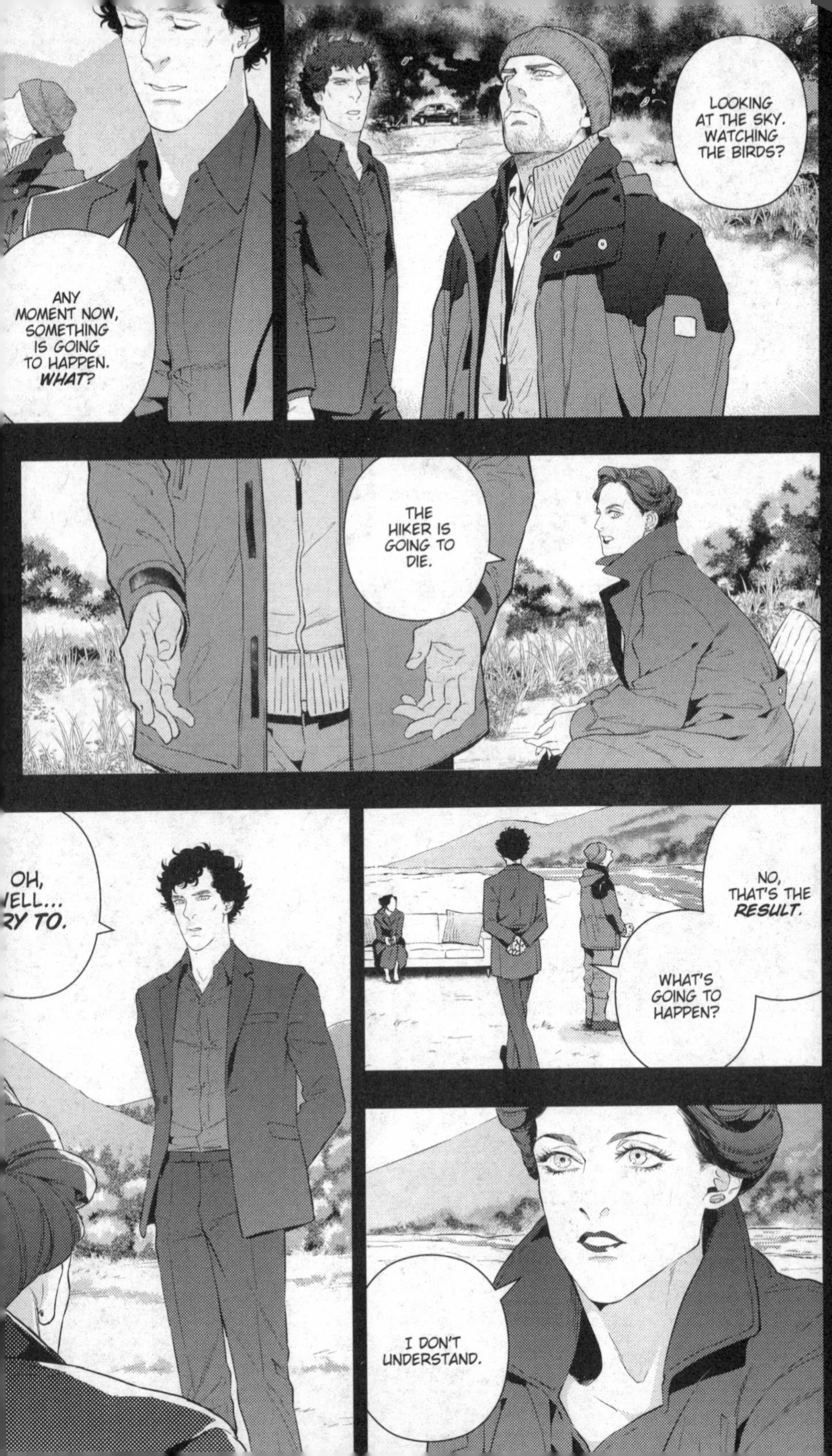
LOOKING AT THE SKY. WATCHING THE BIRDS?
ANY MOMENT NOW, SOMETHING IS GOING TO HAPPEN. *WHAT?*
THE HIKER IS GOING TO DIE.
NO, THAT'S THE *RESULT.*
WHAT'S GOING TO HAPPEN?
I DON'T UNDERSTAND.
OH, ELL... *RY TO.*

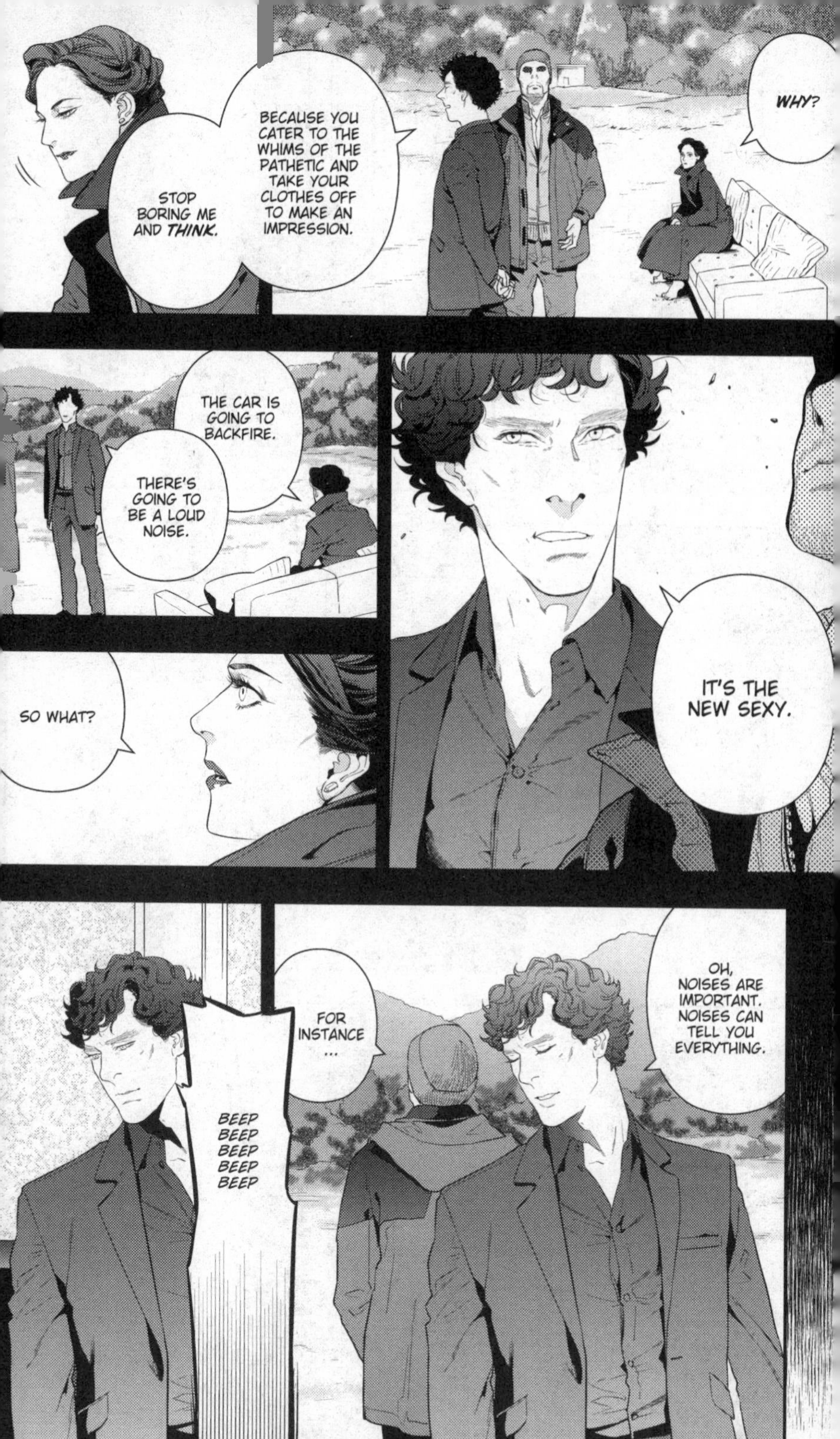
WHY?
BECAUSE YOU CATER TO THE WHIMS OF THE PATHETIC AND TAKE YOUR CLOTHES OFF TO MAKE AN IMPRESSION.
STOP BORING ME AND *THINK.*
IT'S THE NEW SEXY.
THE CAR IS GOING TO BACKFIRE.
THERE'S GOING TO BE A LOUD NOISE.
SO WHAT?
OH, NOISES ARE IMPORTANT. NOISES CAN TELL YOU EVERYTHING.
FOR INSTANCE ...
BEEP BEEP BEEP BEEP BEEP

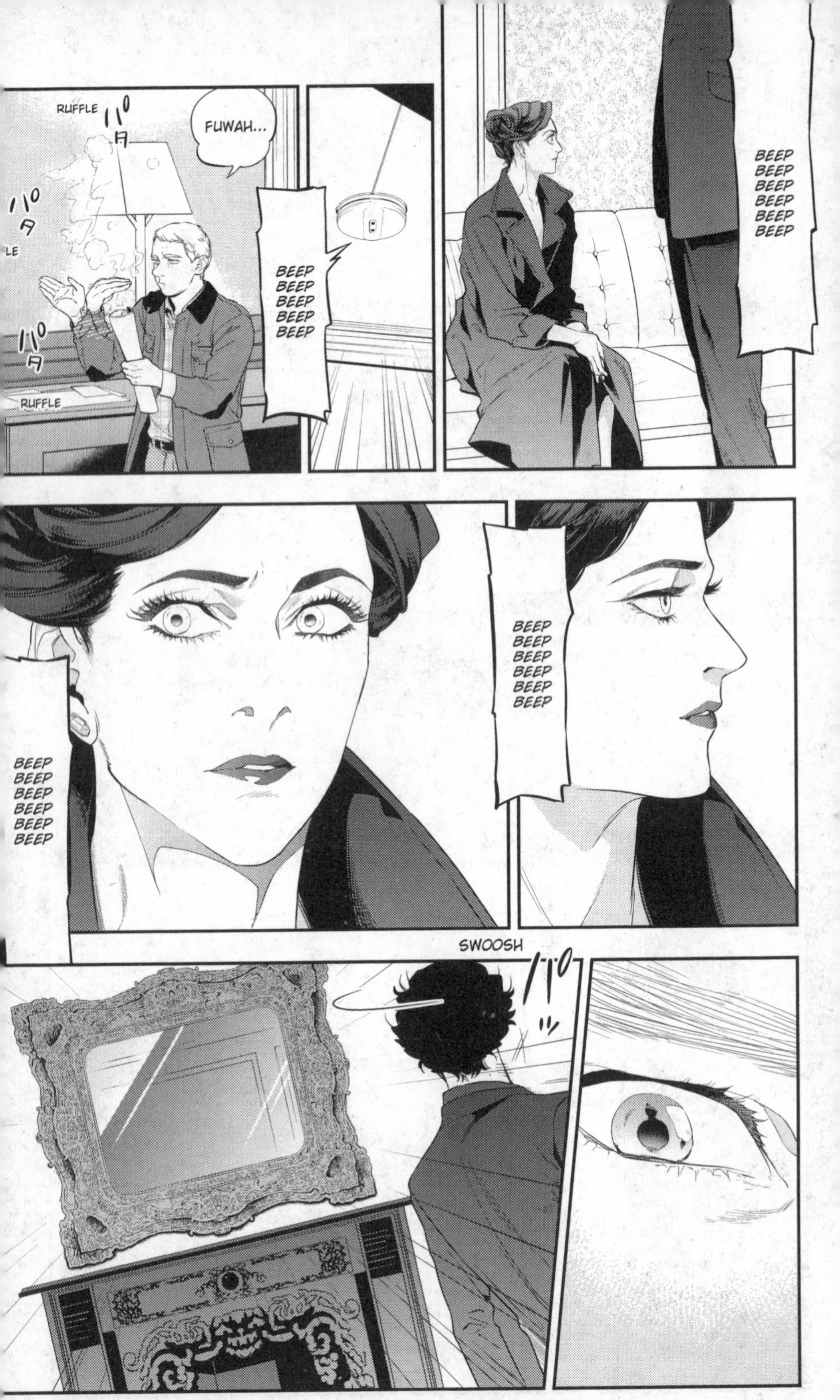

BEEP BEEP BEEP BEEP BEEP BEEP
BEEP BEEP BEEP BEEP BEEP
FUWAH...
RUFFLE
RUFFLE
BEEP BEEP BEEP BEEP BEEP BEEP
BEEP BEEP BEEP BEEP BEEP BEEP
SWOOSH

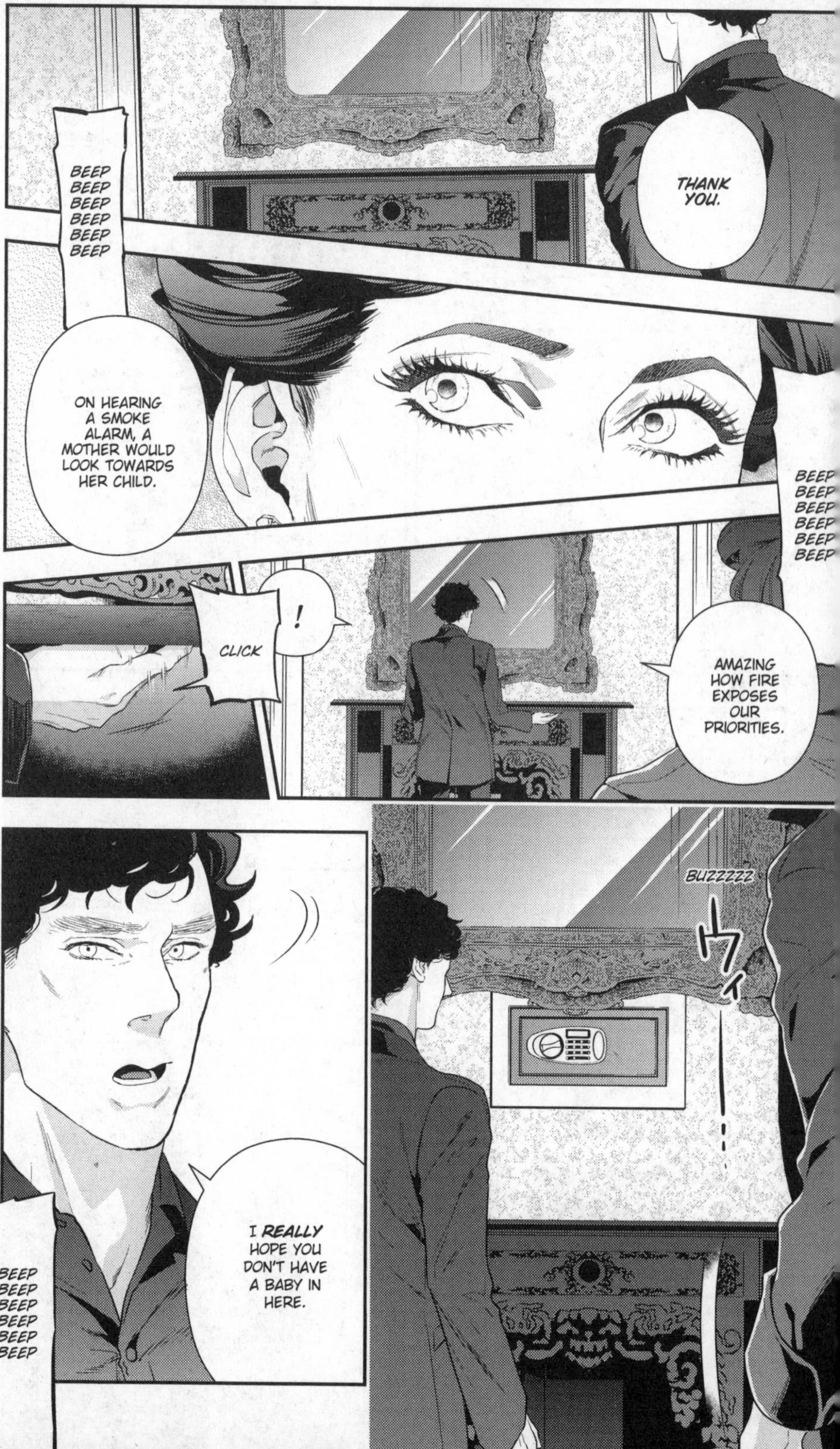

THANK YOU.
BEEP BEEP BEEP BEEP BEEP BEEP
ON HEARING A SMOKE ALARM, A MOTHER WOULD LOOK TOWARDS HER CHILD.
BEEP BEEP BEEP BEEP BEEP BEEP
AMAZING HOW FIRE EXPOSES OUR PRIORITIES.
!
CLICK
BUZZZZZ
ピィ
I **REALLY** HOPE YOU DON'T HAVE A BABY IN HERE.
BEEP BEEP BEEP BEEP BEEP BEEP

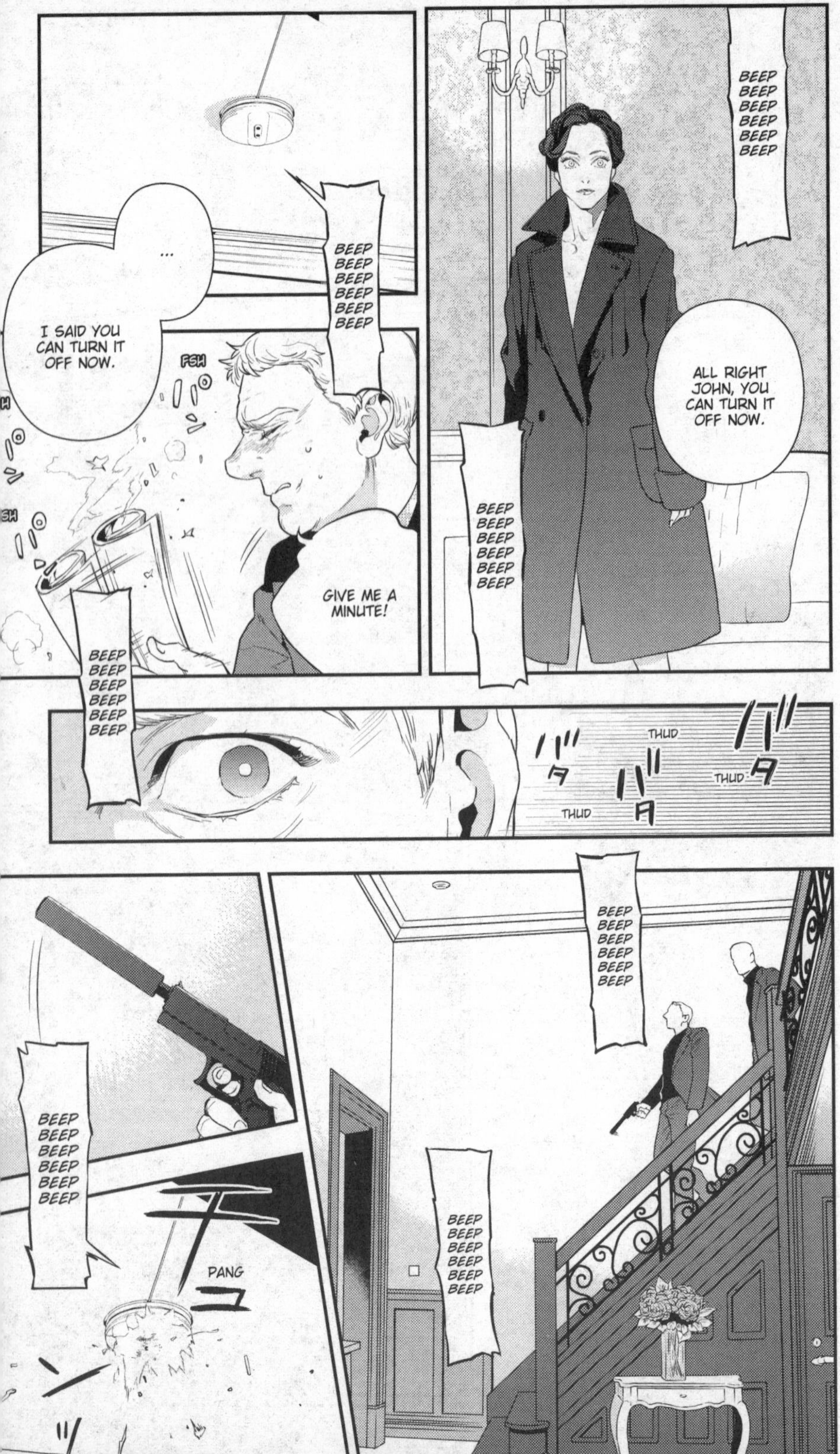
BEEP BEEP BEEP BEEP BEEP BEEP
ALL RIGHT JOHN, YOU CAN TURN IT OFF NOW.
BEEP BEEP BEEP BEEP BEEP BEEP
BEEP BEEP BEEP BEEP BEEP BEEP
...
I SAID YOU CAN TURN IT OFF NOW.
FSH
GIVE ME A MINUTE!
BEEP BEEP BEEP BEEP BEEP BEEP
THUD
THUD
THUD
BEEP BEEP BEEP BEEP BEEP BEEP
BEEP BEEP BEEP BEEP BEEP BEEP
BEEP BEEP BEEP BEEP BEEP BEEP
PANG

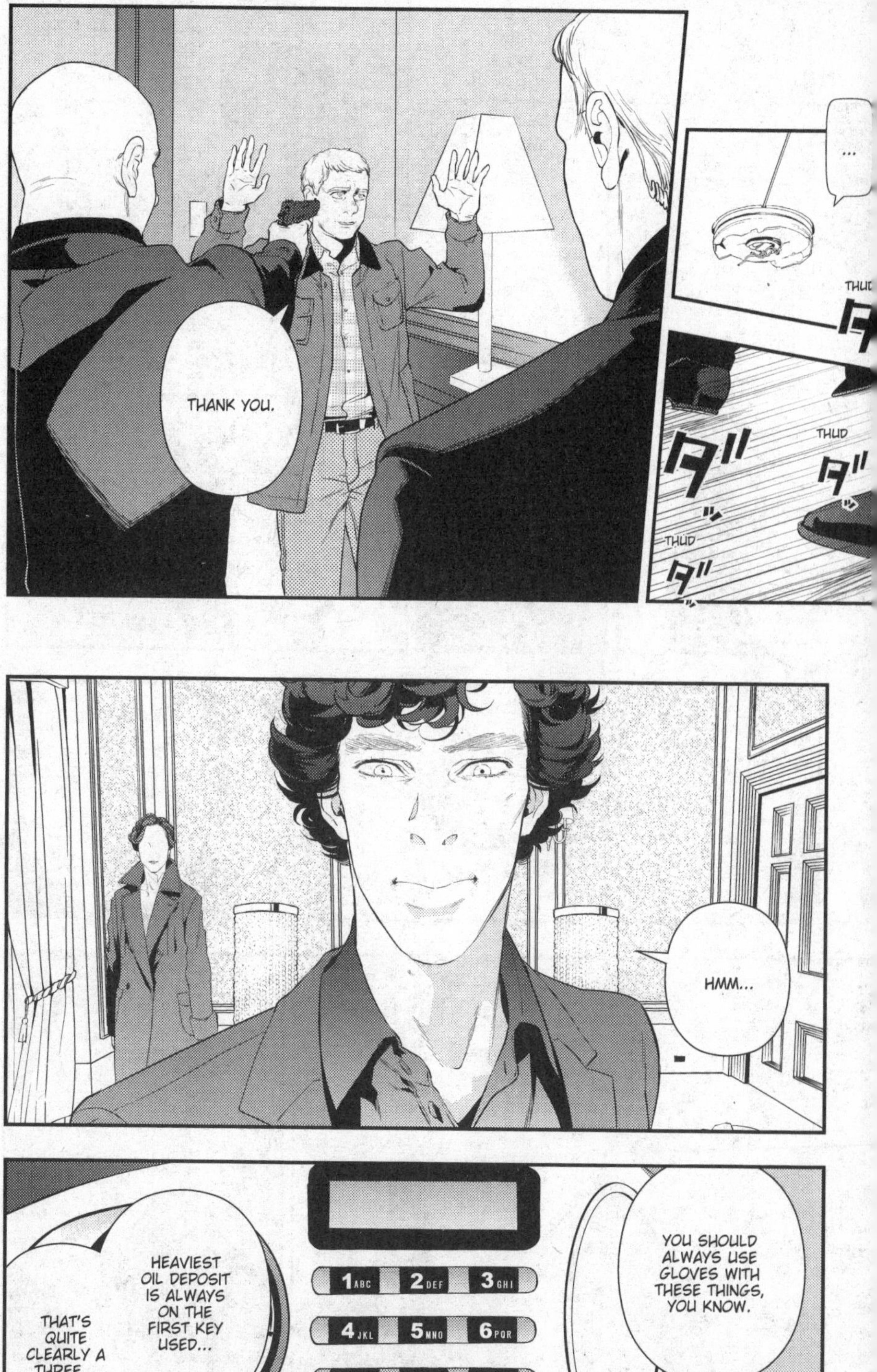
...
THUD
THUD
THANK YOU.
HMM...
YOU SHOULD ALWAYS USE GLOVES WITH THESE THINGS, YOU KNOW.
HEAVIEST OIL DEPOSIT IS ALWAYS ON THE FIRST KEY USED...
THAT'S QUITE CLEARLY A THREE...
1ABC 2DEF 3GHI
4JKL 5MNO 6PQR
7STU 8VWX 9YZ

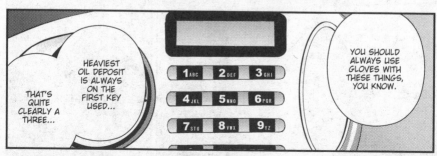

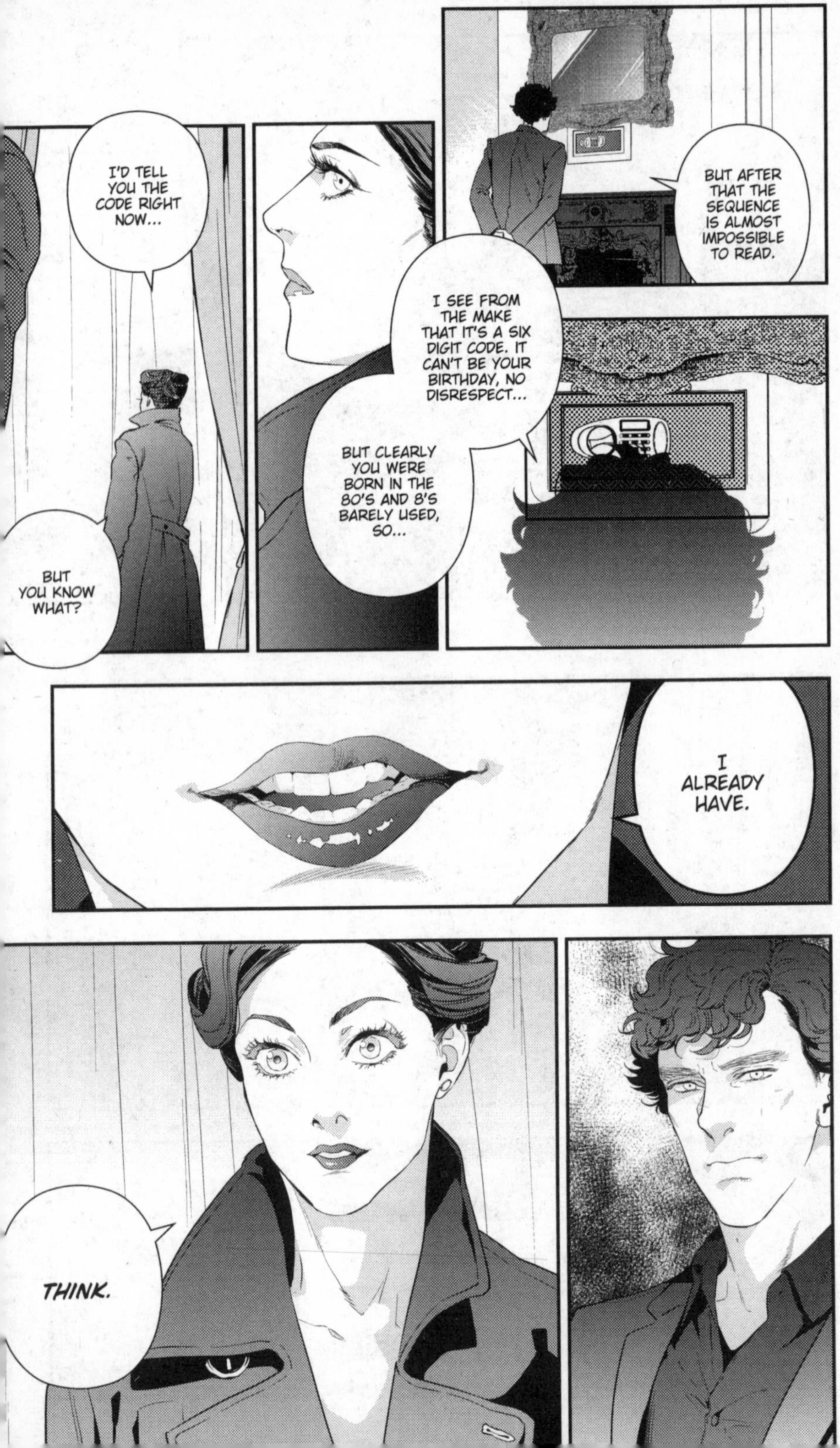
BUT AFTER THAT THE SEQUENCE IS ALMOST IMPOSSIBLE TO READ.
I SEE FROM THE MAKE THAT IT'S A SIX DIGIT CODE. IT CAN'T BE YOUR BIRTHDAY, NO DISRESPECT...
BUT CLEARLY YOU WERE BORN IN THE 80'S AND 8'S BARELY USED, SO...
I'D TELL YOU THE CODE RIGHT NOW...
BUT YOU KNOW WHAT?
I ALREADY HAVE.
THINK.

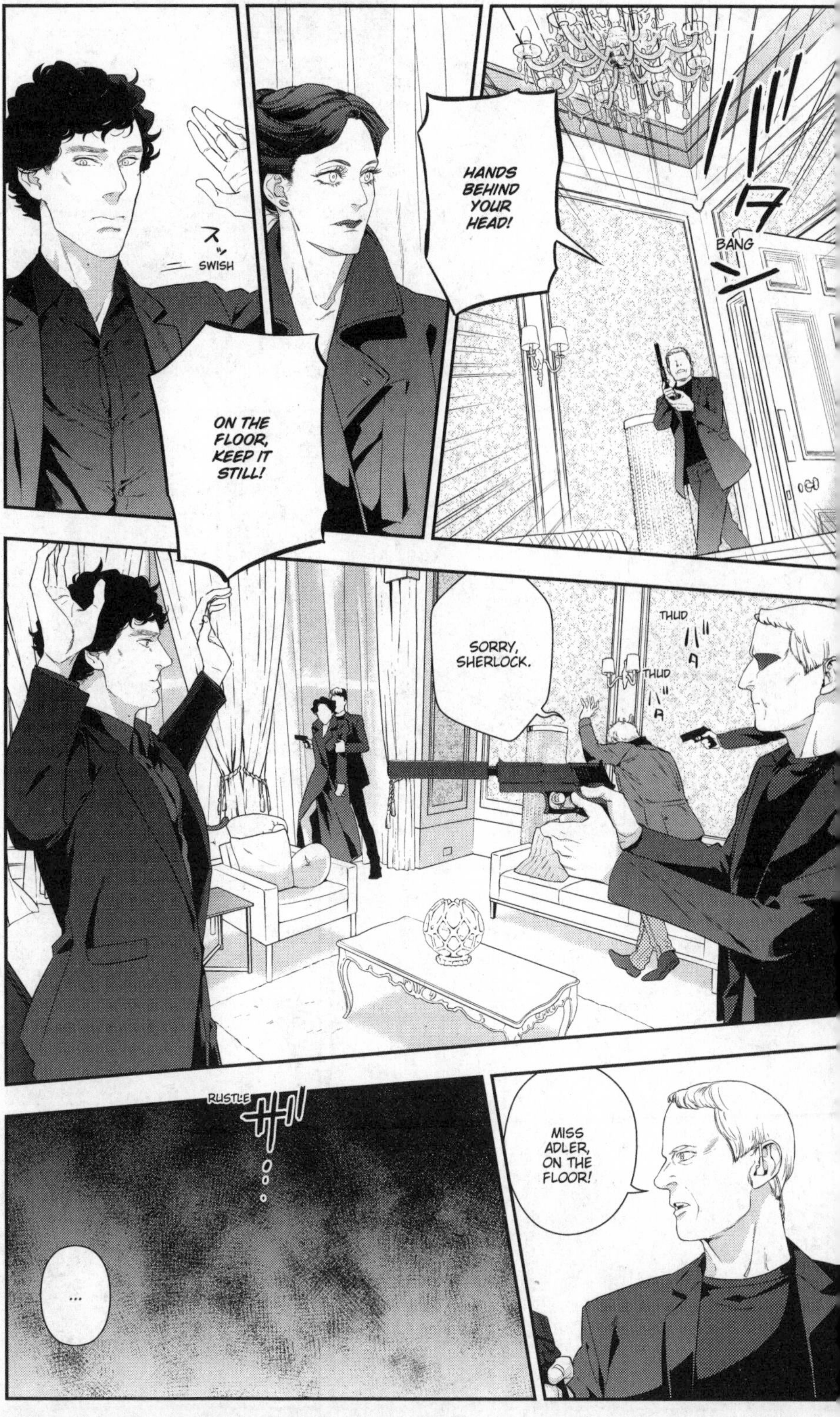
BANG
HANDS BEHIND YOUR HEAD!
ON THE FLOOR, KEEP IT STILL!
SWISH
THUD
THUD
SORRY, SHERLOCK.
MISS ADLER, ON THE FLOOR!
RUSTLE
...

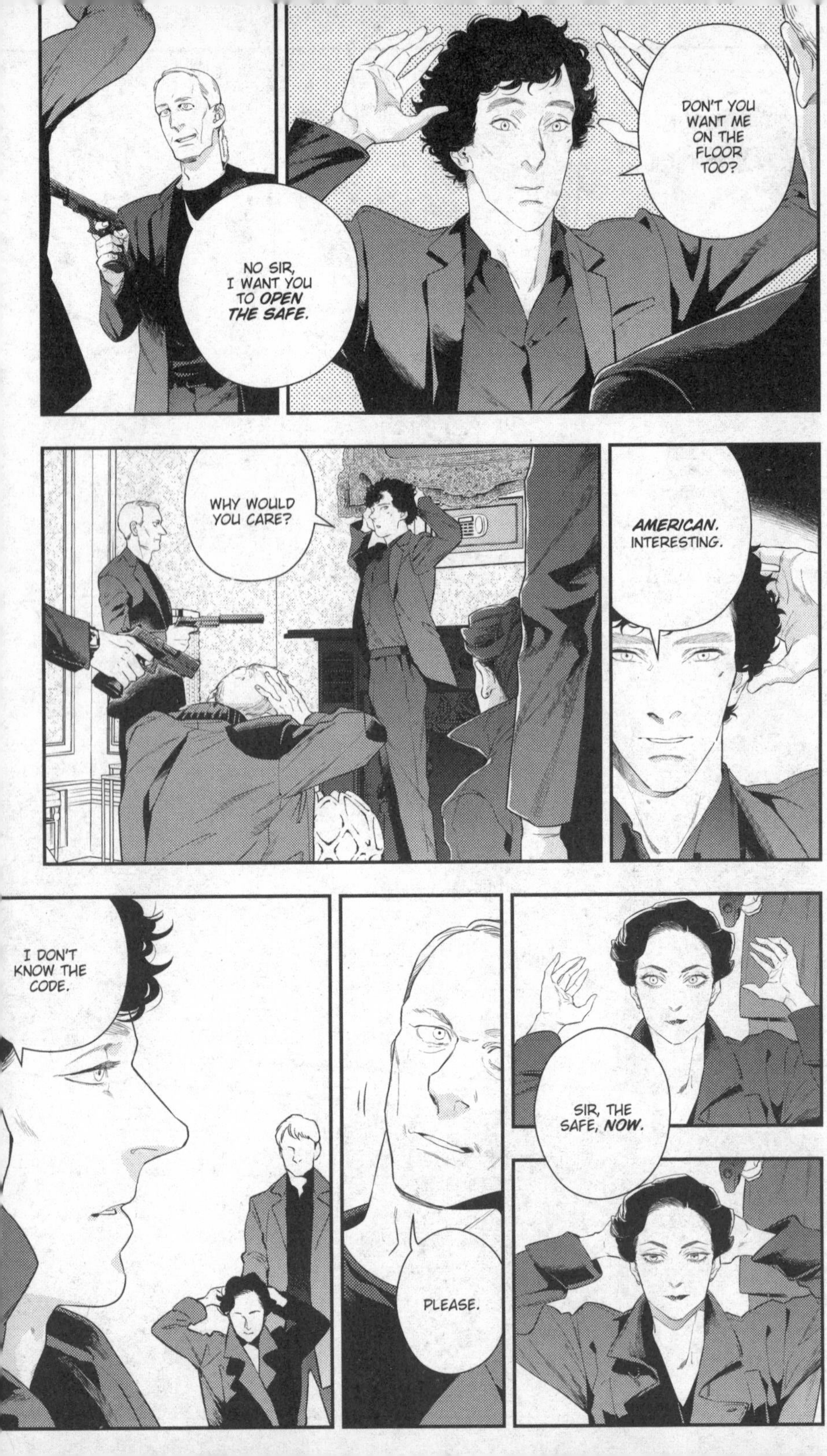
DON'T YOU WANT ME ON THE FLOOR TOO?
NO SIR, I WANT YOU TO *OPEN THE SAFE.*
AMERICAN. INTERESTING.
WHY WOULD YOU CARE?
SIR, THE SAFE, *NOW.*
PLEASE.
I DON'T KNOW THE CODE.

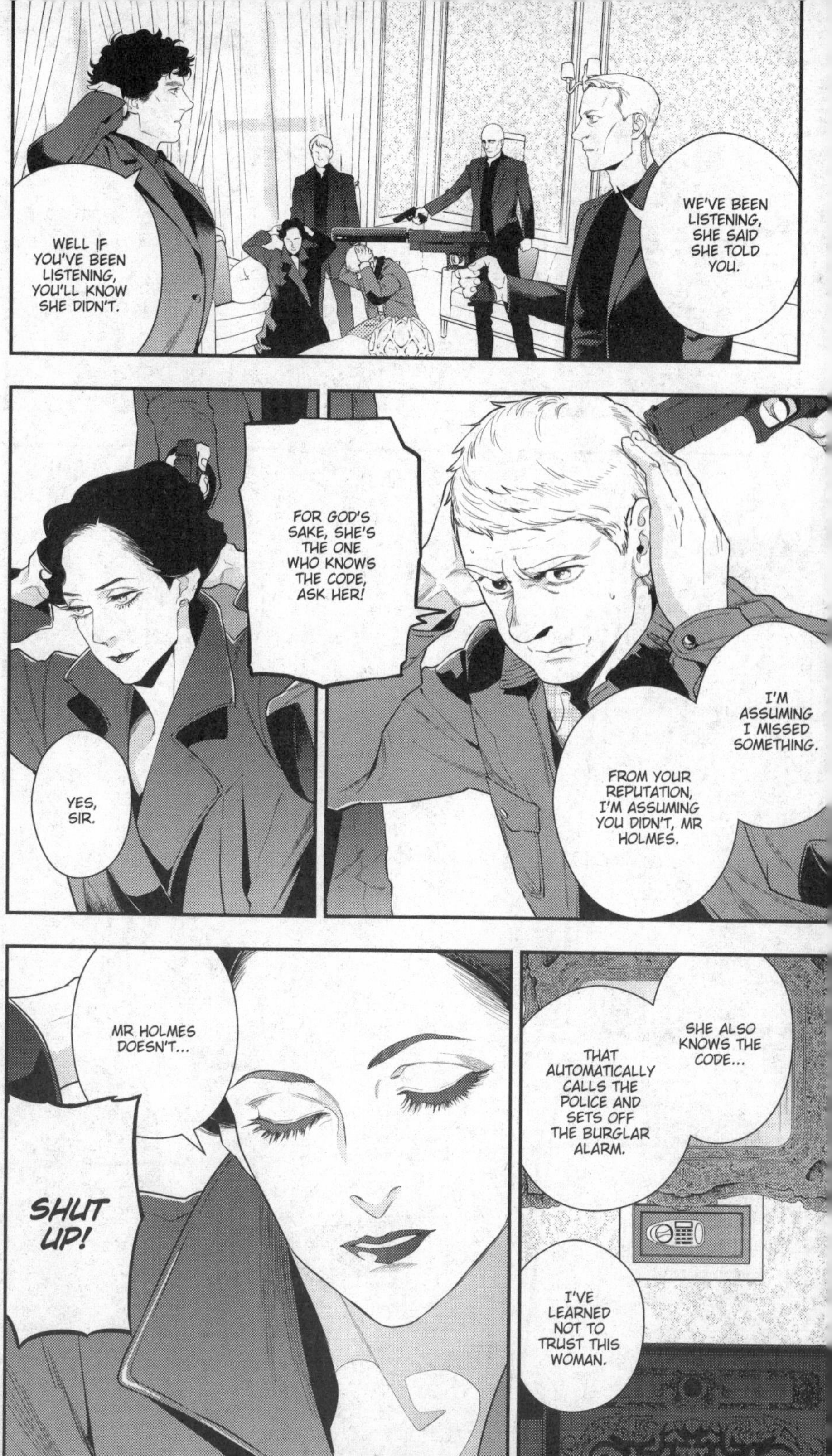
WE'VE BEEN LISTENING, SHE SAID SHE TOLD YOU.
WELL IF YOU'VE BEEN LISTENING, YOU'LL KNOW SHE DIDN'T.
I'M ASSUMING I MISSED SOMETHING.
FROM YOUR REPUTATION, I'M ASSUMING YOU DIDN'T, MR HOLMES.
FOR GOD'S SAKE, SHE'S THE ONE WHO KNOWS THE CODE, ASK HER!
YES, SIR.
SHE ALSO KNOWS THE CODE...
THAT AUTOMATICALLY CALLS THE POLICE AND SETS OFF THE BURGLAR ALARM.
I'VE LEARNED NOT TO TRUST THIS WOMAN.
MR HOLMES DOESN'T...
SHUT UP!

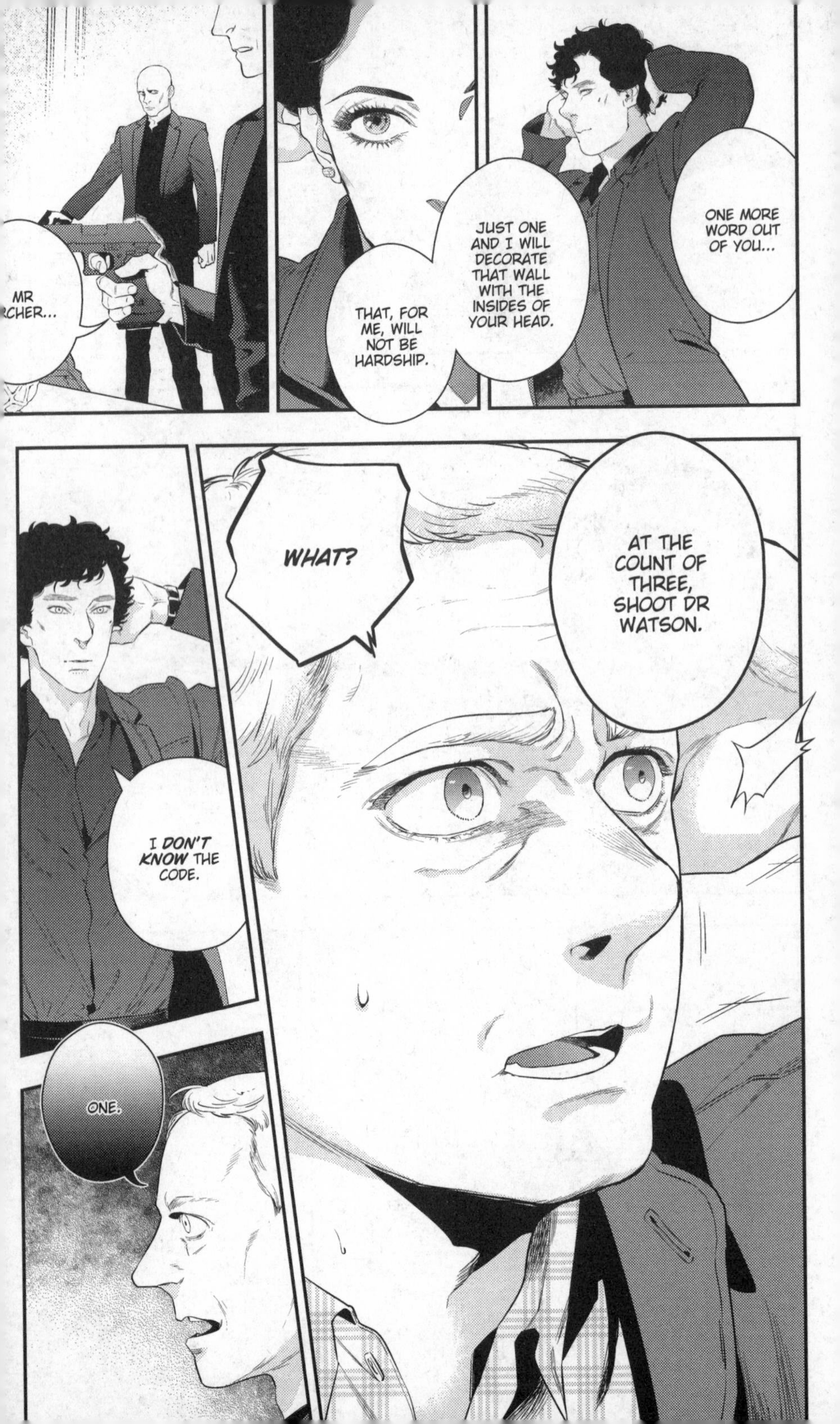
ONE MORE WORD OUT OF YOU...
JUST ONE AND I WILL DECORATE THAT WALL WITH THE INSIDES OF YOUR HEAD.
THAT, FOR ME, WILL NOT BE HARDSHIP.
MR RCHER...
AT THE COUNT OF THREE, SHOOT DR WATSON.
WHAT?
I DON'T KNOW THE CODE.
ONE.

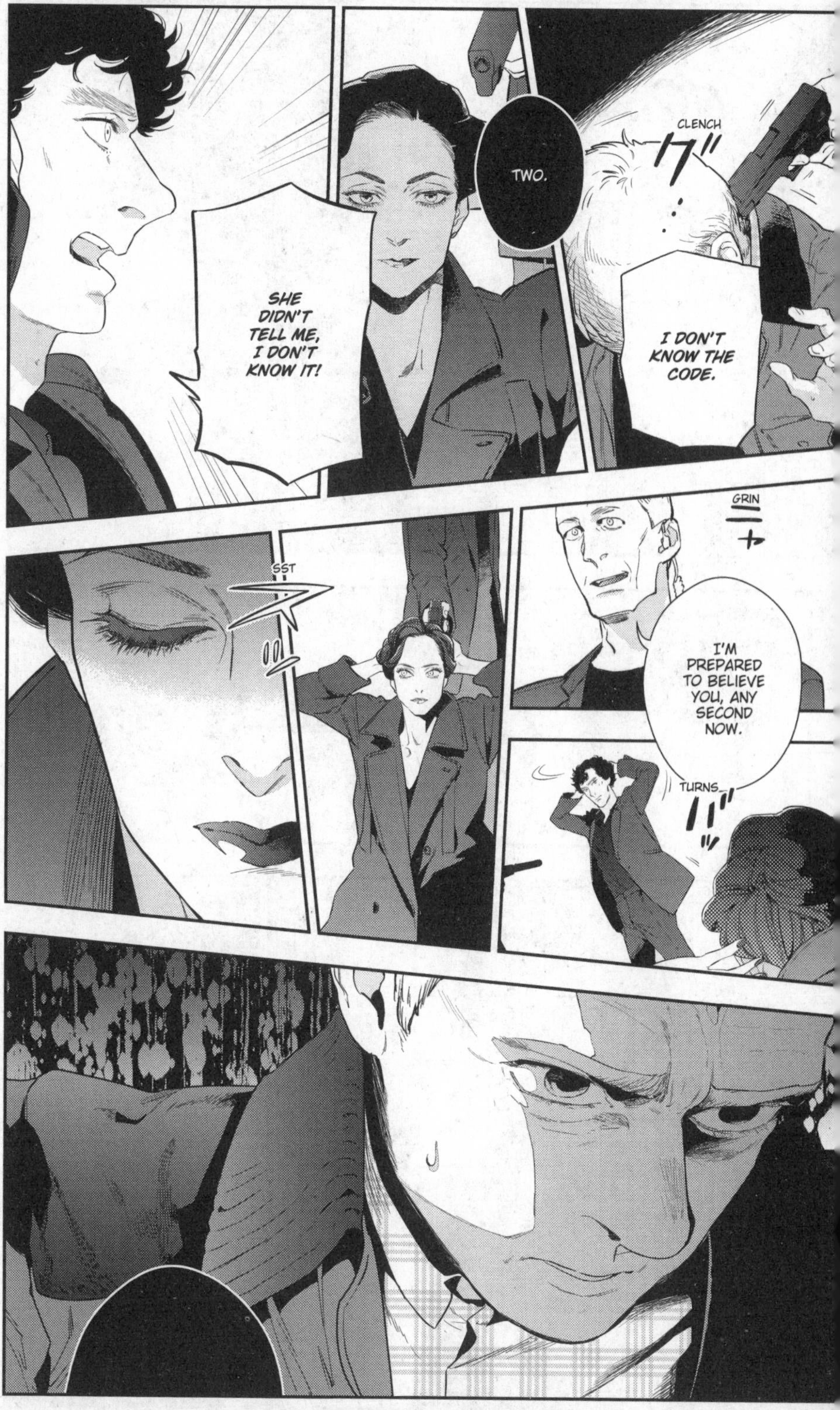
CLENCH
I DON'T KNOW THE CODE.
TWO.
SHE DIDN'T TELL ME, I DON'T KNOW IT!
GRIN
I'M PREPARED TO BELIEVE YOU, ANY SECOND NOW.
TURNS
SST

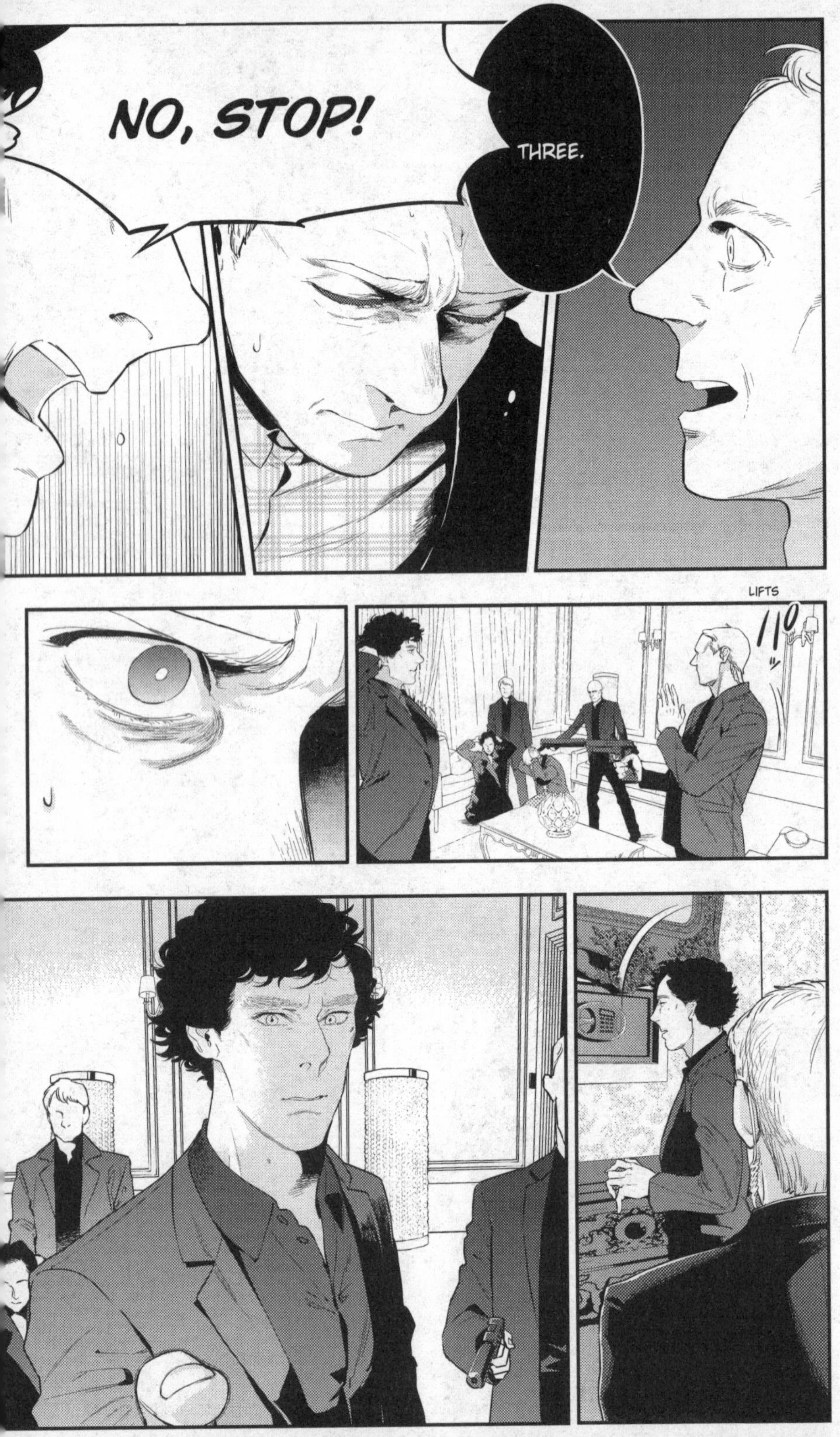
THREE.
NO, STOP!
LIFTS

BEEP
BEEP
ピッ
BEEP
ピッ
BEEP
ピッ
BEEP
ピッ
BEEP
ピッ
ガチャン
KACHAK
SIGHS
フゥ
クイ
THANK YOU MR HOLMES. OPEN IT PLEASE.

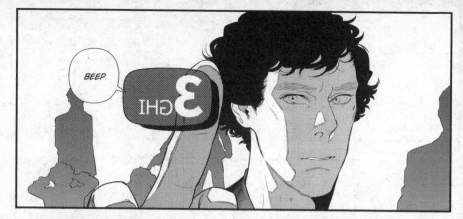

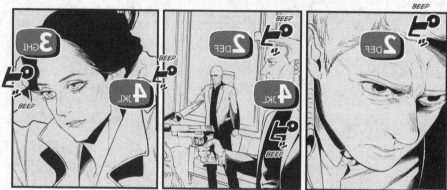

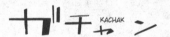

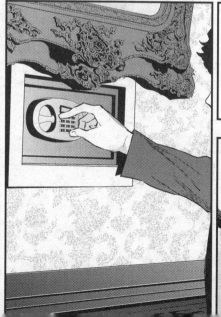

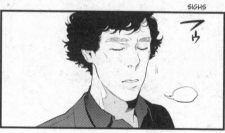

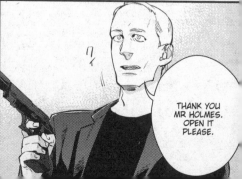

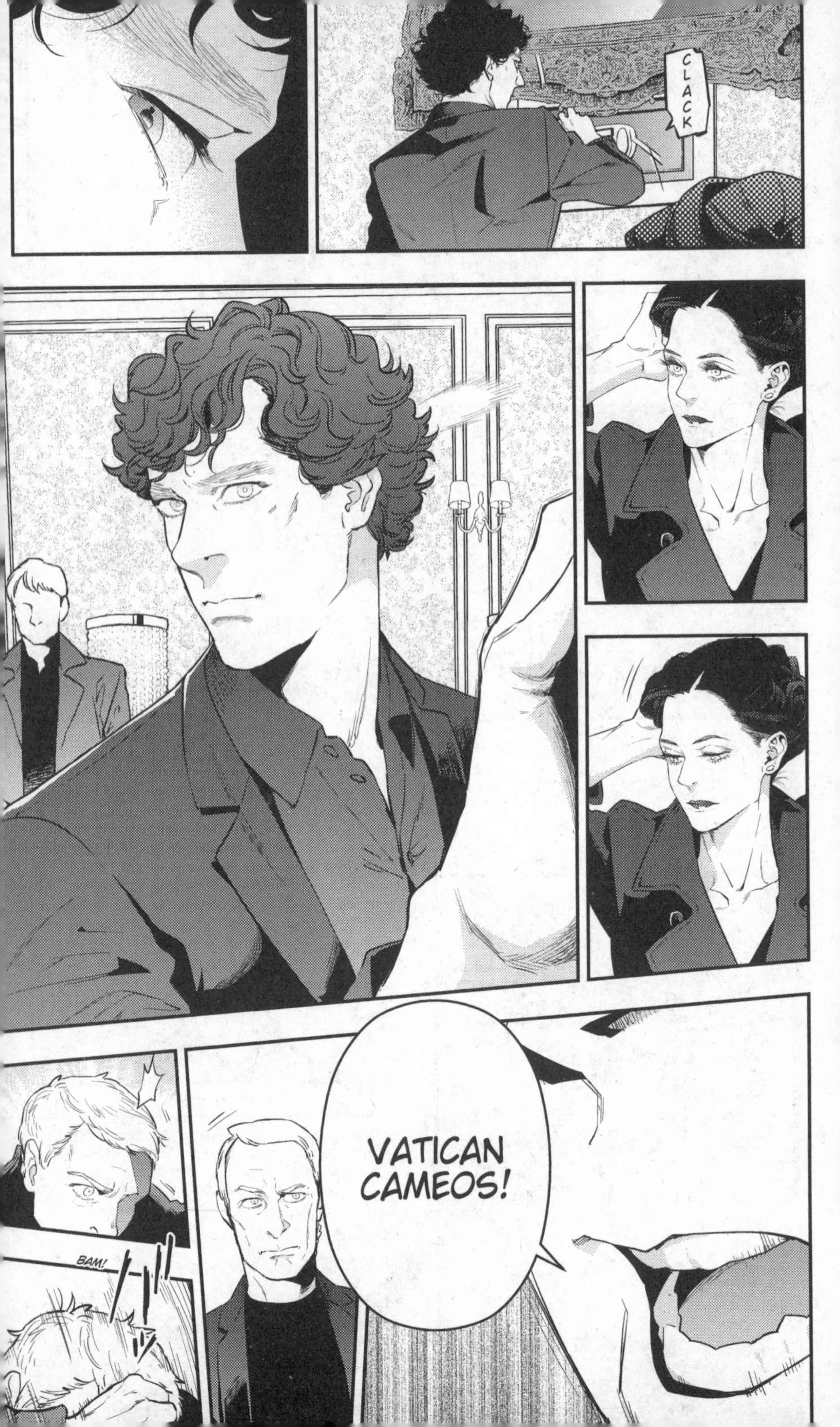
CLACK
VATICAN CAMEOS!
BAM!

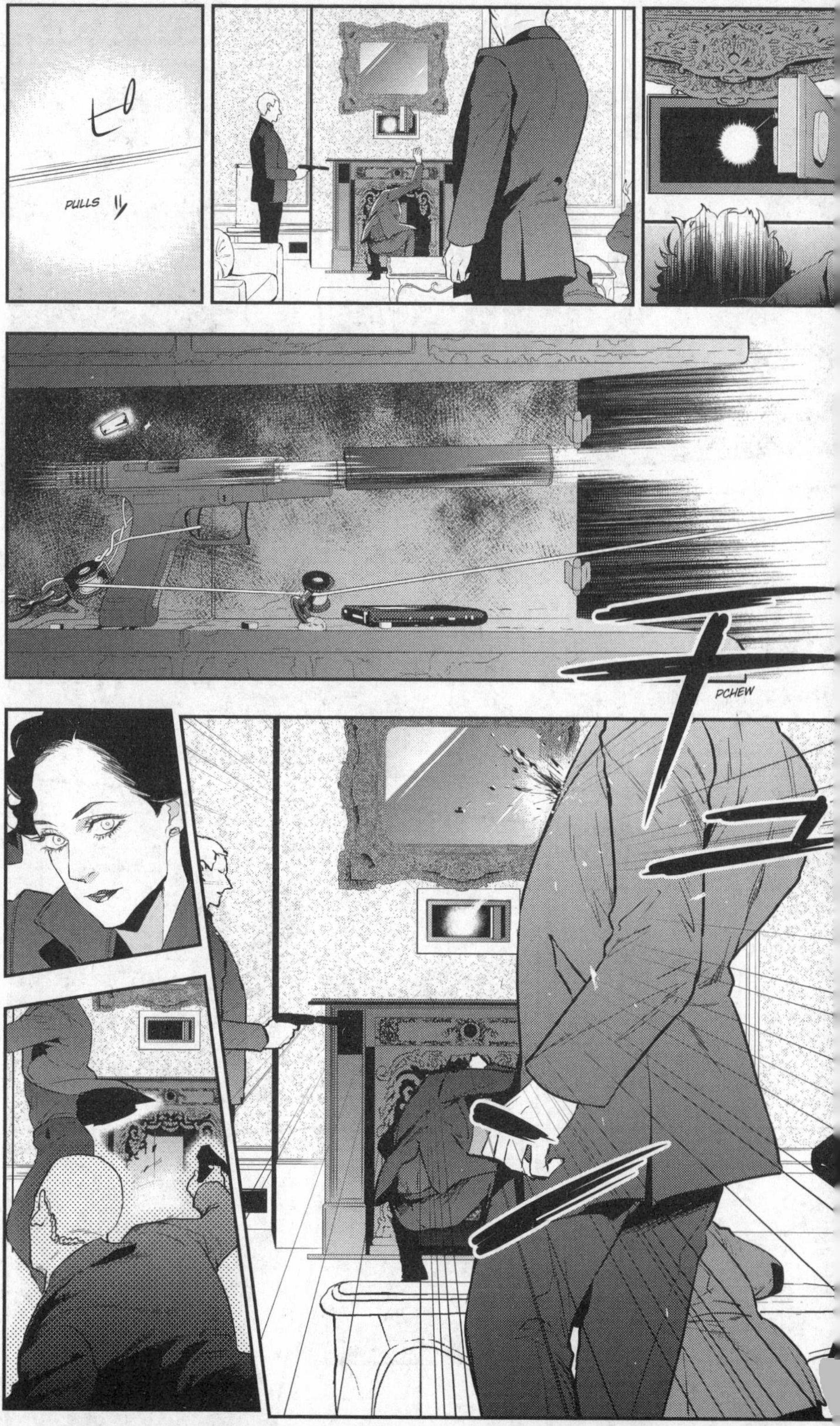
ピッ
PULLS
PCHEW

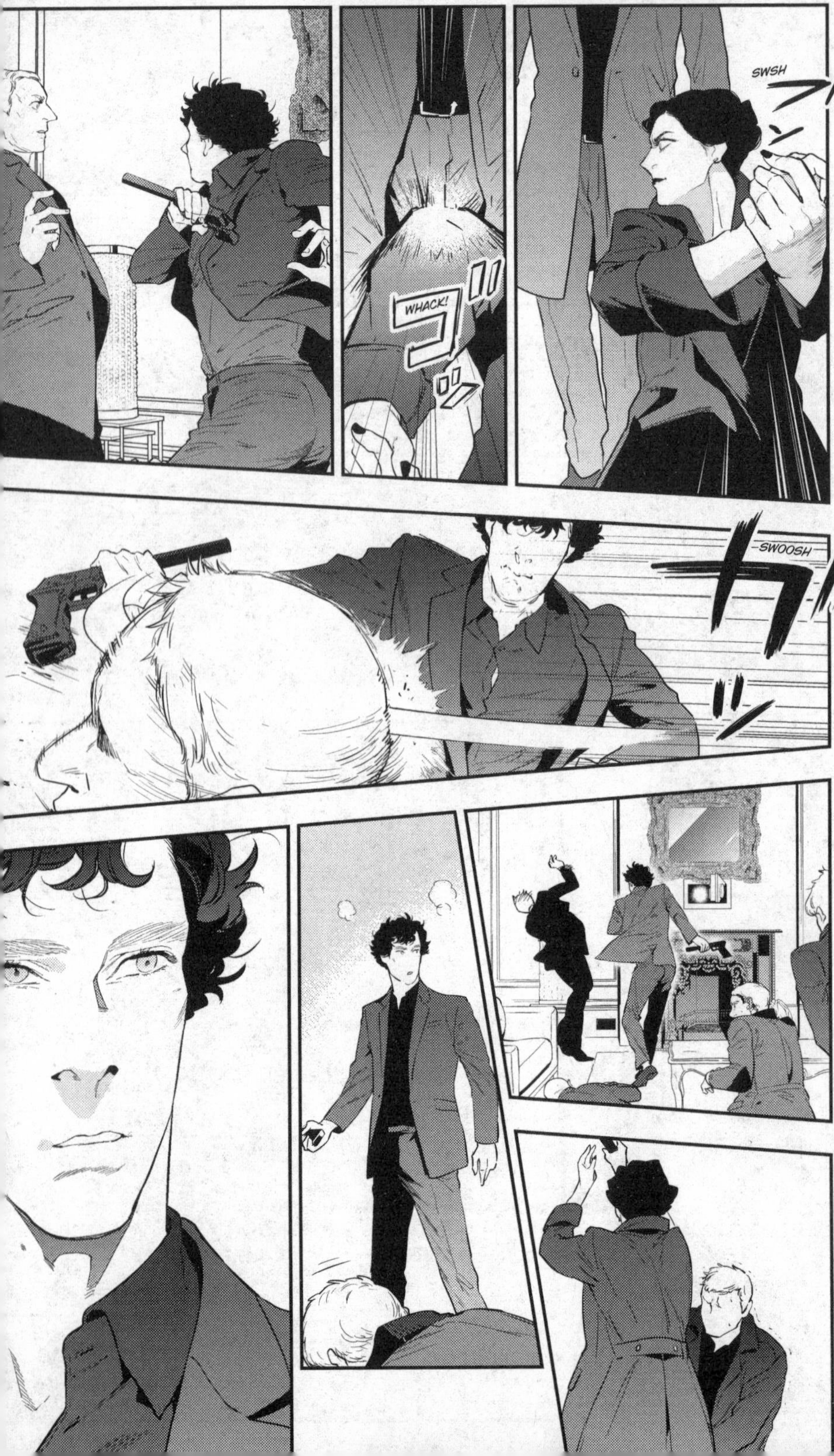
SWSH
WHACK!
SWOOSH

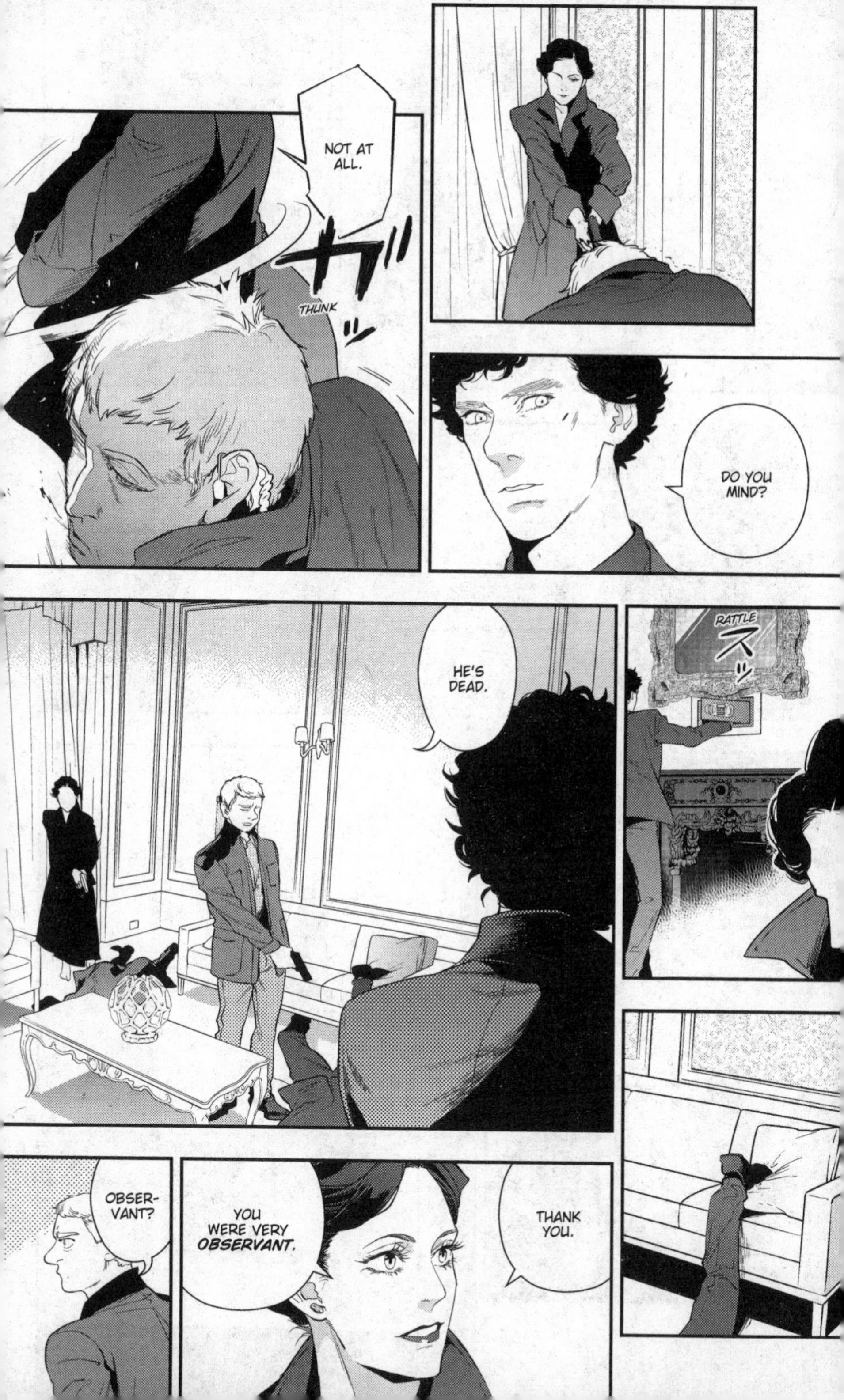
DO YOU MIND?
NOT AT ALL.
ガッ
THUNK
RATTLE
スッ
HE'S DEAD.
THANK YOU.
YOU WERE VERY *OBSERVANT*.
OBSER-VANT?

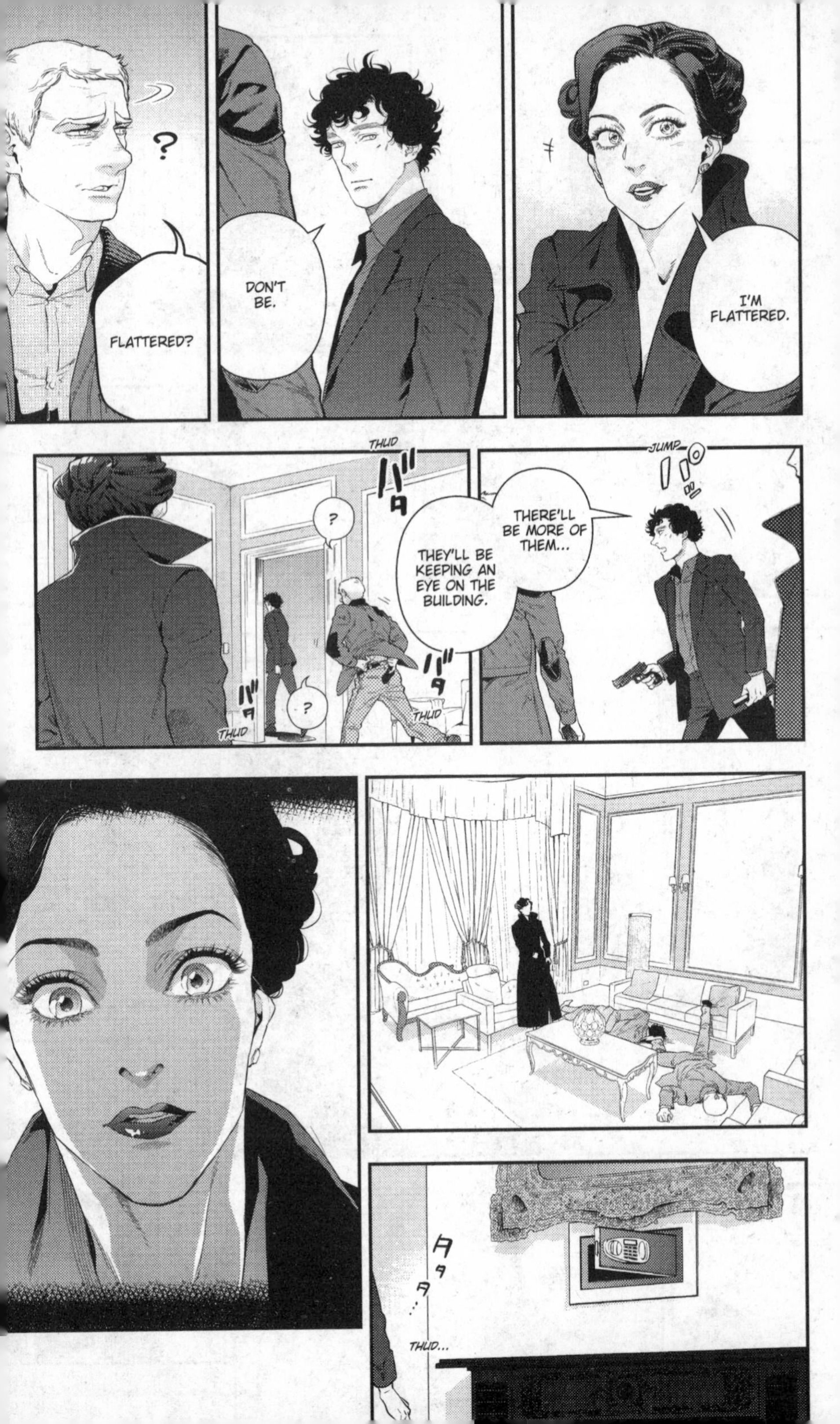
I'M FLATTERED.
DON'T BE.
?
FLATTERED?
JUMP
THERE'LL BE MORE OF THEM...
THEY'LL BE KEEPING AN EYE ON THE BUILDING.
THUD
?
THUD
?
THUD
THUD...

BANG!

44

44

BANG!

BANG!

WE SHOUL[D]
CALL THE
POLICE

LIFTS

HAA...

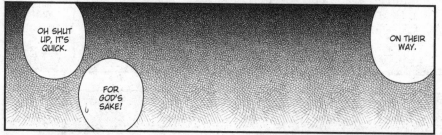

OH SHUT
UP, IT'S
QUICK.

FOR
GOD'S
SAKE!

ON THEIR
WAY.

WELL...

CHECK THE
REST OF THE
HOUSE, SEE
HOW THEY
GOT IN.

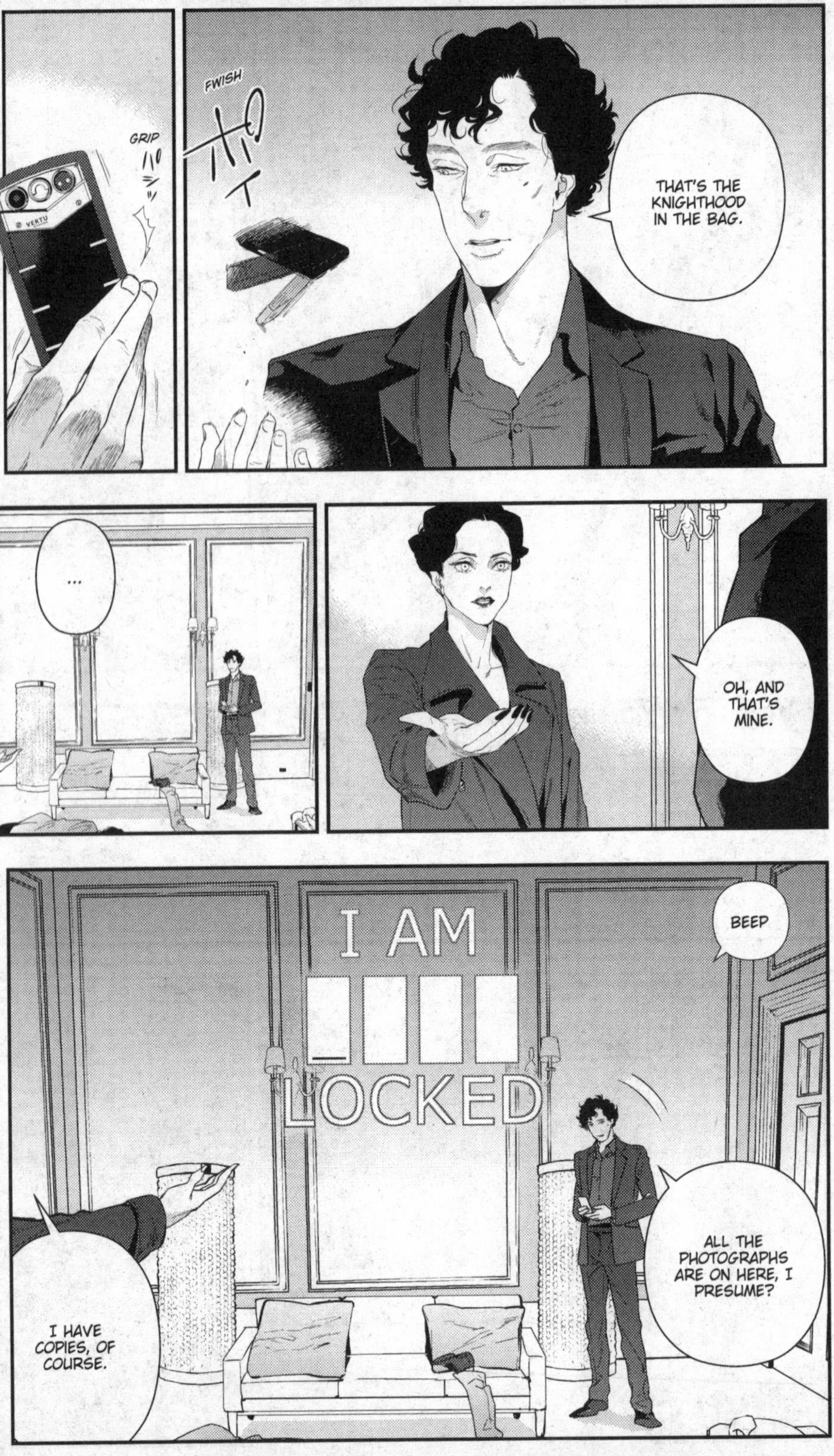
THAT'S THE KNIGHTHOOD IN THE BAG.
FWISH
GRIP
OH, AND THAT'S MINE.
...
BEEP
I AM
LOCKED
ALL THE PHOTOGRAPHS ARE ON HERE, I PRESUME?
I HAVE COPIES, OF COURSE.

Chapter 4

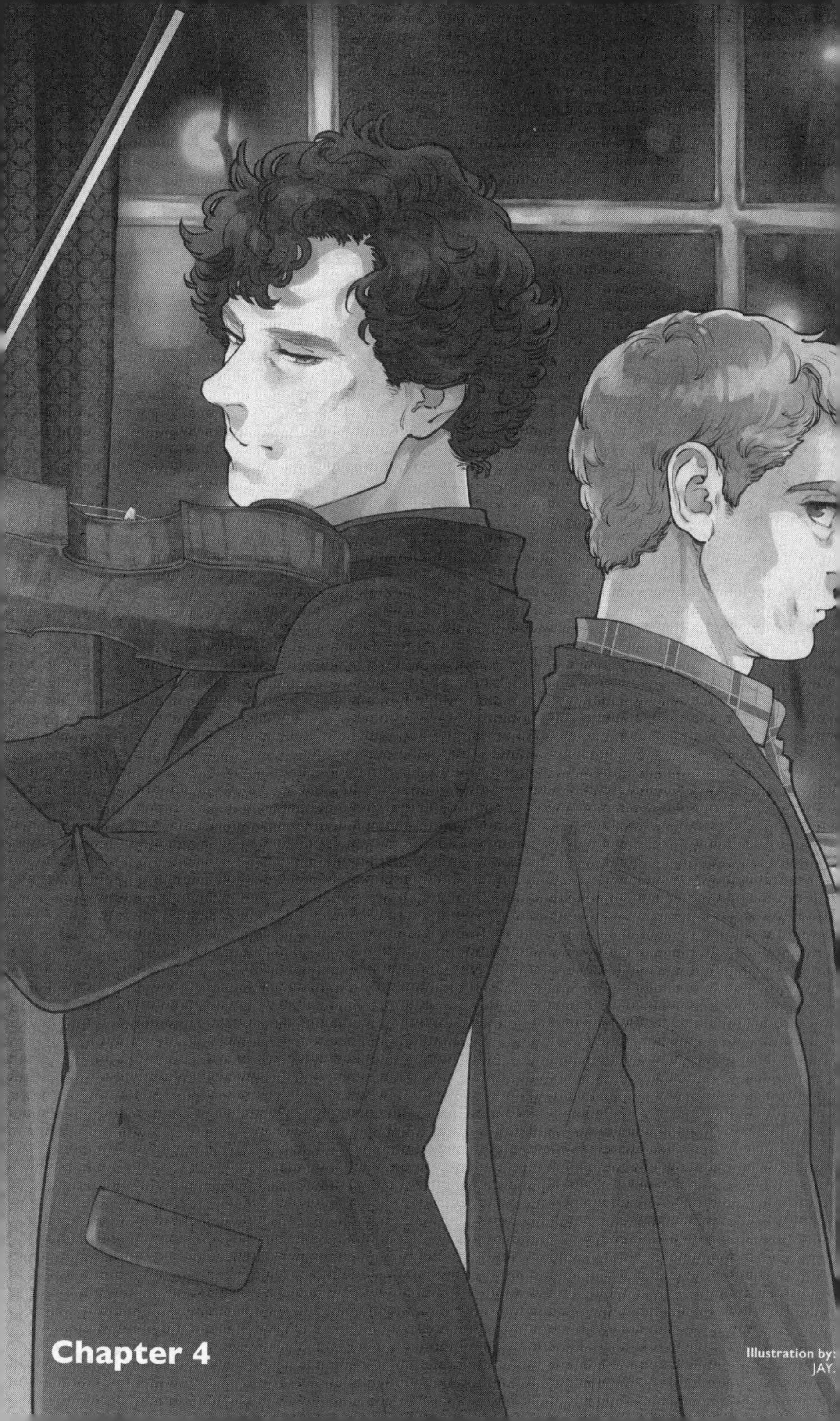

Illustration by:
JAY

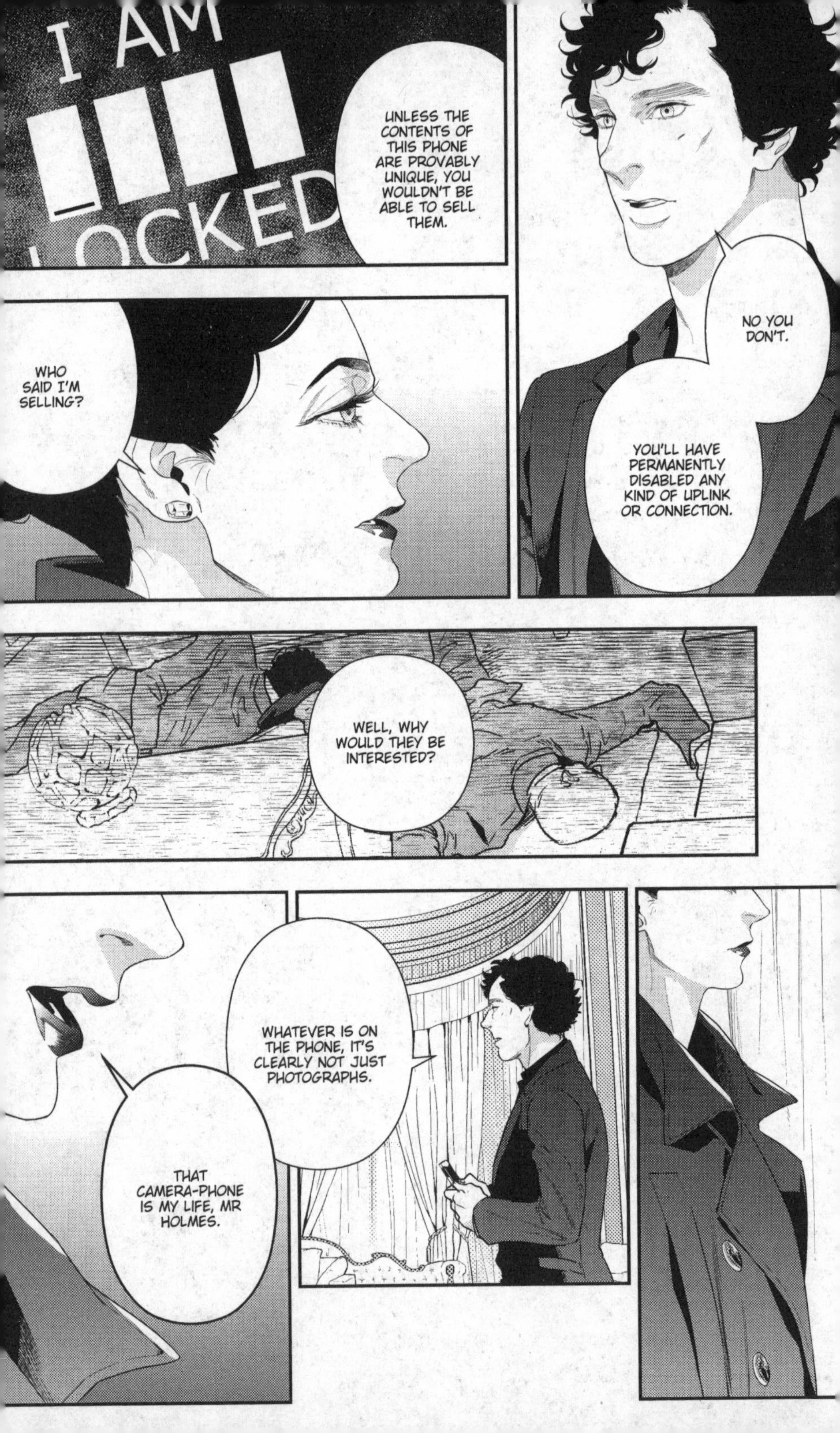
NO YOU DON'T.
YOU'LL HAVE PERMANENTLY DISABLED ANY KIND OF UPLINK OR CONNECTION.
I AM
LOCKED
UNLESS THE CONTENTS OF THIS PHONE ARE PROVABLY UNIQUE, YOU WOULDN'T BE ABLE TO SELL THEM.
WHO SAID I'M SELLING?
WELL, WHY WOULD THEY BE INTERESTED?
WHATEVER IS ON THE PHONE, IT'S CLEARLY NOT JUST PHOTOGRAPHS.
THAT CAMERA-PHONE IS MY LIFE, MR HOLMES.

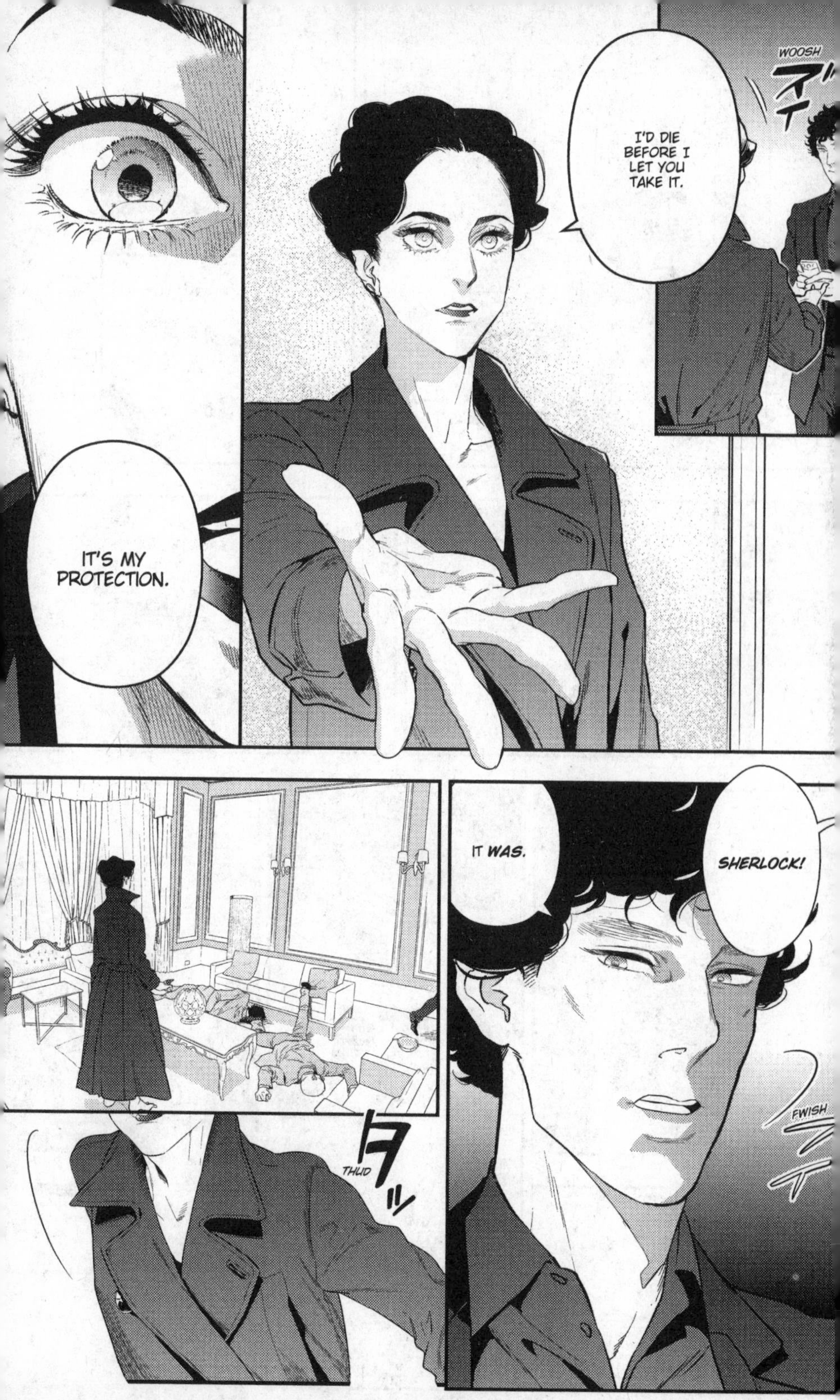
WOOSH
I'D DIE BEFORE I LET YOU TAKE IT.
IT'S MY PROTECTION.
SHERLOCK!
IT WAS.
FWISH
THUD

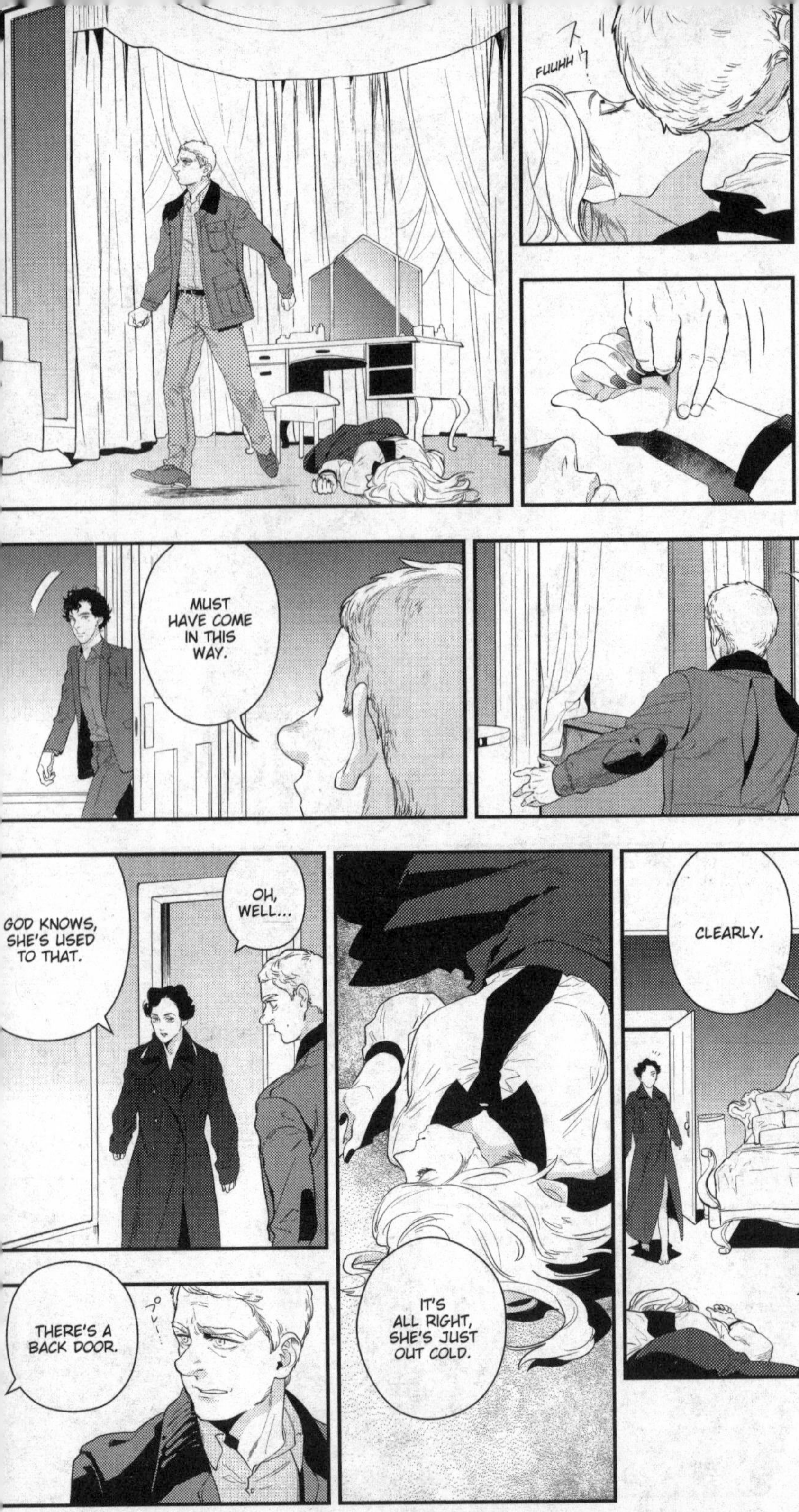
FUUHH
MUST HAVE COME IN THIS WAY.
CLEARLY.
IT'S ALL RIGHT, SHE'S JUST OUT COLD.
OH, WELL...
GOD KNOWS, SHE'S USED TO THAT.
THERE'S A BACK DOOR.

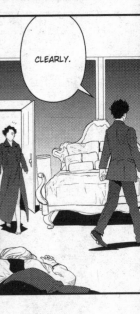

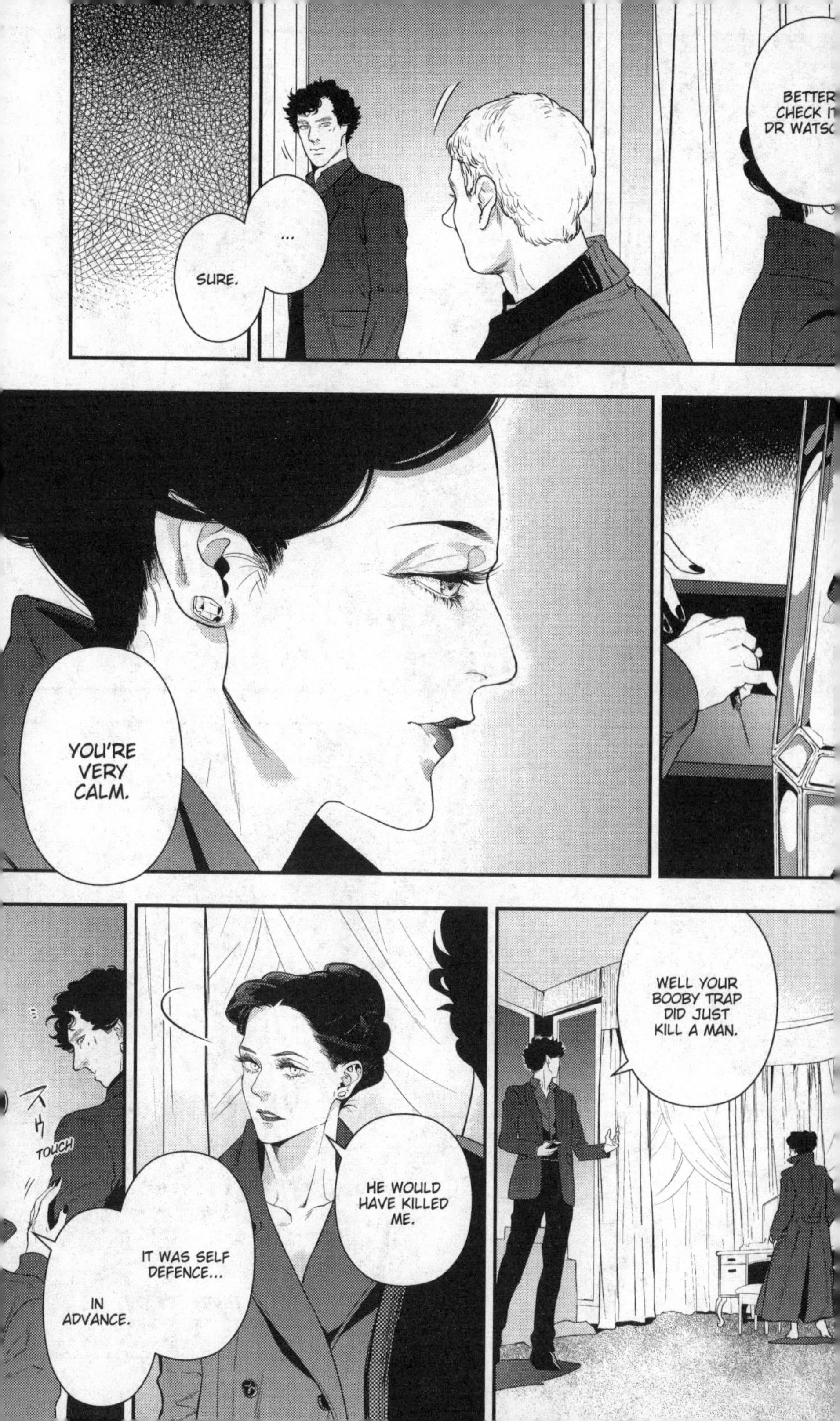
BETTER CHECK IT DR WATSO
...
SURE.
YOU'RE VERY CALM.
WELL YOUR BOOBY TRAP DID JUST KILL A MAN.
HE WOULD HAVE KILLED ME.
IT WAS SELF DEFENCE...
IN ADVANCE.
TOUCH

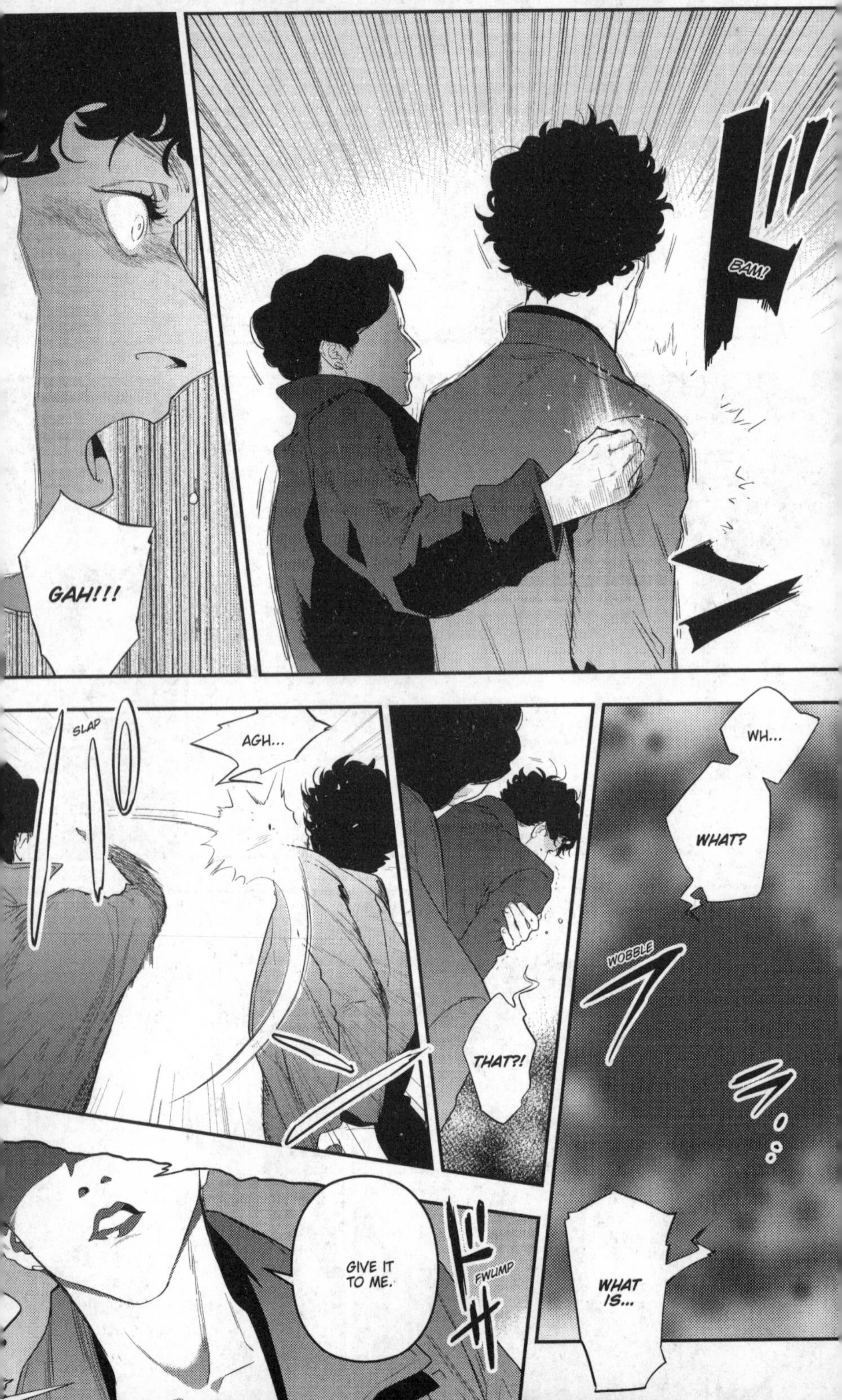
BAM!
GAH!!!
WH...
WHAT?
WOBBLE
WHAT IS...
THAT?!
SLAP
AGH...
FWUMP
GIVE IT TO ME.

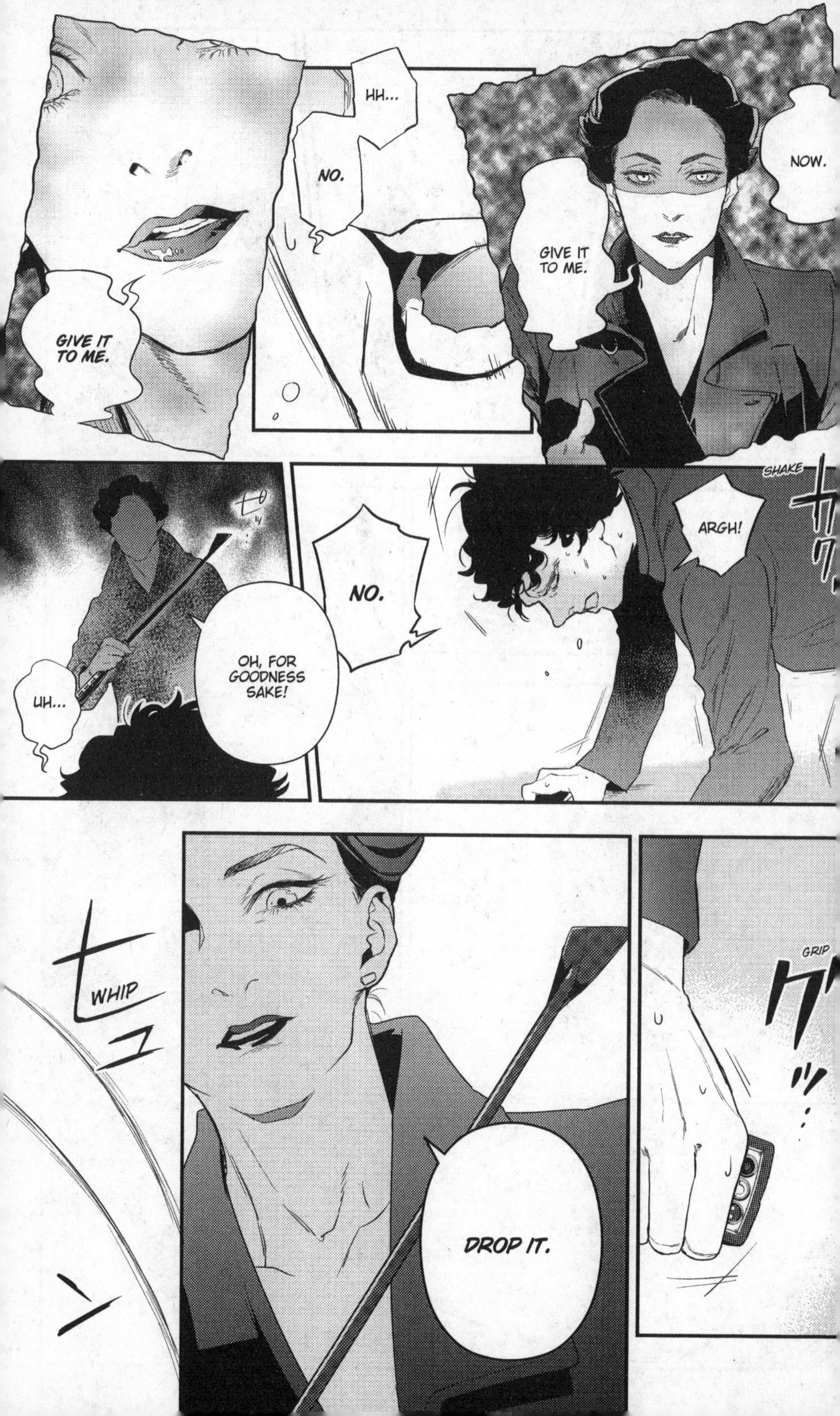
NOW.
GIVE IT TO ME.
HH...
NO.
GIVE IT TO ME.
SHAKE
ARGH!
NO.
OH, FOR GOODNESS SAKE!
UH...
GRIP
WHIP
DROP IT.

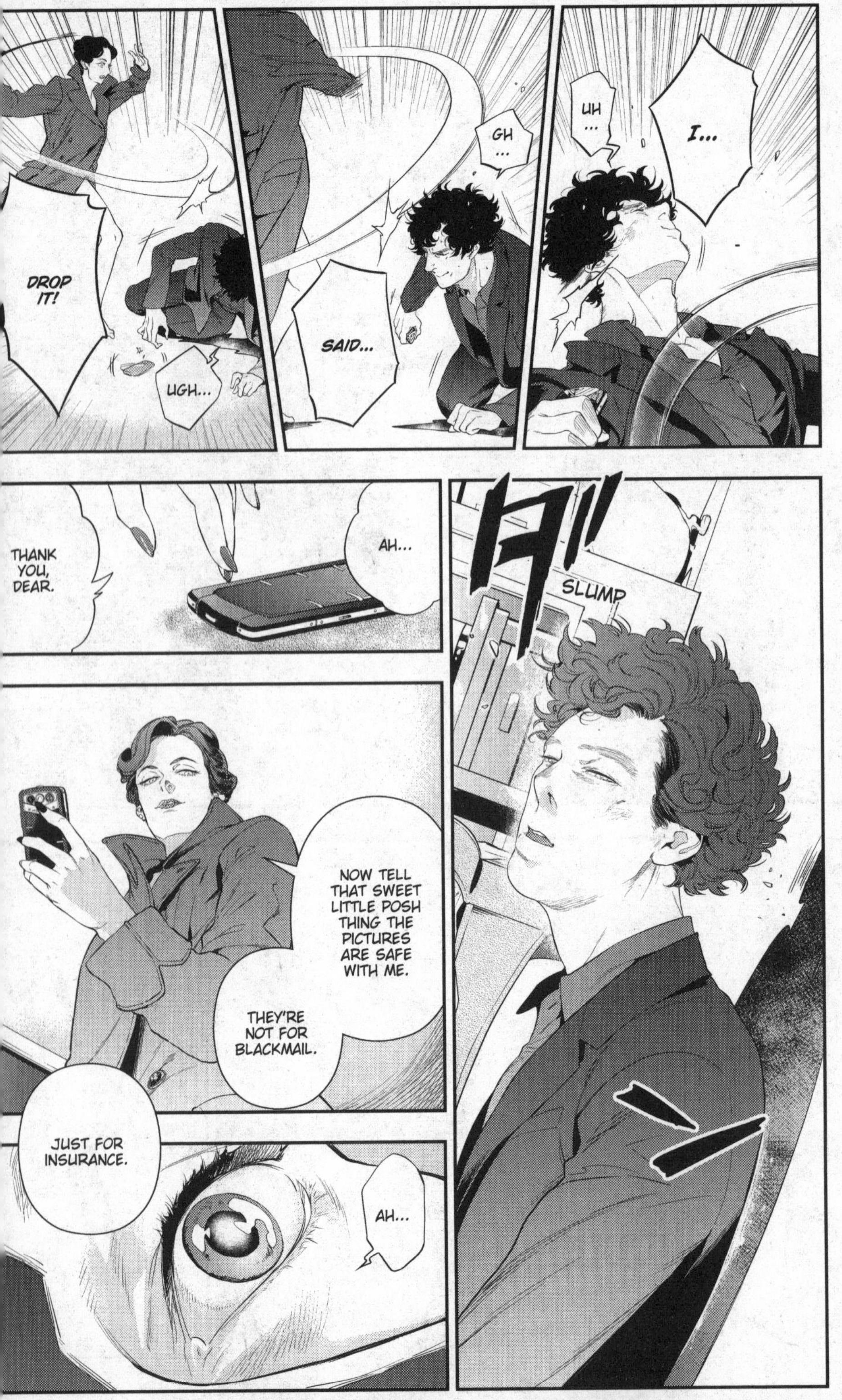
I...
UH...
GH...
SAID...
DROP IT!
UGH...
SLUMP
AH...
THANK YOU, DEAR.
NOW TELL THAT SWEET LITTLE POSH THING THE PICTURES ARE SAFE WITH ME.
THEY'RE NOT FOR BLACKMAIL.
AH...
JUST FOR INSURANCE.

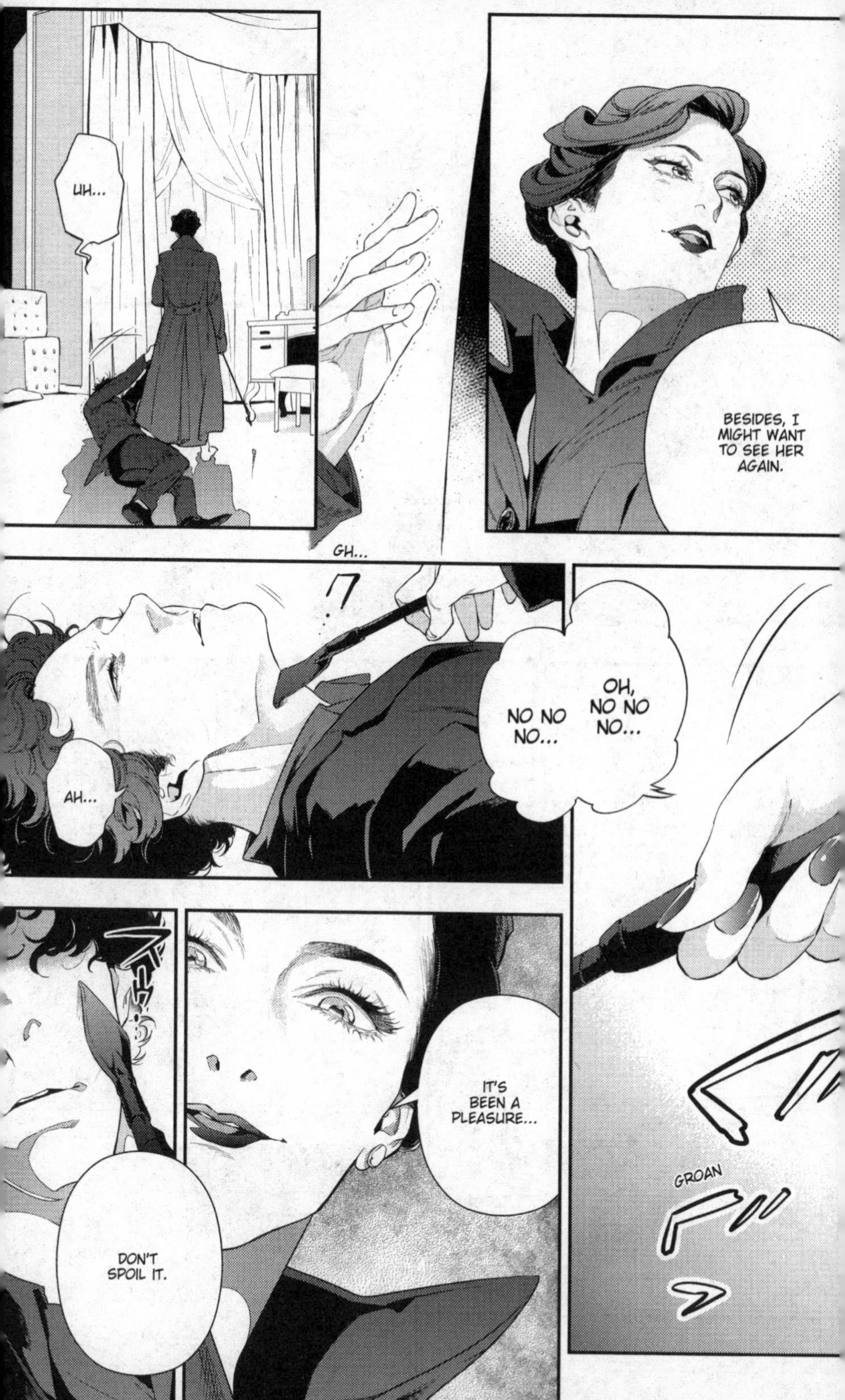
BESIDES, I MIGHT WANT TO SEE HER AGAIN.
UH...
GH...
OH, NO NO NO...
NO NO NO...
AH...
GROAN
IT'S BEEN A PLEASURE...
DON'T SPOIL IT.

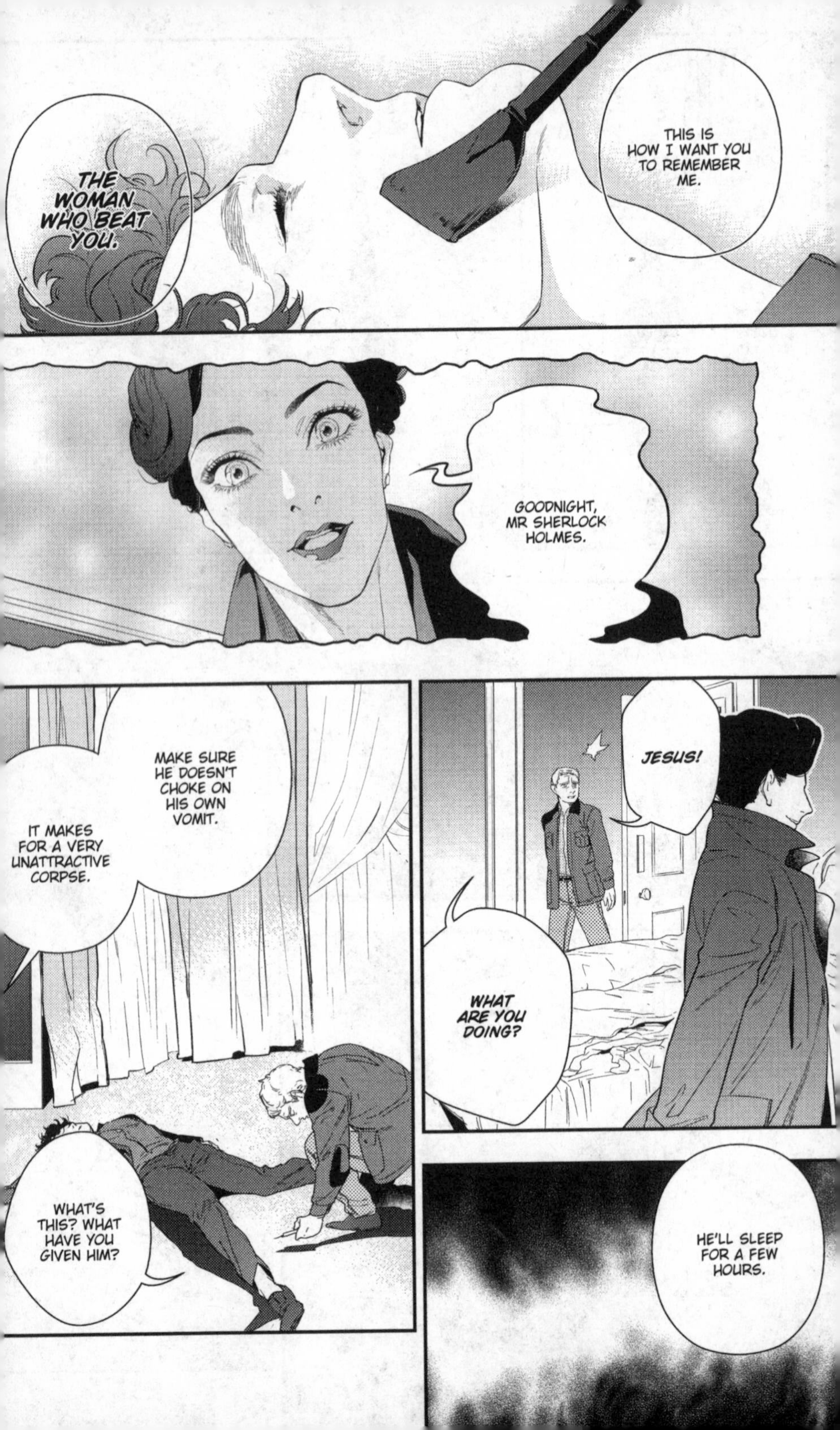
THIS IS HOW I WANT YOU TO REMEMBER ME.
THE WOMAN WHO BEAT YOU.
GOODNIGHT, MR SHERLOCK HOLMES.
JESUS!
WHAT ARE YOU DOING?
HE'LL SLEEP FOR A FEW HOURS.
MAKE SURE HE DOESN'T CHOKE ON HIS OWN VOMIT.
IT MAKES FOR A VERY UNATTRACTIVE CORPSE.
WHAT'S THIS? WHAT HAVE YOU GIVEN HIM?

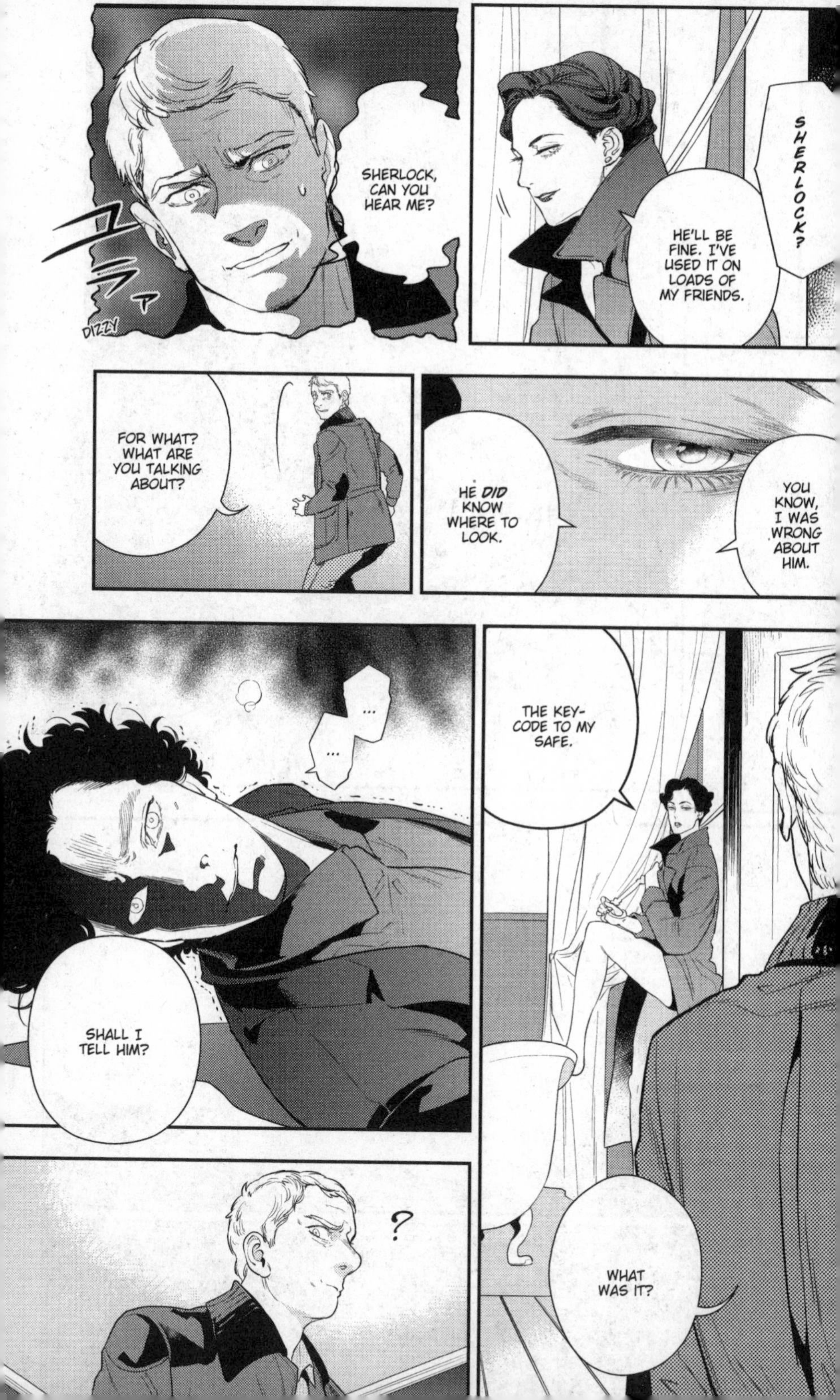
SHERLOCK?
HE'LL BE FINE. I'VE USED IT ON LOADS OF MY FRIENDS.
SHERLOCK, CAN YOU HEAR ME?
DIZZY!
YOU KNOW, I WAS WRONG ABOUT HIM.
HE *DID* KNOW WHERE TO LOOK.
FOR WHAT? WHAT ARE YOU TALKING ABOUT?
THE KEY-CODE TO MY SAFE.
WHAT WAS IT?
...
...
SHALL I TELL HIM?
?

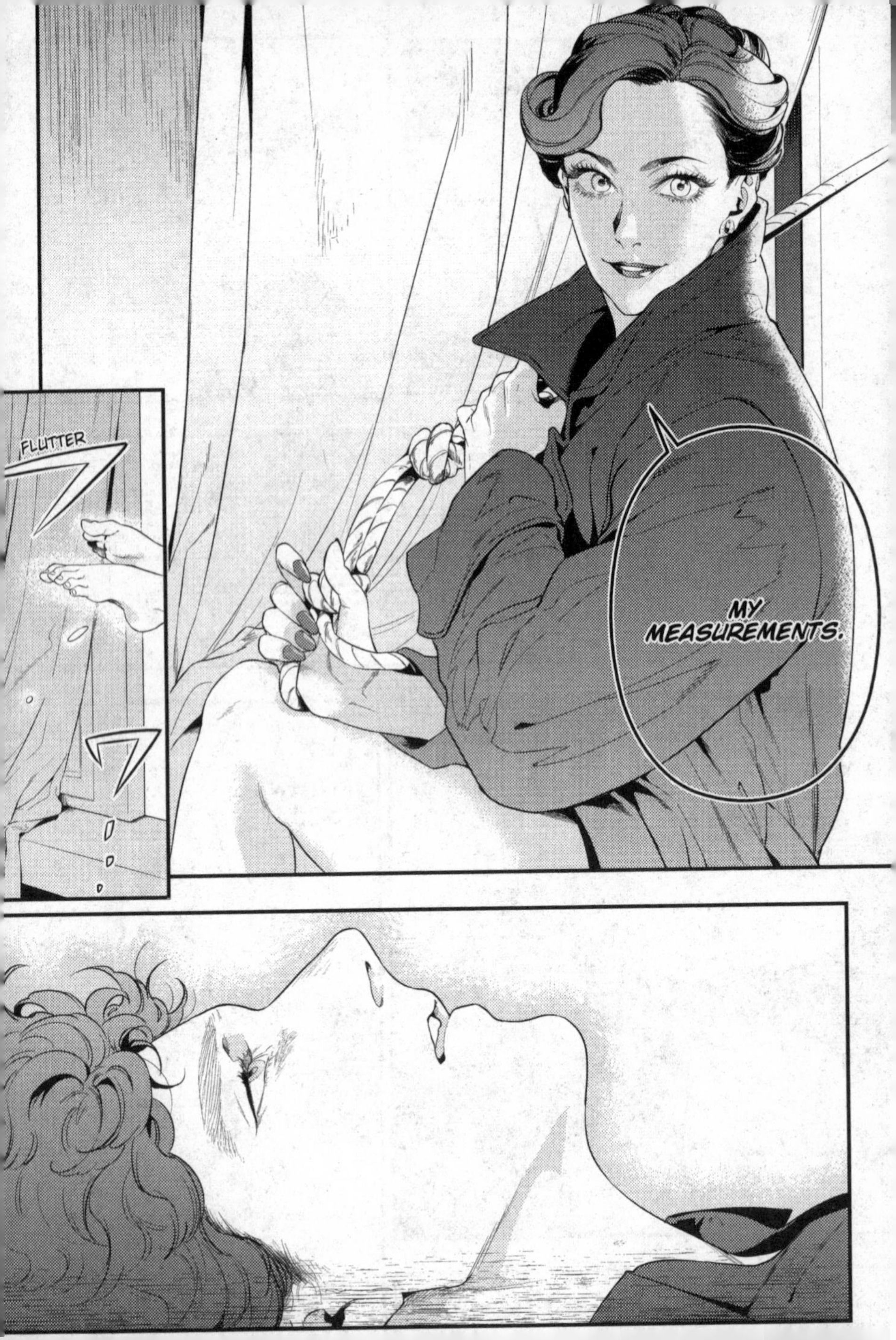
MY MEASUREMENTS.
FLUTTER

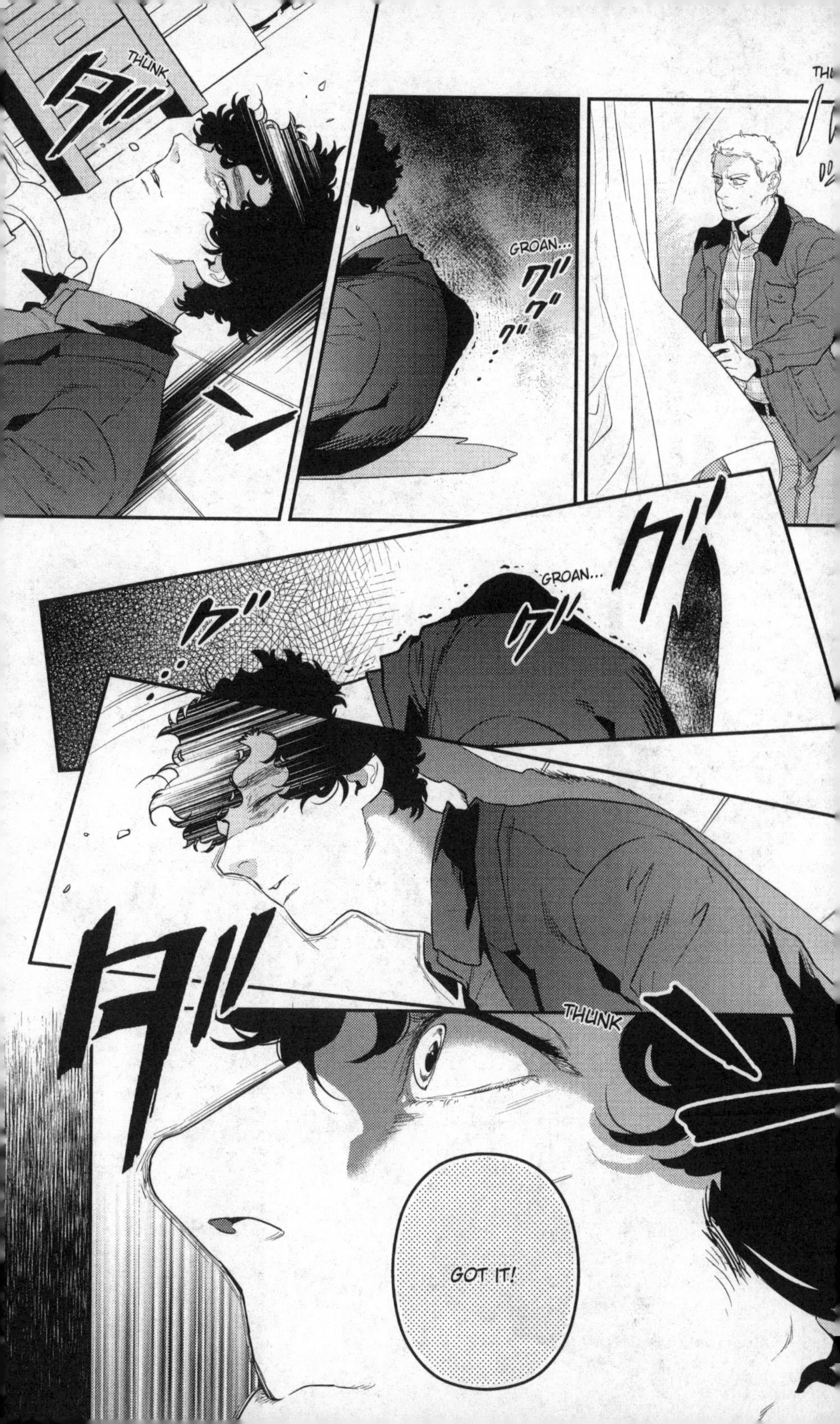
THU
GROAN...
THUNK
GROAN...
THUNK
GOT IT!

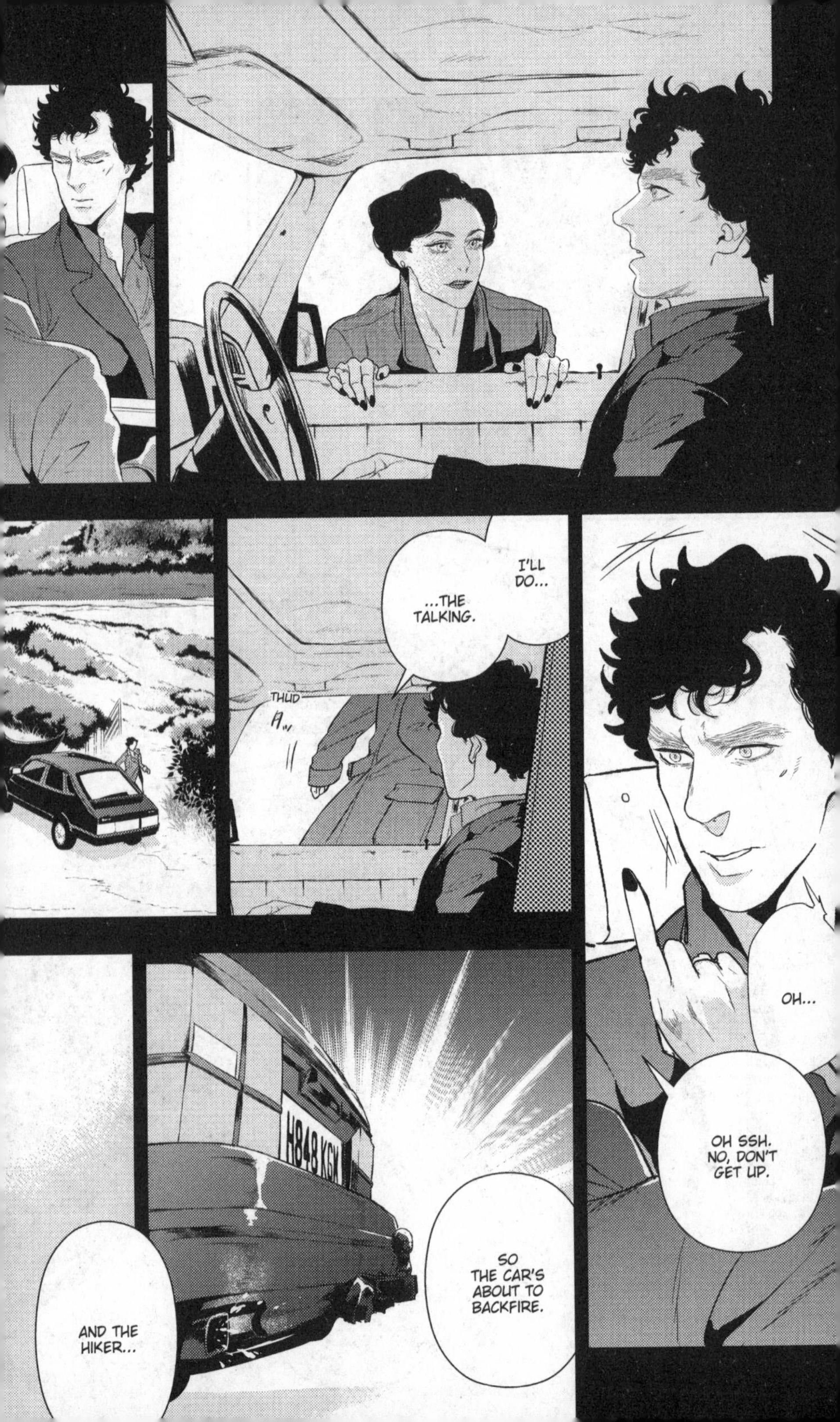

OH...
OH SSH. NO, DON'T GET UP.
I'LL DO...
...THE TALKING.
THUD
SO THE CAR'S ABOUT TO BACKFIRE.
AND THE HIKER...

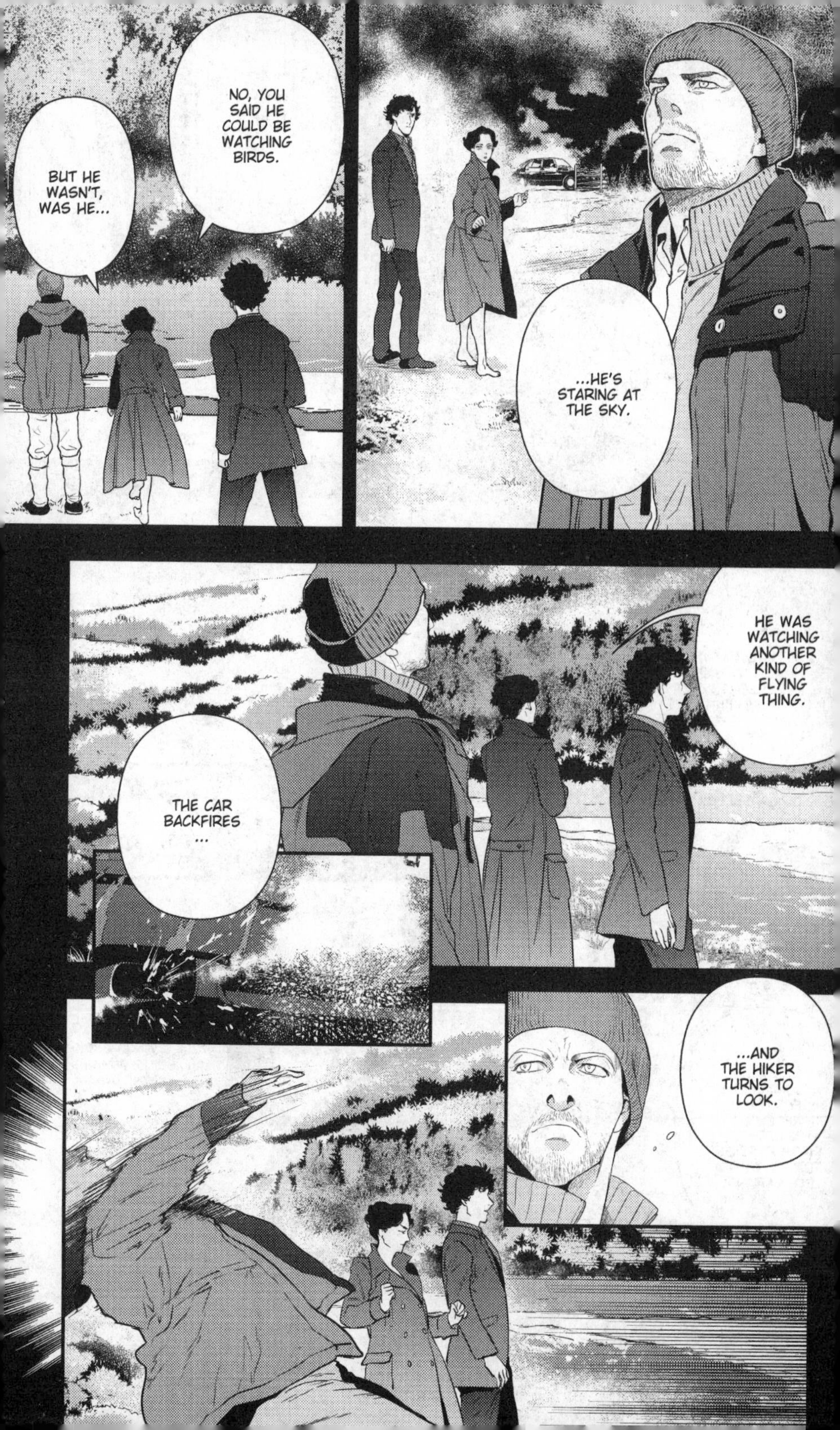
...HE'S STARING AT THE SKY.
NO, YOU SAID HE COULD BE WATCHING BIRDS.
BUT HE WASN'T, WAS HE...
HE WAS WATCHING ANOTHER KIND OF FLYING THING.
THE CAR BACKFIRES ...
...AND THE HIKER TURNS TO LOOK.

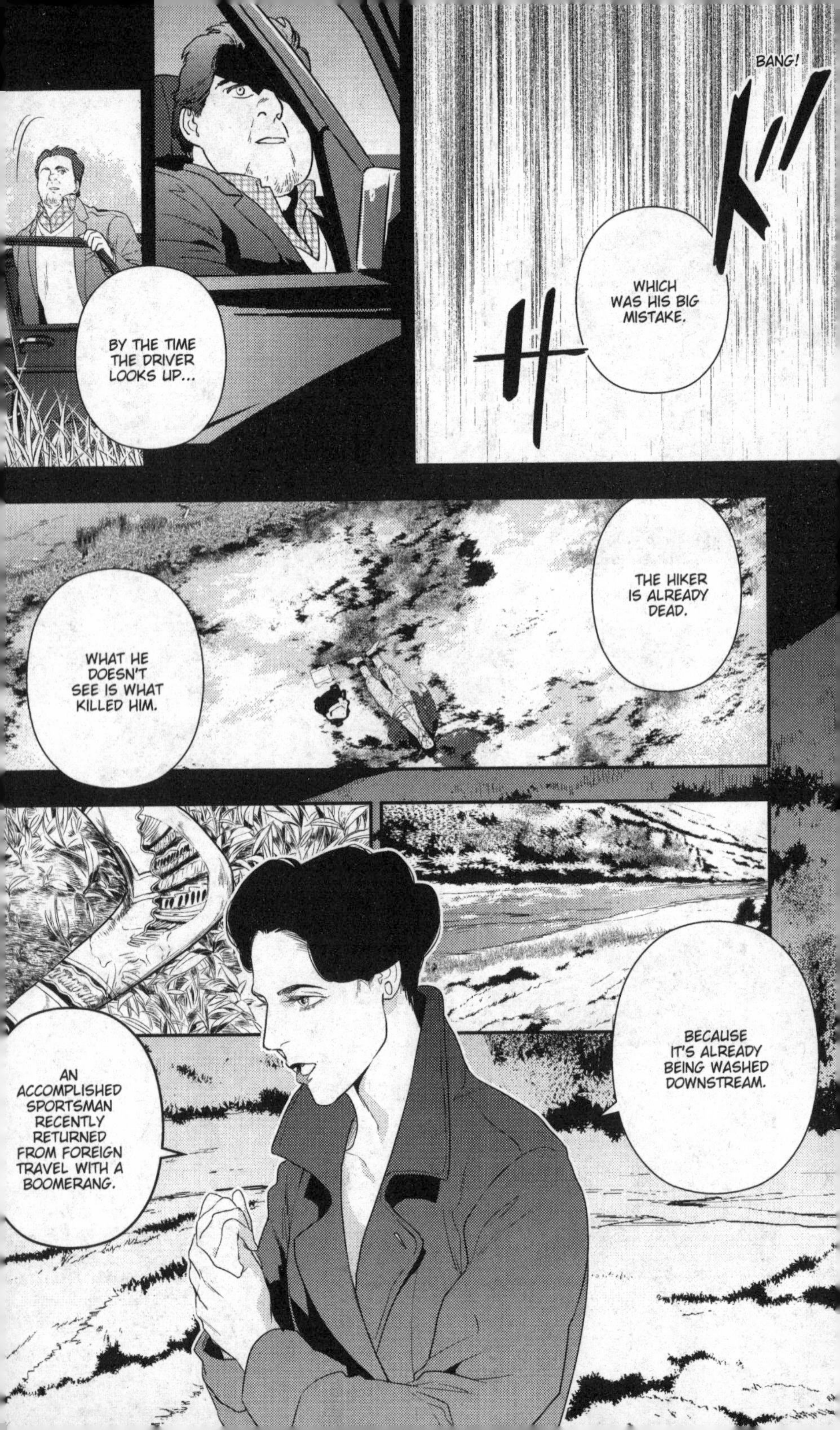
BANG!
WHICH WAS HIS BIG MISTAKE.
BY THE TIME THE DRIVER LOOKS UP...
THE HIKER IS ALREADY DEAD.
WHAT HE DOESN'T SEE IS WHAT KILLED HIM.
BECAUSE IT'S ALREADY BEING WASHED DOWNSTREAM.
AN ACCOMPLISHED SPORTSMAN RECENTLY RETURNED FROM FOREIGN TRAVEL WITH A BOOMERANG.

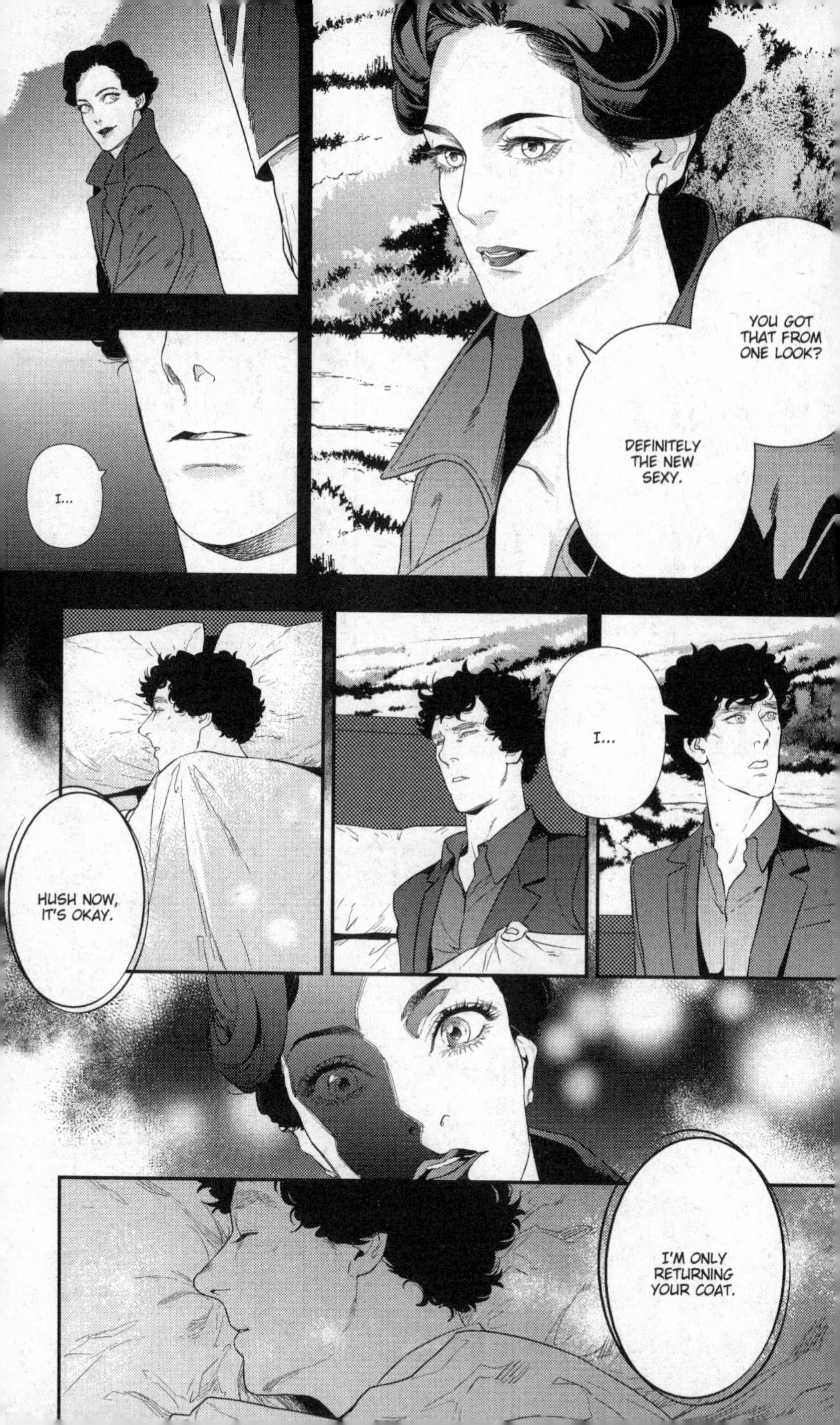
YOU GOT THAT FROM ONE LOOK?
DEFINITELY THE NEW SEXY.
I...
I...
HUSH NOW, IT'S OKAY.
I'M ONLY RETURNING YOUR COAT.

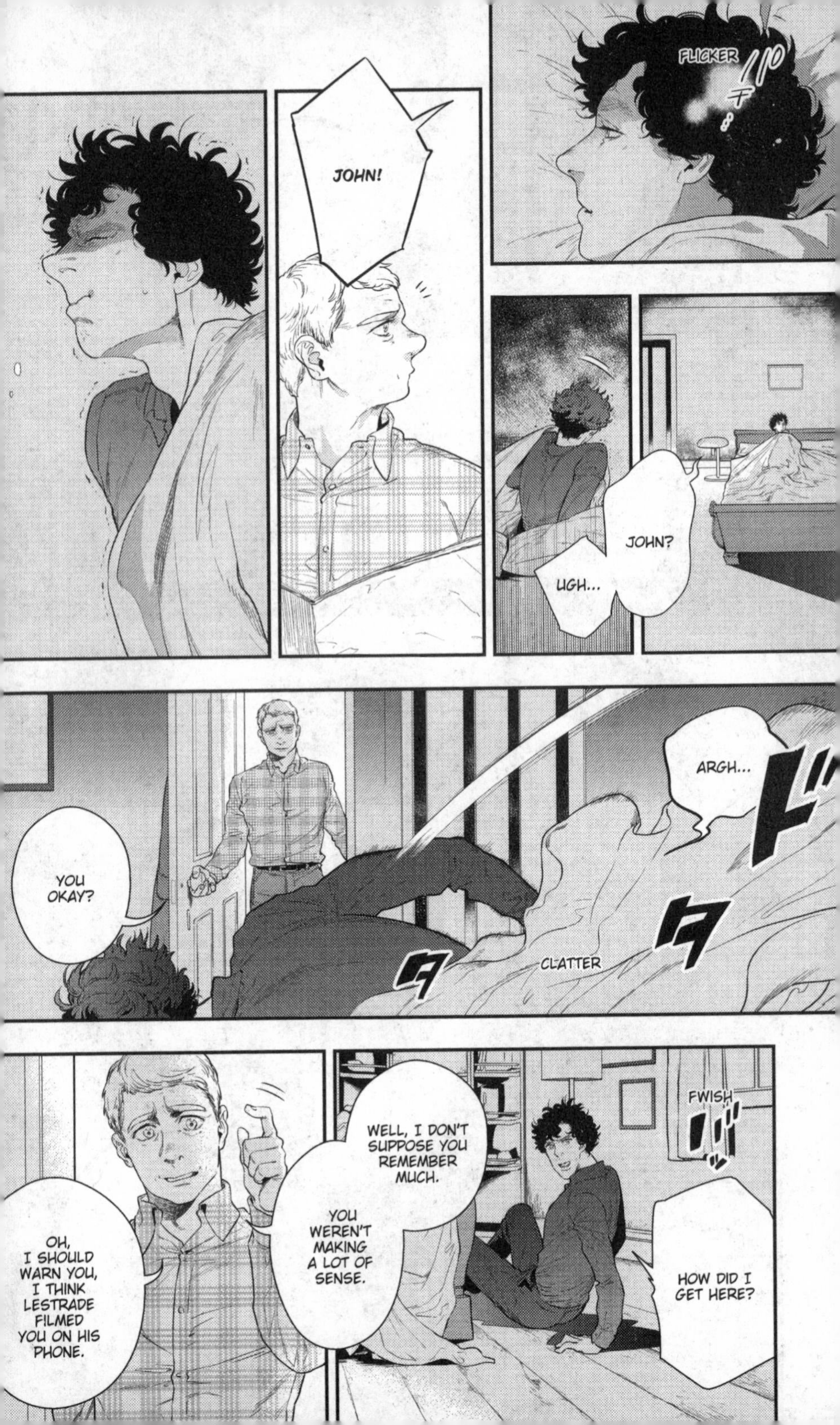
FLICKER
JOHN?
UGH...
JOHN!
ARGH...
CLATTER
YOU OKAY?
FWISH
HOW DID I GET HERE?
WELL, I DON'T SUPPOSE YOU REMEMBER MUCH.
YOU WEREN'T MAKING A LOT OF SENSE.
OH, I SHOULD WARN YOU, I THINK LESTRADE FILMED YOU ON HIS PHONE.

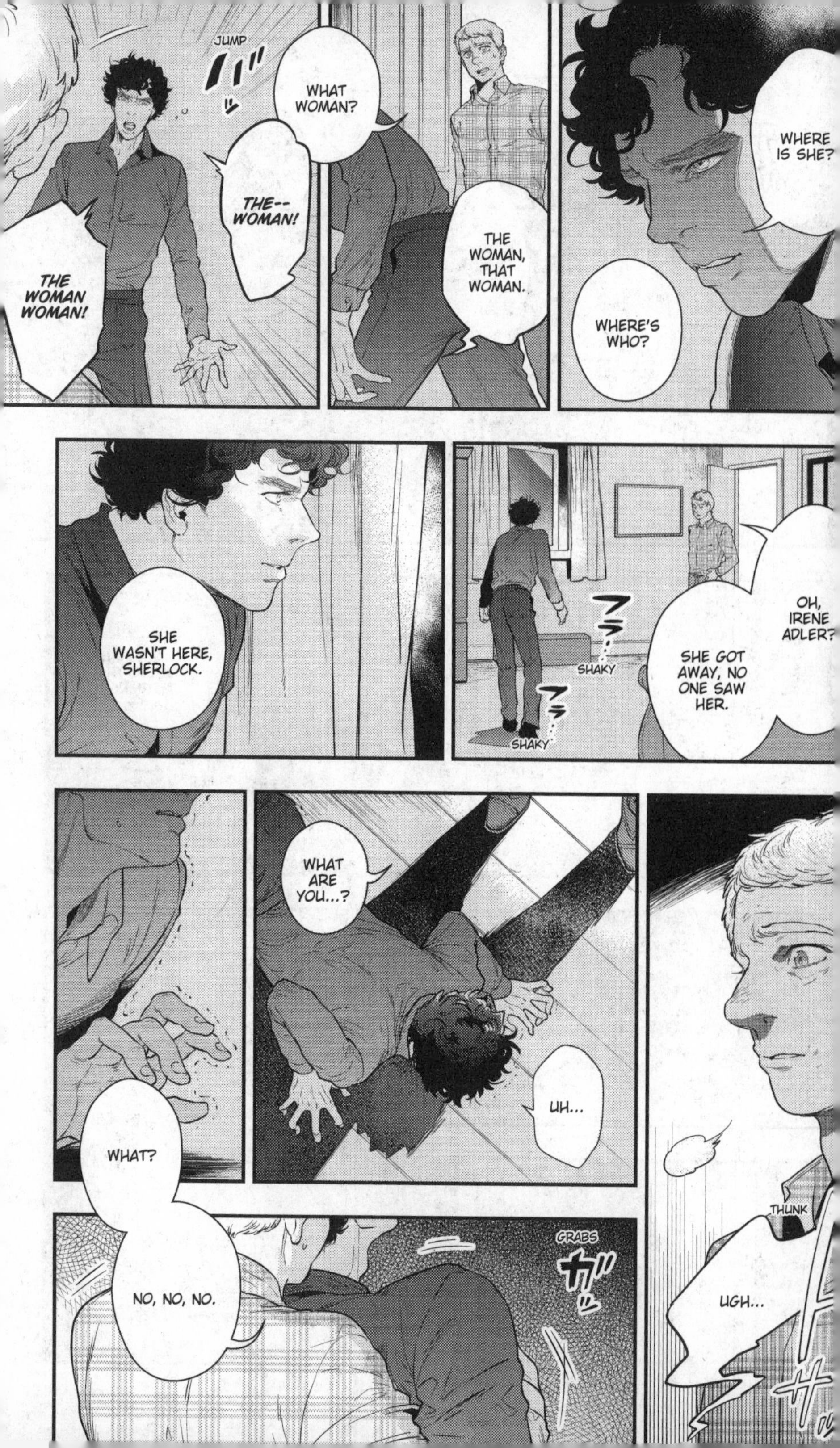
WHERE IS SHE?
WHERE'S WHO?
THE WOMAN, THAT WOMAN.
WHAT WOMAN?
THE--WOMAN!
JUMP
THE WOMAN WOMAN!
OH, IRENE ADLER?
SHE GOT AWAY, NO ONE SAW HER.
SHAKY
SHAKY
SHE WASN'T HERE, SHERLOCK.
THUNK
UGH...
WHAT ARE YOU...?
UH...
WHAT?
GRABS
NO, NO, NO.

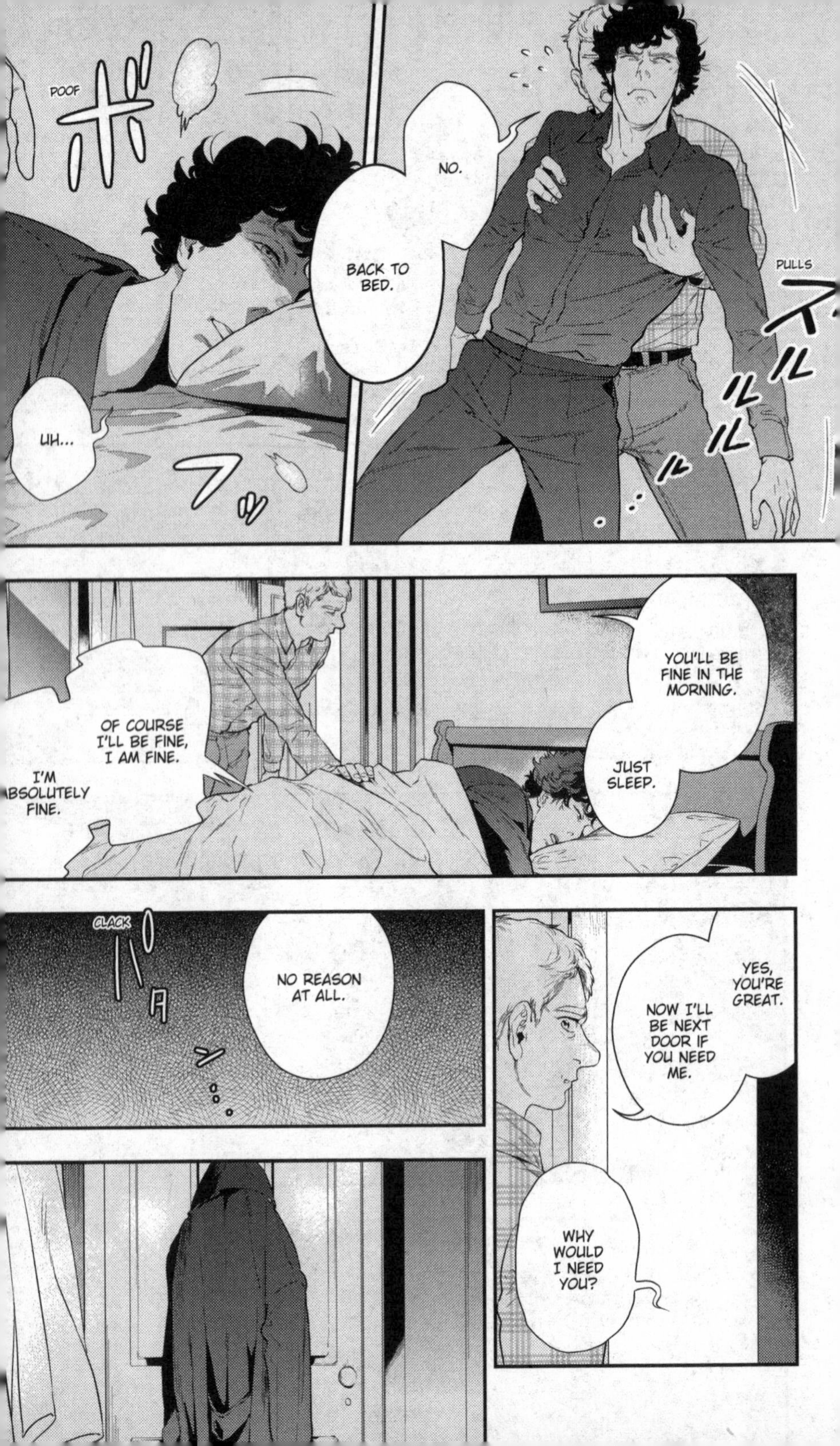

PULLS
NO.
BACK TO BED.
POOF
UH...
YOU'LL BE FINE IN THE MORNING.
JUST SLEEP.
OF COURSE I'LL BE FINE, I AM FINE.
I'M ABSOLUTELY FINE.
YES, YOU'RE GREAT.
NOW I'LL BE NEXT DOOR IF YOU NEED ME.
WHY WOULD I NEED YOU?
NO REASON AT ALL.
CLACK

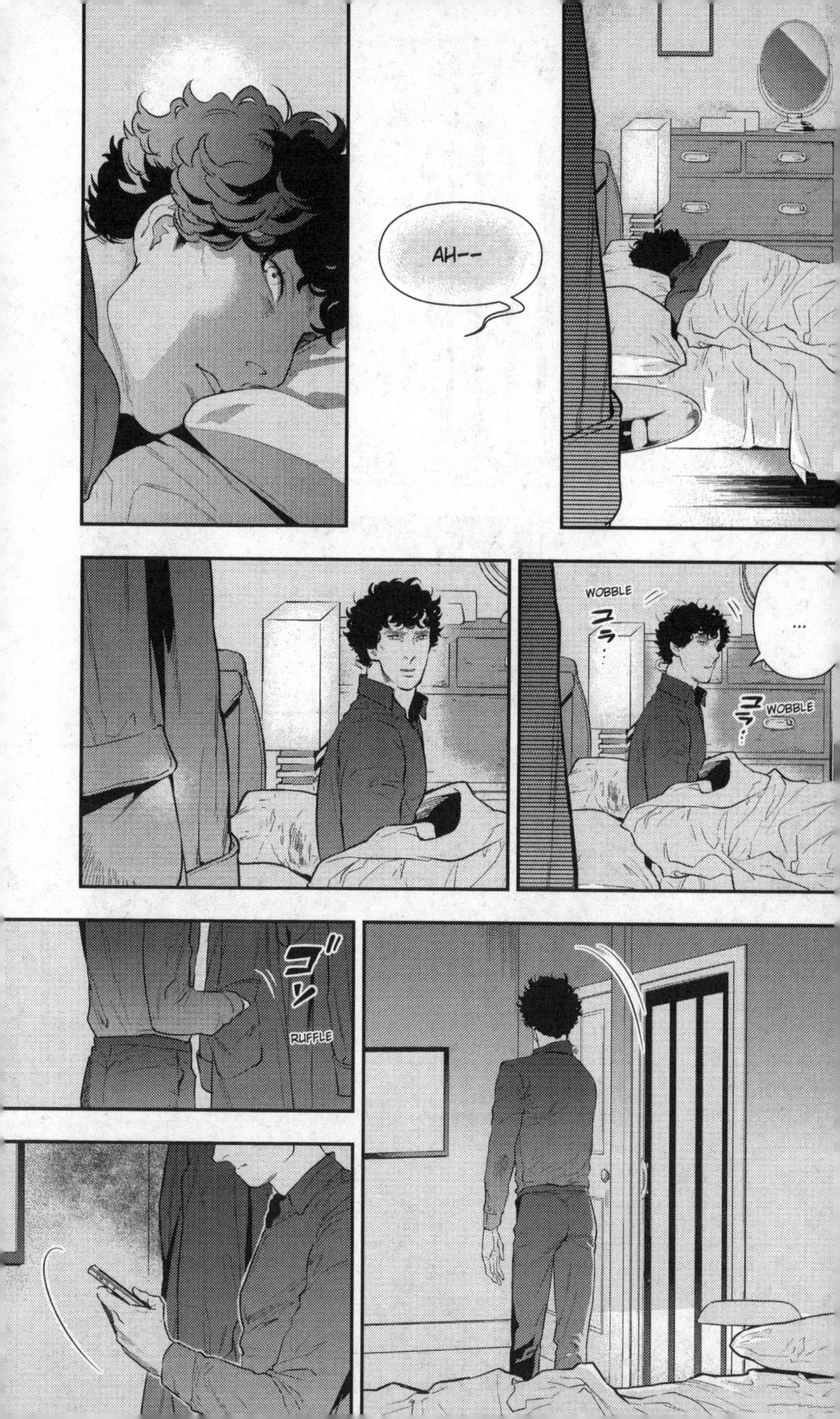
AH--
WOBBLE
ユラ…
...
ユラ…
WOBBLE
ゴソ
RUFFLE

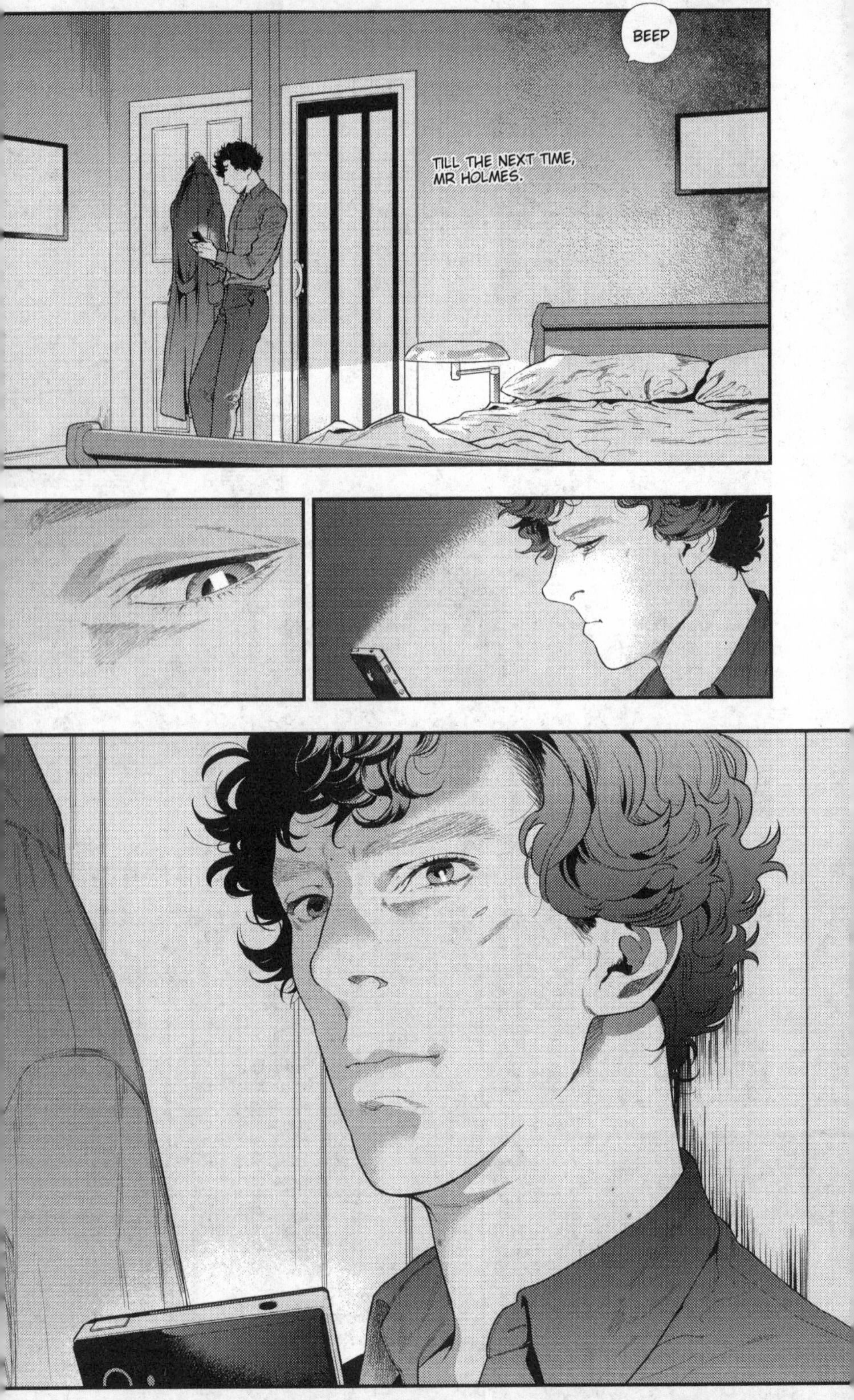
BEEP
TILL THE NEXT TIME, MR HOLMES.

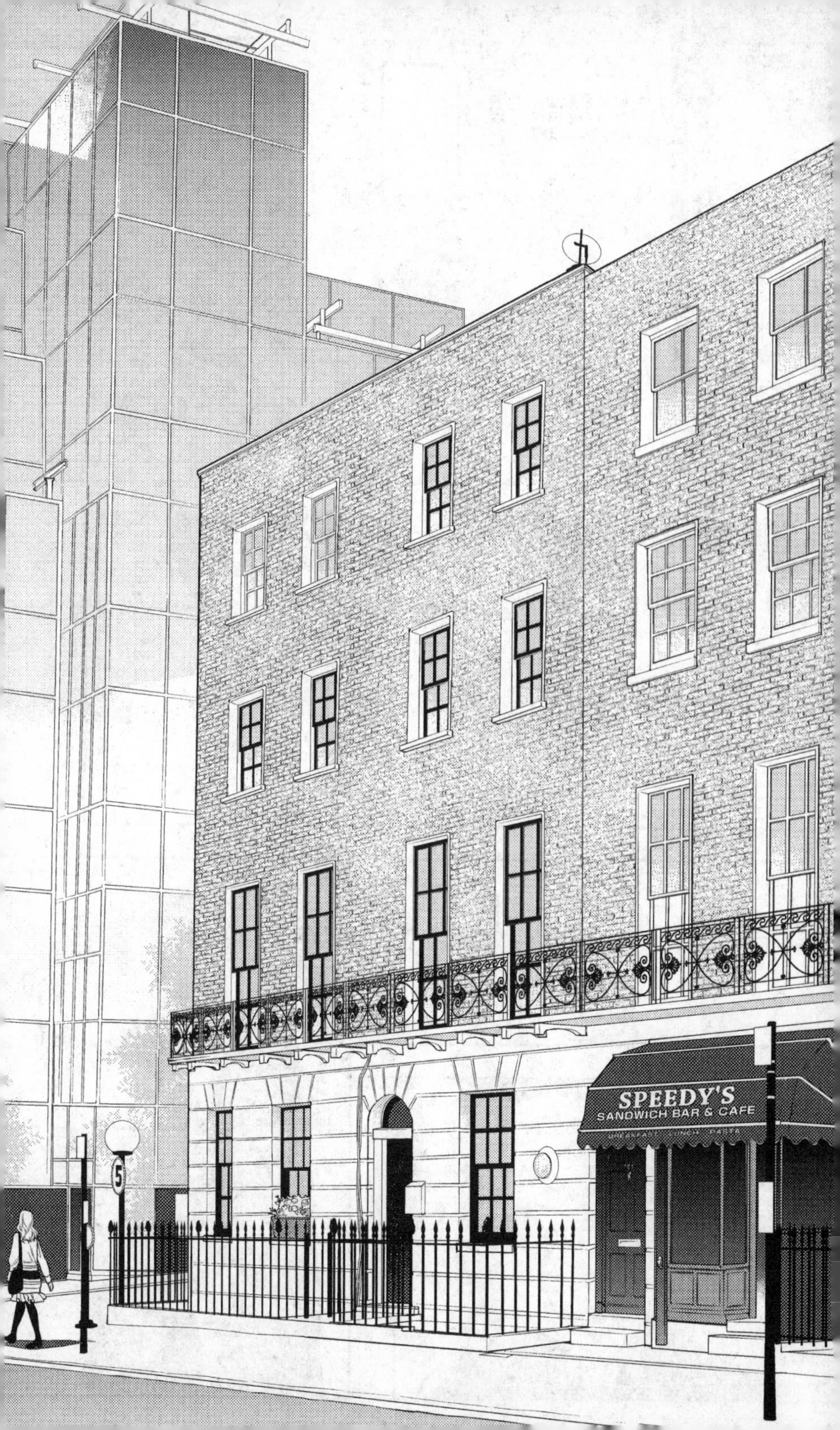
SPEEDY'S
SANDWICH BAR & CAFE

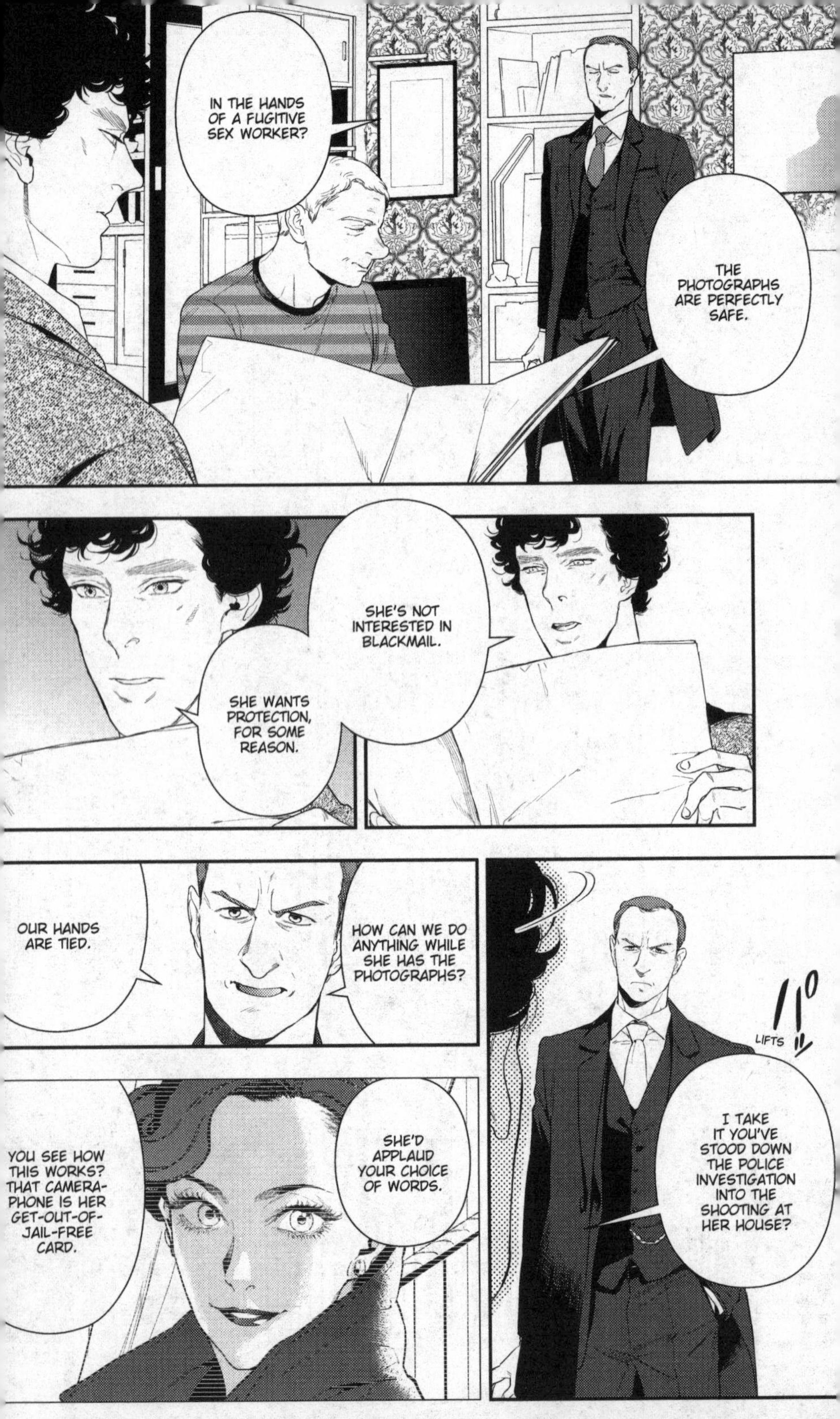
THE PHOTOGRAPHS ARE PERFECTLY SAFE.
IN THE HANDS OF A FUGITIVE SEX WORKER?
SHE'S NOT INTERESTED IN BLACKMAIL.
SHE WANTS PROTECTION, FOR SOME REASON.
LIFTS
I TAKE IT YOU'VE STOOD DOWN THE POLICE INVESTIGATION INTO THE SHOOTING AT HER HOUSE?
HOW CAN WE DO ANYTHING WHILE SHE HAS THE PHOTOGRAPHS?
OUR HANDS ARE TIED.
SHE'D APPLAUD YOUR CHOICE OF WORDS.
YOU SEE HOW THIS WORKS? THAT CAMERA-PHONE IS HER GET-OUT-OF-JAIL-FREE CARD.

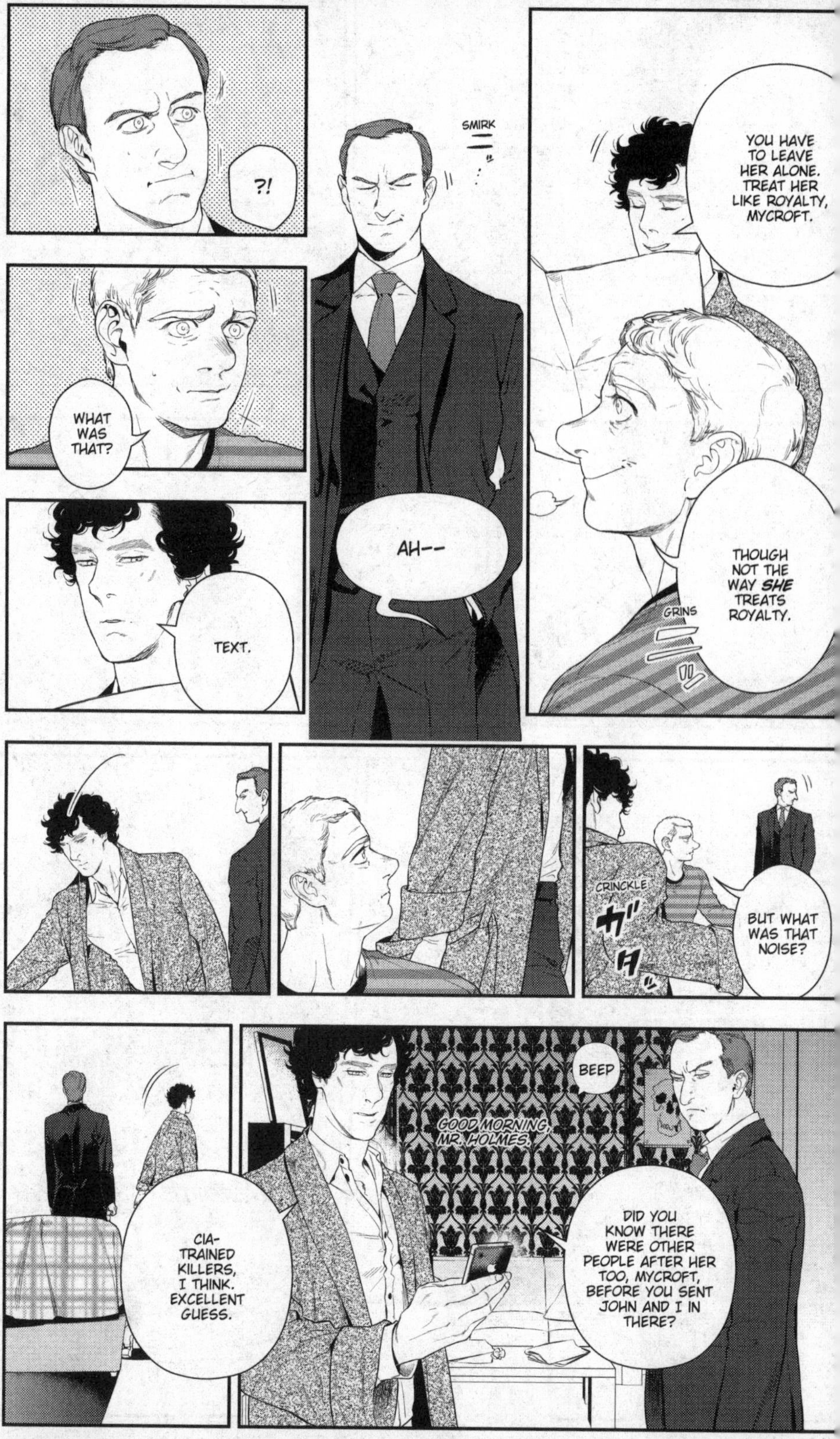
YOU HAVE TO LEAVE HER ALONE. TREAT HER LIKE ROYALTY, MYCROFT.
THOUGH NOT THE WAY *SHE* TREATS ROYALTY.
GRINS
SMIRK
AH--
?!
WHAT WAS THAT?
TEXT.
CRINKLE
BUT WHAT WAS THAT NOISE?
BEEP
GOOD MORNING, MR. HOLMES.
DID YOU KNOW THERE WERE OTHER PEOPLE AFTER HER TOO, MYCROFT, BEFORE YOU SENT JOHN AND I IN THERE?
CIA-TRAINED KILLERS, I THINK. EXCELLENT GUESS.

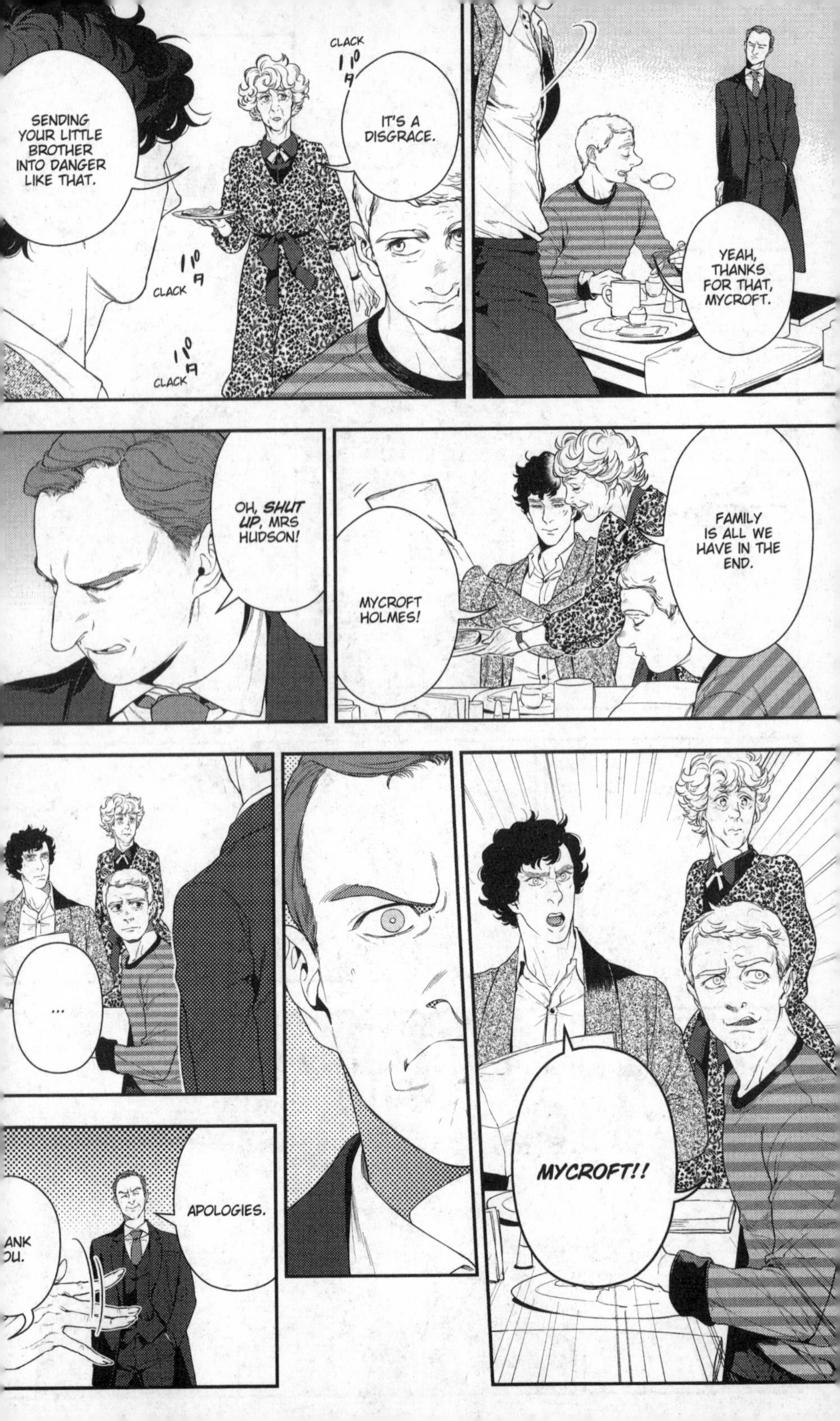
YEAH, THANKS FOR THAT, MYCROFT.
CLACK
IT'S A DISGRACE.
SENDING YOUR LITTLE BROTHER INTO DANGER LIKE THAT.
CLACK
CLACK
FAMILY IS ALL WE HAVE IN THE END.
MYCROFT HOLMES!
OH, *SHUT UP*, MRS HUDSON!
MYCROFT!!
...
APOLOGIES.
ANK OU.

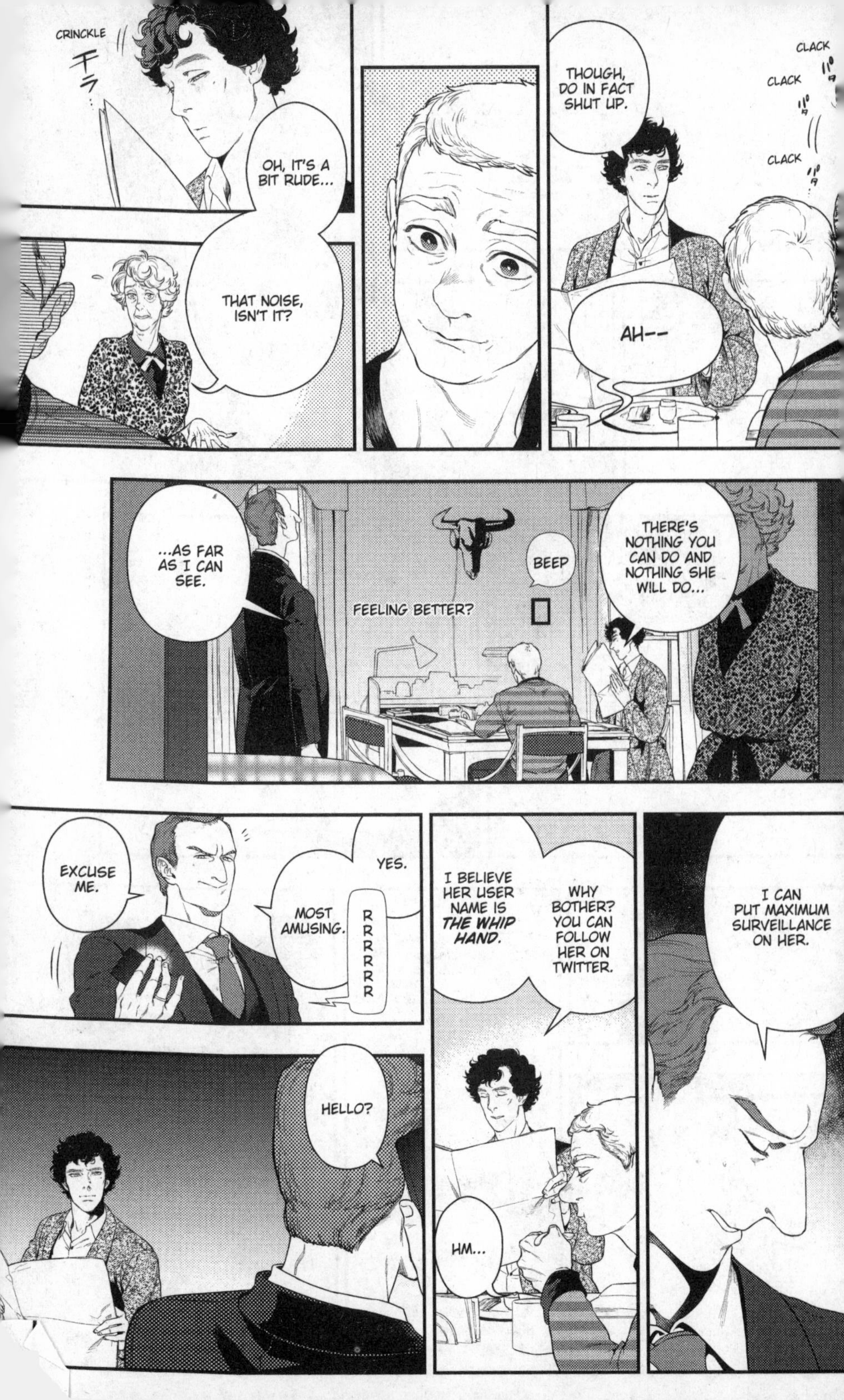
CLACK
CLACK
THOUGH, DO IN FACT SHUT UP.
CLACK
AH--
CRINKLE
OH, IT'S A BIT RUDE...
THAT NOISE, ISN'T IT?
THERE'S NOTHING YOU CAN DO AND NOTHING SHE WILL DO...
BEEP
FEELING BETTER?
...AS FAR AS I CAN SEE.
I CAN PUT MAXIMUM SURVEILLANCE ON HER.
WHY BOTHER? YOU CAN FOLLOW HER ON TWITTER.
I BELIEVE HER USER NAME IS *THE WHIP HAND*.
HM...
YES.
RRRRRR
MOST AMUSING.
EXCUSE ME.
HELLO?

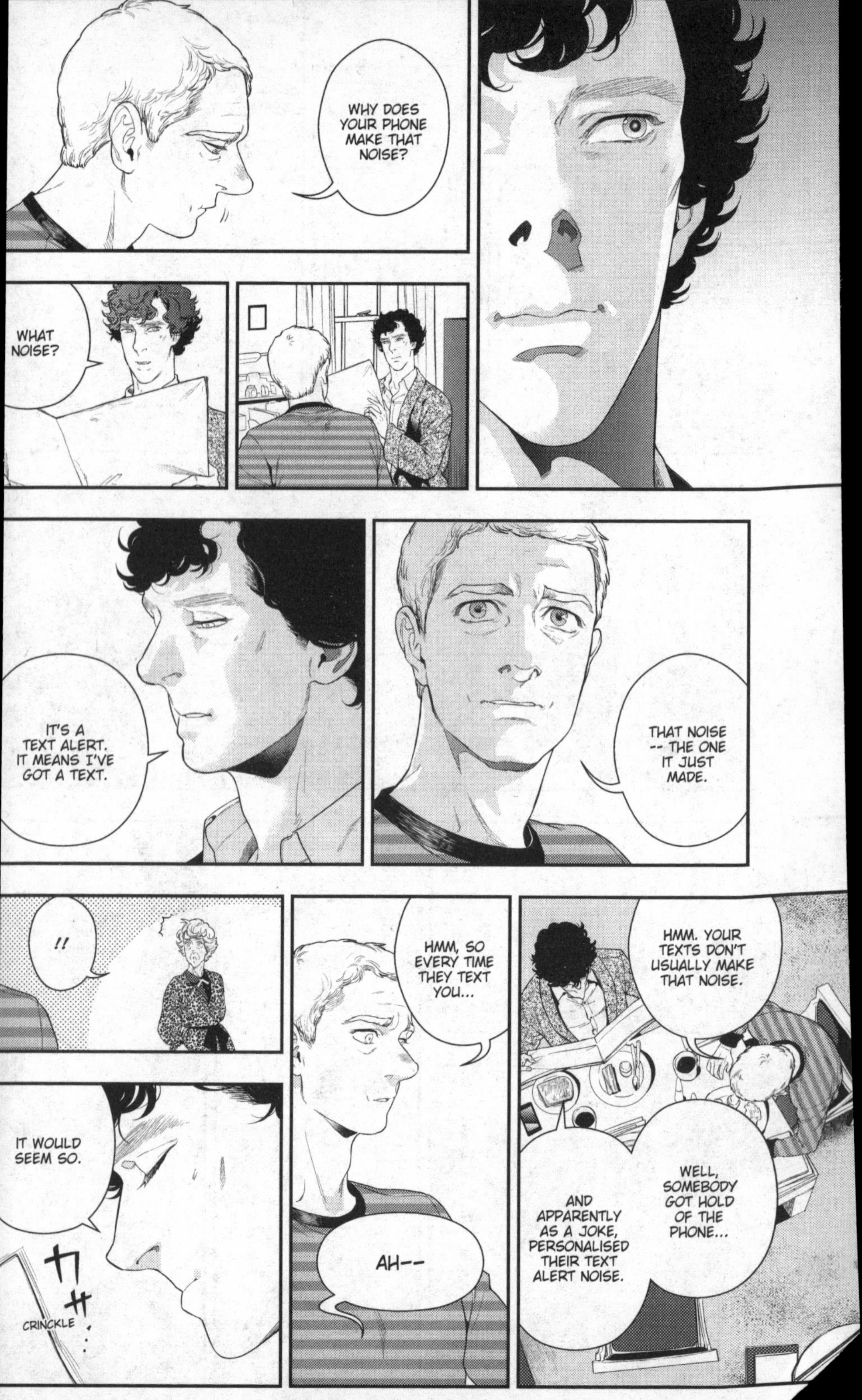
WHY DOES YOUR PHONE MAKE THAT NOISE?
WHAT NOISE?
THAT NOISE -- THE ONE IT JUST MADE.
IT'S A TEXT ALERT. IT MEANS I'VE GOT A TEXT.
HMM. YOUR TEXTS DON'T USUALLY MAKE THAT NOISE.
WELL, SOMEBODY GOT HOLD OF THE PHONE...
AND APPARENTLY AS A JOKE, PERSONALISED THEIR TEXT ALERT NOISE.
HMM, SO EVERY TIME THEY TEXT YOU...
AH--
!!
IT WOULD SEEM SO.
CRINKLE

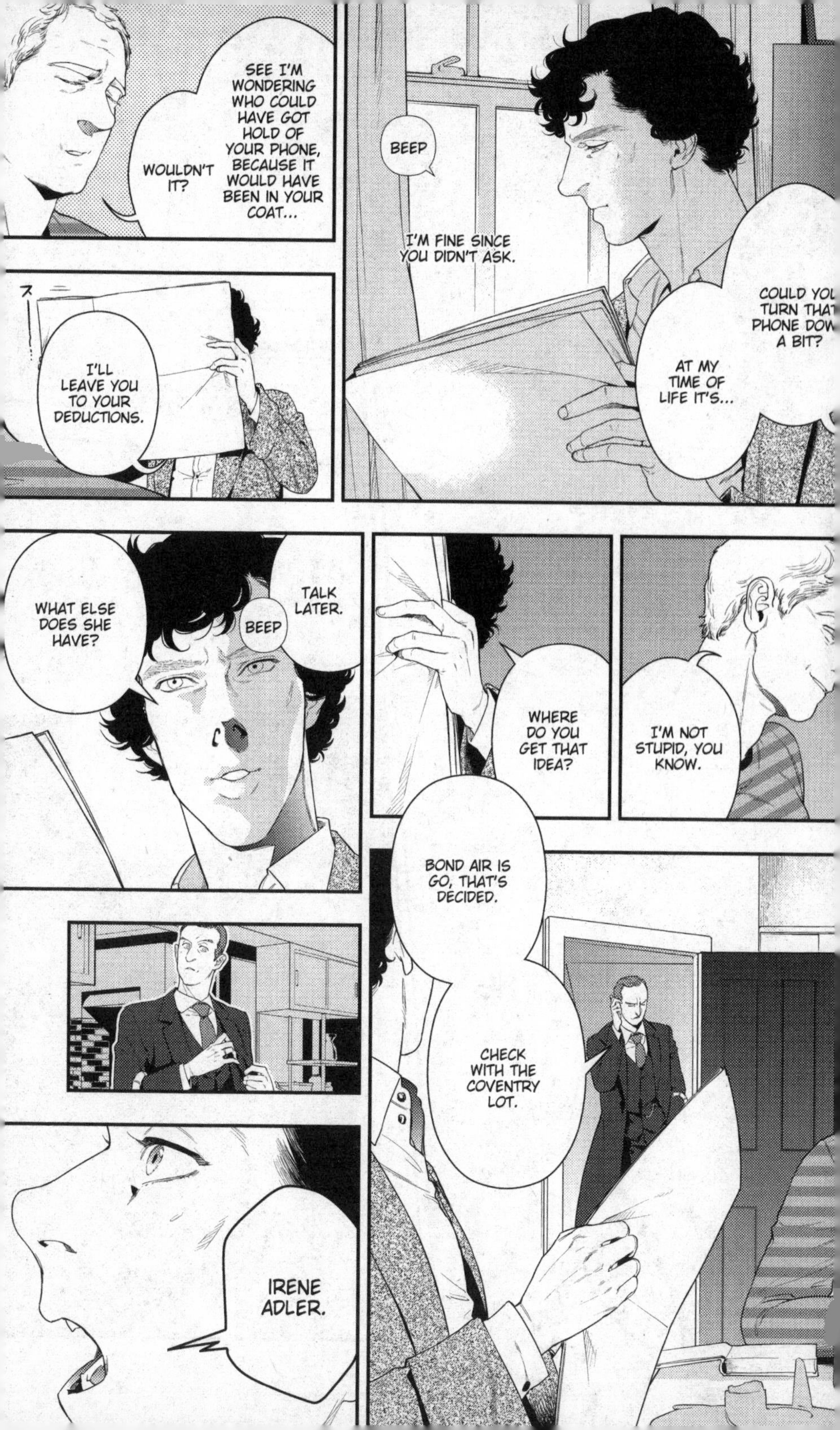
BEEP
I'M FINE SINCE YOU DIDN'T ASK.
COULD YOU TURN THAT PHONE DOW A BIT?
AT MY TIME OF LIFE IT'S...
SEE I'M WONDERING WHO COULD HAVE GOT HOLD OF YOUR PHONE, BECAUSE IT WOULD HAVE BEEN IN YOUR COAT...
WOULDN'T IT?
I'LL LEAVE YOU TO YOUR DEDUCTIONS.
I'M NOT STUPID, YOU KNOW.
WHERE DO YOU GET THAT IDEA?
TALK LATER.
BEEP
WHAT ELSE DOES SHE HAVE?
BOND AIR IS GO, THAT'S DECIDED.
CHECK WITH THE COVENTRY LOT.
IRENE ADLER.

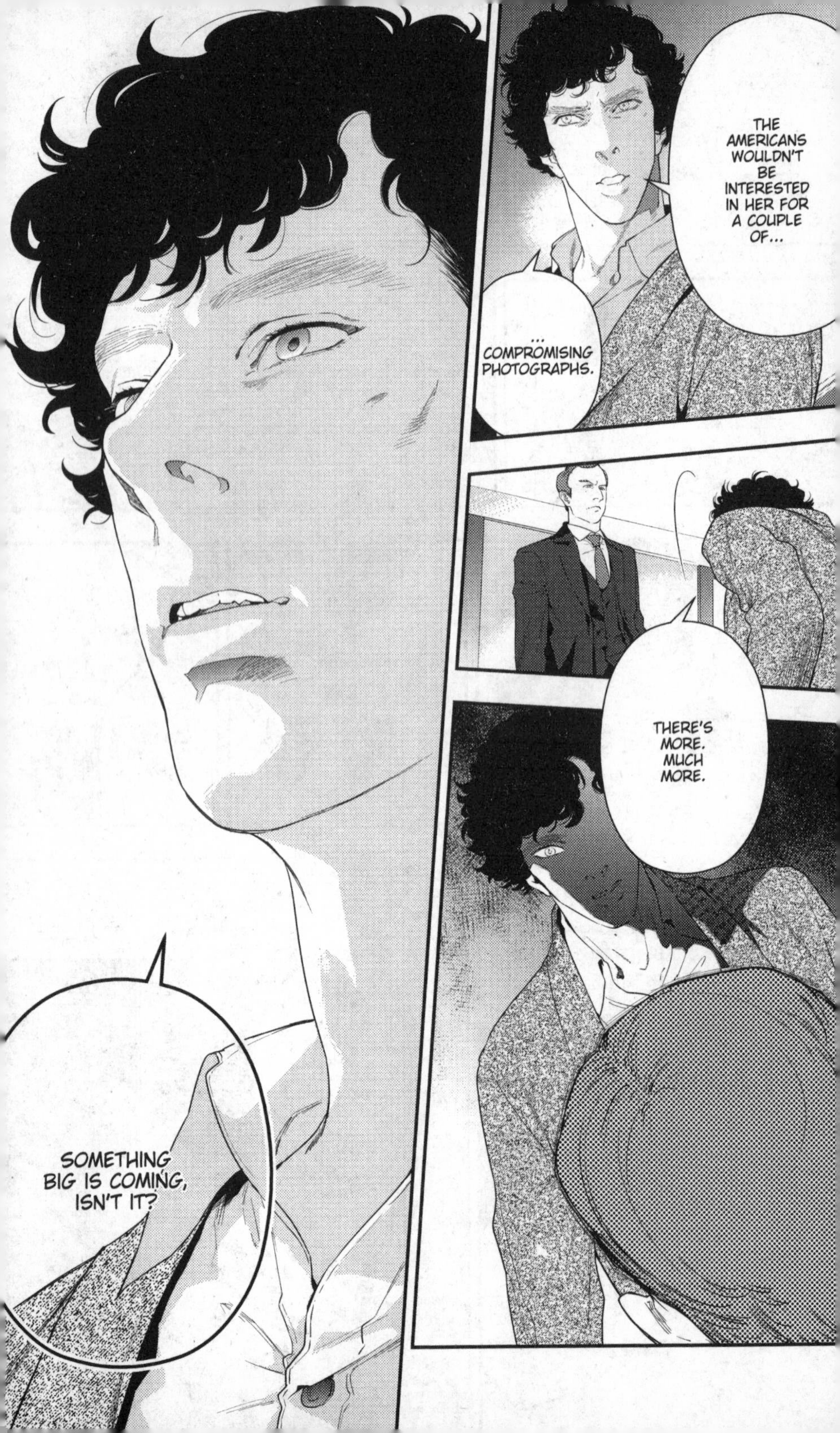
THE AMERICANS WOULDN'T BE INTERESTED IN HER FOR A COUPLE OF...
... COMPROMISING PHOTOGRAPHS.
THERE'S MORE. MUCH MORE.
SOMETHING BIG IS COMING, ISN'T IT?

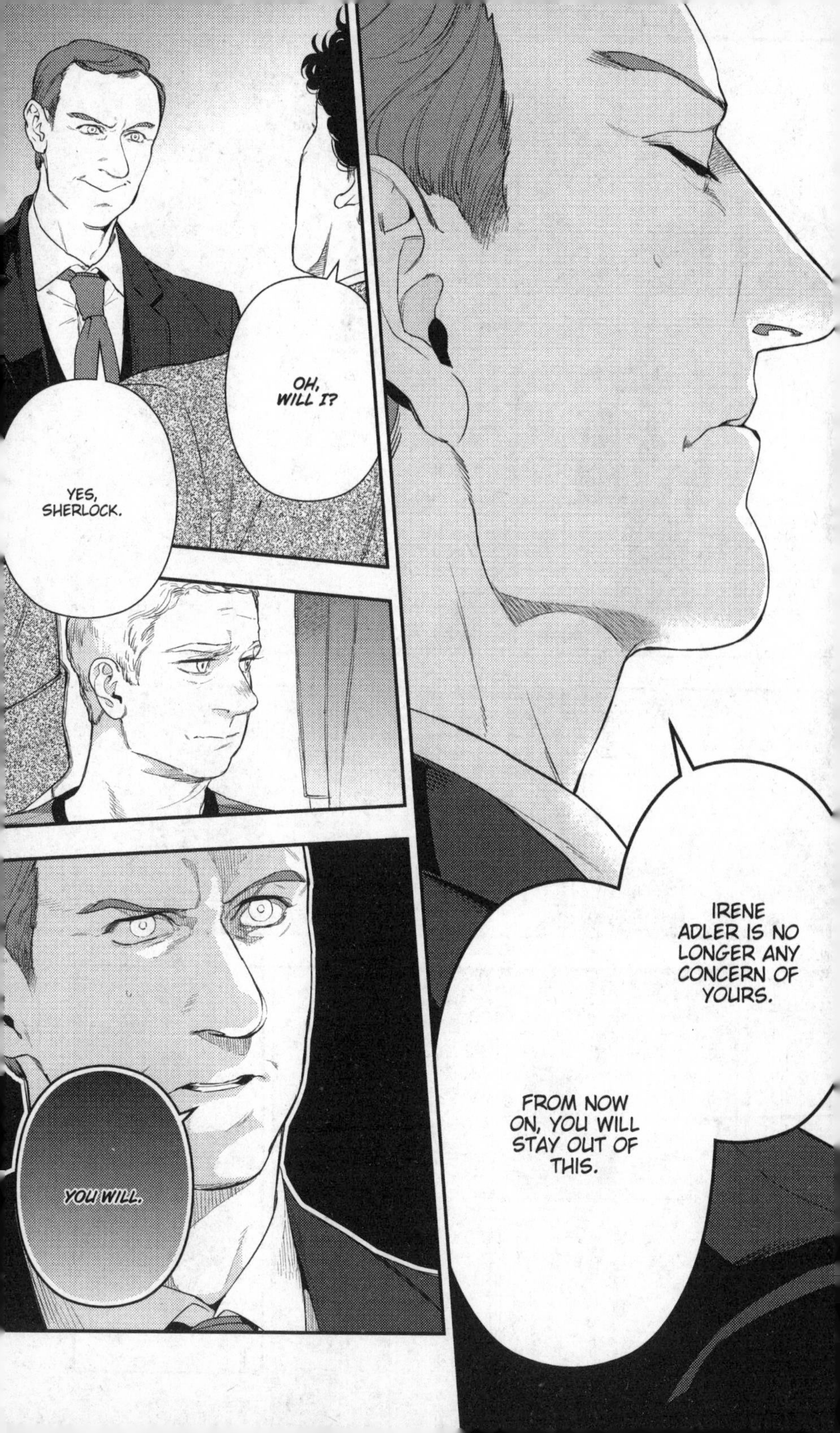
IRENE ADLER IS NO LONGER ANY CONCERN OF YOURS.
FROM NOW ON, YOU WILL STAY OUT OF THIS.
OH, WILL I?
YES, SHERLOCK.
YOU WILL.

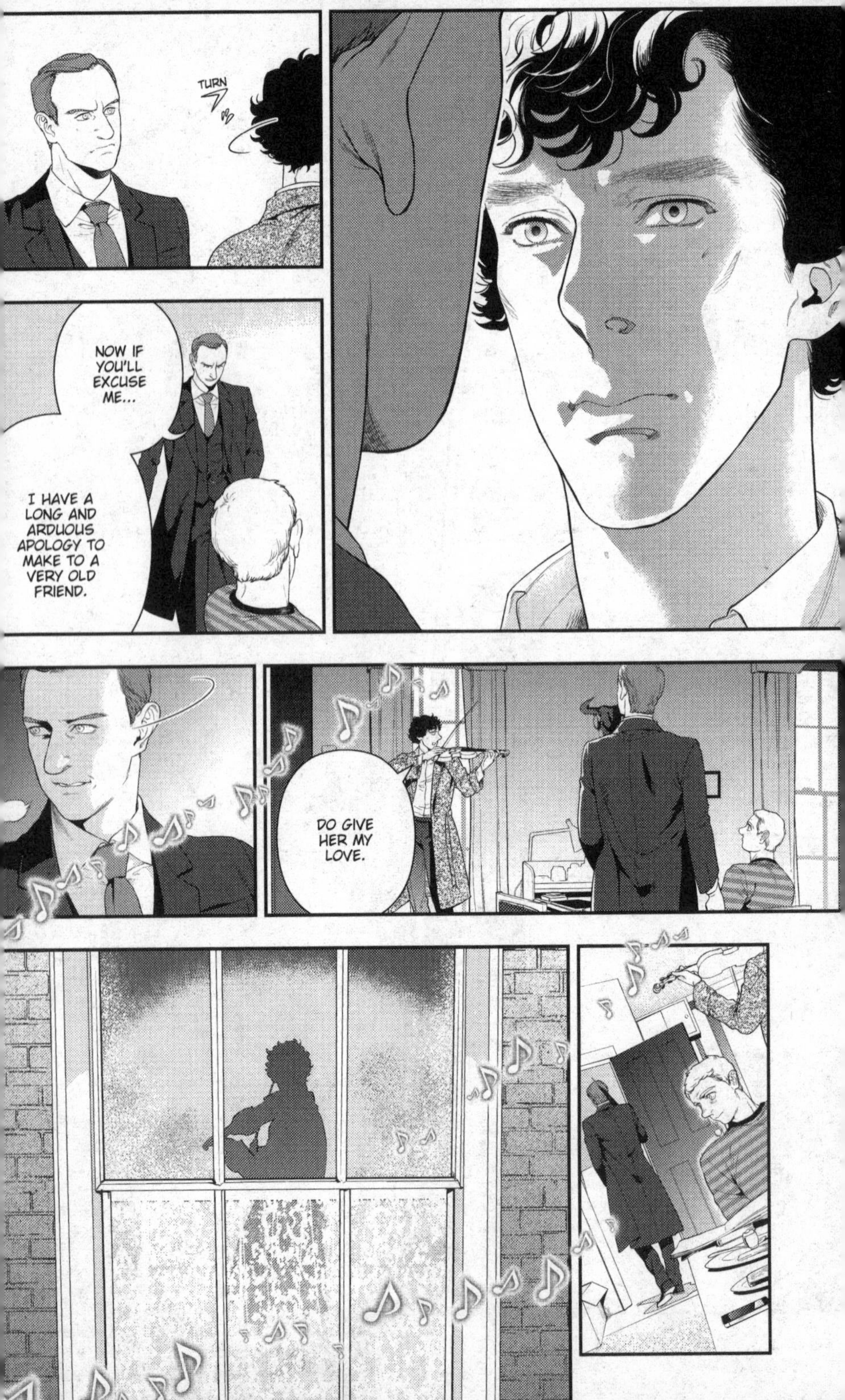
TURN
NOW IF YOU'LL EXCUSE ME...
I HAVE A LONG AND ARDUOUS APOLOGY TO MAKE TO A VERY OLD FRIEND.
DO GIVE HER MY LOVE.

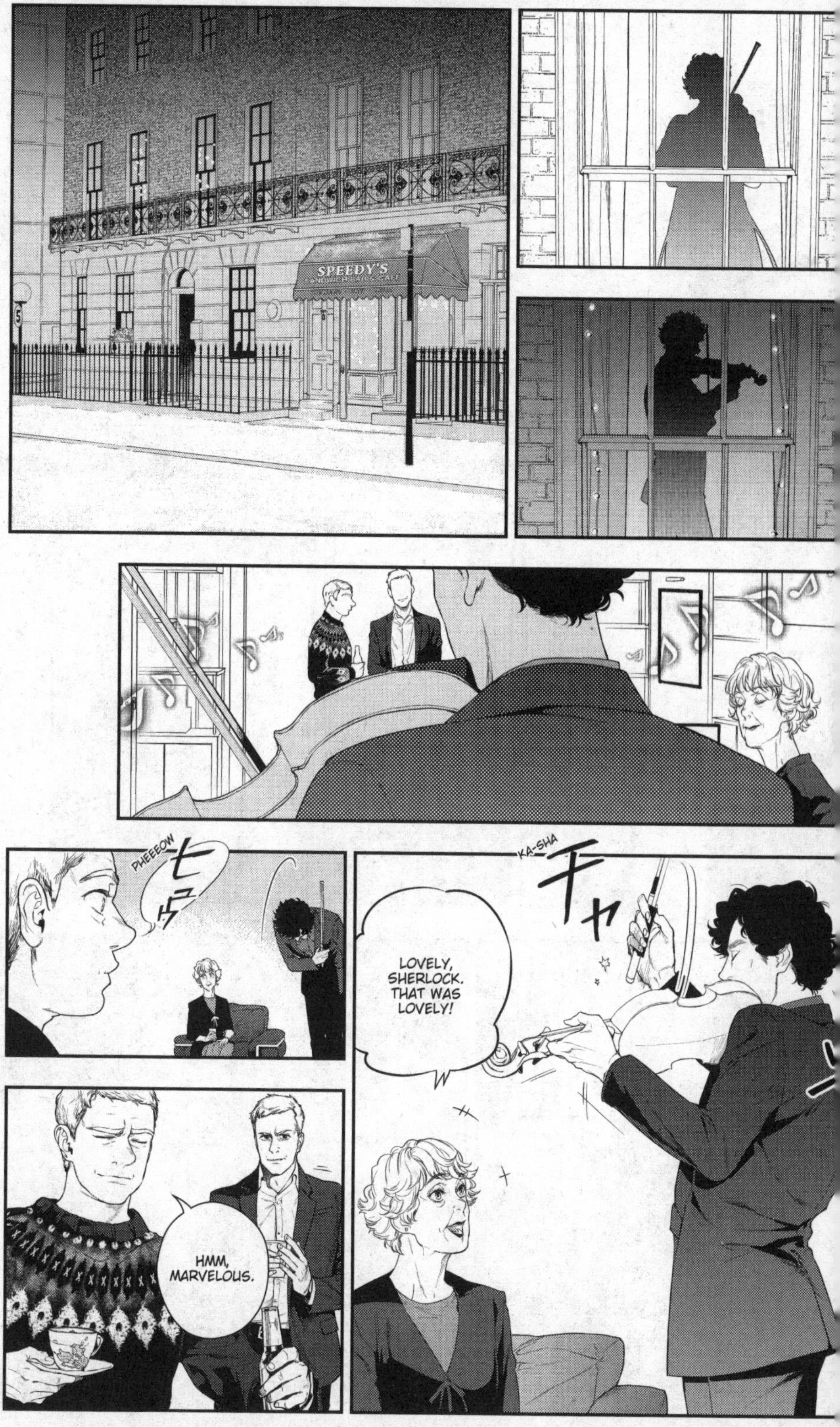
SPEEDY'S
KA-SHA
チャ
LOVELY, SHERLOCK. THAT WAS LOVELY!
PHEEEOW
ヒュゥ
HMM, MARVELOUS.

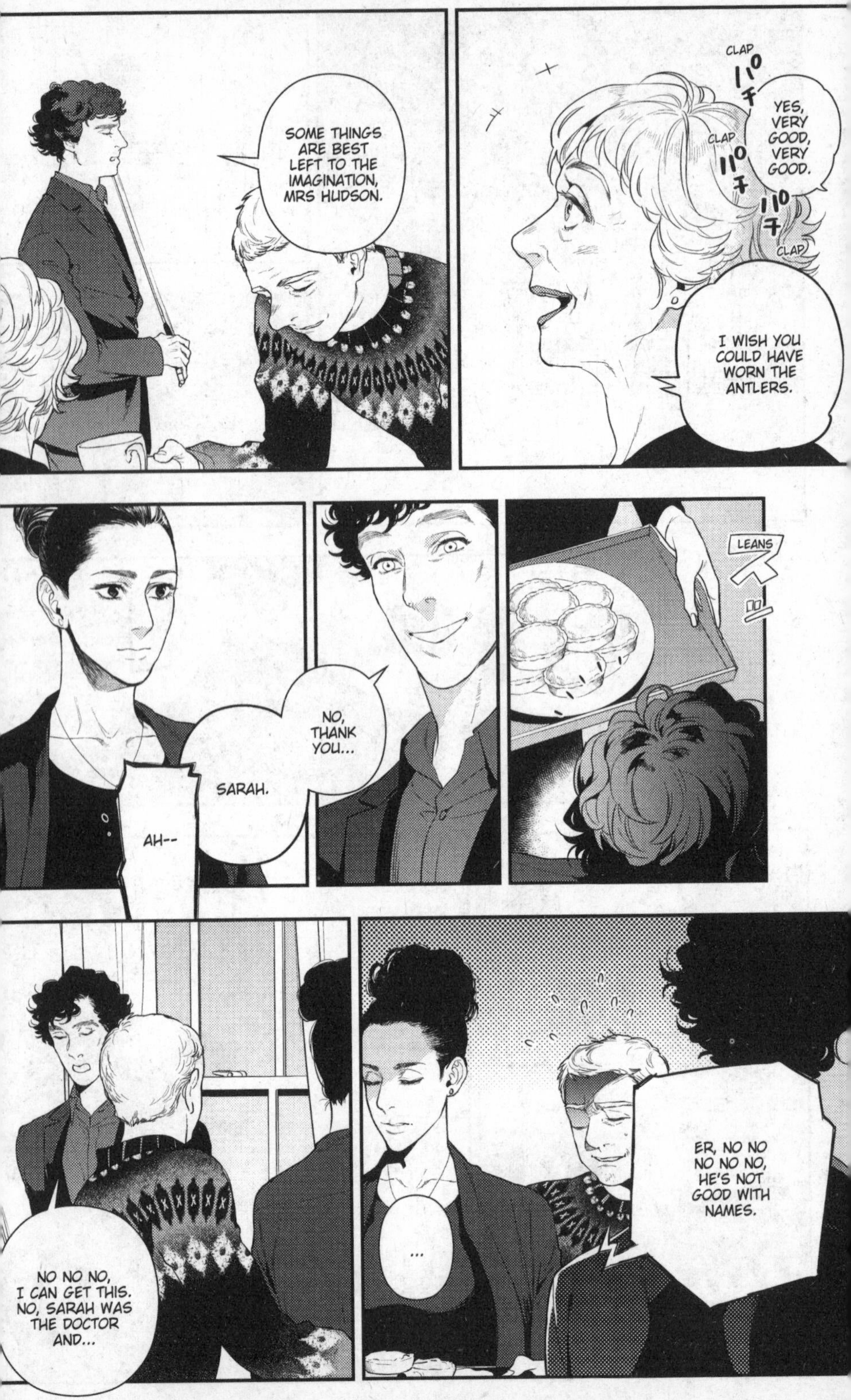
CLAP
パチ
CLAP
パチ
パチ
CLAP
YES, VERY GOOD, VERY GOOD.
I WISH YOU COULD HAVE WORN THE ANTLERS.
SOME THINGS ARE BEST LEFT TO THE IMAGINATION, MRS HUDSON.
LEANS
NO, THANK YOU...
SARAH.
AH--
ER, NO NO NO NO NO, HE'S NOT GOOD WITH NAMES.
...
NO NO NO, I CAN GET THIS. NO, SARAH WAS THE DOCTOR AND...

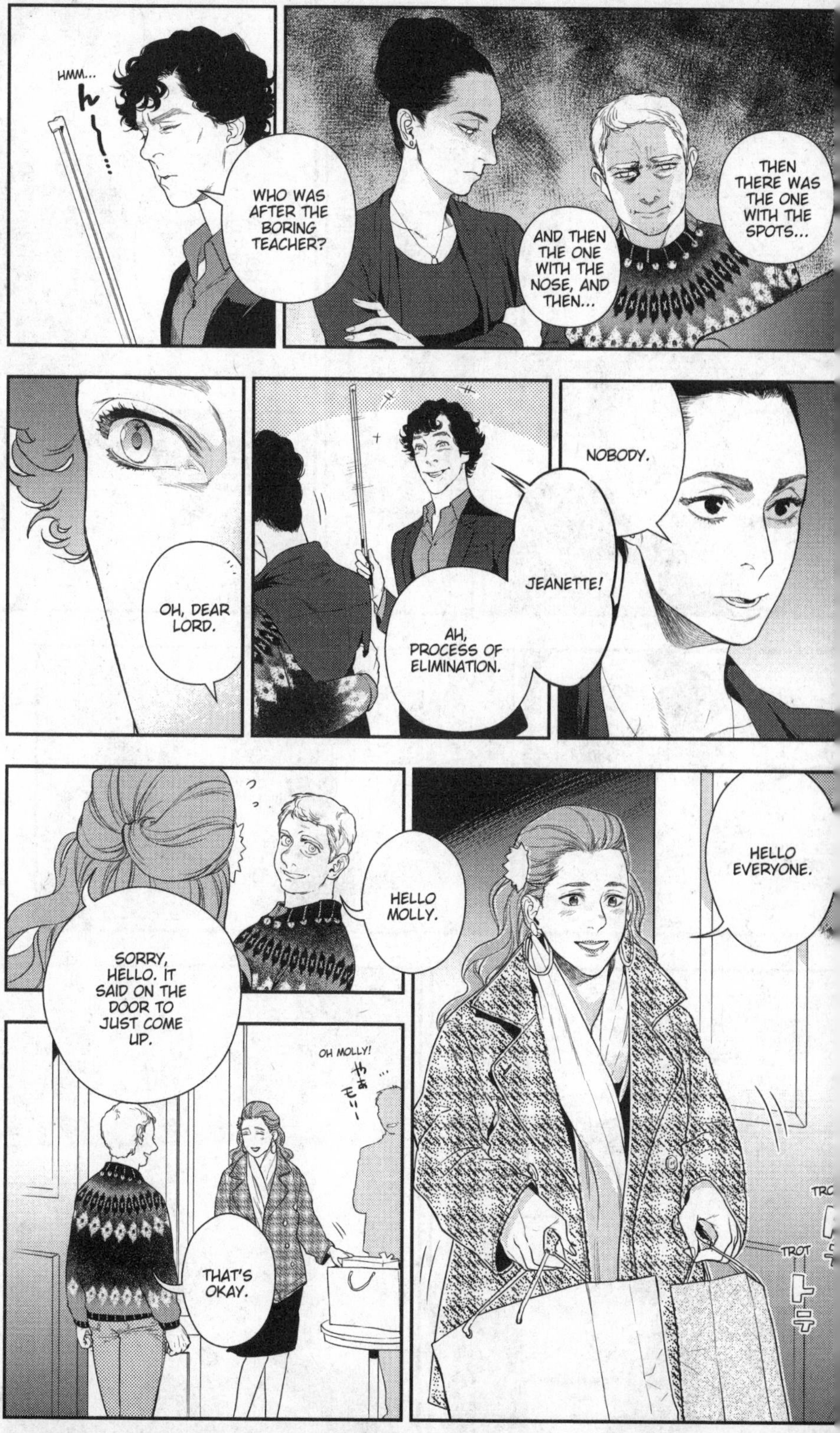
THEN THERE WAS THE ONE WITH THE SPOTS...
AND THEN THE ONE WITH THE NOSE, AND THEN...
HMM...
ん～…
WHO WAS AFTER THE BORING TEACHER?
NOBODY.
JEANETTE!
AH, PROCESS OF ELIMINATION.
OH, DEAR LORD.
HELLO EVERYONE.
TROT
TROT
HELLO MOLLY.
SORRY, HELLO. IT SAID ON THE DOOR TO JUST COME UP.
OH MOLLY!
やあモリー…
THAT'S OKAY.

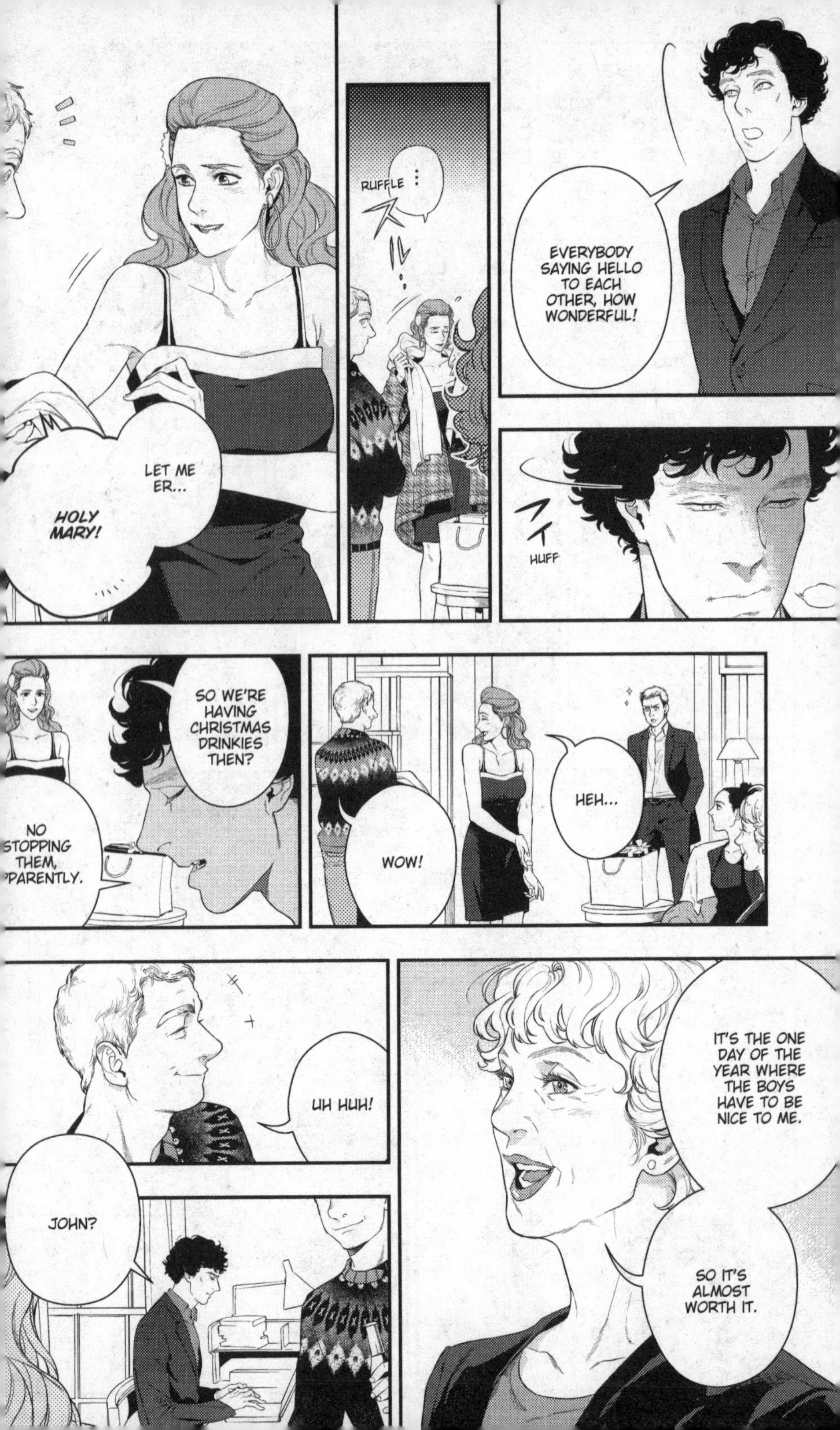
EVERYBODY SAYING HELLO TO EACH OTHER, HOW WONDERFUL!
HUFF
RUFFLE
LET ME ER...
HOLY MARY!
HEH...
WOW!
SO WE'RE HAVING CHRISTMAS DRINKIES THEN?
NO STOPPING THEM, PPARENTLY.
IT'S THE ONE DAY OF THE YEAR WHERE THE BOYS HAVE TO BE NICE TO ME.
SO IT'S ALMOST WORTH IT.
UH HUH!
JOHN?

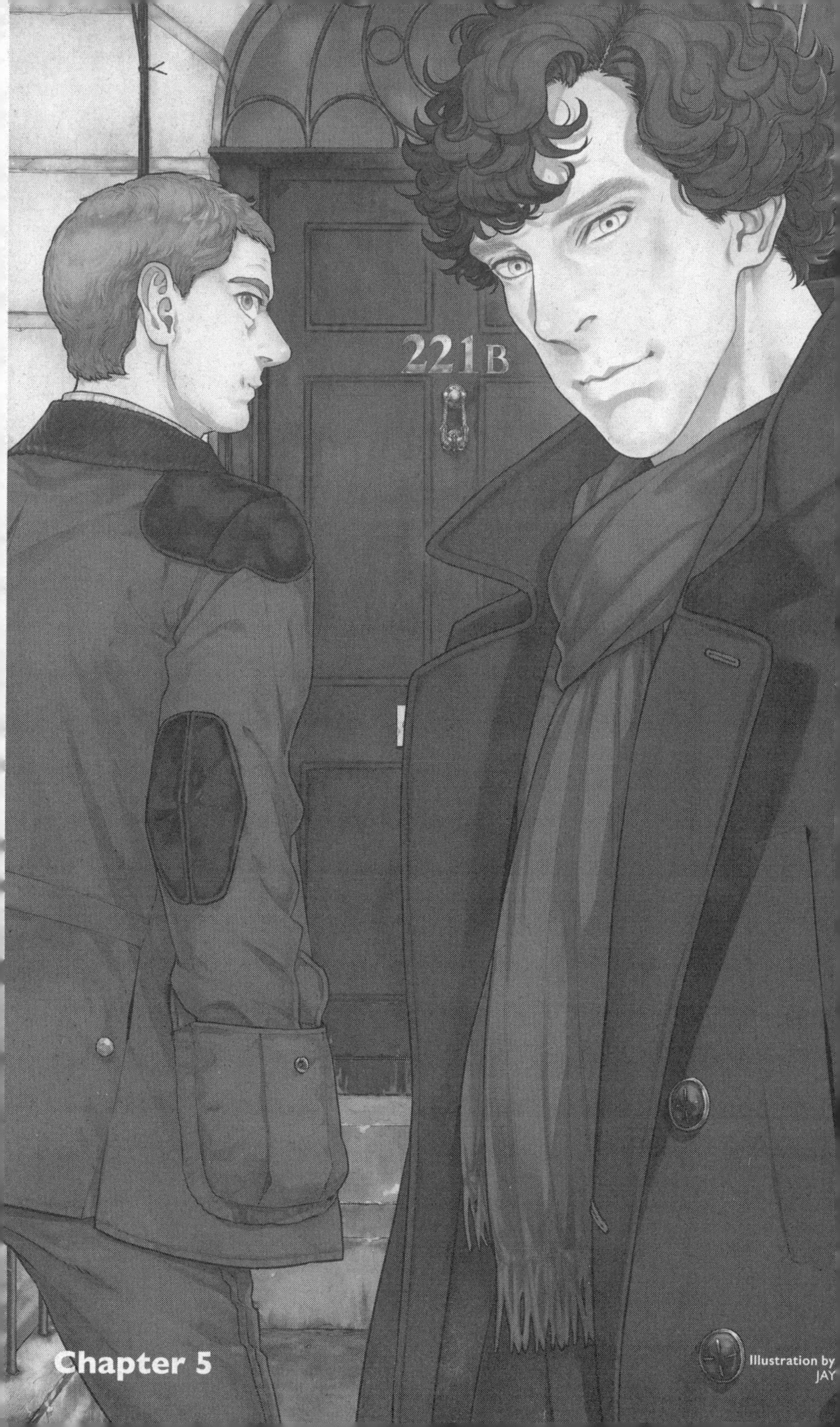
221B

Chapter 5

Illustration by
JAY

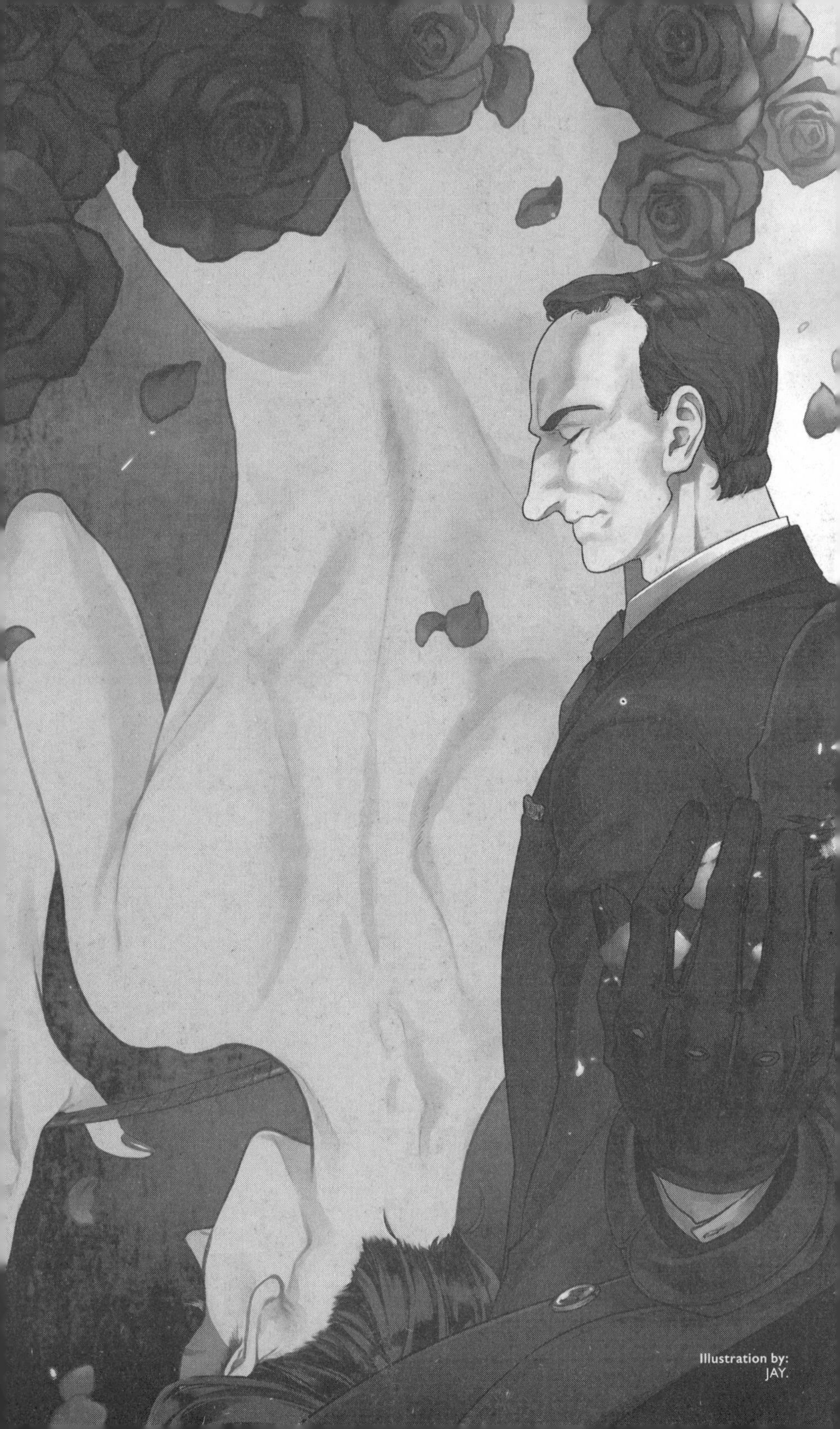

Illustration by:
JAY.

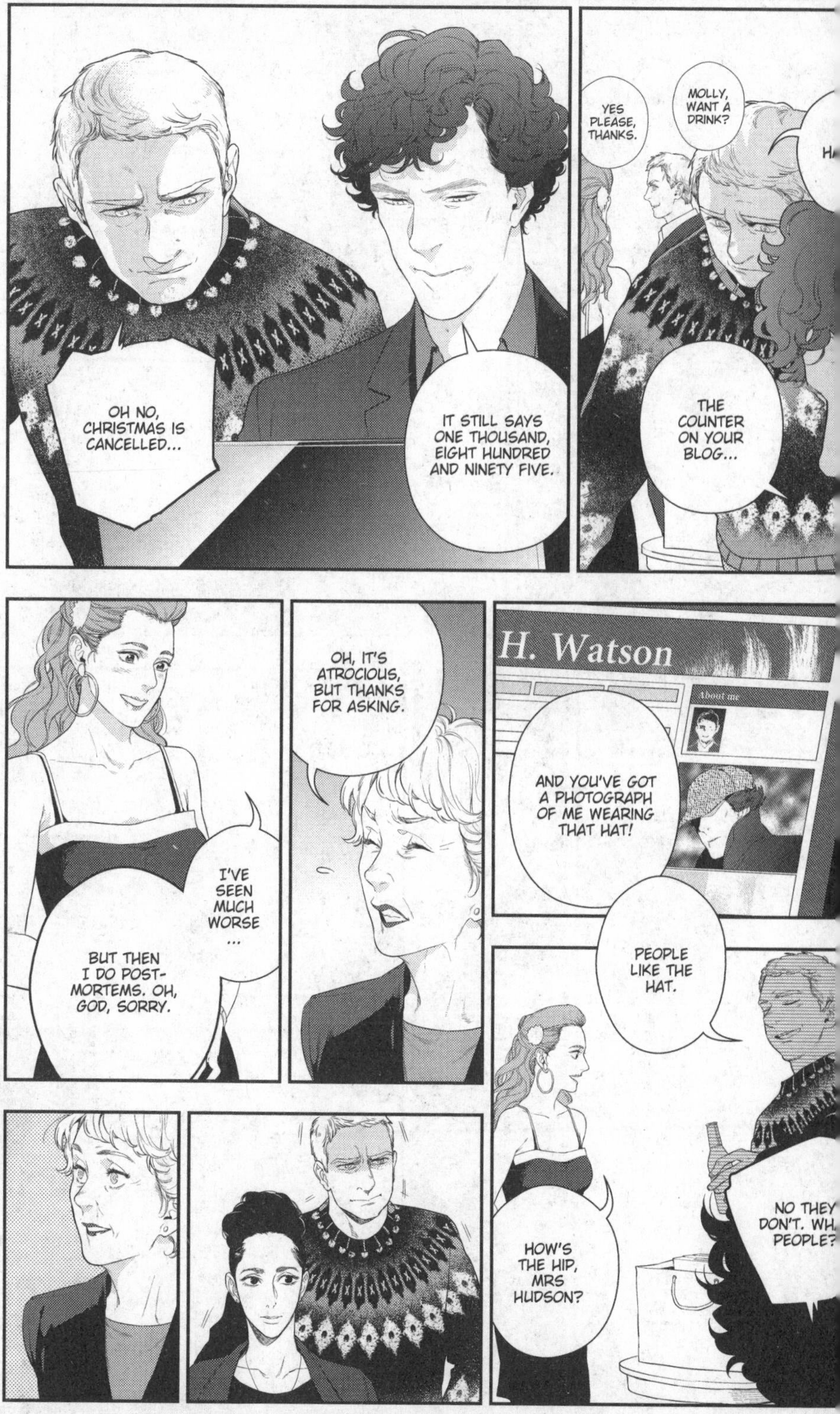
MOLLY, WANT A DRINK?
YES PLEASE, THANKS.
THE COUNTER ON YOUR BLOG...
IT STILL SAYS ONE THOUSAND, EIGHT HUNDRED AND NINETY FIVE.
OH NO, CHRISTMAS IS CANCELLED...
H. Watson
About me
AND YOU'VE GOT A PHOTOGRAPH OF ME WEARING THAT HAT!
PEOPLE LIKE THE HAT.
NO THEY DON'T. WH
PEOPLE?
HOW'S THE HIP, MRS HUDSON?
OH, IT'S ATROCIOUS, BUT THANKS FOR ASKING.
I'VE SEEN MUCH WORSE ...
BUT THEN I DO POST-MORTEMS. OH, GOD, SORRY.

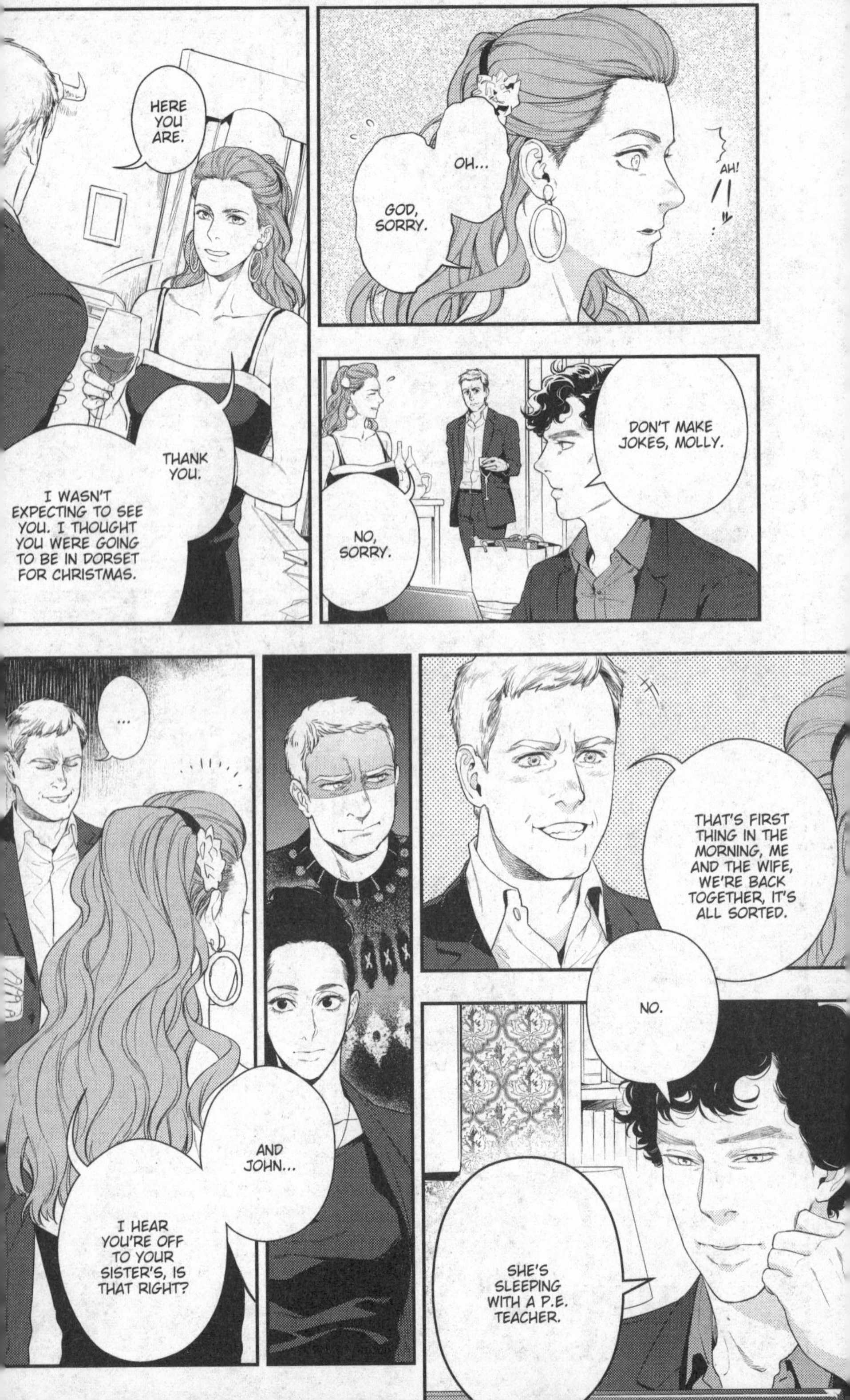
AH!
OH...
GOD, SORRY.
DON'T MAKE JOKES, MOLLY.
NO, SORRY.
HERE YOU ARE.
THANK YOU.
I WASN'T EXPECTING TO SEE YOU. I THOUGHT YOU WERE GOING TO BE IN DORSET FOR CHRISTMAS.
THAT'S FIRST THING IN THE MORNING, ME AND THE WIFE, WE'RE BACK TOGETHER, IT'S ALL SORTED.
NO.
SHE'S SLEEPING WITH A P.E. TEACHER.
...
AND JOHN...
I HEAR YOU'RE OFF TO YOUR SISTER'S, IS THAT RIGHT?

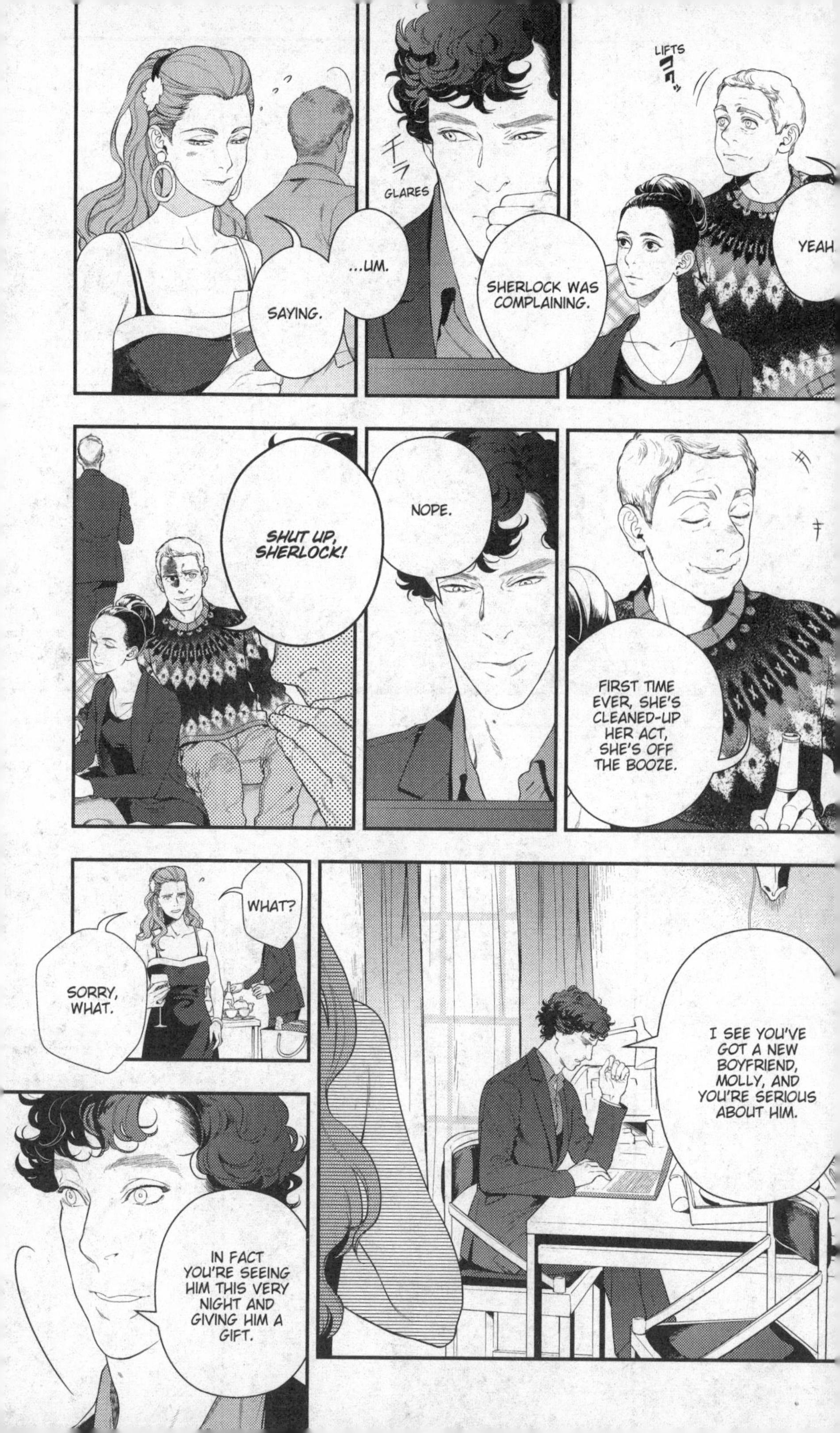
LIFTS
YEAH
SHERLOCK WAS COMPLAINING.
チラ
GLARES
...UM.
SAYING.
FIRST TIME EVER, SHE'S CLEANED-UP HER ACT, SHE'S OFF THE BOOZE.
NOPE.
SHUT UP, SHERLOCK!
I SEE YOU'VE GOT A NEW BOYFRIEND, MOLLY, AND YOU'RE SERIOUS ABOUT HIM.
WHAT?
SORRY, WHAT.
IN FACT YOU'RE SEEING HIM THIS VERY NIGHT AND GIVING HIM A GIFT.

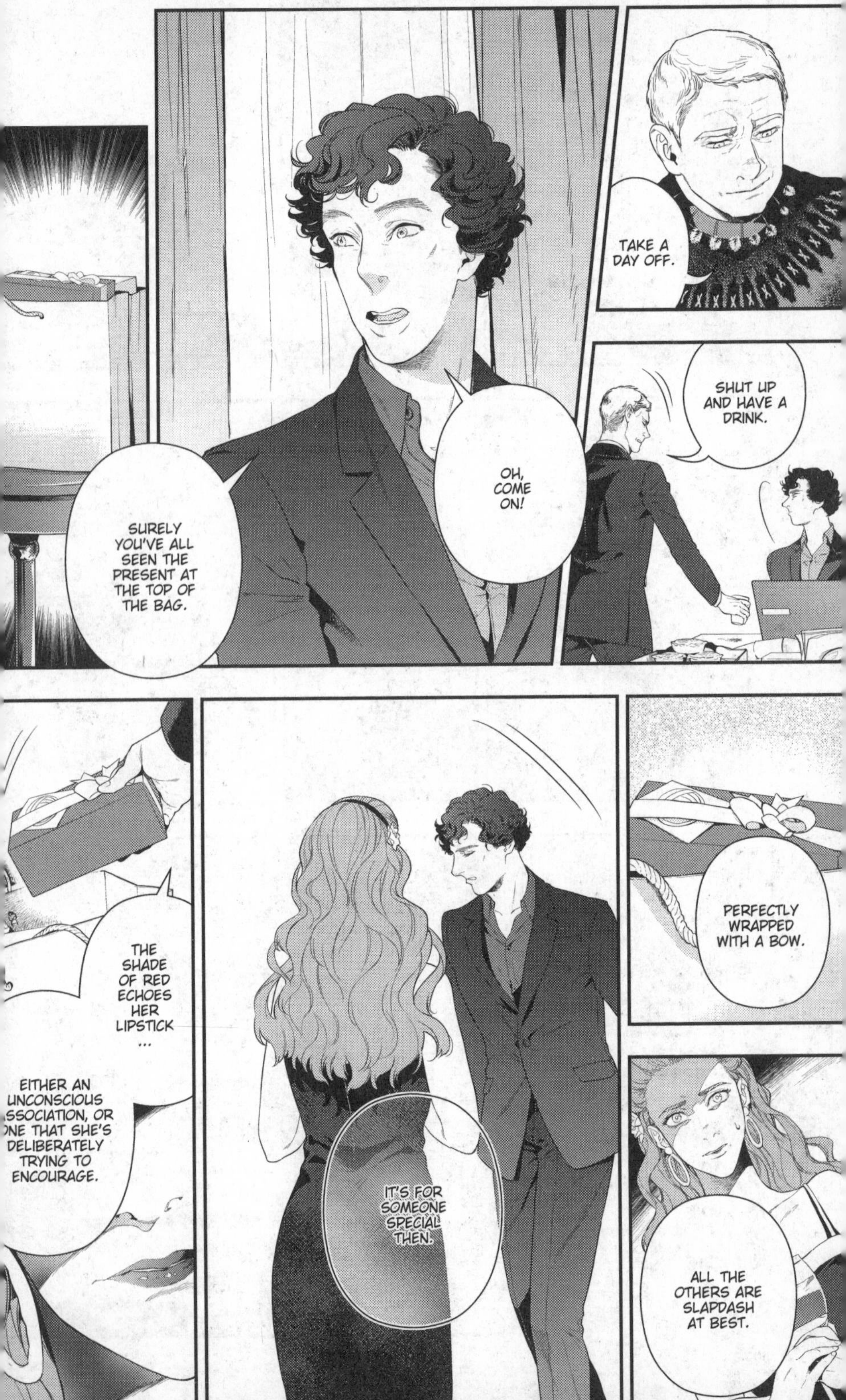
TAKE A DAY OFF.
SHUT UP AND HAVE A DRINK.
OH, COME ON!
SURELY YOU'VE ALL SEEN THE PRESENT AT THE TOP OF THE BAG.
PERFECTLY WRAPPED WITH A BOW.
ALL THE OTHERS ARE SLAPDASH AT BEST.
IT'S FOR SOMEONE SPECIAL THEN.
THE SHADE OF RED ECHOES HER LIPSTICK ...
EITHER AN UNCONSCIOUS ASSOCIATION, OR ONE THAT SHE'S DELIBERATELY TRYING TO ENCOURAGE.

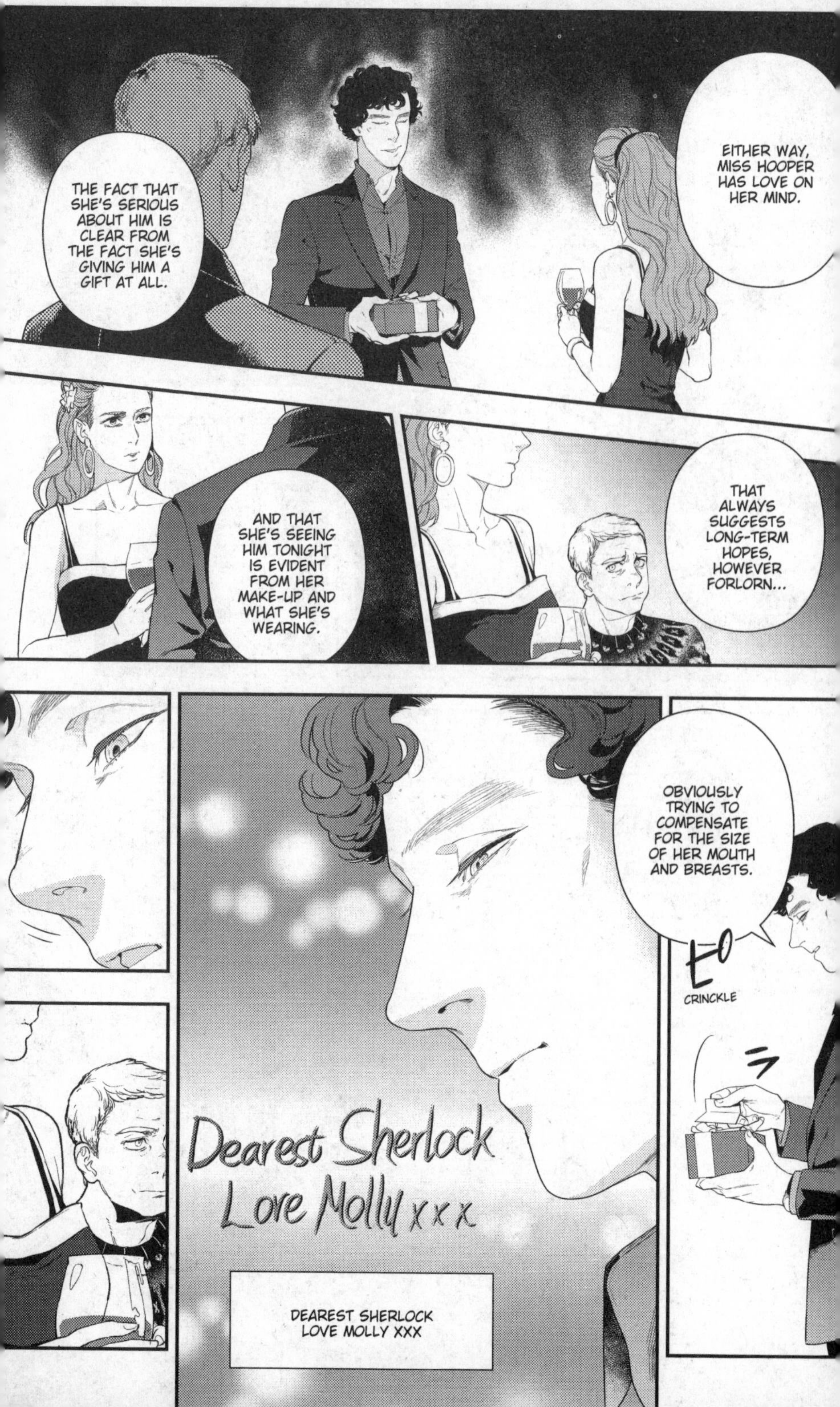
EITHER WAY, MISS HOOPER HAS LOVE ON HER MIND.
THE FACT THAT SHE'S SERIOUS ABOUT HIM IS CLEAR FROM THE FACT SHE'S GIVING HIM A GIFT AT ALL.
THAT ALWAYS SUGGESTS LONG-TERM HOPES, HOWEVER FORLORN...
AND THAT SHE'S SEEING HIM TONIGHT IS EVIDENT FROM HER MAKE-UP AND WHAT SHE'S WEARING.
OBVIOUSLY TRYING TO COMPENSATE FOR THE SIZE OF HER MOUTH AND BREASTS.
CRINKLE
Dearest Sherlock
Love Molly xxx
DEAREST SHERLOCK
LOVE MOLLY XXX

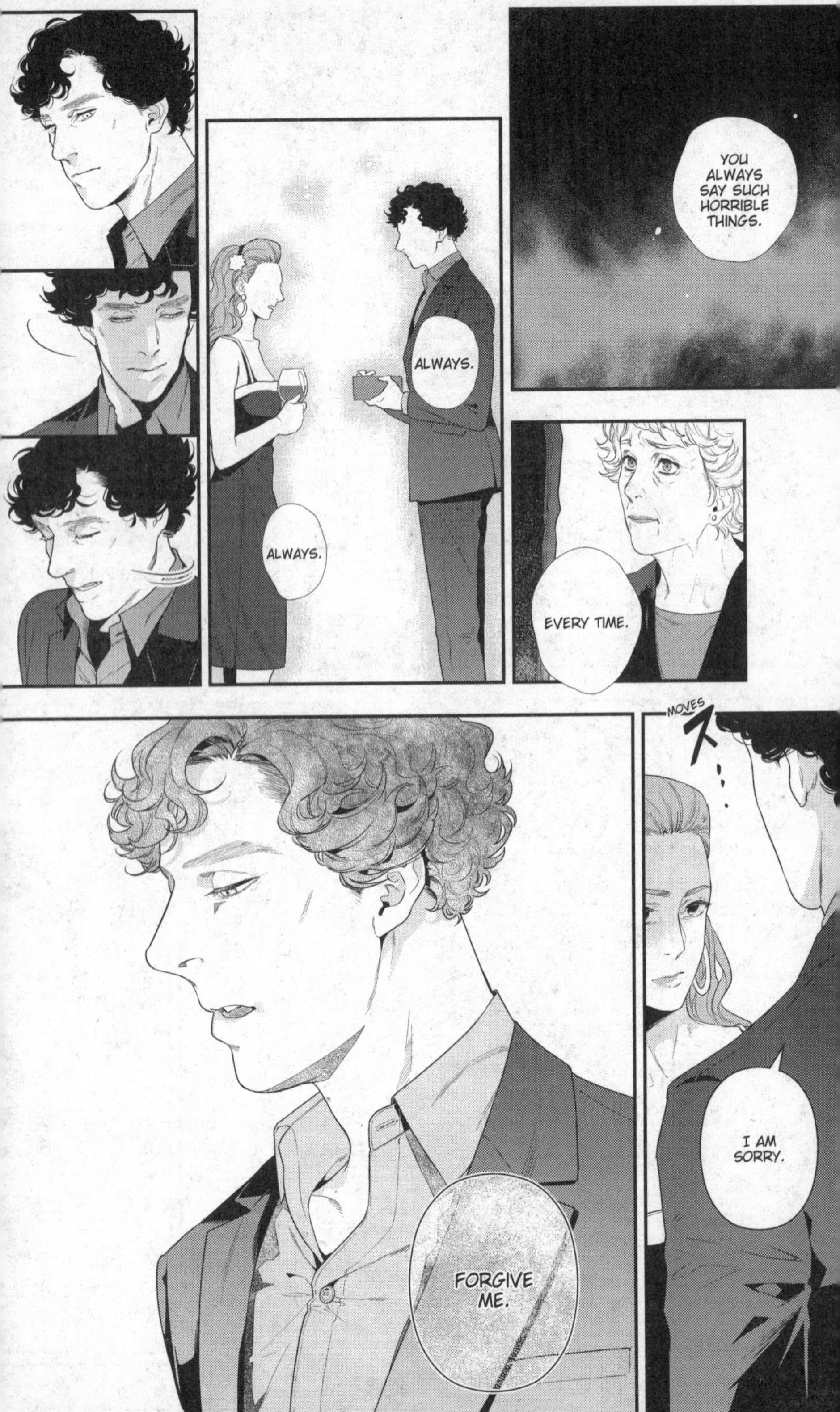
YOU ALWAYS SAY SUCH HORRIBLE THINGS.
EVERY TIME.
ALWAYS.
ALWAYS.
MOVES
I AM SORRY.
FORGIVE ME.

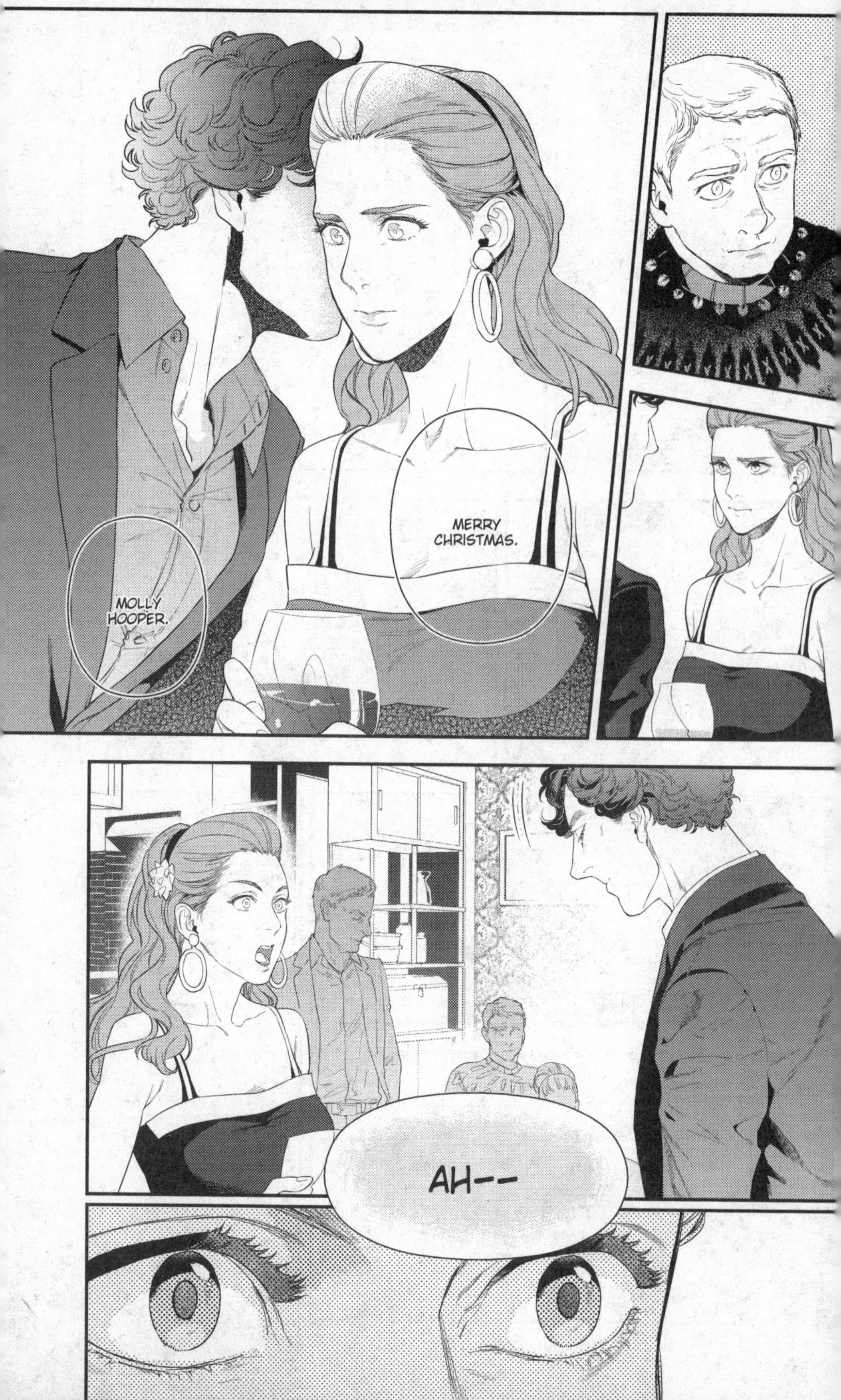
MERRY CHRISTMAS.
MOLLY HOOPER.
AH--

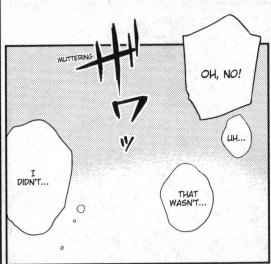

OH, NO!

UH...

MUTTERING

I DIDN'T...

THAT WASN'T...

NO, IT WAS ME.

MY PHONE.

FWISH

MY GOD, REALLY?

WHAT?

FIFTY SEVEN OF THOSE TEXTS, THE ONES I'VE HEARD.

SORRY, WHAT?

MANTLEPIECE

BEEP

FIFTY SEVEN?

THRILLING THAT YOU'VE BEEN COUNTING.

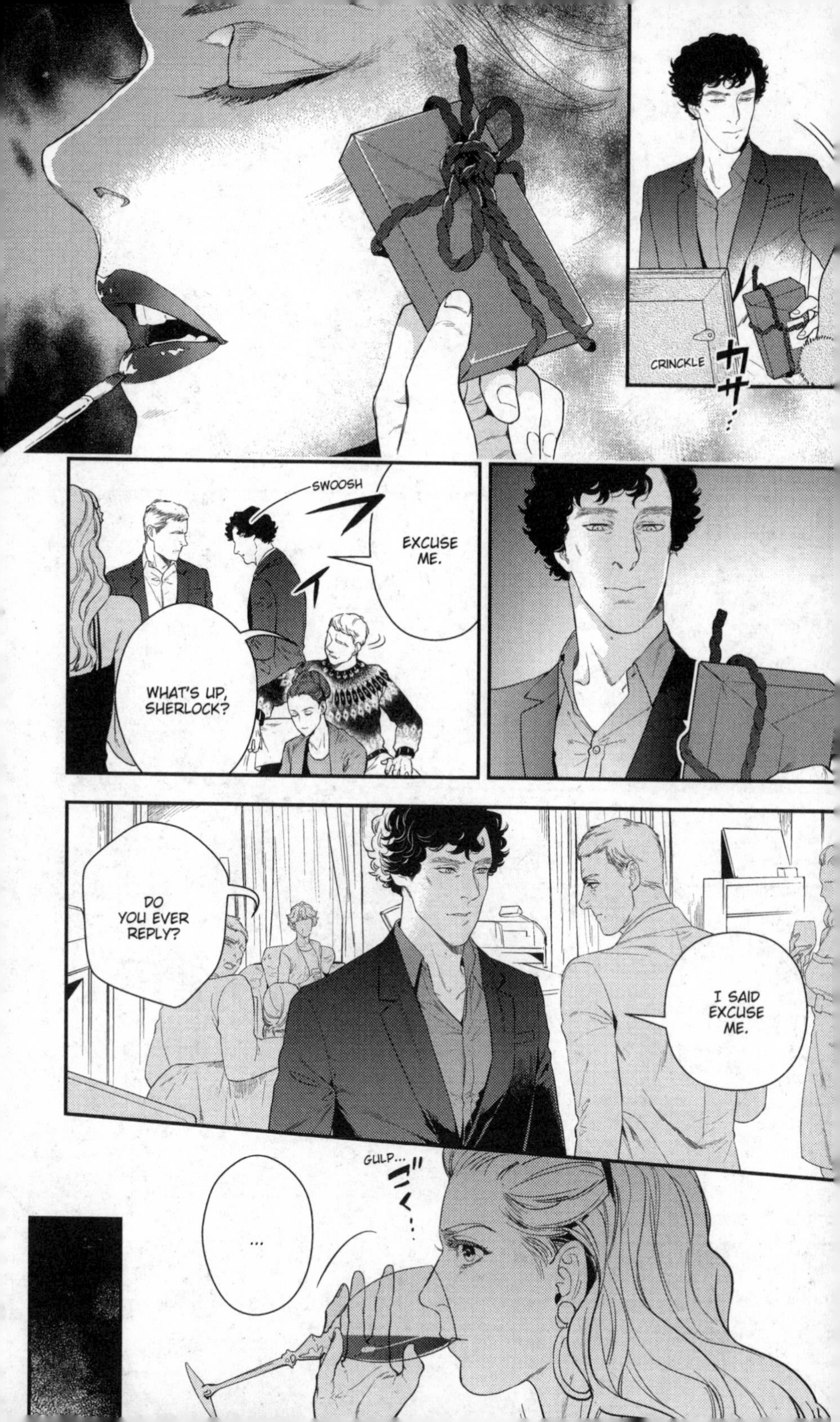
CRINKLE
カサ…
SWOOSH
EXCUSE ME.
WHAT'S UP, SHERLOCK?
DO YOU EVER REPLY?
I SAID EXCUSE ME.
GULP...
ゴク…
...

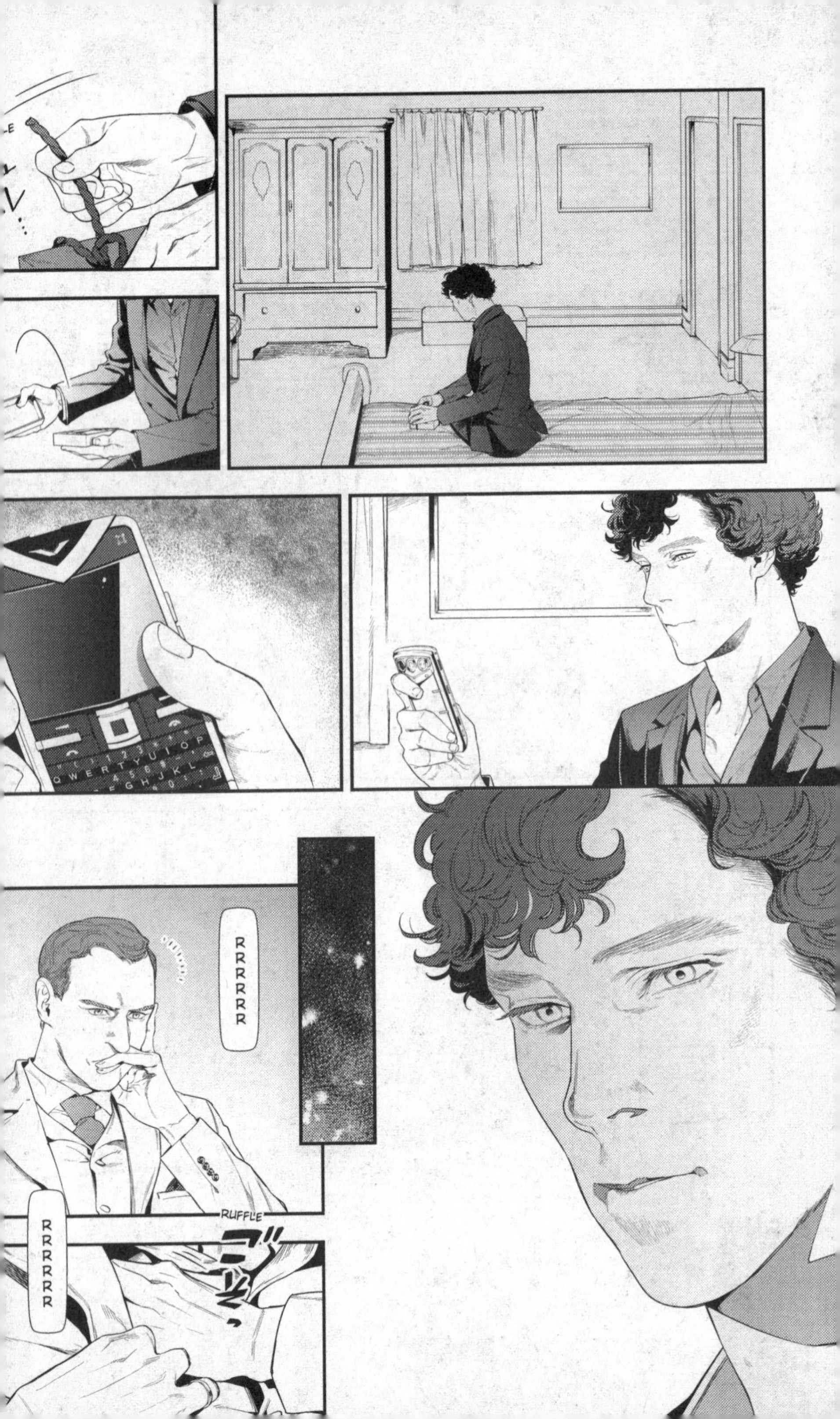
RRRRRR
RUFFLE
RRRRRR

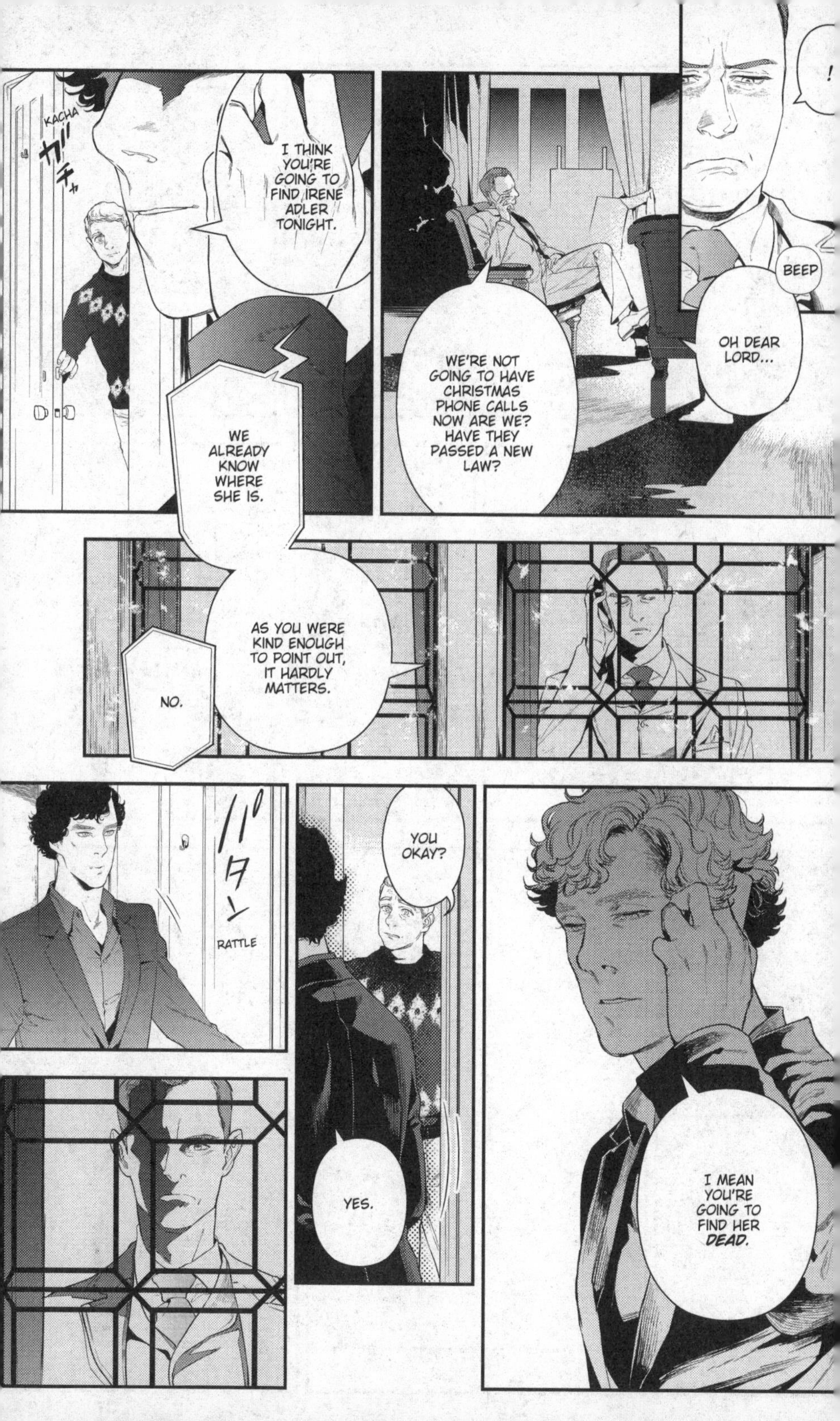
!
BEEP
OH DEAR LORD...
WE'RE NOT GOING TO HAVE CHRISTMAS PHONE CALLS NOW ARE WE? HAVE THEY PASSED A NEW LAW?
KACHA
ガチャ
I THINK YOU'RE GOING TO FIND IRENE ADLER TONIGHT.
WE ALREADY KNOW WHERE SHE IS.
AS YOU WERE KIND ENOUGH TO POINT OUT, IT HARDLY MATTERS.
NO.
I MEAN YOU'RE GOING TO FIND HER *DEAD.*
YOU OKAY?
YES.
パタン
RATTLE

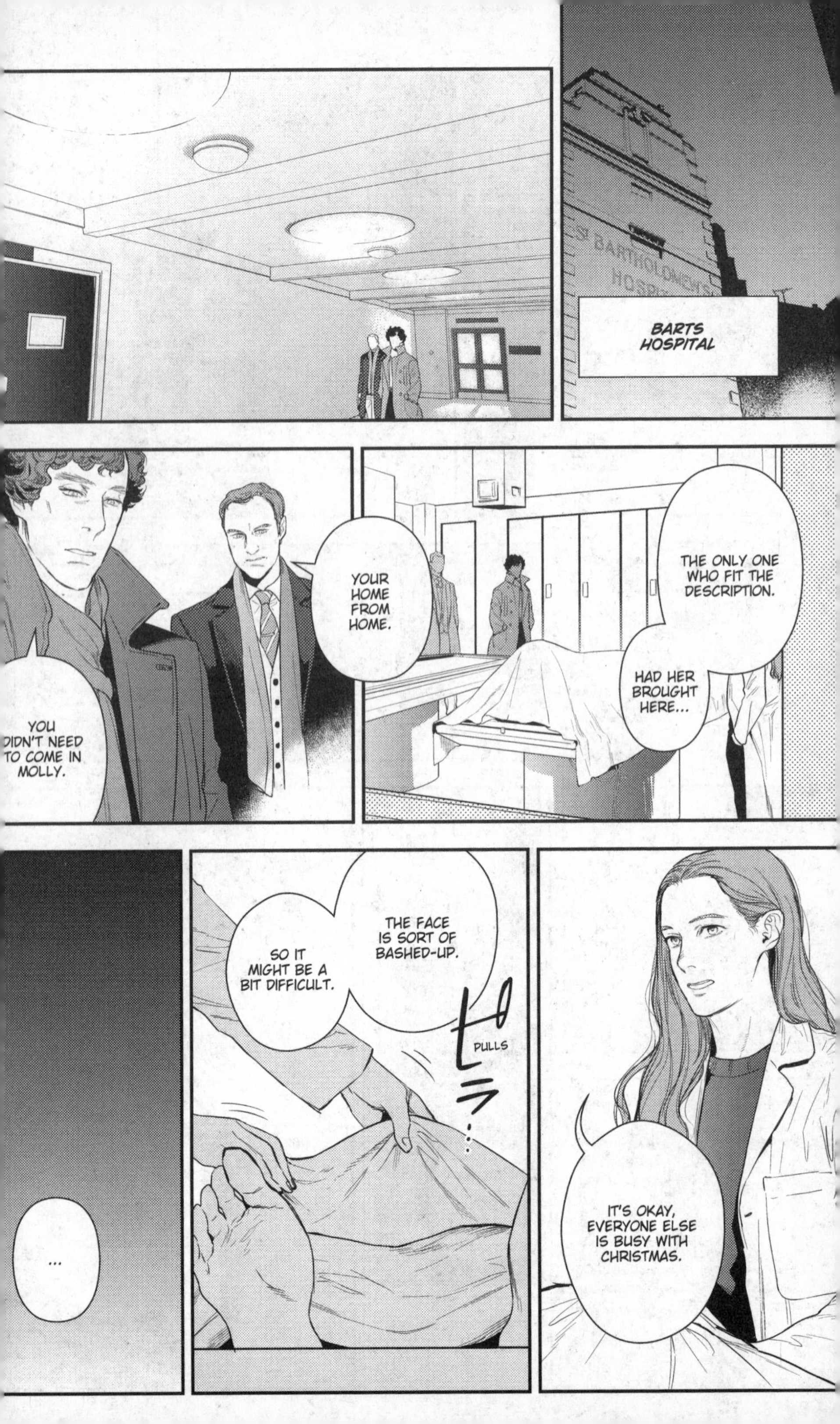
BARTS HOSPITAL
THE ONLY ONE WHO FIT THE DESCRIPTION.
HAD HER BROUGHT HERE...
YOUR HOME FROM HOME.
YOU DIDN'T NEED TO COME IN MOLLY.
IT'S OKAY, EVERYONE ELSE IS BUSY WITH CHRISTMAS.
THE FACE IS SORT OF BASHED-UP.
SO IT MIGHT BE A BIT DIFFICULT.
PULLS
...

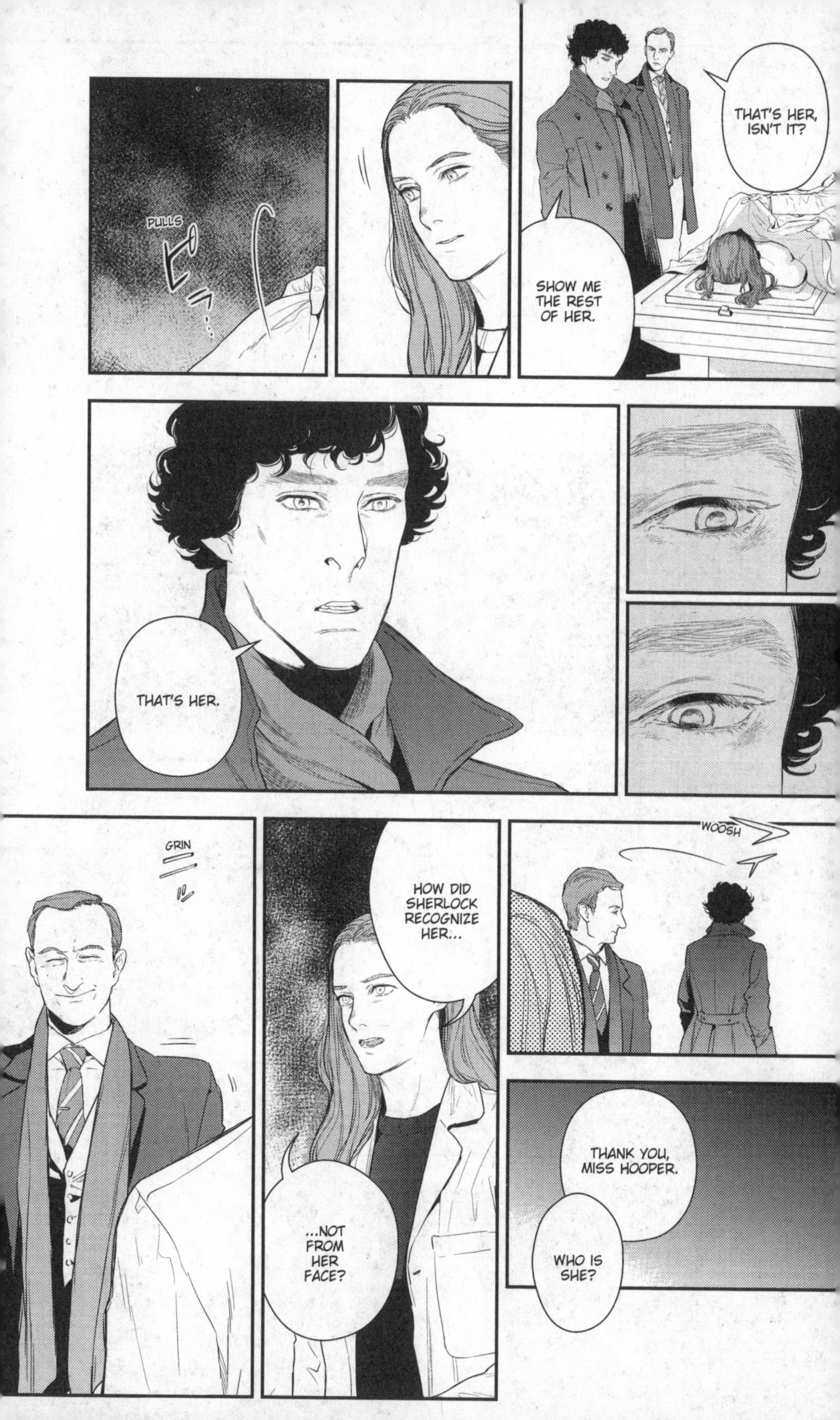
THAT'S HER, ISN'T IT?
SHOW ME THE REST OF HER.
PULLS
THAT'S HER.
WOOSH
THANK YOU, MISS HOOPER.
WHO IS SHE?
HOW DID SHERLOCK RECOGNIZE HER...
...NOT FROM HER FACE?
GRIN

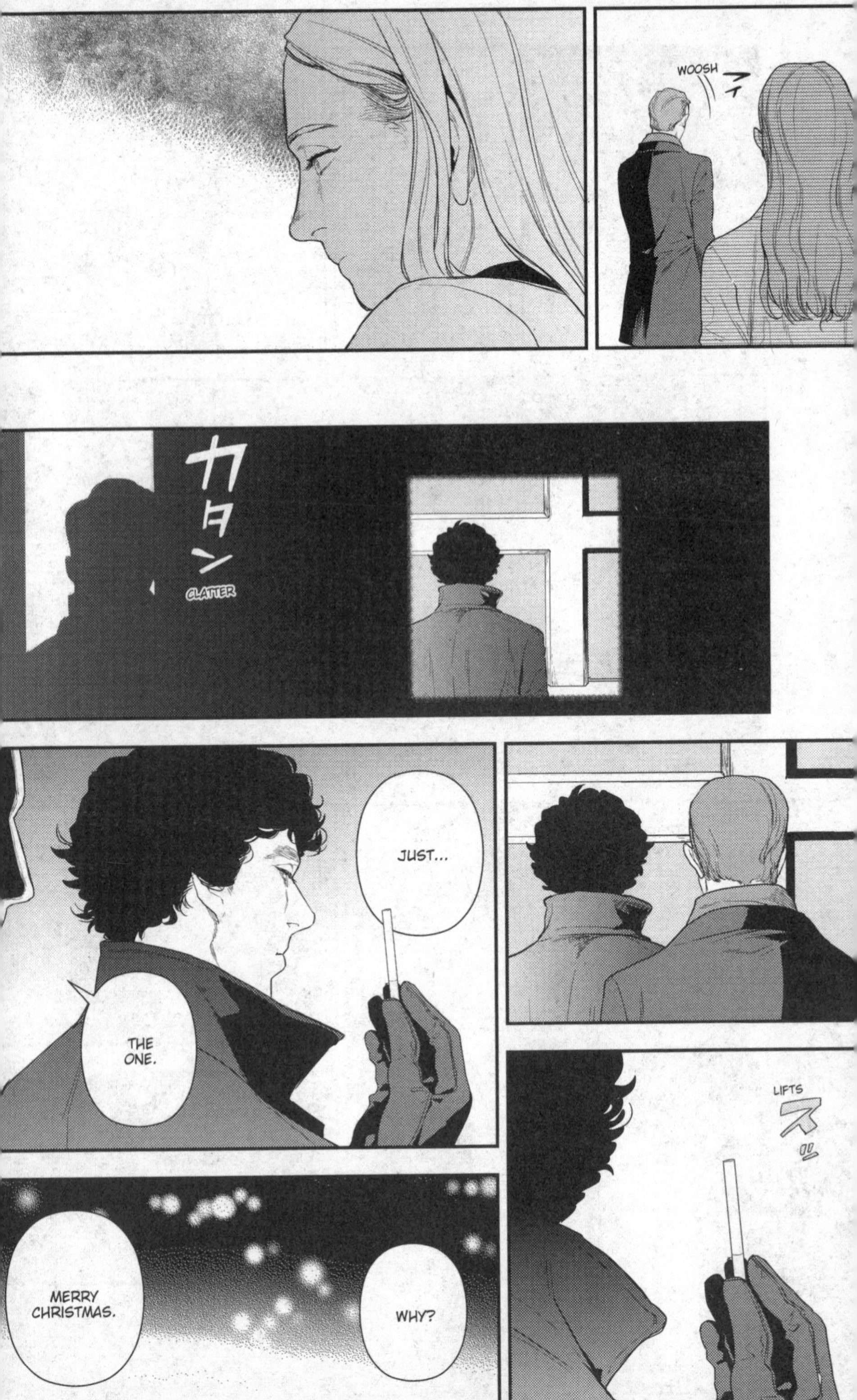
WOOSH
カタン
CLATTER
JUST...
THE ONE.
LIFTS
ス
WHY?
MERRY CHRISTMAS.

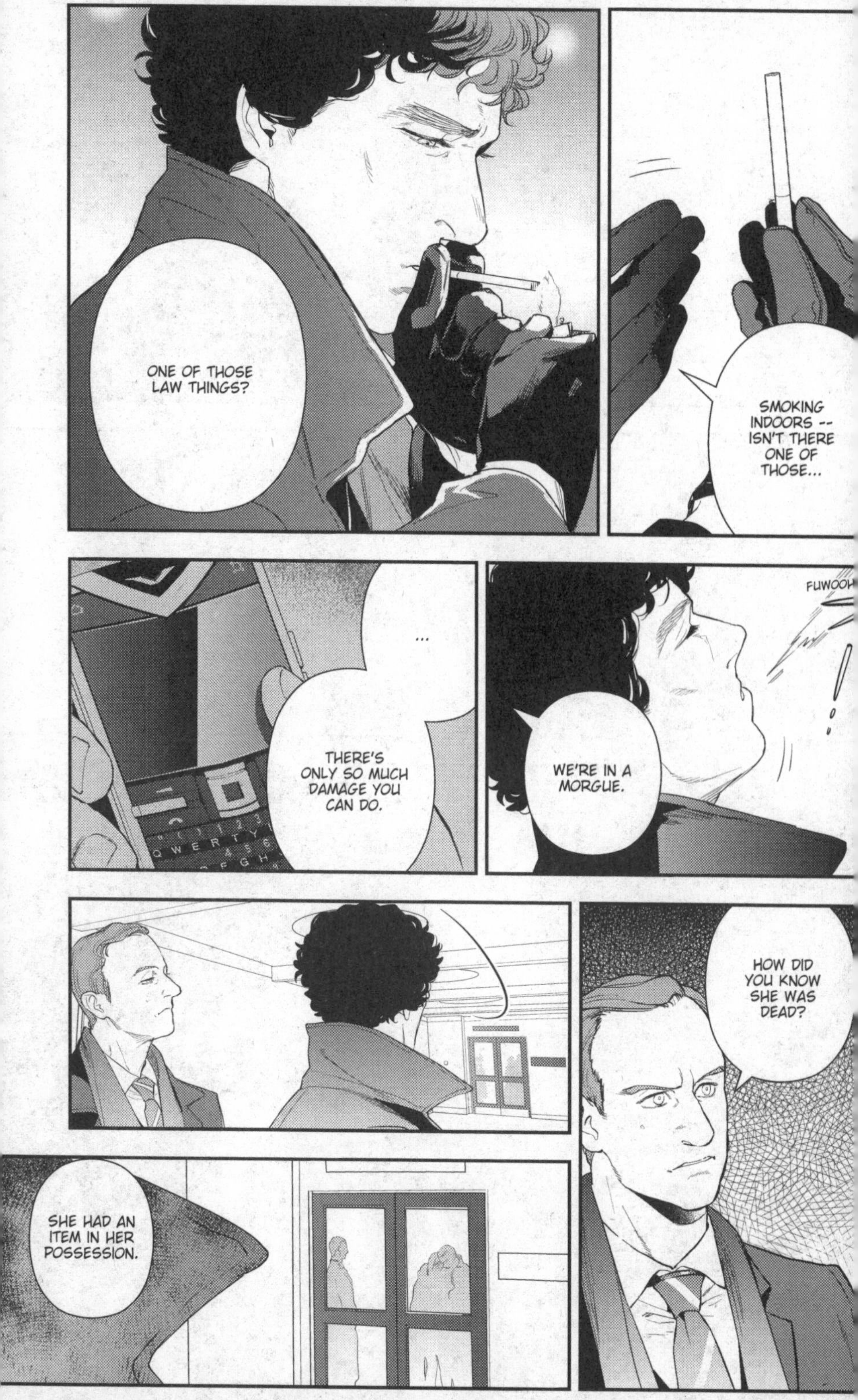
SMOKING INDOORS -- ISN'T THERE ONE OF THOSE...
ONE OF THOSE LAW THINGS?
FUWOOH
WE'RE IN A MORGUE.
...
THERE'S ONLY SO MUCH DAMAGE YOU CAN DO.
HOW DID YOU KNOW SHE WAS DEAD?
SHE HAD AN ITEM IN HER POSSESSION.

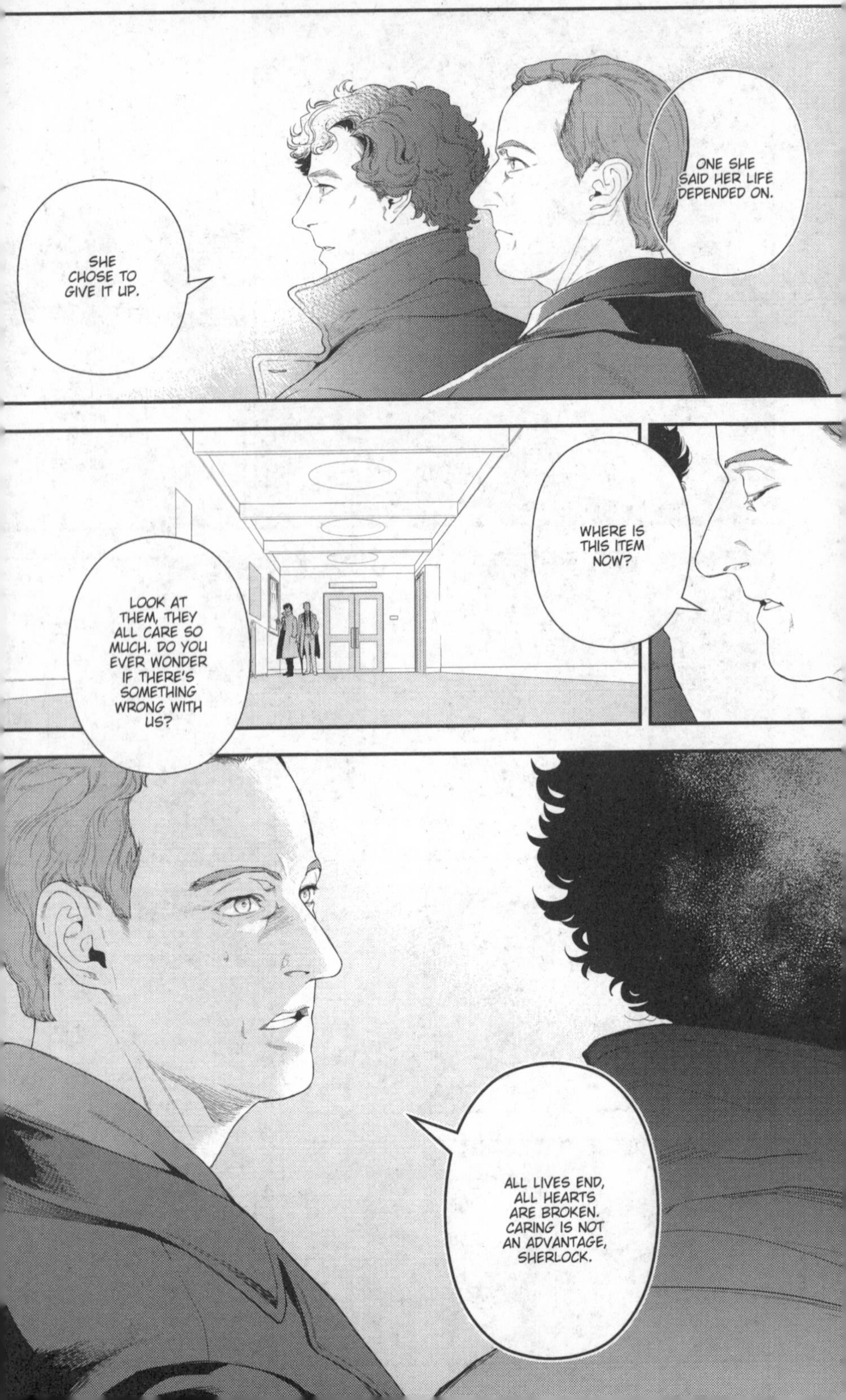
ONE SHE SAID HER LIFE DEPENDED ON.
SHE CHOSE TO GIVE IT UP.
WHERE IS THIS ITEM NOW?
LOOK AT THEM, THEY ALL CARE SO MUCH. DO YOU EVER WONDER IF THERE'S SOMETHING WRONG WITH US?
ALL LIVES END, ALL HEARTS ARE BROKEN. CARING IS NOT AN ADVANTAGE, SHERLOCK.

HUH...

THIS IS LOW TAR.

WELL...

YOU BARELY KNEW HER.

FUU...

MYCROFT.

MERRY CHRISTMAS.

AND A HAPPY NEW YEAR.

TROT

TROT

TROT

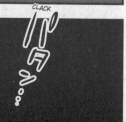

CLACK

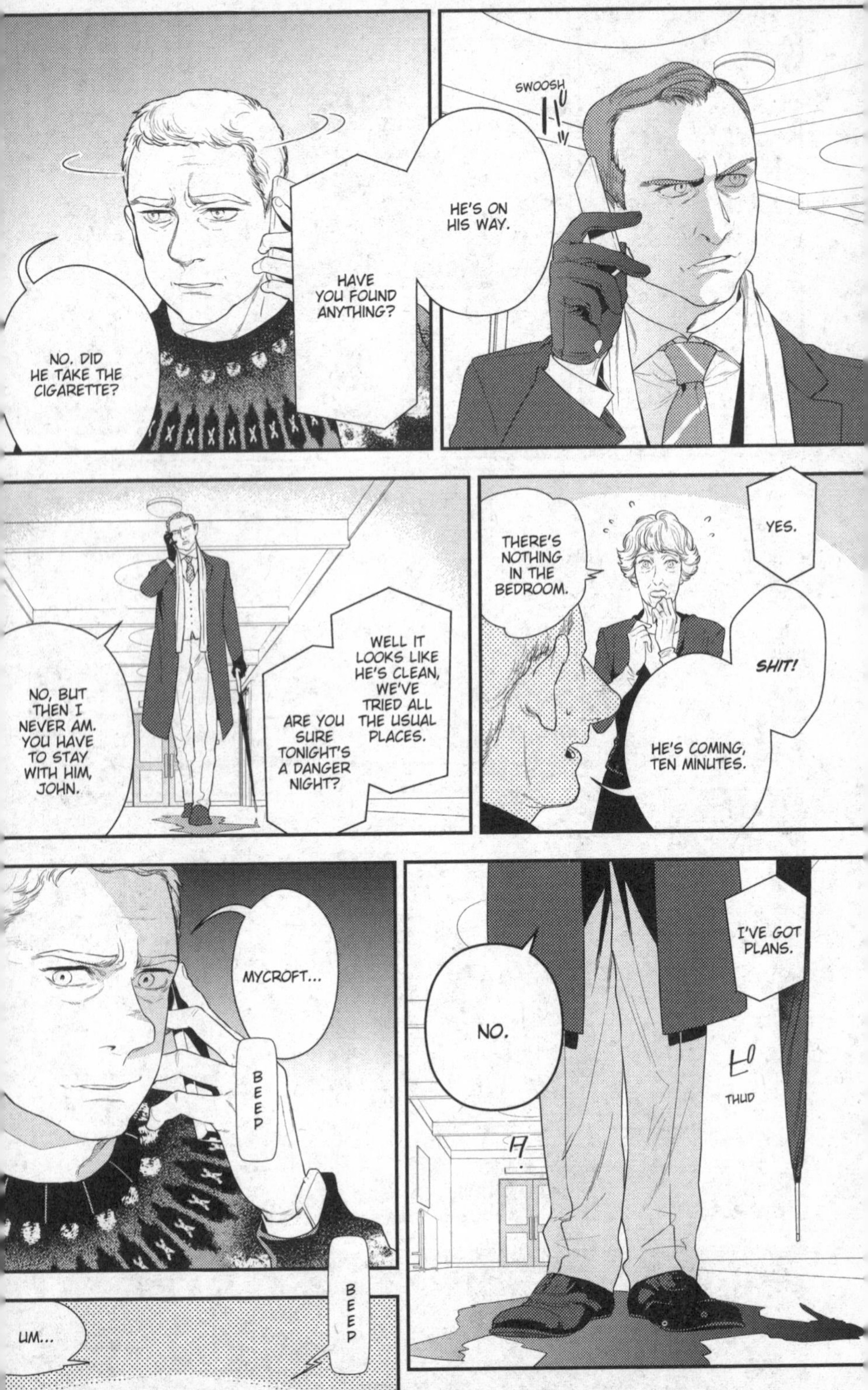
SWOOSH
HE'S ON HIS WAY.
HAVE YOU FOUND ANYTHING?
NO. DID HE TAKE THE CIGARETTE?
YES.
THERE'S NOTHING IN THE BEDROOM.
SHIT!
HE'S COMING, TEN MINUTES.
WELL IT LOOKS LIKE HE'S CLEAN, WE'VE TRIED ALL THE USUAL PLACES.
ARE YOU SURE TONIGHT'S A DANGER NIGHT?
NO, BUT THEN I NEVER AM. YOU HAVE TO STAY WITH HIM, JOHN.
I'VE GOT PLANS.
NO.
THUD
MYCROFT...
BEEP
BEEP
UM...

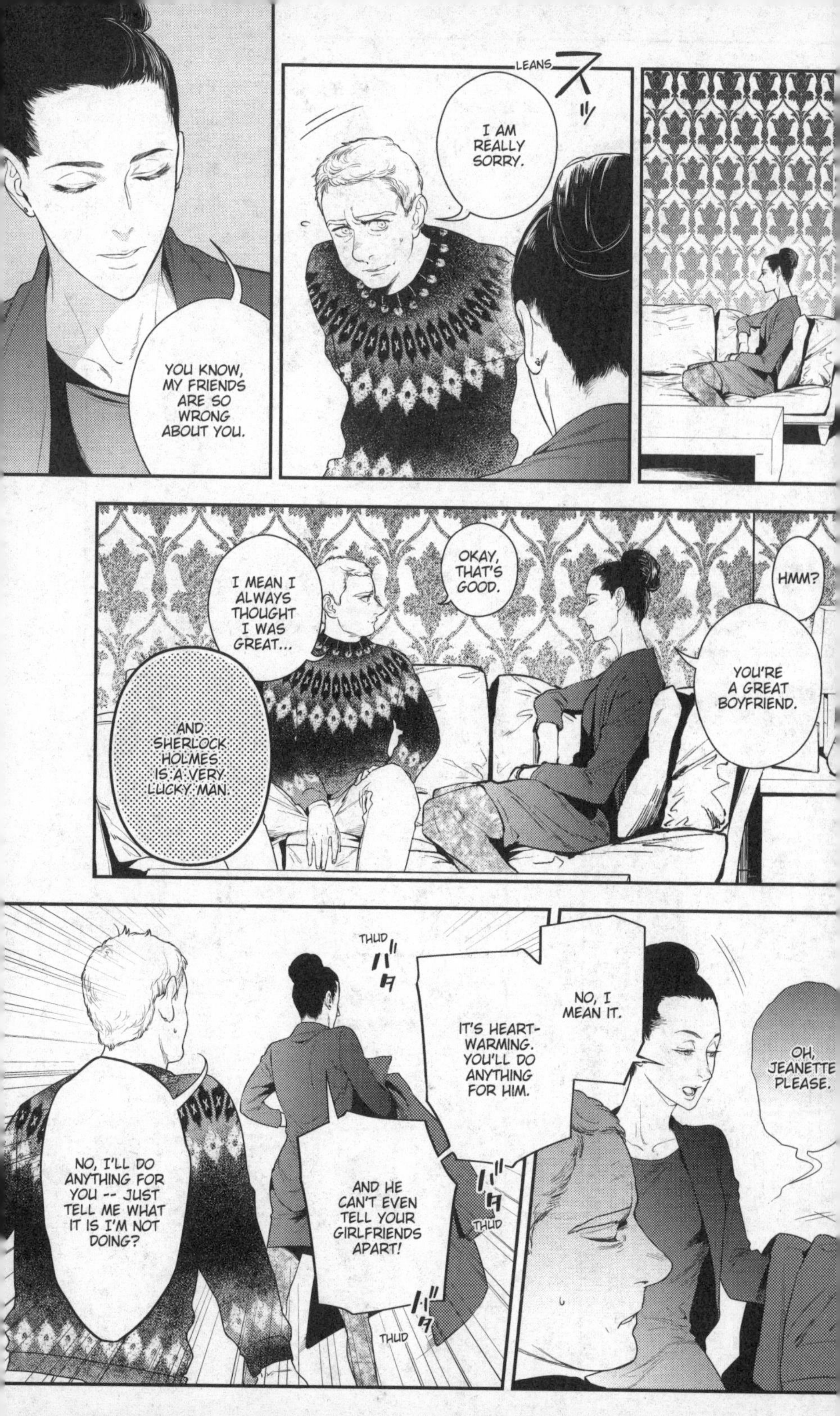
LEANS
I AM REALLY SORRY.
YOU KNOW, MY FRIENDS ARE SO WRONG ABOUT YOU.
HMM?
YOU'RE A GREAT BOYFRIEND.
OKAY, THAT'S GOOD.
I MEAN I ALWAYS THOUGHT I WAS GREAT...
AND SHERLOCK HOLMES IS A VERY LUCKY MAN.
OH, JEANETTE PLEASE.
NO, I MEAN IT.
IT'S HEART-WARMING. YOU'LL DO ANYTHING FOR HIM.
THUD
AND HE CAN'T EVEN TELL YOUR GIRLFRIENDS APART!
THUD
THUD
NO, I'LL DO ANYTHING FOR YOU -- JUST TELL ME WHAT IT IS I'M NOT DOING?

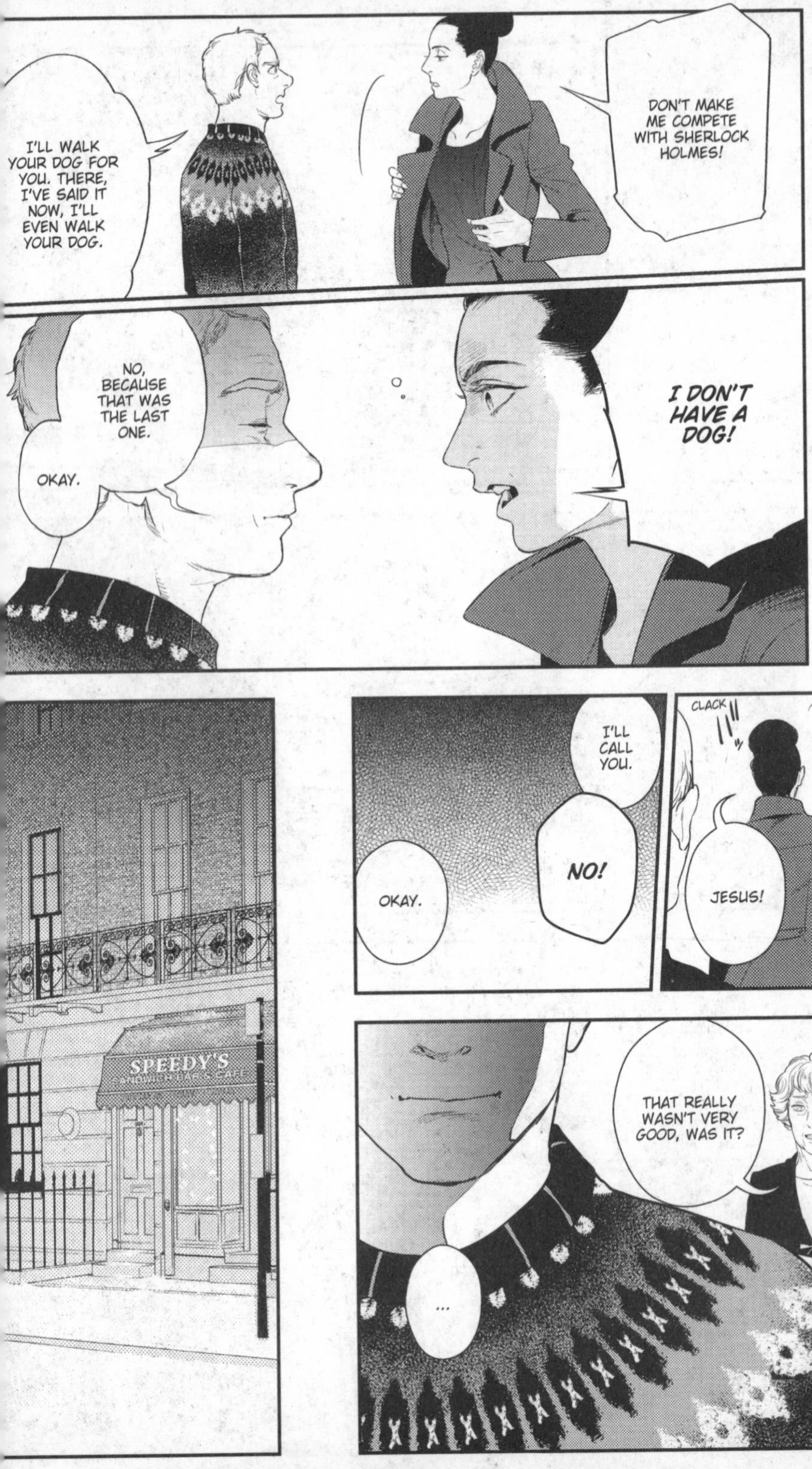
DON'T MAKE ME COMPETE WITH SHERLOCK HOLMES!
I'LL WALK YOUR DOG FOR YOU. THERE, I'VE SAID IT NOW, I'LL EVEN WALK YOUR DOG.
I DON'T HAVE A DOG!
NO, BECAUSE THAT WAS THE LAST ONE.
OKAY.
CLACK
JESUS!
I'LL CALL YOU.
NO!
OKAY.
THAT REALLY WASN'T VERY GOOD, WAS IT?
...
SPEEDY'S
SANDWICH BAR & CAFE

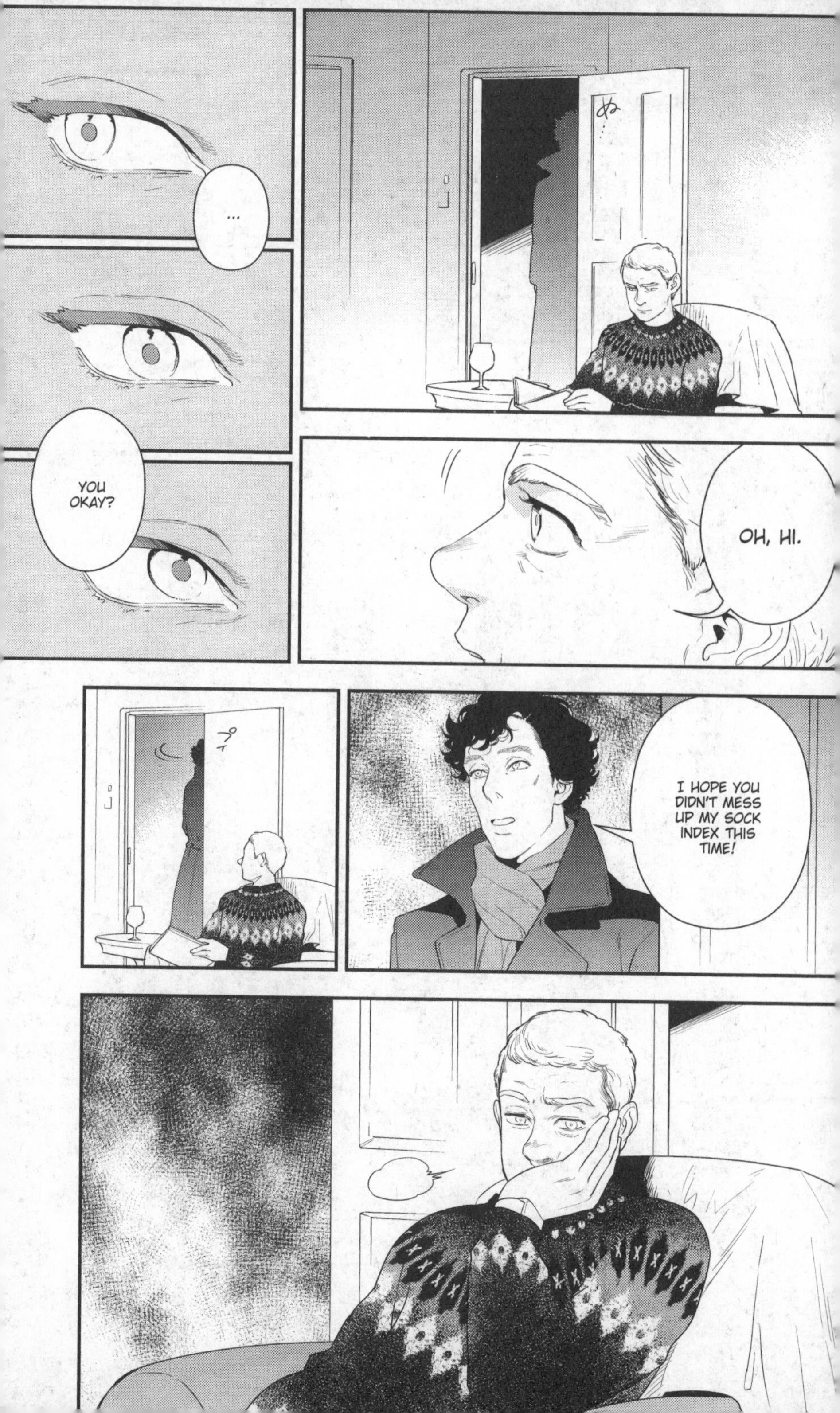

ぬ
...
OH, HI.
YOU OKAY?
I HOPE YOU DIDN'T MESS UP MY SOCK INDEX THIS TIME!

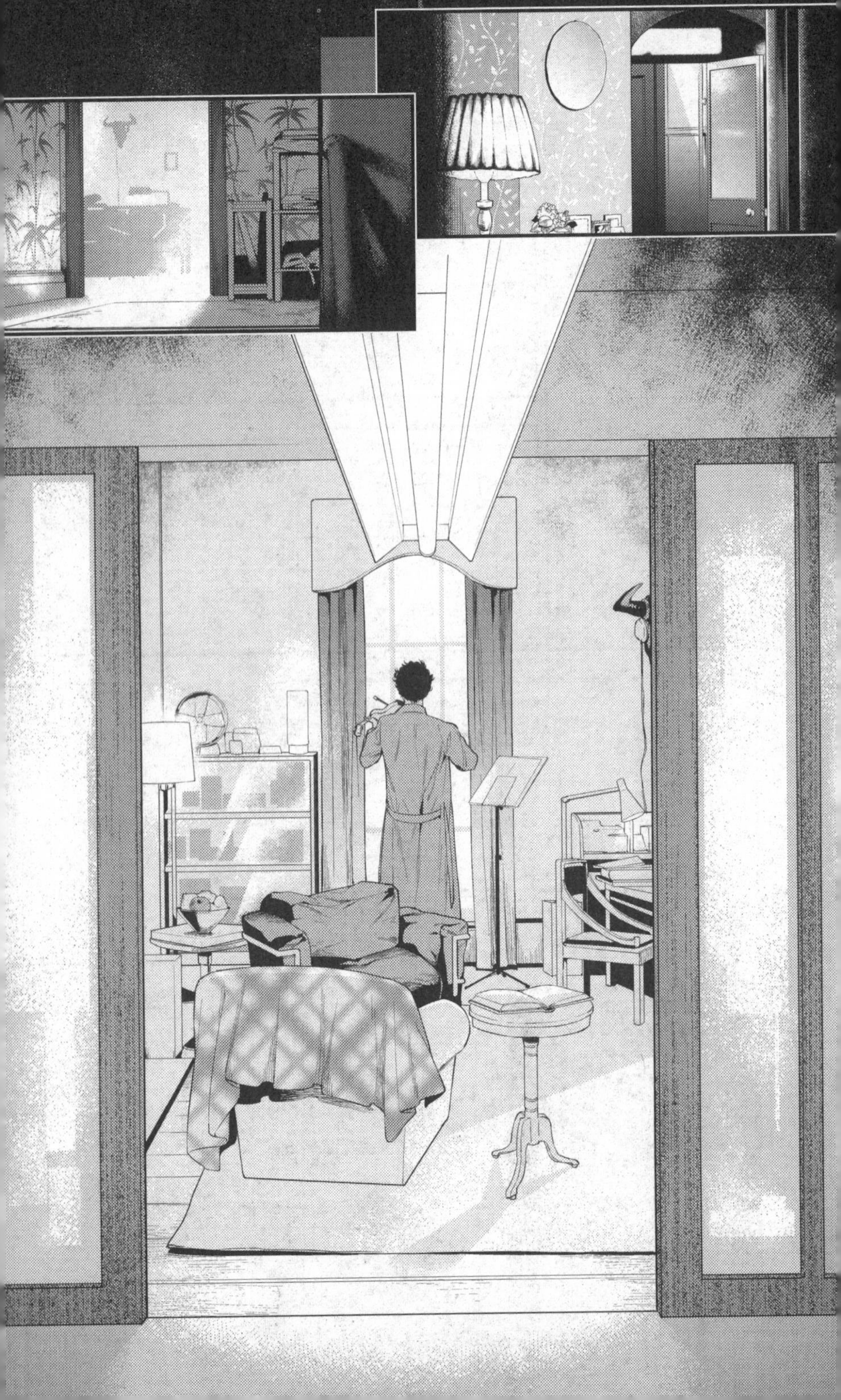

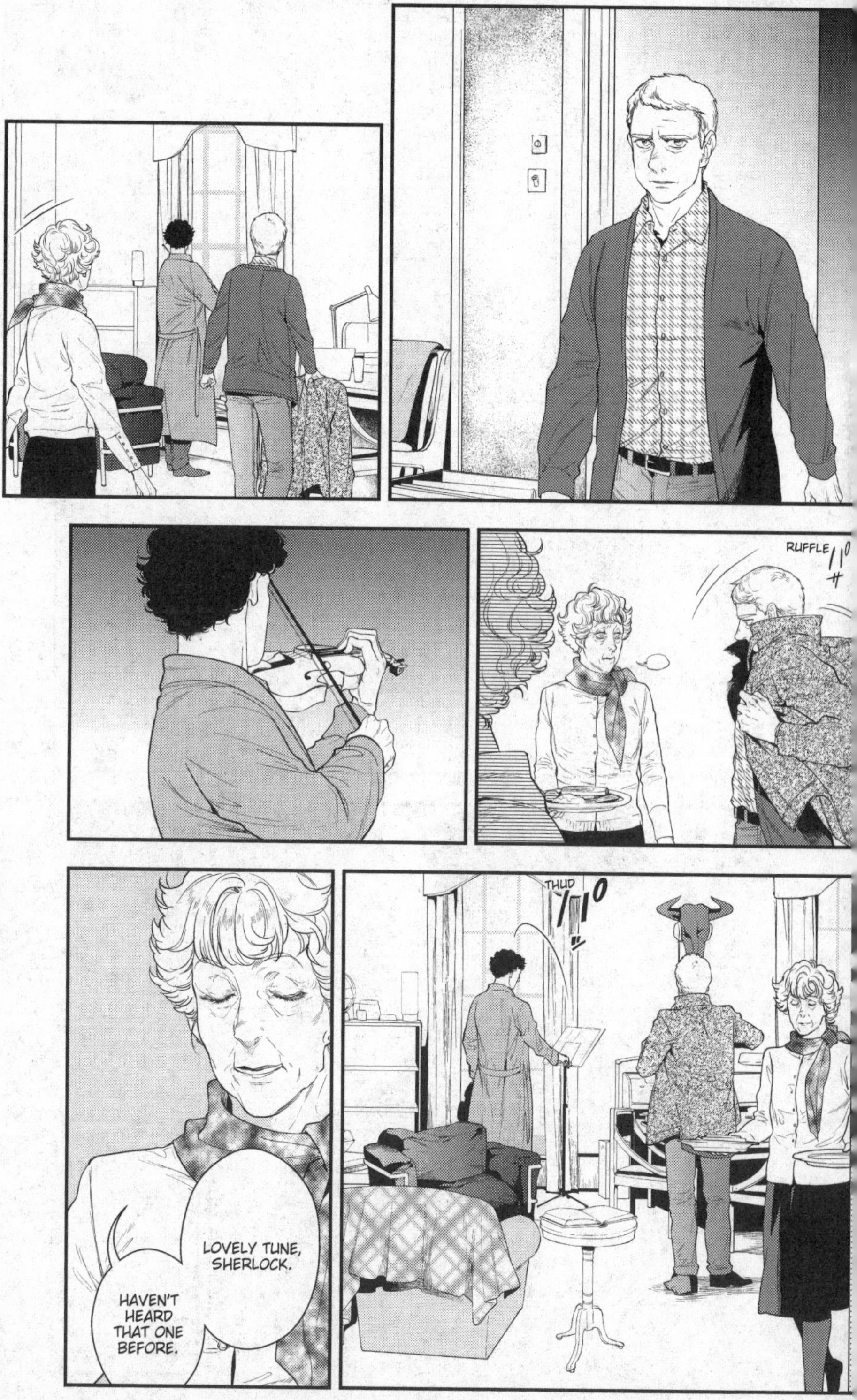
RUFFLE
THUD
LOVELY TUNE, SHERLOCK.
HAVEN'T HEARD THAT ONE BEFORE.

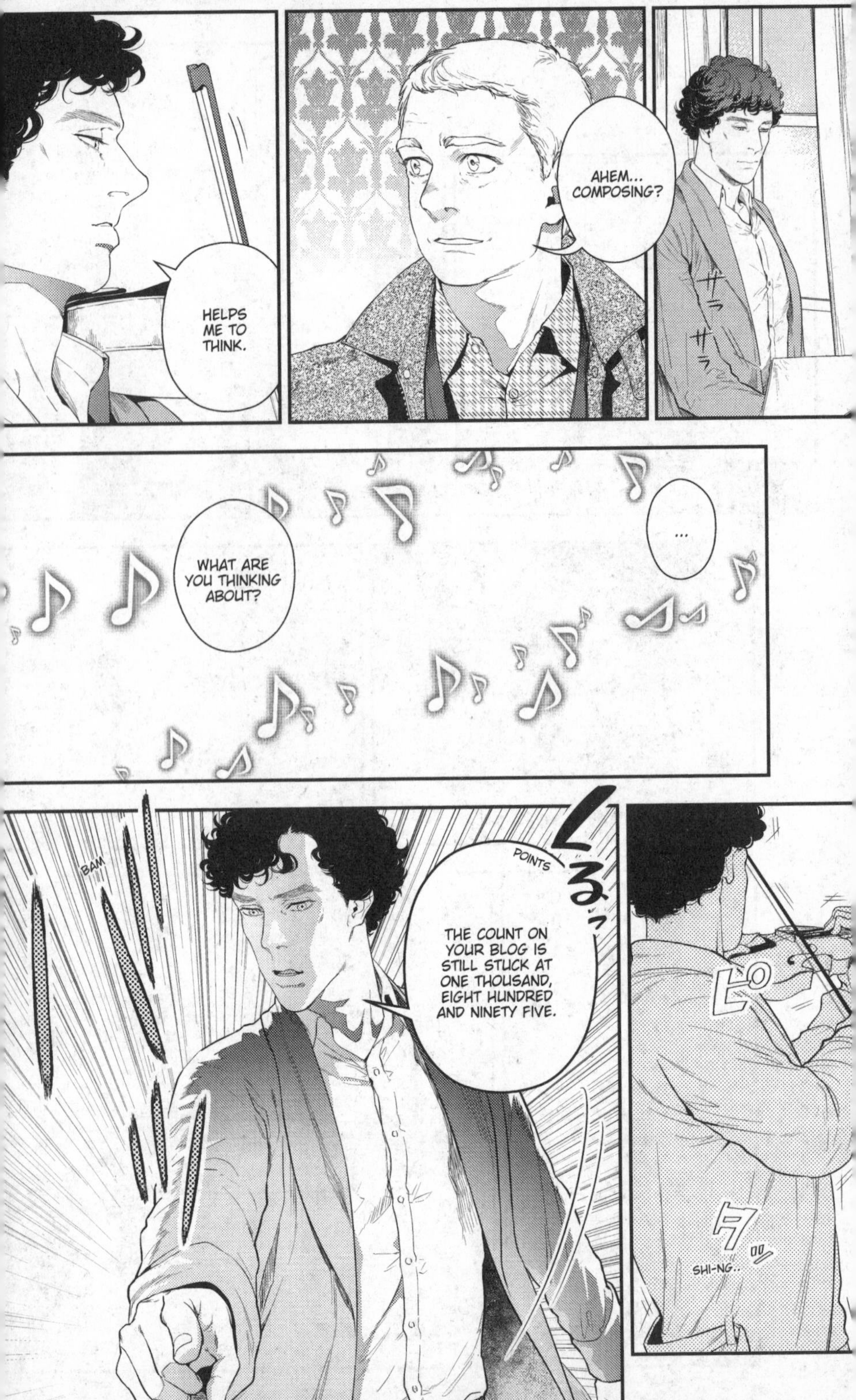
AHEM... COMPOSING?
HELPS ME TO THINK.
...
WHAT ARE YOU THINKING ABOUT?
ピロ
タッ
SHI-NG..
くるっ
POINTS
BAM
THE COUNT ON YOUR BLOG IS STILL STUCK AT ONE THOUSAND, EIGHT HUNDRED AND NINETY FIVE.

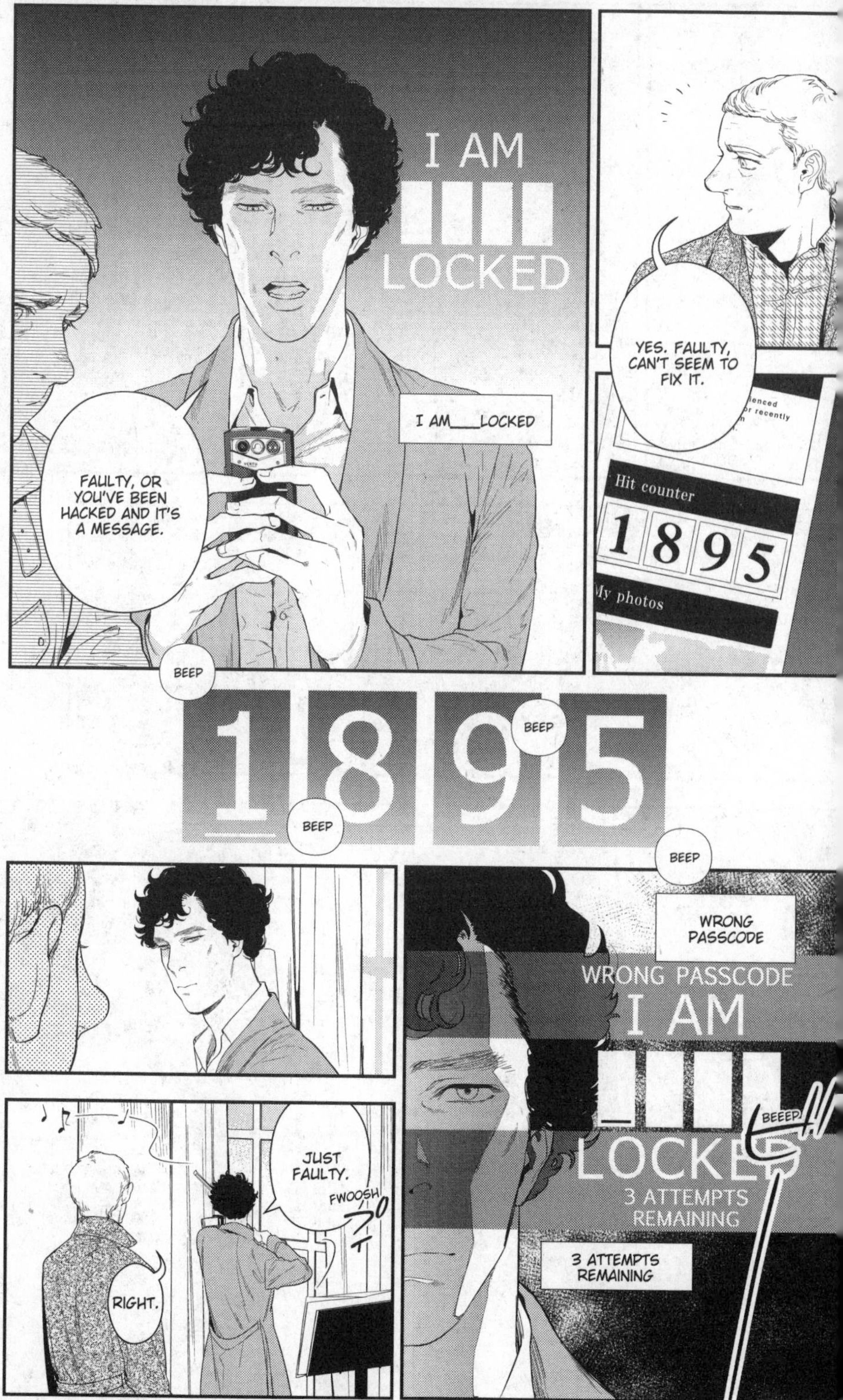
YES. FAULTY, CAN'T SEEM TO FIX IT.
Hit counter
1895
My photos
I AM
LOCKED
I AM___LOCKED
FAULTY, OR YOU'VE BEEN HACKED AND IT'S A MESSAGE.
BEEP
1895
BEEP
BEEP
BEEP
WRONG PASSCODE
WRONG PASSCODE
I AM
LOCKED
3 ATTEMPTS REMAINING
BEEEP
3 ATTEMPTS REMAINING
JUST FAULTY.
FWOOSH
RIGHT.

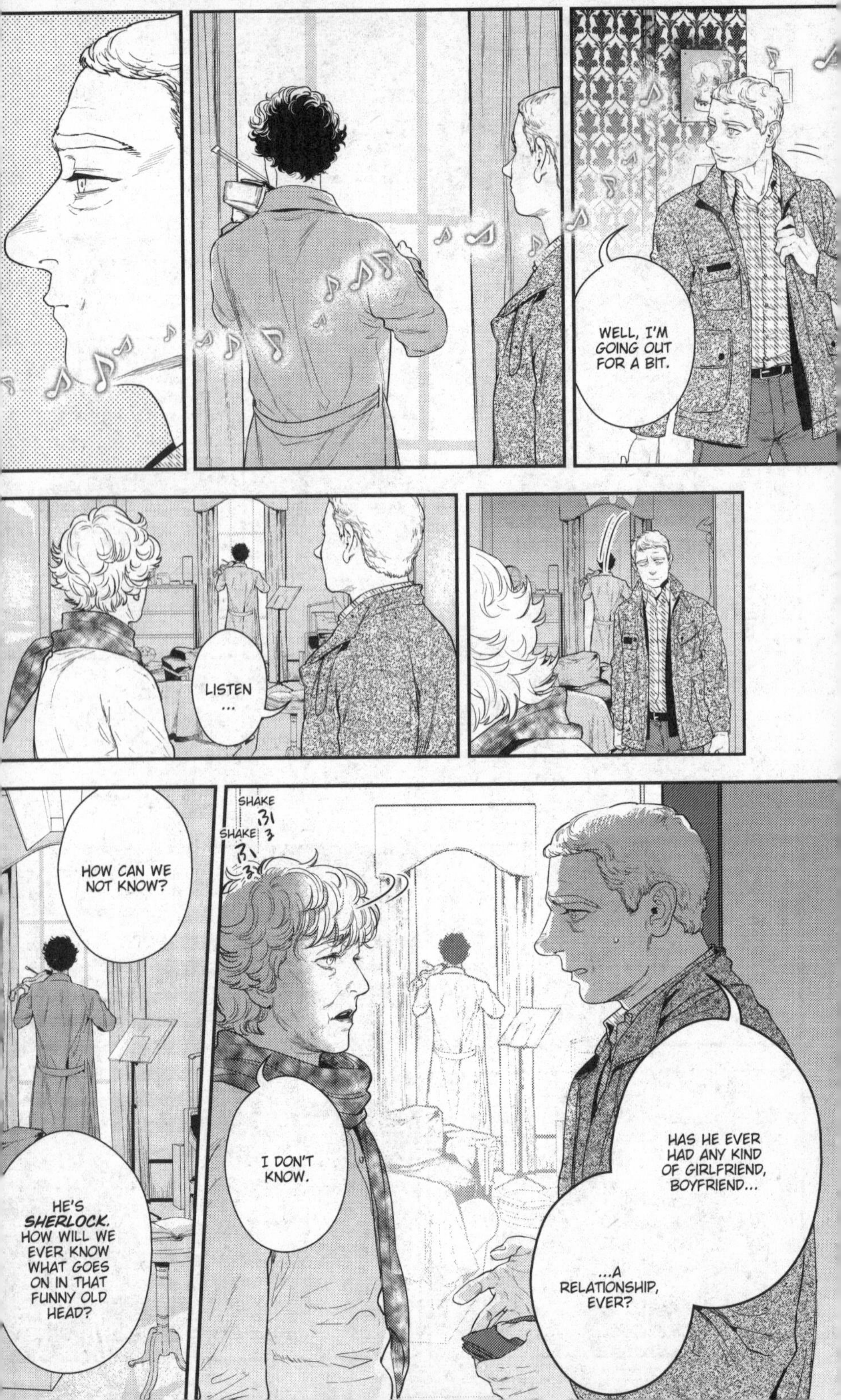
WELL, I'M GOING OUT FOR A BIT.
LISTEN ...
HAS HE EVER HAD ANY KIND OF GIRLFRIEND, BOYFRIEND...
...A RELATIONSHIP, EVER?
SHAKE
SHAKE
I DON'T KNOW.
HOW CAN WE NOT KNOW?
HE'S ***SHERLOCK.*** HOW WILL WE EVER KNOW WHAT GOES ON IN THAT FUNNY OLD HEAD?

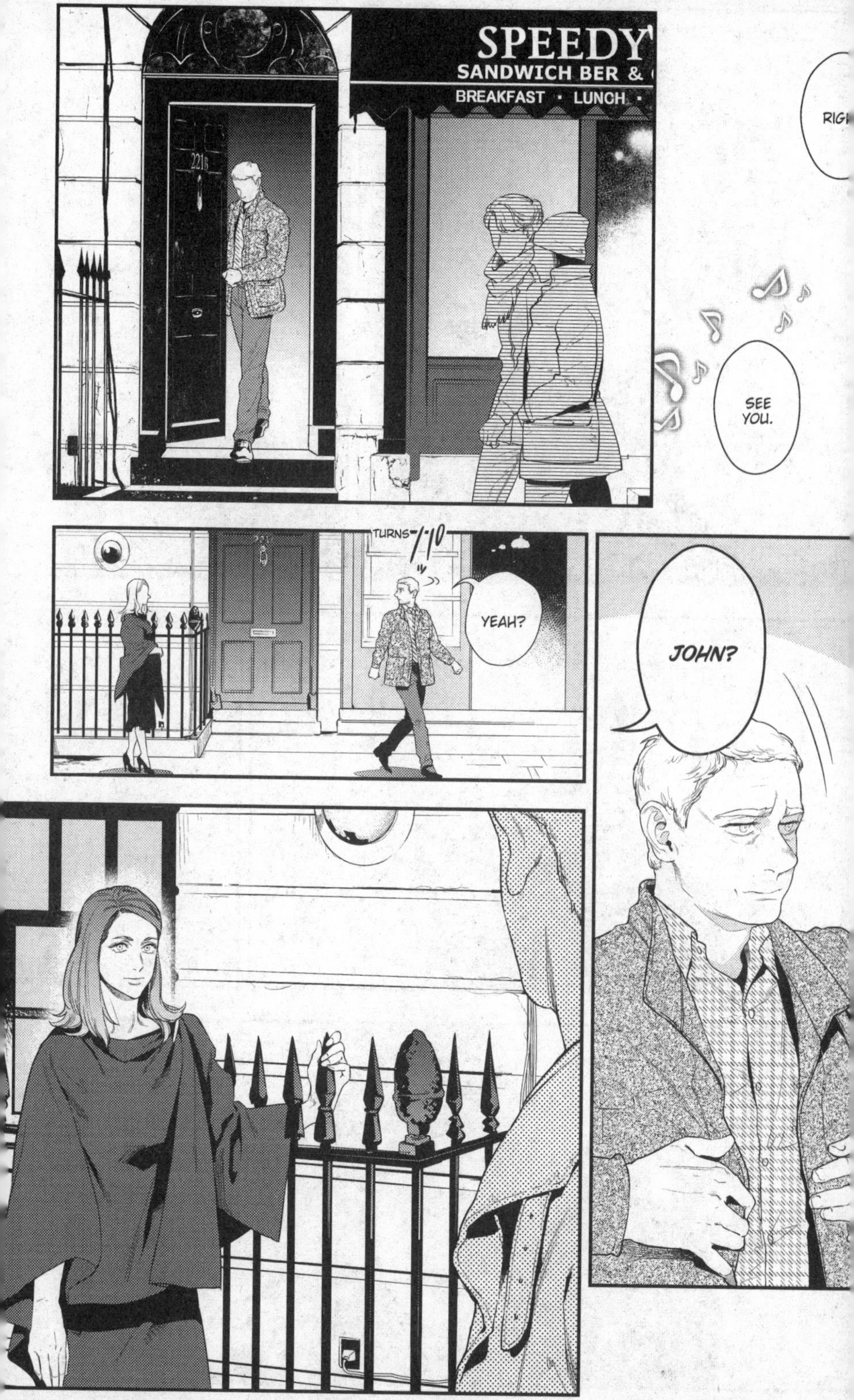
RIG
SEE YOU.
SPEEDY
SANDWICH BER &
BREAKFAST · LUNCH ·
JOHN?
TURNS
YEAH?

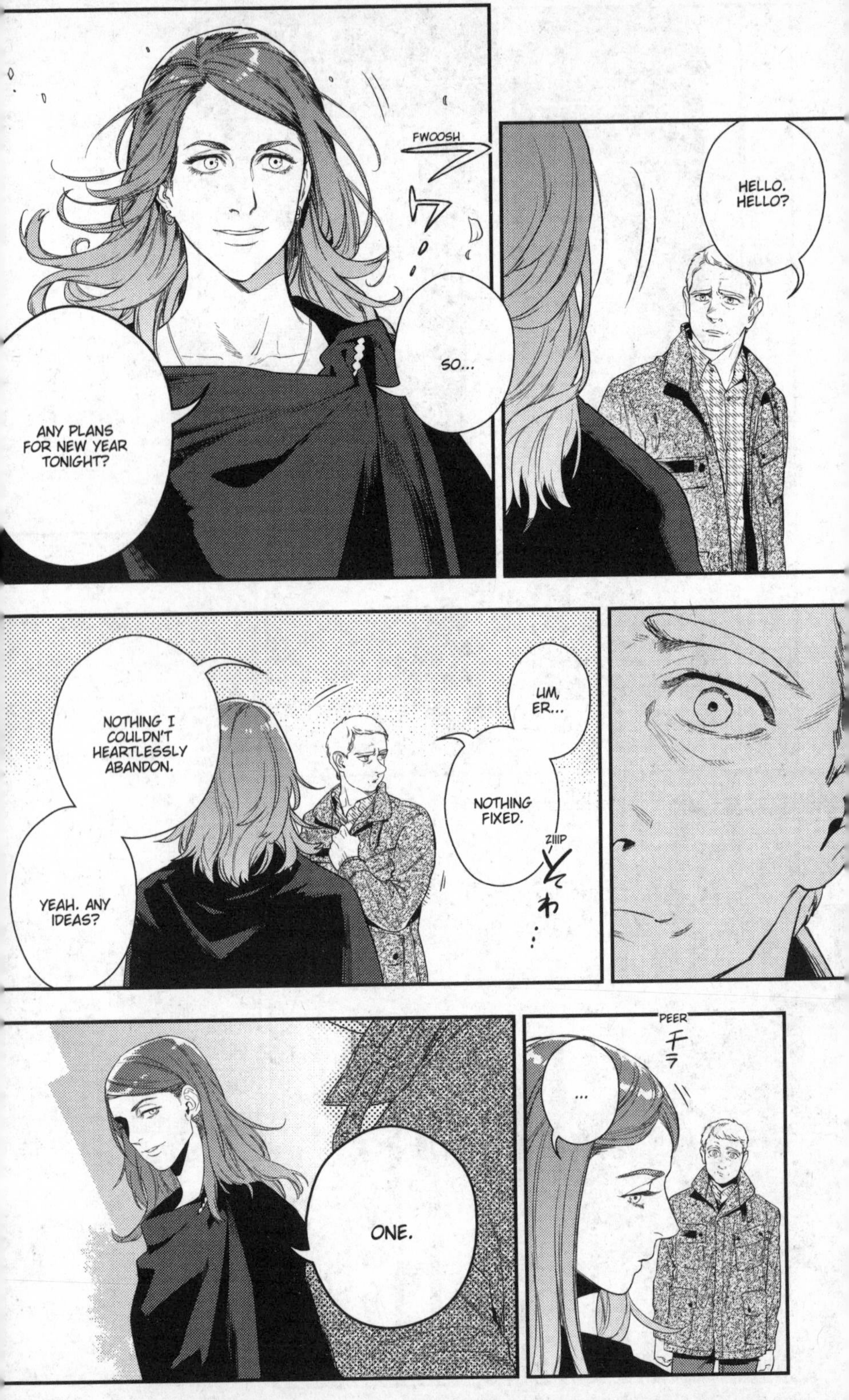

HELLO. HELLO?
FWOOSH
SO...
ANY PLANS FOR NEW YEAR TONIGHT?
UM, ER...
NOTHING FIXED.
ZIIIP
そわ
NOTHING I COULDN'T HEARTLESSLY ABANDON.
YEAH. ANY IDEAS?
PEER
チラ
...
ONE.

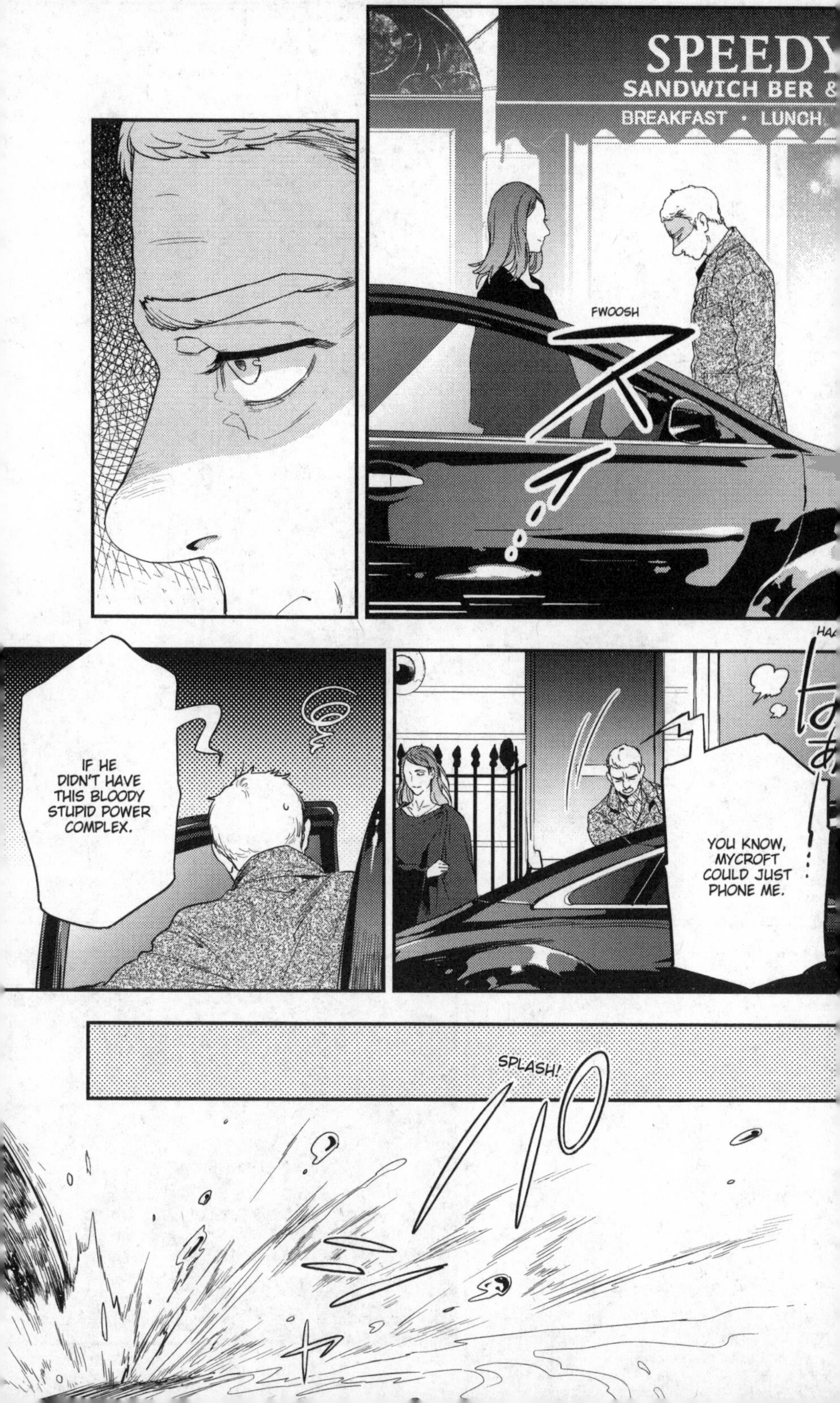
SPEEDY
SANDWICH BER &
BREAKFAST · LUNCH
FWOOSH
YOU KNOW, MYCROFT COULD JUST PHONE ME.
IF HE DIDN'T HAVE THIS BLOODY STUPID POWER COMPLEX.
SPLASH!

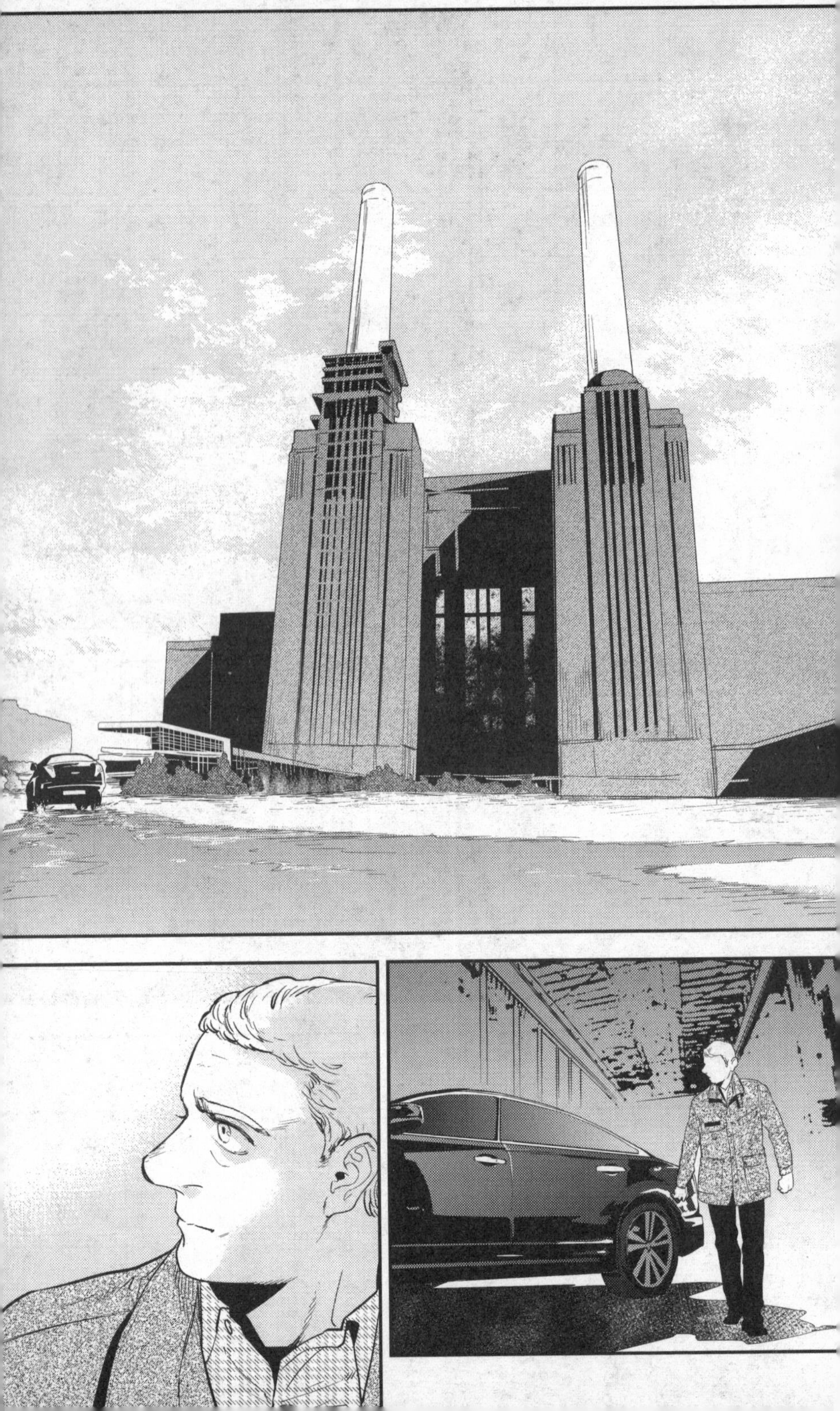

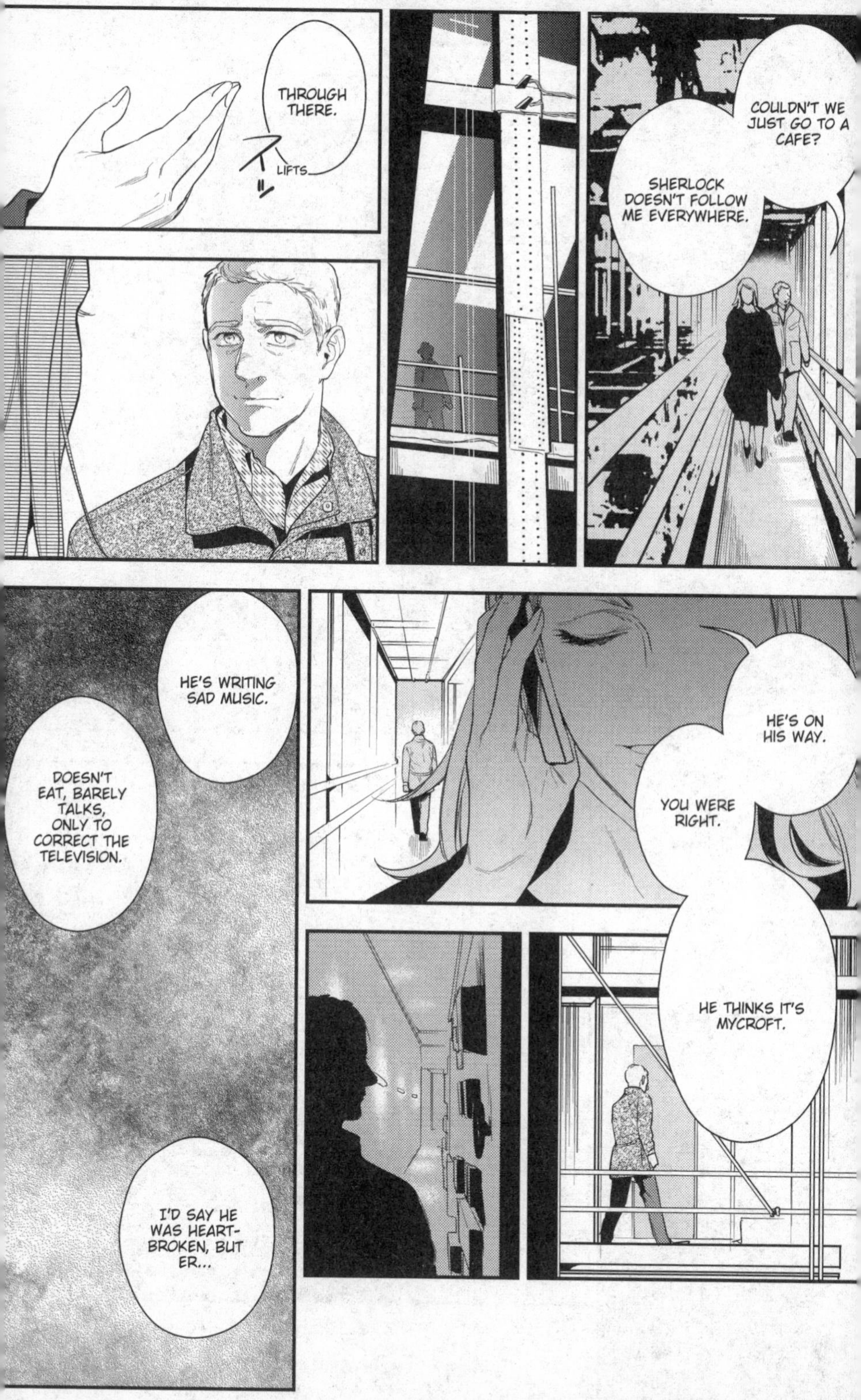
COULDN'T WE JUST GO TO A CAFE?
SHERLOCK DOESN'T FOLLOW ME EVERYWHERE.
THROUGH THERE.
LIFTS
HE'S ON HIS WAY.
YOU WERE RIGHT.
HE THINKS IT'S MYCROFT.
HE'S WRITING SAD MUSIC.
DOESN'T EAT, BARELY TALKS, ONLY TO CORRECT THE TELEVISION.
I'D SAY HE WAS HEART-BROKEN, BUT ER...

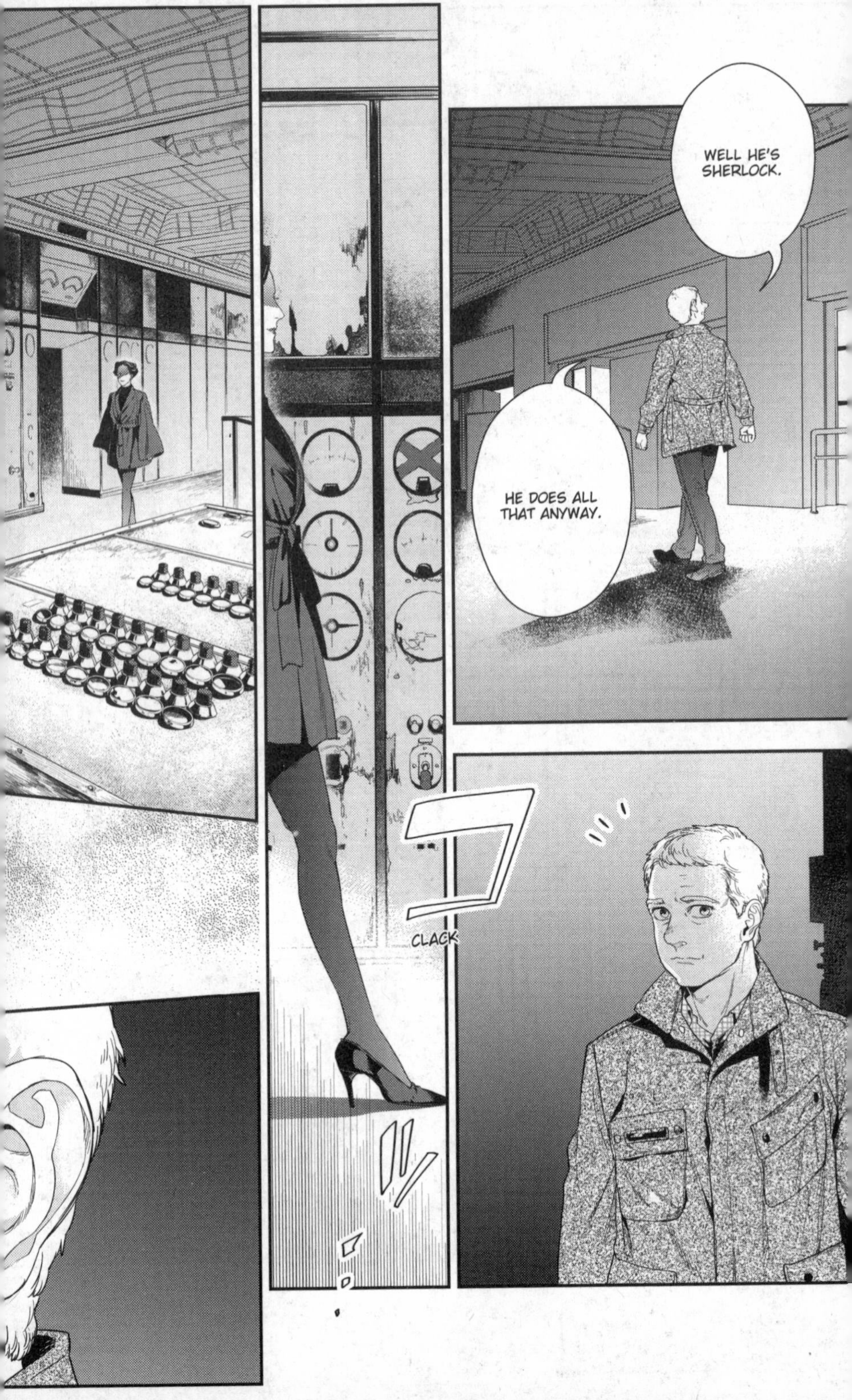
WELL HE'S SHERLOCK.
HE DOES ALL THAT ANYWAY.
CLACK

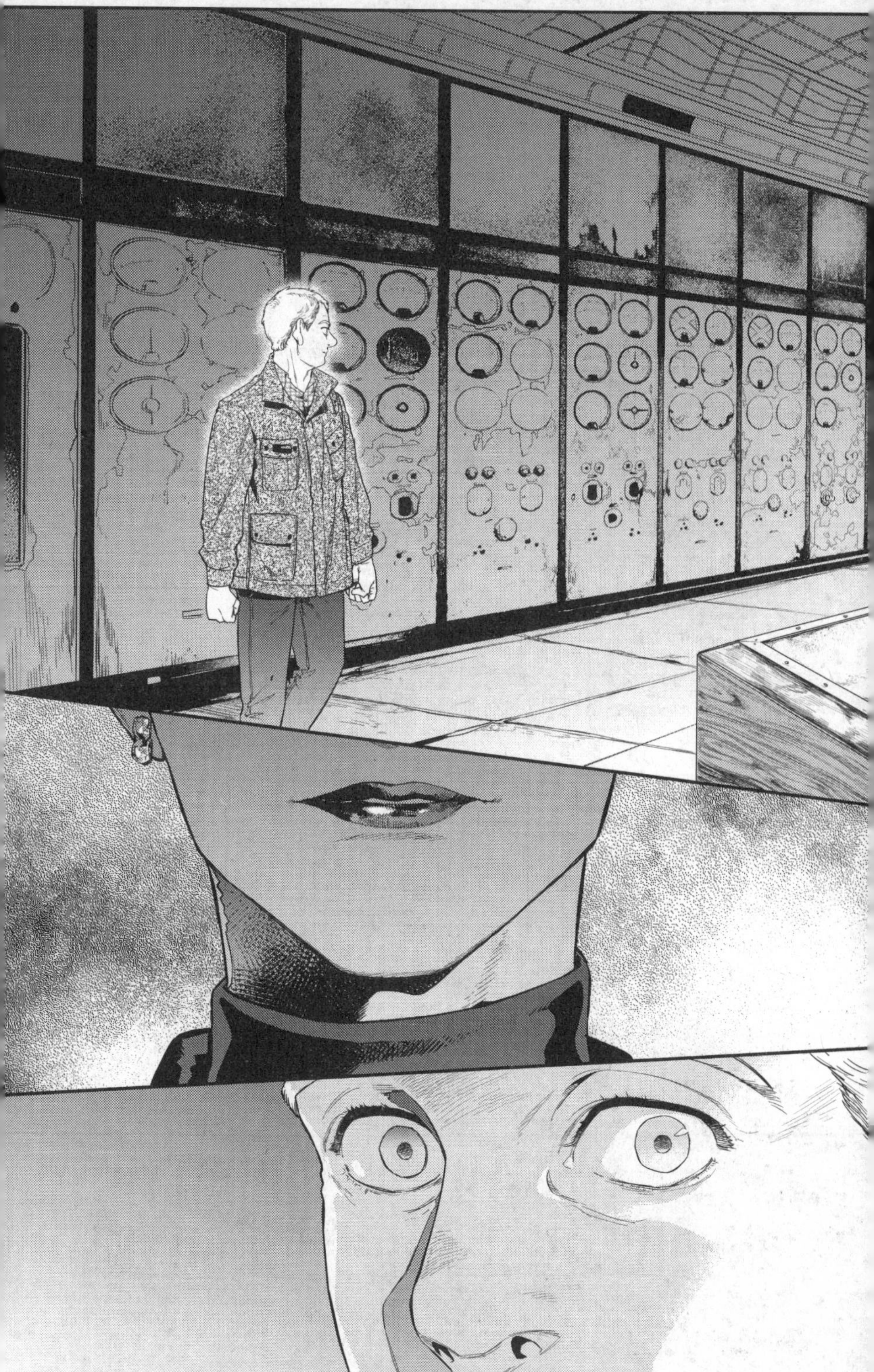

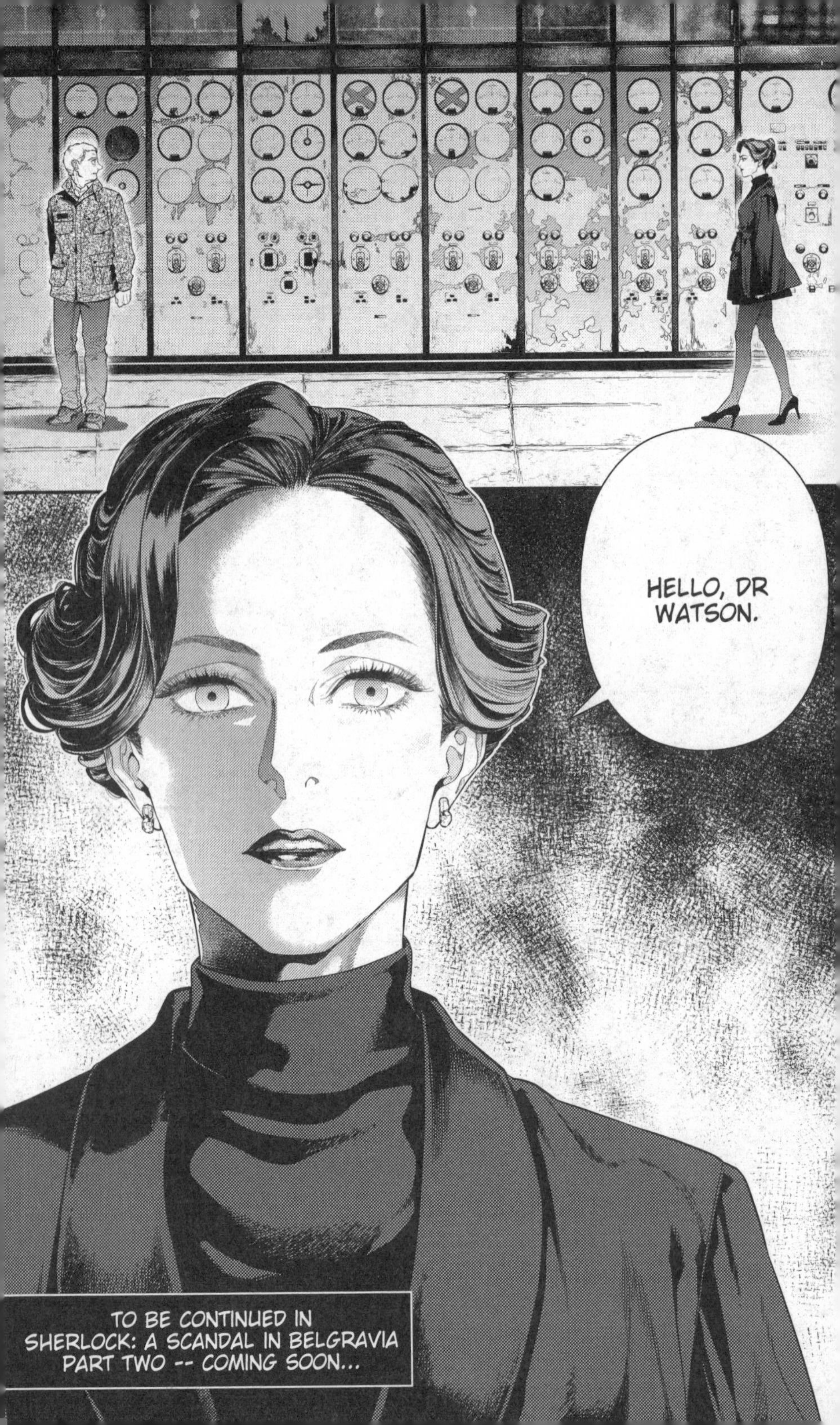
HELLO, DR WATSON.
TO BE CONTINUED IN SHERLOCK: A SCANDAL IN BELGRAVIA PART TWO -- COMING SOON...

COVER GALLERY

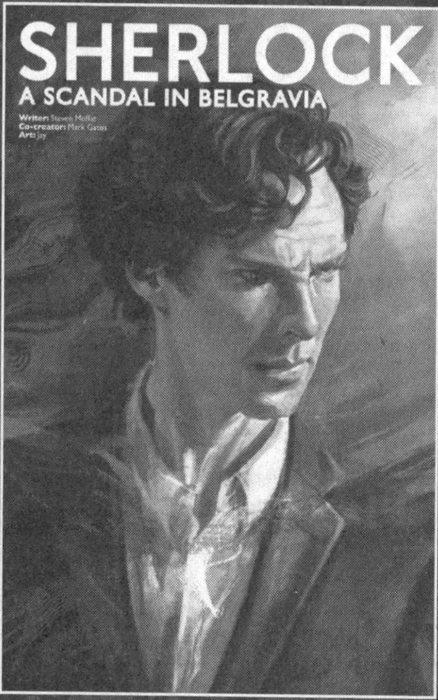
SHERLOCK
A SCANDAL IN BELGRAVIA

#1 COVER A
ALICE X. ZHANG

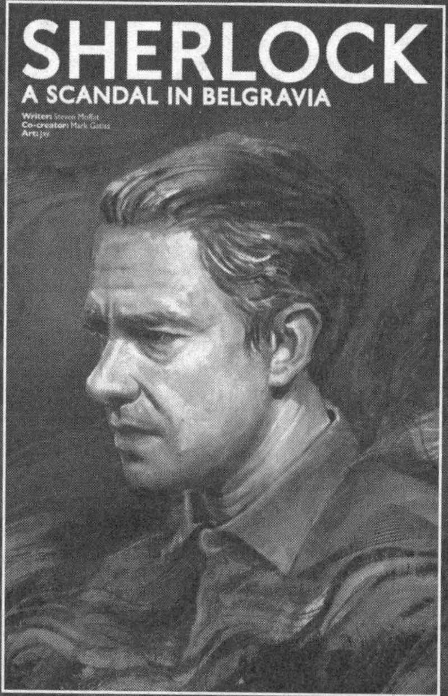
SHERLOCK
A SCANDAL IN BELGRAVIA

#1 COVER B
ALICE X. ZHANG

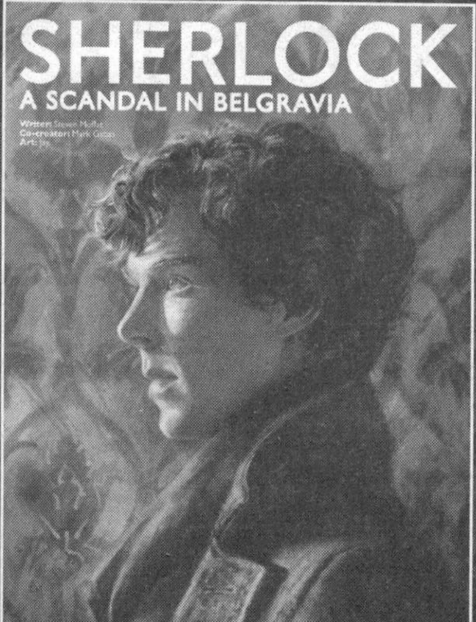
SHERLOCK
A SCANDAL IN BELGRAVIA

#2 COVER A
ALICE X. ZHANG

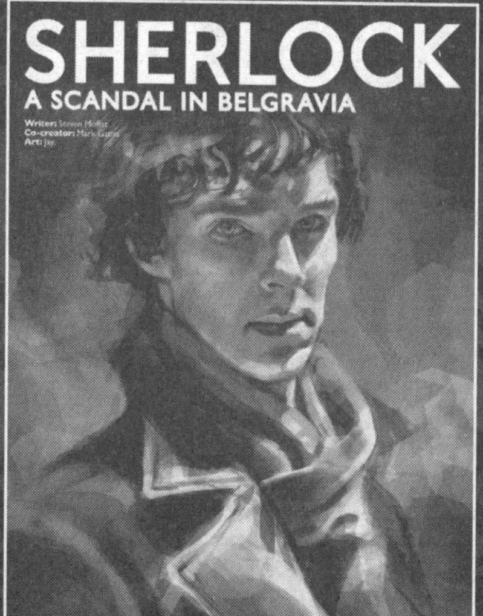
SHERLOCK
A SCANDAL IN BELGRAVIA

#3 COVER A
ALICE X. ZHANG

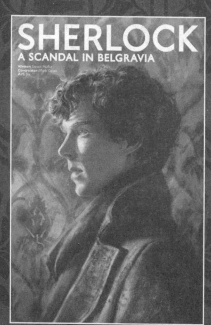

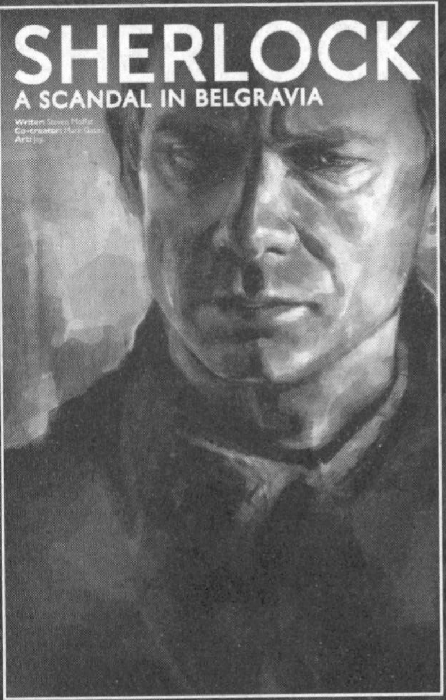
SHERLOCK
A SCANDAL IN BELGRAVIA

#4 COVER A
ALICE X. ZHANG

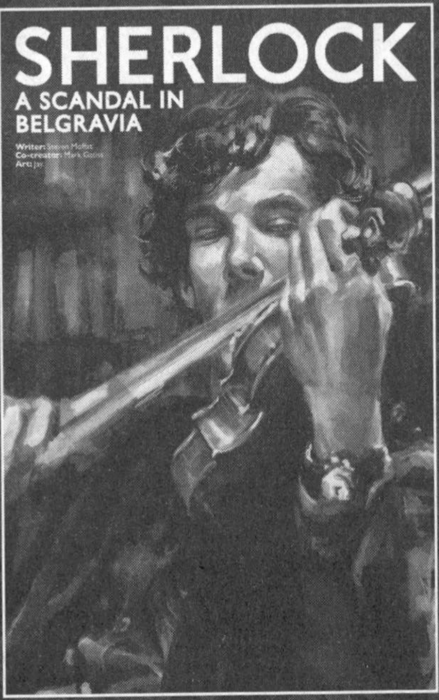
SHERLOCK
A SCANDAL IN BELGRAVIA

#5 COVER A
ALICE X. ZHANG

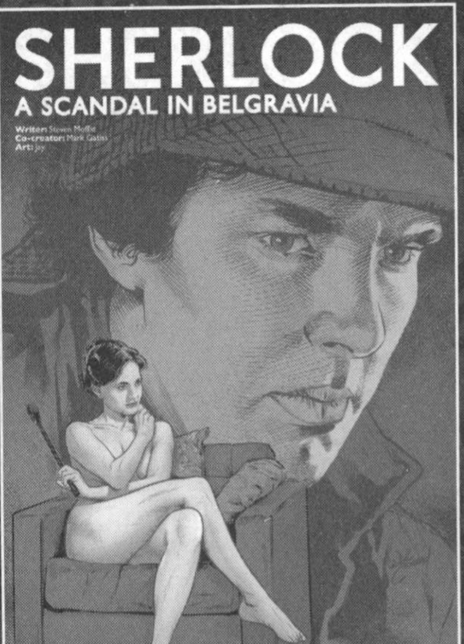
SHERLOCK
A SCANDAL IN BELGRAVIA

#1 COVER E
WILL CONRAD

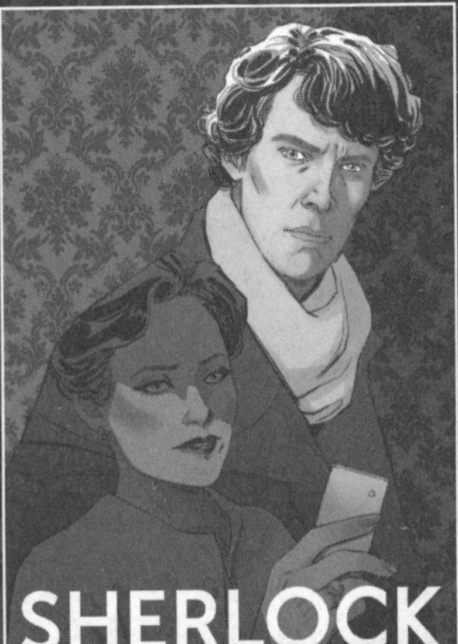
SHERLOCK
A SCANDAL IN BELGRAVIA

#2 COVER D
MARGUERITE SAUVAGE

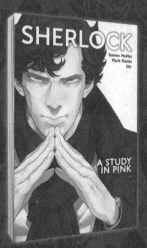

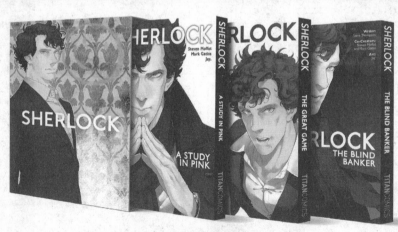

STO

This manga is presented in its original right-to-left reading format. This is the back of the issue!

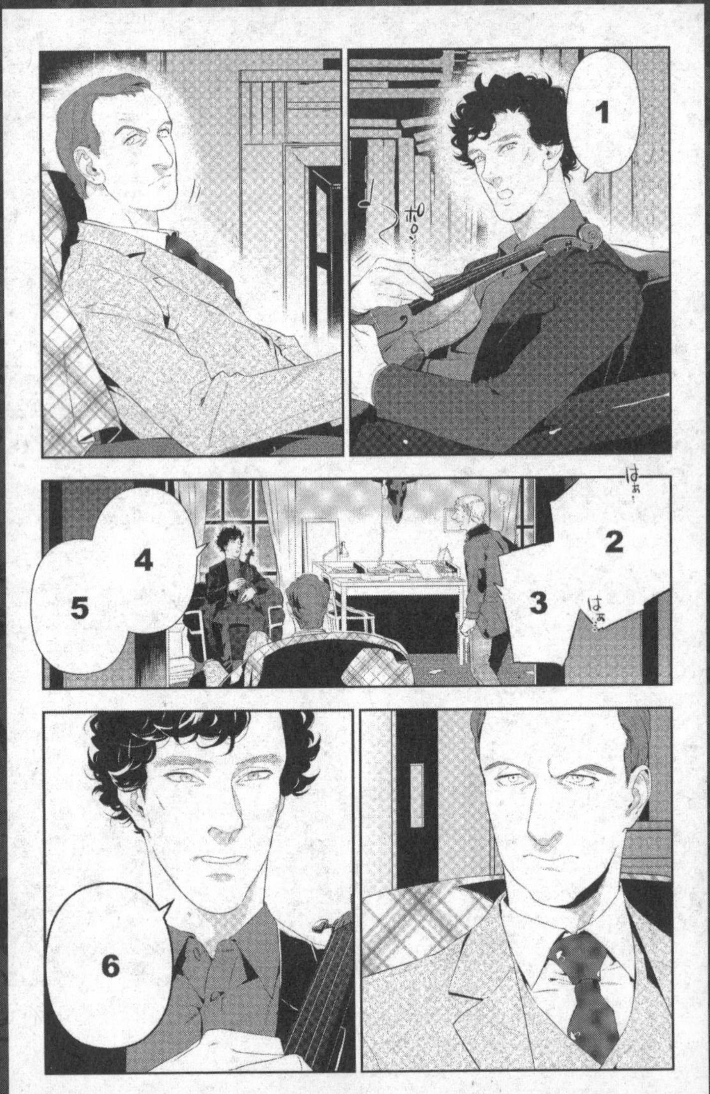
1
2
3
4
5
6

Pages, panels, and speech balloons read from top right to bottom left, as shown above. Sound effects are translated in the gutters between the panels.